A Devotional Guide to the Gospels

Other Books by John Killinger

The Fundamentals of Preaching
Christ in the Seasons of Ministry
The Cup and the Waterfall
Prayer: The Act of Being with God
Bread for the Wilderness, Wine for the Journey: The Miracle of Prayer and Meditation
All You Lonely People, All You Lovely People
For God's Sake, Be Human
The Centrality of Preaching in the Total Task of the Ministry
Hemingway and the Dead Gods
The Failure of Theology in Modern Literature
World in Collapse: The Vision of Absurd Drama
Leave It to the Spirit: Freedom and Commitment in the New Liturgies
The Salvation Tree
The Fragile Presence: Transcendence in Modern Literature
Experimental Preaching
The Second Coming of the Church
The 11:00 O'Clock News and Other Experimental Sermons
The Loneliness of Children
The Thickness of Glory

The Word Not Bound: A One-Act Play

A Devotional Guide to the Gospels

336 Meditations

WORD BOOKS
PUBLISHER
WACO, TEXAS

A DIVISION OF
WORD, INCORPORATED

A DEVOTIONAL GUIDE TO THE GOSPELS

Originally published as individual volumes under the titles: *A Sense of His Presence* (*The Devotional Commentary: Matthew*); *His Power in You* (*The Devotional Commentary: Mark*); *A Devotional Guide to Luke: The Gospel of Contagious Joy;* and *A Devotional Guide to John: The Gospel of Eternal Life.*

Library of Congress Cataloging in Publication Data:

Killinger, John.
A devotional guide to the Gospels.
1. Bible. N.T. Gospels—Meditations. 2. Devotional calendars. I. Title.
BS2555.4.K55 1984 226'.06 84–19702
ISBN 0–8499–3008–1

PRINTED IN THE UNITED STATES OF AMERICA

A Word from the Publisher

We at Word Publishing are pleased to present, in one volume, four individual works that have become classics of their kind. John Killinger's devotional commentaries on Matthew, Mark, Luke, and John are unique in their combination of insightful verse-by-verse exposition with eloquent prayers and devotional material aimed at bringing the lay reader into a closer and stronger discipleship with the Lord.

Each of the four original volumes is printed here in its entirety. To preserve the unique "flavor" of the individual volumes, we have chosen to reproduce each one exactly as it first appeared, retaining the original page numbers and illustrations. The result, we hope, is a book strong in diversity but united by its common theme and purpose.

Together, the four devotional commentaries that make up this volume contain a total of 336 concise readings, enough for almost a year of daily devotions. The readings are designed to guide readers verse by verse through the pivotal first four books of the New Testament. Dr. Killinger gives historical background, points out the poetic beauty of the biblical imagery, and reveals the message or lesson contained in each passage. But the focus of these devotional commentaries is on application as well as understanding of the biblical message. To this end, Dr. Killinger closes each reading with a contemporary prayer intended to be a starting point for personal meditation on how the Scripture passage relates to the reader's own life.

A Devotional Guide to the Gospels is written with the sensitivity and eloquence that have made John Killinger well beloved as a devotional writer. A beautiful and practical aid to daily Bible study, it brings the life and teachings of Jesus into sharper focus, allowing all of us to hear his instructions in words that apply to our own lives and ministries.

We present it in hope that you will find it both helpful and meaningful in your own journey as a Christian.

MATTHEW

Drawings by
Andy Bacon

Contents

Introduction

THE GOSPEL OF MATTHEW

The Gospel of Matthew, like the other Gospels, was written primarily for the Christian community, not as an evangelical tract to convert outsiders to the faith. Its purpose was to help Christians understand more about the life and teachings of the Lord to whom they had pledged their lives, so that they might in turn live as better stewards of God's grace.

It is for this reason, more than any other, that we continue to read the Gospel in our own day.

The Gospel of Matthew, to be sure, does have historical interest for us. It shows us more clearly than the other Gospels how much of Jesus' ministry was shaped by his persistent conflict with the Pharisees, who were concerned for the careful preservation of the Law of Moses and its many addenda. It abounds in comparisons between the old Law and the teachings of Jesus, demonstrating that Christianity, not the Judaism of the scribes and Pharisees, fulfilled the spirit of Moses. It indicates more extensively than the other Gospels that the relationship between Jesus and the disciples was that of teacher and students, and that many of the sayings which we would otherwise assume were broadcast to the crowds were in actuality given only to the disciples, who in turn became the teachers of the crowds. And it delineates, as the other Gospels do not, the special relationship between Jesus and Peter, who became the main leader of the early church, and whose failures as a disciple would have been all the more important as moral lessons to other members of the Christian community.

But it is to learn how *we* can be more faithful in our discipleship today that we still read the Gospel of Matthew. We read it in order to bring our vision of Christ into sharper focus, and to hear his instructions in clearer terms for our own lives and ministries.

For this reason, a devotional commentary on the Gospel may

be even more important to us than a scholarly commentary. It is not intended to supplant scholarly commentaries, which are of inestimable value in their own way. Rather, it attempts in tone and emphasis to bring the reader into keener awareness of a presence —the presence of the living Christ and the absolute presence of God—in a manner totally outside the intention of scholarly compositions. It combines, as fully as possible within the limits of space, the finest fruits of recent scholarship with the devotional stance of the man or woman at prayer. It aims at knowledge; but, more than that, at dedication.

It is not extrinsic to the purpose of this volume, then, to say a word about how it might best be read.

First, it should be read *with* the Gospel of Matthew. It is not a substitute for the reading of the Word itself, but a companion book, a prompter of thoughts the reader may not have had on his or her own while reading the scripture.

Then, as the book is intended to increase the measure of the reader's devotion, each segment should be read quietly, meditatively, in a spirit of listening prayer. As in eating, no more should be ingested at a sitting than can be digested or properly reflected upon. The aim should not be to complete the reading of the book in order to say, "There, that is that," but to live with it as a companion for as long as it continues to guide you into closer association with the One who is its unfailing subject.

This much is certain: We cannot live day by day with the thoughts of the Gospels and not be changed. It is like living in the mountains or living by the sea: gradually and inexplicably, our personalities become altered, are elevated, assuming the character of their environment.

So, I trust, it will be with you as you make your way through this volume.

Nashville, 1977 JOHN KILLINGER

WEEK 1

Only the person who has submitted to John's demand for repentance and cleansing can hope to meet the challenge of Jesus' way of living in the Kingdom. (Week I: Friday)

"Lord, I confess that I am like the crowds: I react much more excitedly to signs and wonders than I do to the mystery of forgiveness. Sharpen my perception more keenly to matters of the soul." (Week III: Saturday)

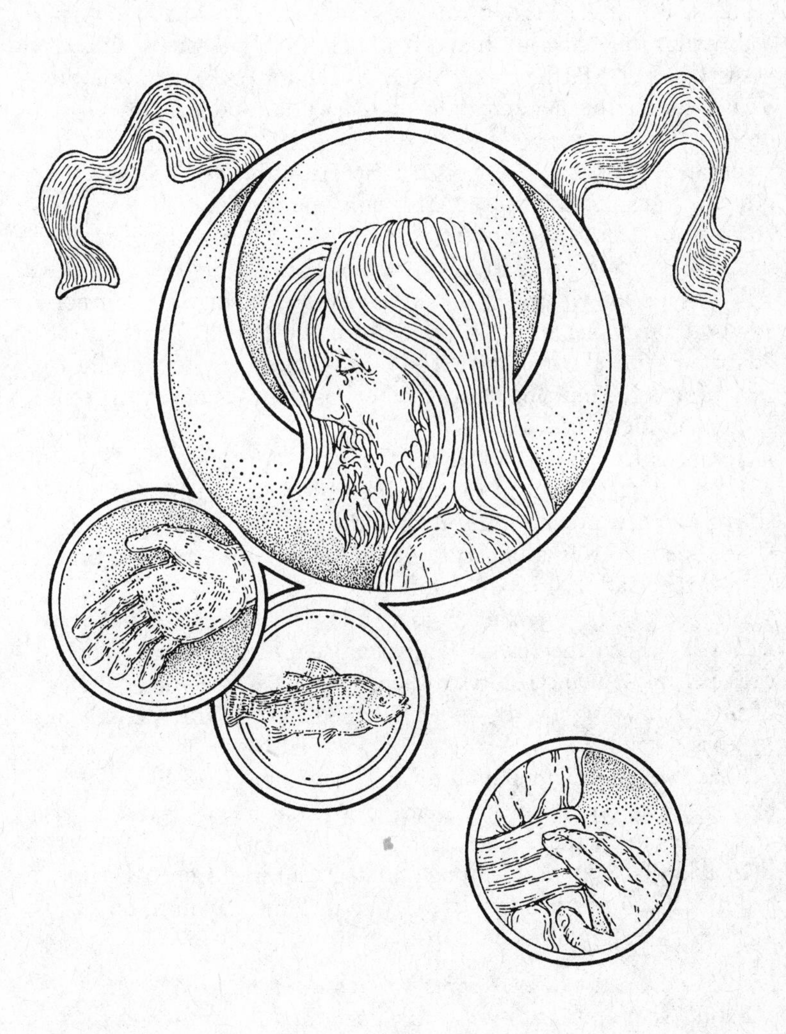

Week I: Sunday

1:1–17 THE NEW GENESIS

"The book of the genealogy of Jesus Christ. . . ." Or, as the original writing may also be translated, "The book of the *genesis* of Jesus Christ." Matthew was about to set forth the story of the new Genesis, the new creation of the world, and it centered in Jesus.

Because Matthew's Gospel was especially directed to Jews, he stressed Jesus' relationship to Abraham, the father of all Jews, instead of to Adam, the first man. Therefore the genealogy, or list of names, tracing Jesus' royal line of descent.

To us, in our fast-paced impersonal society, it may seem a boring note on which to begin. Not so for the Jewish Christians of Matthew's day! To them it would have been sheer poetry, fully as beautiful as the opening verses of the Gospel of John, which seem more majestic to us.

"Jesus Christ, the son of David, the son of Abraham."

I can still recall the old folks in the little town where I grew up sitting on their porches after dark and discussing family histories. There was never anything trite or dull about such talk to them, even if they had heard it all before.

And we can be sure there was nothing trite or dull about this list of names to the Jewish Christians. They knew stories about each person named. History to them was a web, a ladder, a series of interconnecting events, and now it led directly from Abraham to Jesus.

Read over the names in the list. Pronounce them lingeringly, lovingly, the way an ancient Jewish Christian would have. They *are* poetry, aren't they?

Imagine God at work through all the centuries from Abraham to Jesus. Then imagine him at work from Jesus' day until ours.

This is the story of a new creation, isn't it?

O Lord, a thousand years are as a day in your sight.
But we are creatures of a brief span, and history is most

awesome to us. Teach us to honor our years by submitting them to you. Let them be woven into the wonderful pattern of your eternity. Let your new creation continue in us. Through Jesus, who was descended from Abraham and all these ancient people. Amen.

Week I: Monday

1:18–25 THE WORK OF GOD'S SPIRIT

The heavens and the earth, according to the first verses of the book of Genesis, were created by the Spirit of God. The Spirit moved over the face of the dark waters and brought forth the sun and the stars and the world.

Therefore Matthew, who was going to tell the story of the new creation in Jesus Christ, wished to emphasize the role of the Spirit in this new Genesis. His was a simple method, not at all unknown among the biographies of heroes in the ancient world: He spoke of a miraculous conception in which the Spirit actually fathered the child born to Mary.

The prophet Isaiah had promised long before that a virgin would conceive and bear a special child. His name would be called Emmanuel, or God with us.

God had been present in his first creation. The author of Genesis pictures him walking in the garden in the cool of the evening. Now, in the new creation, says Matthew, he is to be present in a different way. He is to be tempted, to suffer, and to die like one of us. It is a form of intimacy for which, as the Apostle Paul had already put it, the whole creation groaned until now. God will be in Christ, making the world his again.

Lord, it is exciting to think of your Spirit at work in the world where I live, making the new creation out of the old. I want to be part of the new creation. I want my family and friends to be part of it. Help me to submit my entire being to your Spirit, so that my life flows with your purpose and not against it. Through Jesus, who has shown us your Spirit. Amen.

Week I: Tuesday

2:1–12 WHAT MAKES MEN WISE?

Of all the miracles associated with the birth of Jesus, none seems more miraculous than the arrival of these strangers from the East. Apparently there were several of them. It has traditionally been assumed that there were three because three gifts are mentioned, but this is only an assumption.

Matthew's purpose in telling about them was to indicate the worldwide significance of the birth of the Christ. These travelers symbolized the eventual homage of all nations before the Son of God. They brought gifts usually associated with royalty. And for good reason—Jesus was destined to rule over all.

What could induce men like these to leave their homes and travel to distant lands? They said they had seen the star and knew that the prophecy concerning Jesus' birth in Bethlehem was about to be fulfilled.

That is amazing, when you think about it. The whole beings of these men appear to have been open to receive the messages of God in the universe around them. How different from the way most of us live! We are so preoccupied with matters of daily existence that we rarely take time to watch and listen to the universe we live in. We develop spiritual myopia—an inability to see anything that doesn't concern our living or maintaining a household or enjoying a ballgame.

How many messages we miss—and how impoverished our lives are as a result.

Lord, I have eyes but I have learned to live without seeing. I am so insensitive. Teach me to have a sense of wonder again, the way I did as a child. Let me look at everything as if for the first time, and marvel not at what *things are, but* that *they are. Through Jesus, who is the greatest object of wonder.* Amen.

Week I: Wednesday

2:13–18 CHRIST AND THE BEAST

Here is a part of the Christmas story we are prone to leave out—the part about terror and cruelty and the provocation of evil. But it ought to be there, every Christmas, for it is inseparable from the birth of the holy child.

The book of Revelation ends with the struggle between Christ and the Great Beast, the symbol of evil; and there is where the gospel must really begin, as Matthew saw it. Herod, like most tyrants, felt extremely insecure. He probably did not believe that God was ready to send a Messiah to Israel, but he did worry that any popular figure might topple his precarious throne. So he lashed out demonically at the news of Jesus' birth, and had all the male children under two years of age in the town of Bethlehem slain. Wails of agony must have gone up in many homes as Herod's soldiers entered and dashed the babies against walls or pulled them limb from limb.

What a tangled skein life is. The best that happens seems somehow to call forth the worst too. Even the birth of the Savior brought extra suffering into the lives of some.

How impossible it is to separate the wheat and the tares, the good and the bad, in this life. As the Apostle Paul said, it is impossible even within a single life—the good we do, we have trouble doing, and the evil we would not do, we seem to do in spite of ourselves. Can we hope that it will be any better with groups, institutions, and nations?

This is why, in many liturgical traditions, a prayer of confession is set right at the heart of worship. Our only hope is in the righteousness of God, for we cannot claim any righteousness ourselves. We admit our mixed motives, impure thoughts, and failure to love our neighbors. It is the least we can do, for however much we belong to Christ, we are still troubled by the beast within.

O God, I long to be pure and honest and to deal thus with all persons. But I am too weak and unwise to fulfill the longing. Life is too complicated, and I often make wrong choices. Help me not to despair, but to rely more on you. Let me find in you the acceptance which enables me to live as well as I can with humility, courage, and compassion, accepting in others the weakness I find so deeply embedded in my own nature. Through Jesus, whose very presence often serves as the catalyst to clarify good and evil. Amen.

Week I: Thursday

2:19–23 THE IMPORTANCE OF DREAMS

More dreams! First there was the one with the angel telling Joseph that God's Spirit was the father of the child she carried. Then there was the one warning him to take Mary and the child into Egypt. Now these additional dreams, in which he is advised to return to Israel and to settle in Galilee.

I wonder if we would follow advice we received in a dream.

Probably not. We belong to a culture which has put great emphasis on rationality. We have even developed rational explanations for dreams, so that we need not pay much attention to them. Many of us categorize dreams among hallucinations and disorders of the mind.

But some modern voices are saying that we do not pay enough attention to our dreams. And, if it is true that we reason better with our whole selves, not merely with our minds, then these messages may be of considerable importance.

Could it be that God uses our subconscious minds to implant

suggestions in us that our tougher conscious minds would reject? Perhaps our lives would be richer and more exciting if we only learned to trust our impulses from the unconscious more than we presently do.

When I have a hard decision to make, I pray as I fall asleep, "Speak to me in my dreams, O Lord," for I know I am more likely to hear there than in my busy waking hours.

> *Sometimes, Lord, you come to us in conscious modes. Other times you come when the mind is asleep and not watching. Help me to be so alive to the possibility of hearing your voice that I may hear in any way it comes to me. Through Jesus, who always heard.* Amen.

Week I: Friday

3:1–12 A FORERUNNER FOR THE TEACHER OF RIGHTEOUSNESS

Some scholars believe that John the Baptist was reared in or near the Essene community in Qumran, on the Dead Sea. The Essenes placed great emphasis on simple, righteous living and on ritual lustration or baptism.

Wherever John came from, his message and actions were an appropriate prelude to the ministry of Jesus, for what they called for most was a radical reordering of priorities, a total conversion of lifestyle. They became the background against which Matthew would shortly set the Sermon on the Mount, with its teachings of a transformed ethic for the new creation, and we cannot begin to understand those teachings if we forget this. Only the person who has submitted to John's demand for repentance and cleansing can hope to meet the challenge of Jesus' way of living in the Kingdom.

Already the word is laid down for the Pharisees and Sadducees, the people who think their religious affiliation will give them an advantage in entering the Kingdom. Tradition and heritage are only excess baggage in the day of the Lord. God can raise up new children for the Kingdom out of the very stones that crowd the riverbanks. (In Hebrew, there is a pun in this remark: *banîm* is children and *abanîm* is stones.) Christ's arrival will be a judgment on the falsely religious; they will be cut down like trees which do not bear fruit and burned like the useless chaff that is winnowed from the wheat.

Lord, help me to hear this stringent demand for personal conversion and righteousness, that I may soon be ready to consider the ethical teachings of Jesus when I read them. Let me depend on no artificial standards of worthiness as I come before you for judgment, but rely wholly on your grace to make me your child. Through Jesus, who baptizes the world with fire. Amen.

Week I: Saturday

3:13–17 THE SIGN OF THE NEW CREATION

When the earth was created, God's Spirit hovered over the face of the waters. Now, in the new creation, the Spirit is identified with baptism, the ritual entry to the Kingdom.

This is why Jesus himself came to John to be baptized. John demurred because he stood in the presence of the one who was God's Spirit in the flesh. But Jesus insisted.

Human pride might have prevented our doing what Jesus did. We like to be begged, cajoled, and complimented into joining a movement.

But Jesus did not wait. He knew that a new age was coming into being. He came directly to the fiery prophet, to be baptized with all the others.

It was an important moment in human history, as was testified by the descent of the dove and the *bat qôl*, or voice out of heaven, saying, "This is my Son, my Beloved."

The full meaning of this strikes us only as we compare it with the story of Adam in the garden and God's disappointment in his failure to obey. Jesus' humility in accepting baptism "to fulfill all righteousness" was a sign of his willing obedience, and God was pleased. The new creation would not be hindered by the new Adam.

Lord, man baptizes with water and you baptize with the Holy Spirit. I need both, in order that your Kingdom may be fulfilled in me. Without the water, I hold myself apart from others in the Kingdom. Without the Spirit, the water is without effect. Fill me now with your Spirit, that I may be ready to meet the radical demands of the new age. Through Jesus, who has led the way as my Lord. Amen.

WEEK II

Week II: Sunday

4:1–11 HOW THE KINGDOM COMES

Matthew wrote his Gospel primarily as a catechism for teaching the Christian community what it needed to know. He must therefore have regarded prayer and fasting as very significant, to have placed this selection at the beginning of Jesus' public ministry.

We can only conclude that if prayer and fasting were so essential in Jesus' life, they must also be essential in ours today. But how many of us behave as if they were? We give them so little attention in our daily existence.

What if our lives were built around prayer and fasting?

First, we would live with a new awareness of the presence of God in all our affairs.

Second, the anxieties and fears which cripple us in the attempt to live full and meaningful lives would soon blow away like chaff from the wheat.

Third, we would perceive the world as gift instead of punishment. What had been wilderness to us would become a paradise where we had everything we truly needed.

We tend to associate prayer with miracles—with making things happen outside ourselves. But the greatest miracle prayer ever works is the transformation of the self so that it recognizes the blessings of God that lie around us all the time.

In other words, prayer reveals the Kingdom to us.

> *Lord, I have eyes to see but am often blind to the miracles around me. I have ears to hear but I usually talk so much that I cannot perceive what others are saying. Teach me quietness and wonder, O Lord, so that the glory of life can enter my senses and I can feel the abundance of your grace that is always present to me. Through Christ, who learned obedience through prayer and fasting.* Amen.

Week II: Monday

4:12–25 DOING GOD'S WILL IN GALILEE

Religion makes some of us headstrong. If God is with us, we think, then we ought to assume the most prominent positions as quickly as possible.

But here is our Lord doing exactly the opposite. Leaving Judea, the region around Jerusalem, he preached and taught in the remote area of Galilee. He even called two sets of brothers who were Galilean fishermen to become his most intimate followers. Together they traveled the countryside, interpreting the scriptures in synagogues as they went—in the country churches of their day!

Surely there is a lesson in this for us about working faithfully wherever God wants us to work. We are never required to serve in highly visible positions—only to apply ourselves cheerfully wherever we are.

Ironically, the greatest movements often begin in the least conspicuous places. The crowds which gathered around Jesus in Galilee soon spread his fame abroad, and people began coming from as far away as Jerusalem to hear his teachings and find healing for their infirmities.

> *Lord, I suspect that Jesus' time of prayer and fasting in the desert prepared him for serving in inconspicuous places. I pray that my own seasons of devotion will leave me as filled with peace and contentment as he was, that I too may glorify you in humility and readiness to serve the poor.* Amen.

Week II: Tuesday

5:1–12 A GREATER THAN MOSES

Matthew was writing his Gospel for people whose whole religious life had once centered in the Torah, the Law brought down from the mount by Moses. It was important therefore that they see Jesus as the Moses of the new creation, the one whose teachings from the mount would establish a Kingdom greater than the old kingdom of Israel. Hence this "sermon," put together with editorial license from sayings of Jesus which probably occurred in many settings during his ministry.

It begins by defining who are the members of the new Kingdom —the humble, the heavyhearted, the gentle, the righteous, the merciful, the pure in heart, the peacemakers, the persecuted, the maligned. At a stroke, Jesus sets these over against all the self-righteous people who regarded themselves as the cream of the godly society. We have but to recall the poor and outcast people to whom he constantly ministered if we wish to see these descriptions fleshed out. They were, after all, the little stones which John the Baptist had said God could raise up into the true children of Abraham.

The first Law, the Law of Moses, had been subject to misinterpretation. The Pharisees had followed it scrupulously, but had missed the point of it. There would be no missing the point of the new Law. Jesus made it plain that the Law was not to supplant true devotion to God—even prostitutes and tax-collectors could be numbered among the blessed ones. And finally, lest even words like these in Matthew 5:1–12 be misconstrued, Jesus died as one accursed under the Law of Moses. It was a new era!

Lord, I need to remember what it is to be blessed, fortunate, happy. It is not necessarily to be well off. Nor are being in mourning, being persecuted, or being maligned in themselves signs of well being. Instead, to be blessed is to be in Christ, to be in the Kingdom, regardless of the state of my external affairs. It is to be yours in faithfulness despite whatever happens in the world. Therefore I can mourn and say, "Yet how fortunate I am," or I can be ill used and think, "There is still room for happiness." Let the truth of this insight sustain me through this day and the next. In the name of Jesus, who died for what he taught. Amen.

Week II: Wednesday

5:13–16 SALT AND LIGHT

"YOU are the salt of the earth. . . . YOU are the light of the world." Read it with the right emphasis. Jesus was setting his disciples over against the old Israel, over against Judaism, over against Mosaic religion. He wanted them to see that it was *they*, not the priests and keepers of the old Law, for whom the world was waiting. *They*, not the scribes and Pharisees, would be heralds of the Kingdom. *They*, not the old rabbis, would bring spice and light to the people of the earth.

Do we dare read ourselves into the "you"? Then the words commit us to action. If we are salt, then we must season. If we are light, then we must shine. For salt that does not season is thrown out and light that does not shine is worthless.

Let your light shine, Jesus said, so that it gives illumination to everyone and that those who see your good works will recognize the glory of God in you.

This is no theology of good works Jesus was recommending, but a theology of the glory of God. We bring seasoning and light to the world, not that the world may praise us, but that it may see and fall down before the presence of God in our midst. Salt is lost in the flavoring of food; we do not praise the salt but the taste of the food. Light is overlooked when it reveals the contents of a room; we do not praise the light but the items on display.

So it is with us: The joy of our calling is to help people discover the glory of God!

Lord, being salt and light is a problem to me. I am so inclined to seek people's attention for myself. I want to have my flavor brought out and my qualities illuminated. Help me to discover the richness of life when it is dedicated to helping others to see you instead of me, so that they praise your name instead of mine. Through Jesus, who always reminded us that what he did was through your presence and not his own power. Amen.

Week II: Thursday

5:17–48 A MORE PERFECT WAY

Here is the Teacher of Righteousness at his most incisive!

Think of the battles of grace versus works that had already swept through Christianity when Matthew wrote his Gospel. Paul had had conflict after conflict with the Judaizers, the Jewish Christians who insisted on the primacy of legalism in their newly founded religion. The question was by no means settled.

How does Matthew resolve it? By grouping the teachings of Jesus into a remarkable *both/and* combination.

No, you cannot work for the Kingdom, Jesus says—God *gives* the Kingdom. He gives it to the humble, the mourners, the gentle, those who long for righteousness—all those who are described in Matthew 5:3–12.

But of those to whom much is given much is expected. Now that you are given the Kingdom, you must go beyond the dry righteousness of the scribes and Pharisees, and fulfill the law in love.

You have heard it said that you must not kill—you must not even be angry with your brother.

You have heard it said that you must not commit adultery—you must not even have lust in your heart for a person of the opposite sex.

The law says you may put away your wife by divorcing her—but that way you make a mere thing of her, and treat her as an adulteress, who has lain with you without love.

You have heard it said that you should not make false oaths—but you should not have to make any oaths at all, because your word should be your bond and you should do everything you say you will do.

You have heard that it is right to extract payment from everyone who owes you, even to the extent of an eye for an eye and a tooth for a tooth—but you should go all out for other persons, even those who are considered your enemies.

Jesus did not come to do away with the Law. The Law was never our problem. It was the human will that was the problem. When the will is bad, we can find ways of getting around any law or statute. Jesus came to tell us that God gives us the Kingdom without regard to the Law, but that, once we know that, we should desire to go far beyond the Law, obeying the highest impulses of the human soul. That way, and that way only, do we reveal the perfect way of God to the world.

That way only do we become the salt and light to the world.

Lord, I am an unworthy person. I have accepted the gift of your Kingdom without really considering what is an appropriate lifestyle for me as a child of the Kingdom. I am afraid I have obscured for others the true vision of life in the Kingdom. I have also robbed myself of the joy of total commitment to your way. Now that I see this, help me to catch the real spirit of the Kingdom. Let me not live with the law as a requirement to be met but as a guideline to go beyond. Through Jesus, whose understanding of these things sustained him even in the horror of crucifixion. Amen.

Week II: Friday

6:1–23 A DEPTH OF HONEST PIETY

In the preceding passage, Jesus said that true righteousness lies not in fulfilling the demands of the Law but in going beyond them. Now he warns against mere superficial piety—practicing our religion in order to be seen by others.

When we give gifts to the poor, we are to do it quietly—so quietly, in fact, that one hand doesn't know what the other is doing.

When we pray, we are to do it without ostentation—even in a small room with the door shut. Nor are we to seek virtue through extremely long prayers, as though God sold his favor by the yard. We are to pray simply and economically, as the manifestation of a sincere and devoted spirit.

When we fast (remember that Jesus gave the model for fasting and praying in Matthew 4:1–11), we are not to screw our faces up and try to look like martyrs in our faith; on the contrary, we are to put on happy faces and not let on to others that we are fasting at all.

Doing these things to be seen by others is laying up treasures on earth, where they will not last. What we should be interested in is what God thinks about our piety. Our real treasure is with him.

As our bodies receive their vision from the eye, so our spiritual lives receive their light from the way we look at things. If we are shortsighted, and are concerned only about how other persons perceive our righteousness, then we shall be full of darkness. But if we see things truly, and realize that our religion is to be judged by God, not man, then we are living in the light.

Lord, I am condemned by this brief prayer which Jesus told us to pray. To pray it, my whole life must be sincerely dedicated to you—must be in fact a prayer. When I pray, I am more wordy because I feel an awkwardness in our relationship—I have not been totally committed to your will in my life. Forgive me, as I hope I am at peace with all persons, and let me glorify your name through honest religion in the days to come. Amen.

Week II: Saturday

6:24–34 SHALOM: THE TRUE PEACE OF GOD

Shalom, the Hebrew word for fullness and peace, was frequently heard among the Jews. But Jesus struck at the irony of a religion in which so many people spoke of *shalom* and so few people actually possessed it. Most Jews, he observed, were like the Gentiles—they clamored for food and clothing and security as if these were the most important things in their lives. True *shalom* had not become part of their lifestyle.

None of us, said Jesus, can worship both God and worldly possessions. If we care about mere things—if we pile them up in order to have plenty tomorrow—they inevitably interfere with our giving full attention to God.

How this cuts across the grain with us, just as it did in Matthew's day! We much prefer the theology occasionally found in the Old Testament which says that possessions are a sign of God's favor. But the New Testament seems to have a bias in favor of being poor—not because there is any special virtue in poverty itself, but because the poor are freer to respond to the radical demands of the Kingdom.

God's wayfarers in the world—that is how the New Testament pictures the disciples of Jesus. People like Peter and John, who, when accosted by the crippled beggar in Acts 3, had no silver or gold coins to give him but gave him instead the healing power that sprang from their dedication and purity of heart.

Peter and John had *shalom—really* had it—because they had left everything to follow Jesus. When will we learn there is no other way to have *shalom?*

Lord, I am really uncomfortable with one foot in the boat and one foot on the shore. I don't know why I try to live this way. It is an agony, really. I guess I am afraid to leave the land. But I see the inadequacy of this position, and ask for faith to commit myself entirely to the boat. Help me to launch out into the deep. Through Jesus, who will be in the boat with me. Amen.

WEEK III

Week III: Sunday

7:1–28 LIVE A SIMPLE LIFE AND LIVE IT WELL

Energy is the power of life, and each of us has only a certain amount of it, whether psychic or physical. We should be careful, then, how we spend it, and Matthew concludes the Sermon on the Mount by repeating some of Jesus' observations about living simply and living well.

We should not waste time and effort criticizing others. We have enough to do looking after our own failures.

We should not give ourselves to idle arguments or disputations with people who have no real interest in the Kingdom. Besides being pointless, it often works to our own detriment.

We should live in simple expectation that God will take care of us. Even an earthly father tries to meet the needs of his child. Can we not expect more of God?

We should do good to all other persons—even those outside the faith—just as we would like them to do good to us. This is, after all, the point of the Law and the prophets.

We should really concentrate on entering the Kingdom, because it is more demanding that many people realize. Few, in fact, really enter it; most simply follow the crowds, thinking they are entering.

We should cling to sound teaching and avoid self-appointed prophets and teachers who are only taking advantage of some people's confusion. You can usually tell who these false leaders are by measuring them against the teachings in this sermon. Unfortunately, they lead many people astray, and these people are going to be disappointed in the end and protest that they were great servants of the Lord; but the Lord will tell them they were mistaken.

The way to be sure you are moving in the right direction is to live by the words of this sermon. It is like a rock you can build your house on. Then, when the time of the winds and rains comes, and other people's efforts are being swept along in the swirling waters, yours will stand fast.

Lord, I know why people thought Jesus had real authority, and did not speak empty things he had borrowed from other people. It was because his life was real and because he spoke to the depths in their own hearts. I know he speaks to the deep places in mine. He makes all other philosophies seem so cheap and selfish in comparison. I want the Kingdom to be a reality in my life, Lord. I don't want to be like those poor people who spent their lives on the wrong things. Help me to build well on these teachings without turning them into a new legalism. Through Jesus, whose gift to us on the cross is the surest guarantee of the validity of everything he taught. Amen.

Week III: Monday

8:1–4 THE POWER TO HEAL

After the section on Jesus' teachings, Matthew now turns to reports of his healing power. The very first story, of the healing of a leper, continues the theme we touched on earlier, that Jesus is greater than Moses, who gave the Torah.

The Torah, in Leviticus 13 and 14, gave very specific instructions about persons having leprosy. At the very first sign of an itching sore, they were to present themselves to the priest. If he verified that they had contracted leprosy, then they must go outside the community and live alone until they either died or were cured of the dread disease. In the event of a miraculous cure, the healed person was to present himself to the priest, who would determine whether the person was indeed relieved of the disease. If the priest decided that the person was cured, he would kill a bird, dip a living bird in its blood, sprinkle some blood on the cured person, and release the living bird to fly away as he pronounced the person well.

Moses' memory was sacred among the Jews because he was the

giver of the Law. But here was one who could do more than give a law about a person with leprosy—he could heal the person! Jesus reached out and touched a man, says Matthew, and immediately the man was cleansed of his disease.

Finally, as if to emphasize again that he had come to fulfill the Law, not to destroy it, Jesus told the man to go to the priest and make an offering of the two birds as Moses had commanded.

> *I am awed, O Lord, by the power of this man Jesus, who could touch a leprous man and make him whole again. I am also awed by his self-control in telling the man to go and show himself to the priest and fulfill the Torah. He must really have been in touch with himself to do that—and in touch with you. Help me to enter into this mystery too. In the name of the Healer.* Amen.

Week III: Tuesday

8:5–17 MORE HEALINGS

Two more, to be precise. The servant of the Roman centurion, and Peter's mother-in-law. And then all those nameless ones who were brought with demons and illnesses.

Why did Matthew choose these two stories out of the hundreds he might have known?

The centurion probably represented the non-Jewish world, much as the narrative of the magi had symbolized it in the birth episode. Even though his Gospel was intended primarily for Jewish Christians, because he was at such pains to point out how Jesus fulfilled the Old Testament prophecies, Matthew obviously wanted to say something here to include all the non-Jews who had become Christians.

"Many will come from east and west," said Jesus, "and sit at table with Abraham, Isaac, and Jacob in the kingdom of heaven, while the sons of the kingdom will be thrown into the outer darkness."

As for Peter's mother-in-law—well, Peter had become something very special in the history of the church, and this little domestic touch would have meant much to the early Christians. The story is not entirely unlike the other. After all, Peter was an outsider to the Pharisees too—one of the little folk, the people of the land, who were practically illiterate on important religious questions. And a mother-in-law would have enjoyed almost as little status as a servant. She was, in effect, a nobody. But even the nobodies are included in the gifts brought by Jesus.

Lord, nobody could be more of an outsider to the faith of Israel than I. I'm not of the first century, I don't speak the language, I don't know the traditions. Yet you have opened your Kingdom to me. Why, Lord? It is a wonder too deep to contemplate. I can only marvel and live in constant thankfulness. In the name of the one who extended power to nobodies. Amen.

Week III: Wednesday

8:18–22 SAYINGS FOR DISCIPLES

These two sayings, involving would-be disciples, are interesting for their emphasis on the radical demands which Jesus laid upon those who would follow him.

First, the scribe who was awed at Jesus' teachings and vowed to follow him wherever he went. He did not know what he was saying, apparently, and Jesus apprised him: "Foxes have holes, and birds of the air have nests; but the Son of man has nowhere to lay his head." Two suggestions leap from this saying—one, of the restless, itinerant nature of Jesus' ministry, and the other, of the stature of the man. "Son of man," *huios tou anthrōpou,* is one of several messianic titles found in the scriptures. Albright and Mann, in the Anchor Bible translation, render this title "The Man," insisting that it means "Representative Man" as in the book of Daniel. Either way, Jesus identifies himself with the end-time of history and as a cosmic figure who should lack a specific residence. The person who wished to follow him was thus reminded that it was no little movement he would attach himself to, and that it was not one from which he could turn back at any time he desired.

Second was the follower who wished to come with Jesus after a brief delay for burying his father (Jewish law required burial within twenty-four hours). "Follow me," said Jesus, "and leave the dead to bury their own dead." What is the meaning of this apparently harsh answer? Would a day have made that much difference? Perhaps Jesus was underlining the demand for obedience in those who became his disciples. Or perhaps he was emphasizing the difference between the old era, the era of the Torah, and the new, the era of the Messiah, in which case he was saying in effect, "When you follow me, you are entering a completely new age; let those who belong to the old age take care of their own." Whatever the meaning, it is clear that the emphasis was on total commitment to the Messiah.

Lord, I have trouble with the tone of these verses. There is a streak of stubborn independence in me that doesn't want to surrender to you. Is the character of the new age such that I must surrender in order to be a disciple? It really bothers me, Lord. Help me to deal with the distress this causes me, and to do it in such a way that I become a more faithful servant. Through Jesus, who both assures and frightens me. Amen.

Week III: Thursday

8:23–27 THE LORD OF THE WINDS AND SEA

Matthew now narrates three separate incidents depicting the extraordinary power of Jesus—the calming of the sea (8:23–27), the casting out of demons from two Gadarene demoniacs (8:28–34), and the forgiving and healing of a paralytic (9:1–8).

One of the remarkable things about the narrative of the storm, when we think about it, is that the cry for help came from disciples, some of whom were fishermen, men of the sea. For years the sea had been their second home. They had surely ridden out many a storm, for storms were likely to arise quickly on the Sea of Galilee. Why this sudden evidence of fear and distrust in their own ability to survive? We can only surmise that the storm's fury was greater than any they had seen before, and that in the height of the churning clouds and the depth of the troughs opening in the water they were genuinely afraid they would perish.

Jesus was the center of *shalom* through all of this. The violence of the storm did not even awaken him. The men had to shake him and cry out to him that they were on the verge of dying. Turning his face toward them (Mark records that he had been sleeping on a pillow), he asked why they had so little faith. Then he stood and transferred the calm that was in him to the sea itself, and to the winds, so that everything became still.

"What sort of man is this," marveled the experienced seamen, "that even winds and sea obey him?"

> *Lord, does this story suggest that you are more the master of my situation—my home, my context, my business—than I am, just as you were master of the fishermen's sea? If it does, then maybe I had better rethink the matter of who is in charge here.* Amen.

Week III: Friday

8:28–34 LORD OVER DEMONS

"What have you to do with us, O Son of God?" cried the demons. "Have you come here to torment us before the time?" Matthew surely used this story to emphasize that Jesus was recognized as the Messiah even by the spirits that inhabit people. In

Enoch, a Jewish apocalypse, demons are said to have power until the day of judgment. Here, in Matthew, they realize that Jesus is the bringer of that day of judgment, though the final catastrophic day has not arrived.

The passage also indicates again the universal character of Jesus' messiahship, for he is in Gentile country, not Jewish (hence the herd of pigs), and these particular demons inhabit two men who are not Jewish.

In Mark's Gospel (5:1–20) there is only one demoniac, and, when Jesus has used his power to exorcise the demons, the man becomes the focus of attention for the townspeople who come out to see the effects of the miracle. But Matthew, who has possibly combined the Marcan account with another in Mark 1:23–28, so that there are two possessed men instead of one, has the crowds come out to see Jesus, not the cured demoniacs. It is a subtle change, perhaps, but an important one: It is who the Messiah is that is important in all of these stories, not what is done in the stories. He is the Lord of the new creation, and that is the theme that matters to Matthew.

Mark makes it plain why the men begged him to leave their part of the country: they were afraid. Unaccustomed to witnessing such displays of power, they asked Jesus to go away. They preferred to keep matters the way they were.

Lord, I would probably have been right in there with those townspeople, if I had been there, asking you to move on to some other territory. It is the dullness in me. I prefer an almost intolerable status quo, which I know, to any kind of interference-with-that-status-quo which I don't know. Help me to get beyond that, Lord, and be ready for any new thing you introduce into my life. Cast out the demon of my dullness, and let me follow you. Amen.

Week III: Saturday

9:1–8 THE AUTHORITY TO FORGIVE AND THE POWER TO HEAL

This story goes beyond the preceding miracle stories in Matthew because it raises the question of Jesus' authority to forgive sins. Mark's account of the same story (2:1–12) makes the problem more explicit: Only God can forgive sins. Jesus was accused of blasphemy, therefore, because he was exercising the divine right to forgive.

This would have been a ticklish issue with the Jews, for whom the matter of forgiveness was institutionalized into a system of priests and sacrifices. Jesus was flying in the face of the entire system by telling the paralytic that he was forgiven. But Matthew apparently set the story here for two reasons: to indicate the growing conflict between Jesus and the scribes (and by implication the Pharisees), and to further enhance the picture he has already drawn of Jesus as the leader greater than Moses, who was able to deliver the Law but unable to exercise the priestly function of absolving guilt.

The healing miracle, which to human flesh would seem to require more power than forgiving sin, was performed in the story as a sign of authority which the people could understand. And, while we do not know the reaction of the scribes to this, the crowds, as is often the case in Matthew's Gospel, respond as though electrified, glorifying God for having sent such authority among them in the flesh.

> *Lord, I confess that I am like the crowds in this story: I react much more excitedly to signs and wonders than I do to the mystery of forgiveness, which is much less visible. Sharpen my perception that I may look more keenly to these matters of the soul which are often more important than the merely physical functions of the body. Through Jesus, who saw at once that this paralytic needed forgiveness more than he needed locomotion.* Amen.

WEEK IV

"Tell John what you see—the blind recover sight, the deaf hear, the lame walk, the dead and dying are raised up." (Week IV: Thursday)

"Lord, teach me to care so much for everyone affected by my power that I may not abuse it, but may turn it into a blessing shared with others." (Week VI: Sunday)

Week IV: Sunday

9:9–13 A KINGDOM OF SINNERS

Most scholars do not believe that the Matthew mentioned here was actually the author of this Gospel, but the story is told with the probable intention of linking the name of the disciple to the Gospel.

Tax collectors were held in disdain by religious Jews not so much because they worked for the occupying power as because they handled money with pagan inscriptions and drawings on it. The sinners referred to, moreover, were probably nonobservant Jews, not grossly disreputable people. Both the tax collectors and the sinners were apparently friends of Matthew who gathered in his home with Jesus and the other disciples after Matthew decided to give up his office to be a follower of Jesus.

The Pharisees, who were among the thirty or forty persons who probably stood around the room in Matthew's home, mumbled to the disciples their amazement that this famous rabbi was eating with nonobservant persons. Jesus, as happens several times in the Gospel, overhears remarks not intended for him and answers them. He cites Hosea 6:6—"I desire mercy, and not sacrifice"—and says he came to call sinners, or nonobservers, not the traditionally righteous people.

We must remember that Judaism was very strong toward the end of the century when this Gospel was written, despite the overthrow of Jerusalem in A.D. 70, and that there was much wrangling between the Christians and the Judaizers. This narrative would have been a strong document in struggles such as that between Paul and the Judaizers in the Galatian churches.

Again, as promised by John the Baptist, it is a case of God's raising up new children of Abraham from the stones along the river of baptism.

Lord, I have the same problem as the Pharisees: I tend to expect you in the old familiar places, behaving in traditional ways. Therefore I do not watch for you to break out in new places, doing new things. Forgive this shortsightedness in me, and help me to be more open. I do not want to miss the evidences of your presence in my own day and my own society. Through Jesus, whose freshness and authority seem always to have lain in his power to see clearly. Amen.

Week IV: Monday

9:14–17 THE PRESENCE OF THE BRIDEGROOM

This passage is easily linked to the preceding one because it has to do with nonobservance. John the Baptist's disciples ask Jesus why it is that they fast as the Pharisees do, while the disciples of Jesus do not. The specific references of the passage may have been intended by the author as a rejection by Jesus of identification with the Essenes or other practitioners of cultic righteousness.

The ground for the rejection would be the fact that Jesus is someone special. He is the bridegroom and center of a celebration. He is the one greater than Moses. He is the Messiah, the Lord of the new creation.

There is apparently a reference to the death of the Messiah—the bridegroom will be taken away from the wedding guests—and then the guests shall fast again as others do. But for the moment they are enjoying a foretaste of the great eschatological wedding, the end of all things in God's new era.

In that final time, Jesus seems to indicate, the Torah or Law of Moses will be left behind. To try to graft the Kingdom onto it would be like putting a new, unshrunken patch on an old garment that has been washed many times, or like putting powerful new wine into old skins that no longer have the flexibility to endure much expansion. Therefore observances such as calendrical fasting (as opposed to fasting for self-discipline) are matters of mere fussiness among the followers of Jesus, and hardly worth attention.

As Jesus said to the Pharisees in Matthew's house, God desires mercy, not sacrifice—which is far more demanding than the old system of laws and regulations.

Lord, there is something comfortable about a rule or a law. It helps us to know where we stand. And there is something frightening about Jesus' way of saying we are beyond that now and are ruled by a spirit, not a regulation. It sort of takes my breath. I hope I am ready for this. Give me the faith to live in the new era. Through Jesus, the bridegroom. Amen.

Week IV: Tuesday

9:18–38 JESUS AND THE CROWDS

Here Matthew gives us an impressionistic picture of the busy ministry of Jesus. Everywhere he turned there were people to be helped, people from all levels of society, including even the president of the local synagogue. And each time Jesus performed a miracle of healing or resuscitation, his reputation grew that much more, so that ever greater crowds pressed at his elbow.

"Nothing like this has ever been seen in Israel," proclaimed the people. Not even Moses or Elijah had been able to do such things. Jesus was clearly the one appointed to usher in the new creation.

Traveling from town to town announcing the new era and curing the people, Jesus felt deeply for the persons who had such need. They were like poor bleating sheep, stumbling over one another in every direction because they had no leaders.

The old Mosaic order had run its course and was doing the masses little good. It was time for a new leader, time for a new order, a new creation. But the new creation would not come in of its own; it required many colaborers, the way a ripe crop requires many persons for immediate harvesting.

Pray for such workers, said Jesus. Beg the owner of the crop to send them in where the need is so great. It is time for a new thing to be done in Israel.

I see an image, Lord, of thousands of people entering an enormous field where the corn fairly bursts to be picked. They are a motley crew—literate and illiterate, rich and poor, gifted and clumsy. And they all enter for one reason—to harvest the heavy crop. I pray for them, Lord—the missionaries and ministers and teachers and nonprofessional Christians alike—and offer myself to be one of them. Through Jesus, who looked on crowds with great compassion. Amen.

Week IV: Wednesday

10:1–42 INSTRUCTIONS FOR DISCIPLES

Imagine yourself in Jesus' place. You have called twelve disciples and they have been with you for months now, learning about the Kingdom and helping with the crowds of people as you taught them and healed the sick. Now you are ready to send them out singly or in small groups all over the country. What would you say to them on the eve of their departure?

Here are Jesus' instructions to them. They are very practical, and in keeping with what he has told them about life in the Kingdom.

The disciples' major responsibility is to proclaim the arrival of the Kingdom, heal the sick, cleanse the lepers, cast out demons, and raise the dead or dying.

They are to take no money for any of this, except such as is necessary to live from place to place. (Already by the time Matthew wrote this, some persons had tried to use the gifts of the Spirit for personal gain. See the account of Simon Magus in Acts 8:4–24.)

They are to behave properly, and, if any household or town fails to receive them, simply shake the dust from their feet as they leave—what one writer has called "the sacrament of failure," to be performed over the hard cases that must be left behind.

They should expect difficulties—prison, quarreling, divided households, death. (By the time of this Gospel's writing, the disciples had probably encountered all these obstacles in abundance.) Yet they are not to fear, for they do the work of God and he is with them. He who considers every sparrow of the field will not fail to note their every peril.

Not the least of the disciples' difficulties will be from their own families. Parents will not want sons and daughters to go as workers in this seemingly impossible undertaking, nor will children wish their parents to go. But a life given for the Kingdom, whatever the immediate cost, is a life fulfilled.

It is an exciting venture the disciples set out upon, for they go in the name of Jesus and anyone who receives them is actually receiving him. Even a cup of cold water handed to one of them along the way will have its reward.

> *Lord, it must have been terribly demanding to be one of the first disciples. There weren't any churches for them to preach in, or any Christian communities to offer them support. They were obviously committed people. I pray for today's ministers, Lord, that they may know similar commitment. Remind them that the power and the Kingdom are yours, and that all that is required of them is to be faithful to the vision. Through Jesus, who still calls and sends out disciples.* Amen.

Week IV: Thursday

11:1–19 JESUS AND JOHN THE BAPTIST

It was natural for John to raise the question, wasn't it? He was alone and in prison, probably treated like an animal, miles from the countryside and riverbanks he loved. A man can become desperately uncertain about things in a situation like that.

"Tell John," Jesus said, "what you see—the blind recover sight, the deaf hear, the lame walk, the dead and dying are raised up."

It was a definitive answer. What more was there to say? The Kingdom and its Lord were obviously there.

Afterwards, Jesus mused on the rough old prophet. Surely no mother's son on earth was greater than John. Yet, said Jesus, in the Kingdom every one is as great as John—the Kingdom is an equalizer.

The times were violent, the way the weather is when a cold front and a warm front collide, and John, tough as he was, had gotten caught in the violence. Jesus himself would be crucified, but he was up to it. Is it possible that he was even a rough and violent man, as John was? The satire in his language in verses 7–10 may indicate that he was.

People are funny, Jesus was thinking. John came as an abstemious religious figure, eating little and refusing strong drink, and people said he was crazy. Jesus came as the opposite, eating and drinking with nonobservant Jews, and the very same people said he was a glutton and a drunkard. Yet God's purpose was being worked out in both of them.

It is amazing, isn't it, how many ways God works?

> *Lord, this is such a human passage. I can almost hear Jesus laughing with joy as he told those men to go tell John what they saw. He had such utter confidence in it all. And that reverie about John—he really cared for John, the way a man cares for another man who has done a good job. And that reflection on people too—Jesus was no fool, Lord. He knew the price of things, didn't he? I can follow more joyfully for this passage, Lord.* Thanks.

Week IV: Friday

11:20–30 GOD AND THE SIMPLE FOLK

Ah, the disappointment breaks through here for the towns that had already proven inhospitable to the Kingdom's work. Even Capernaum, which had been Jesus' headquarters, had rejected the new creation. They had all written their own judgments, but the chief strategist of the new age was disappointed.

There is a touch of sadness and irony in his thanksgiving. God has indeed begun his new creation in the simple folk—the untutored people of the land, who don't stand very high in anybody's social register. They have rallied to the Kingdom.

Let them flock to him—the hard-working poor, the little people of the land—and he will give them relief. Let them join him in the yoke—they will find him gentle and humble-hearted like themselves. Together, they will bring in the Kingdom.

The sophisticated townspeople and the religious leaders are too preoccupied with other things to care about the Kingdom; but God will build it yet from the little stones along the riverbank!

> *Lord, I always liked countryfolk. They don't take things for granted the way city people do. They are affected by the rain, the smell of the earth, the movement of birds. There is an openness and honesty about them, bred by the land they work on. They are more in touch with themselves than city dwellers. And they are still working for the Kingdom. God bless the peasants and the farmers. Through Jesus, who found them receptive.* Amen.

Week IV: Saturday

12:1–14 LORD OF THE SABBATH

As is often the case in Matthew's Gospel, the spirit and thrust of the new creation are here set over against those of the old. Under the Torah, which was the chief religious expression of the old order, some people had fallen into a way of life characterized by mere legal nitpicking; among the thirty-nine varieties of work which their excessive legalism forbade was the plucking of grain on the Sabbath. But the spirit of Jesus' Kingdom shatters this narrow philosophy the way new wine shatters old wineskins.

First Jesus reminds the Pharisees that David himself had once set a precedent for eating food forbidden by religious scruples when the scruples are transcended by the fact of simple hunger. Then he cites an additional biblical reference, Numbers 28:9–10, and throws the discussion into another key altogether: The priests in the temple profane the Sabbath by performing their duties on the holy day, and are guiltless in doing so; and, as he himself is Lord of the new creation, his disciples are as free to do whatever he permits them as the priests of the old order!

There is a different accent here than in Mark's account of the same event (Mark 2:23–28). In Mark, Jesus says, "The sabbath was made for man, not man for the sabbath; so the Son of man is Lord even of the sabbath" (verses 27–28). In other words, man himself takes precedence over mere legalism. But Matthew omits the humanistic reference, repeats his earlier usage of Hosea 6:6 ("I desire mercy, and not sacrifice"), and interprets this verse as a repudiation of the old order in favor of the new. That is, God took no pleasure in the excessive legalism of the old system; he has given his creation over to the Son of man, the Messiah, who is Lord of the Sabbath as he is Lord of everything else. The Pharisees are guilty not only of offending humanity, but of accusing the Lord himself.

Proceeding to the synagogue, where there is a man with a withered hand, Jesus is taunted by some persons there over whether it is permissible to heal on the Sabbath. With the same *élan* he has shown in the earlier episode, Jesus reminds them that their laws permit them to rescue animals on the Sabbath, and asks if a man isn't of more value than an animal. Ignoring the likely rejoinder that rescuing animals is considered an emergency but that there is no reason a static condition such as a lame hand cannot wait until the following day, Jesus tells the man to put forth his hand and heals it.

It is no wonder the Pharisees go away angrily and seek ways to destroy Jesus. His whole tone and temper are different from theirs. His disregard for legalism is only a handy excuse; the fact is, they cannot bear the new order which he represents.

> *Lord, how clearly Jesus saw what the true priorities in life are, and how easily we confuse them. We are always setting into motion systems which run away from us and begin to oppress people—in government, in education, in business, in human relations. Help us to see when this happens and be willing to terminate or modify them as much as is necessary for the good of those affected by them. Through the one whose courage led to a cross.* Amen.

WEEK V

Week V: Sunday

12:15–21 THE SECRET OF JESUS

When the time comes that you are well known to all men, said the poet Rainer Maria Rilke, then it is time to take another name —any name—so that God can call you in the night.

Here, in fulfillment of a prophecy in Isaiah, Matthew indicates the becoming modesty of Jesus as his fame grew throughout Israel. To be sure, there was an external reason for his asking those he healed not to tell anyone—the opposition of the Pharisees was growing and he did not wish to provoke a final encounter before his hour had come (cf. John 12:27, 13:1). But the quiet manner which Isaiah predicted for the Messiah accords well with the injunctions in Matthew 6 against making any display of piety or good works. Jesus was not letting his left hand know what the right hand had done.

People appreciate modesty. The greatest persons in the world are usually the most self-effacing. Their strong sense of inner worth renders unnecessary the praise of the multitudes. It is the diminutive persons, the would-be heroes, who make a show of their gifts and achievements.

> *Lord, why is it that those of us who do least for others are most concerned to be recognized for what we have done? We desire thank-you notes, brass plaques, and public praise for all our good deeds. Help us to be more like the Master of men, who, having rendered the greatest of services, besought others to remain silent about the gift.* Amen.

Week V: Monday

12:22–37 JESUS SPEAKS BACK

Jesus may have been a gentle and modest person, but he was also firm with those who opposed him. In this passage there are echoes of John the Baptist, whose fiery denunciation of the scribes and Pharisees once rang out along the Jordan.

The Pharisees had said that Jesus derived his power from the Evil One. How, he demanded to know, could the Evil One bring forth good works? Obviously it was the Pharisees themselves who were related to the Evil One. They were a nest of snakes, hissing and writhing and ready to inject their poison into any victim who came near them!

It was not that Jesus minded their words against him—those would be forgiven. But their impediment to the movement of the Spirit of God, to the coming of the Kingdom, was unforgivable. In the day of judgment, their own words would prove their condemnation.

Here is a healthy attitude for all of us! We should not worry about what others say or think of us, but we should always be concerned about the spirit of evil which blocks the Kingdom's work in the world. *That* is the real problem we face.

> *Lord, I often get steamed up over the wrong things—little slights from friends or a lack of recognition from those I work for—while I hardly think of the graft and corruption at the corporate level which are grinding down your little ones, making slums of our cities, and poisoning the atmosphere of our world. Help me to become more passionate about the important things. Through Jesus, who had the right perspective.* Amen.

Week V: Tuesday

12:38–50 SIMPLE FOLK REQUIRE NO PROOF

How easy it is to think, "If only I had lived in Jesus' day and seen the miracles he worked, I would have had no problem believing in him!" But Jesus said to the scribes and Pharisees that only a perverse generation needs a sign in order to believe, and he refused to accommodate their desire for a sign—except to speak of his own death and resurrection, which Matthew obviously regards as the most important sign he ever gave. They would fare worse in the judgment than the people of ancient Nineveh or the Queen of the South—non-Jews who respected God more than they did!

The scribes and Pharisees had tried, in their vain efforts to be righteous, to cleanse their lives of evil. But the evil had returned to its source seven times stronger than when it began. What hope could there be for such stiff-necked people?

By contrast, there were the disciples, who had never thought of themselves as righteous or skilled in the Law. They were like brothers and sisters and parents to Jesus. They had followed him without asking for signs of his power and authority. They were like the gentle, humble people of the Beatitudes. Theirs would be the Kingdom of God.

Forgive me, Lord, for having ever desired signs of your favor. I am surrounded by such signs if I will only learn to see them. Life bears abundant clues of your presence, from the gentle sunlight that awakened me this morning to the water I drank from an old dipper to the lovely yellow squash on my plate at dinner and the smiles of my family around the table. Why am I so obtuse that I seldom recognize you? Thank you for being there, and for Jesus, who made such things much plainer to us. Amen.

Week V: Wednesday

13:1–23 SPEAKING IN PARABLES

Matthew 13 is given solely to parables about the Kingdom and discourse about parables. It is both tantalizing in its material and enlightening about Jesus' method of teaching. Contrary to the image we received from Matthew 5:1, of Jesus addressing the multitudes with the Sermon on the Mount, Matthew 13:34–35 asserts that Jesus "never spoke to them without a parable." This may mean that Jesus left the crowds to go up to the mountain and teach the disciples, and that the rich body of ethical teachings in Matthew 5–7 was really delivered to the inner circle of followers, not to the masses.

Why would Jesus have spoken to the crowds only in parables? Perhaps it was so the ones God intended to hear and be saved would recognize the true meaning of the parables, while others would hear only puzzling words and would not be affected by them. In this sense, a parable has been called "a trap for meaning." Its relevance is apparent only as one enters the story and acts out the drama. If the person hearing is successful, then the story becomes his or her story—it is no longer an impersonal narrative. Otherwise the story remains a mere absurdity.

We can only conclude that the explanation of the parable of the seeds in verses 18–23 and the later explanation of the parable of the wheat and tares in verses 36–43 are additives or glosses on the original text for the purpose of instructing neophyte Christians in the day when the Gospel was written. Jesus clearly expected the original disciples to understand the parables without explanation; if they did not, then there was no reason for him to speak in parables at all.

Lord, the disciples heard and understood because their lives were committed to you. But I am often like the crowds who heard but never understood. At least, like them, I am seldom swept away from my usual moorings to enter the unchartered seas of the Spirit. The very monotony of my existence accuses me of never having heard and responded fully to you. My meager response has been like that of the ground where the thistles lay—my own cares have grown faster than my concern for the Kingdom and have choked it out. I long for matters to be different, Lord. Increase my power to hear these parables as I read them again. Let me truly live them, from the inside out. Through Jesus, who tempts me with such mysteries. Amen.

Week V: Thursday

13:24–43 THE SECRET GROWTH OF THE KINGDOM

The one element common to all three of these parables is the way the Kingdom grows quietly, unobtrusively, and then one day becomes suddenly apparent to all.

The wheat grows silently among the tares until the time of harvest. Then the tares are cut down and destroyed, while the wheat is harvested and garnered into barns.

The lowly mustard seed, smaller than the seed of a cantaloupe or squash, grows quietly into a stalky plant towering over the plants from other small seed, and the birds come to light in it and survey the other plants below.

A tiny amount of leaven or yeast is mixed with a much larger amount of flour. It is invisible to the eye when they have been combined. Yet in a few hours it has quietly spread throughout the dough and caused it to expand to double and triple its original size.

It is always easier, isn't it, to see the evil at work in the world. Our daily papers and newscasts focus on the horrors and atrocities of the world around us. But the good news of the Kingdom is that it is growing too, though quietly and without notice, and that those who have ears to hear may realize this and exult in hope.

When I am appalled at the intensity of violence and rage in the modern world, Lord, help me to remember that the Kingdom has been growing quietly and steadily for centuries now, and that it is stronger and more wide-spread than anyone knows. Remind me of the unexpected people and places where I have had glimpses of its existence, and let me figure from that the almost limitless possibilities for its success in the world. Through Jesus, who could speak thus confidently despite the impending horror of the cross and the defection of his friends. Amen.

Week V: Friday

13:44–52 MORE PARABLES

"For sheer joy," says the New English Bible, the man who found the buried treasure "went and sold everything he had, and bought that field."

We can picture the man racing about from acquaintance to acquaintance, asking whatever they would give him for his possessions.

"But you don't want to sell those candlesticks, Barnabas—they belonged to your uncle Joseph."

"I want to sell—give me anything!"

"But Barnabas—your library! You have always loved it so!"

"No matter—it is nothing. What will you give?"

Joyously, confidently, vigorously selling *all* for the field with its treasure. So it is, said Jesus, with the Kingdom. If a man only knew its worth, he would give up everything for it.

This was the difference between Jesus and the scribes and Pharisees—he was enthusiastic, filled with the Spirit of the Kingdom. His mind raced from image to image, describing the coming of a new creation.

Even a teacher of the Law, he said, can become a learner in the Kingdom. Then he will not merely draw on the store of what has been written and said before, but will feel the tides of creation rise within him, so that he speaks new things as well as old.

How beyond price the Kingdom is—if men would only realize it!

> *The old and the new, Lord. How wonderful if all people were so open to both the past and the future, and could draw upon one while learning of the other. Grant that I may maintain a spirit which combines both reverence for what has been thought and taught in the past and receptivity for all the emergent factors which make for a new order in my time. Through Jesus, who said we could learn from him.* Amen.

Week V: Saturday

13:53–58 DISDAINING THE FAMILIAR

I went to school with one of the most famous theologians of modern times. We were not friends, but I used to see him frequently in the library, the halls, and the room where we ate our lunches. Like others who knew him even marginally during those days, I have great difficulty believing that he is the same man whose name is spoken with respect throughout the world. He was simply too common and unattractive to have evolved into that other person. In order to read his writings with proper reverence, I have to detach myself from any memory of the student I saw, and think of him only as a renowned theologian.

Apparently it was this way for the people of Jesus' hometown. They could not believe that the profound teachings they heard from Jesus or the miraculous healings he performed came from one whom they had watched growing up as the son of Mary. And the attention which they paid to the contrast between their expectancies and the man who stood before them diverted them from the things he was trying to say and do, so that his effectiveness was limited in their midst.

What they needed to remember, as we do, is that wisdom is a gift of God, whatever the vehicle, and we should not permit our incredulity toward the source to blind us to its value.

Lord, sometimes my children stagger me with their insights into life's mysteries. Help me never to miss the truth of what they say because I am so preoccupied with its source. The same goes for all the other places where I seldom expect to find wisdom. Through Jesus, who both said and did the truth. Amen.

WEEK VI

Week VI: Sunday

14:1–12 THE DEATH OF THE BAPTIST

God is not the only judge of men. History—the long look—also renders its judgment. And history reveals the vast difference between the two men at the center of this little drama.

John we know to have been a simple man of simple tastes. Herod's life was complicated by ambition, pride, and foolishness.

John was morally zealous. Herod was corrupt and entangled in his own sins. He had broken Jewish law to divorce his wife and marry Herodias, and he broke it by executing John without a trial and by executing him by decapitation.

John was totally committed to the coming Kingdom of God. Herod was committed to keeping his own throne intact if he could.

John died with honor, and is remembered throughout the world as the forerunner of Christ. Herod died in disgrace, banished by the emperor to the remoter districts of Gaul, cut off from the very kingdom he sought so desperately to preserve.

Real security, history seems to say, does not lie in earthly thrones and fortifications, but in commitment to God and his righteousness. It cannot be bought by gold and jewels. It is given to those who live in the Spirit of God.

> *Lord, power in the hands of a careless person is a frightening thing. It even prompts me to consider whether I do not often misuse the modest power at my disposal. Teach me to care so much for everyone affected by my power that I may not abuse it, but may turn it into a blessing shared with others. Through Jesus, who cared about the use of power.* Amen.

Week VI: Monday

14:13–21 FEEDING THE CROWDS

Finding a lonely place in the Israel of Jesus' day was not always easy, especially around the populous western shore of the Galilean Sea. It has been estimated that in a country hardly larger than most American counties there were at that time more than two hundred cities with more than 15,000 inhabitants each. Jesus often had to go across the lake, five or six miles at the wider points, to find some solitude. As several disciples were fishermen by trade, transportation was no problem.

But on this occasion the enthusiastic crowds, knowing what Jesus intended to do, simply swept around the shore of the sea and were waiting for him on the other side. Instead of instructing the disciples to turn the boat about and head for the other side again, Jesus had such feeling for the people that he went ashore among them and continued healing their sick.

At the day's end, the disciples suggested that he send the people to get food. Doubtless they had a small store of food in their boat—Mark 8:14 indicates their habit of keeping a supply—but they were reluctant to take it out and begin eating in the presence of the crowds.

"Give them something to eat yourselves," said Jesus. "All we have," they replied, "is five loaves and two fish." "Let me have them," said Jesus. He blessed the loaves and fish and gave them to the disciples to distribute, and when everyone had eaten his or her fill, there were twelve basketfuls of scraps remaining.

The miracle is reminiscent of the Israelites' receiving manna from heaven as Moses led them through the wilderness. But, as Jesus is greater than Moses, the provision is much more abundant for those he feeds.

This was an important narrative among the early Christians, not only because Jesus was the new Moses but because the multiplication of the bread accorded so well with the Eucharistic meal which was the central rite of Christian fellowship. In a time when Christians sometimes met literally in the wilderness to avoid detection, or at least in very private places, the story spoke eloquently of the way God daily provided their food for spiritual life.

We are so inclined, Lord, to put our trust in programs organized for our future maintenance—in Social Security and insurance funds and savings accounts—so that we spend much of our present energy providing for tomorrow's needs. "In God We Trust," we say—and put the motto on our money. *Help us to rediscover the meaning of freedom and spontaneity by depending on you for our daily bread. Through Jesus, who is sovereign of every wilderness place we can possibly inhabit.* Amen.

Week VI: Tuesday

14:22–36 CHRIST AND HIS CHURCH

After feeding the people and sending them away, Jesus went up the hillside that swept duskily down to the sea. The average person would have done so in order to lie down and sleep after such a strenuous day. But Jesus went up to pray. He had learned long ago that prayer releases inner energies that restore the person even more than sleep.

Apparently Jesus had sent the disciples home for the night too, or else they had spent the night on the boat and then had put out very early in the morning to do some fishing. But the sea was rough and they were having difficulty. In the fourth watch, possibly as daylight was struggling to break through the storm, Jesus appeared to the disciples walking on the water. Shaking in terror, they thought they were beholding an apparition. Only his voice dispelled their fears.

Peter, always the most impetuous disciple, tried to walk to Jesus on the water. But the sight of the deep waves and the force of the wind made him falter, and the waters began to swallow him up. Swimmer that he doubtless was, he cried out for help. Reaching out and supporting him, Jesus chided him: "Why did you hesitate? How little faith you have!" And, when they were both in the boat, the wind suddenly died and the men all fell down exclaiming, "Truly you are the Son of God."

Imagine the situation in the early church's life to which a passage like this must have spoken. Persecutions had made survival difficult for the church. Jesus' reappearance was delayed beyond their expectations, just as he was late in coming to the disciples on the boat. Peter, who was probably already known as the chief spokesman of the church, had faltered badly at the time of the crucifixion. But Jesus had steadied him and helped him back into the boat. Clearly the exhortation to those in the church during this stormy period was to fall down and worship Jesus as the Son of God!

The remarkable picture in verses 34–36 is in keeping with such a passage. It is of the transcendent Christ passing through the crowds with people begging only to touch the hem of his garment. "And everyone who touched it," translates the New English Bible, "was completely cured."

> *Lord, I am greatly moved by this picture of the early church and its worship. Grant that when the storms seem too much for us today we shall remember this passage and take heart. Through Jesus, who joins us in the troubled vessel.* Amen.

Week VI: Wednesday

15:1–20 THE PARABLE OF THE UNRIGHTEOUS MAN

This material is closely related to Jesus' teachings in Matthew 5:17–48, where he said that he had not come to abrogate the Law of Moses but to fulfill it. The scribes and Pharisees in the passage are concerned once more with the failure of the disciples, who are nonobservant Jews, to keep the regulations or traditions which have become associated with the Law. The disciples do not perform the ritual lustrations before meals.

Stung by this persistent nettling over nonessentials, Jesus replies in two ways.

First, he reminds them that they themselves have *altered* the Law of Moses to make the commandment to honor one's parents avoidable, just as in Matthew 5:31–32 he reminded his audience that the law concerning divorce had been *weakened* to suit the contemporary legalists. In other words, they put their own traditions above the Law of God and teach as holy doctrines the commandments of men!

Second, Jesus gives his critics a brief parable: It is not what goes into the mouth that defiles a person but what comes out.

The disciples, uncomfortable with the tension that is building between Jesus and the legalists, ask him if he realizes he has angered his hearers. But he too is angry, and lashes back: "Let them alone; they are blind guides." Though they set themselves up as leaders of the people, they and the people will both fall into the ditch.

Peter, again the spokesman for the early church, asks for an interpretation of the parable. As in earlier cases, this is probably for the benefit of catechumens in the church of Matthew's age, who needed to understand the meaning of the saying. It is not the food entering the body that defiles it, says Jesus, but the talk coming out of it.

We recall that Paul had written to the Corinthians (8:1–13) about eating meat sold from pagan altars. In that instance Paul handled a similar question by saying that "food will not bring us into God's presence" but that he personally would eat no meat at all if it proved an offense to those whose faith was weaker than his.

Paul, of course, was dealing with a question *within* the community of believers, and so was inclined to be charitable. Jesus, on the other hand, was dealing with the incorrigible lawyers and Pharisees, whose scruples were of another order than those of the Christians who wished to abstain from meat given to idols. He was therefore inclined to do as he had instructed his disciples—shake the dust from his feet and abandon them to judgment.

Lord, those who meet about such things say that it is scruples over how the communion meal is to be taken that keep the major bodies of the church from uniting today. We are no better than the scribes and Pharisees, it seems, for we put our own traditions above fellowship and worshiping together. Save us from being blind guides of the blind. Through Jesus, who perennially rebukes our foolishness. Amen.

Week VI: Thursday

15:21–28 JESUS AND A FOREIGNER

If we are bothered by Jesus' tendency at this stage to define his mission in terms of Israel and not of the entire world, we must remember that Matthew's Gospel was written from a Jewish perspective to emphasize how Jesus had first fulfilled the prophecies regarding a Messiah for Israel. But this story very self-consciously represents Jesus as bringing benefits to the Gentile world as well.

The woman, a Canaanite, accentuates the Jewishness of Jesus by calling him Son of David. And she asks for so little—the crumbs that fall from the table. The Greek word used here for dogs, *kunaria,* specifically means small dogs—house dogs or lap dogs, as contrasted with the larger dogs that guard sheep or roam the fields. It is a gentle imploring that the woman makes.

Jesus cannot resist, and grants her request—her daughter is freed from the demonic spirit. The Gentile world begins in a small way to benefit from the coming of the Jewish Messiah!

From what small beginnings, Lord, sprang the riches that have come to the Gentile world from the Jewish Savior. My mind boggles at any attempt to enumerate your blessings to our culture. Freedom, peace, love, and all they mean in specific ways, are the gifts of your Spirit. We thank you through Jesus, who has broken down every wall that divided us, if we will only see that he has. Amen.

Week VI: Friday

15:29–16:12 WORRYING ABOUT BREAD

Again the story of the crowds and Jesus' compassion on them. Again the hesitance of the disciples—"We have only seven loaves and a few fishes." Again the blessing of what there was and the feeding with abundance in the wilderness. And again the nagging question of the Pharisees, "Show us a sign," with the cryptic answer that they were to have only the sign of the prophet Jonah.

"Beware," says Jesus to the disciples, "of the leaven of the Pharisees and Sadducees." Leaven was often used by rabbis as a symbol of evil and how quickly it permeates everything. But the poor dull disciples! They hear the word leaven and realize in an instant that they have failed to bring any bread with them, though there were so many basketfuls left over from the feeding of the four thousand. "He has caught us unprepared," they think.

"Don't you understand?" Jesus says. "I was speaking of the evil influence of the Pharisees and Sadducees, not of real bread."

The real point of the lesson may lie with the bread and not with the leaven, however; at least it appears so in the parallel passage in Mark 8:11–21. Twice Jesus had performed miracles in supplying bread for vast crowds—and here they were, a mere handful of disciples, worrying because they had no bread. Are we not prone to do the same—to forget the providence of God through the ages when we come to a moment of present need in our lives?

Lord, I too am a dull disciple. I forget the many miracles that have sustained my life until this moment, and cry out as though lost because of some small need that must now be met. Help me to know there are no emergencies in your Kingdom—only opportunities to wait upon your generous hand. Through Jesus, whose lot it is to have dull disciples. Amen.

Week VI: Saturday

16:13–20 THE GREAT CONFESSION

There is lively debate about this passage. Some scholars think it is an early attempt to bolster the papal authority of Peter by designating him as the foundation of the church and consigning to him the keys of stewardship. Others insist that it is the confession of Peter which is to be the foundation of the church.

Regardless of what the passage says about Peter, however, it provides an important picture of Jesus. Several times in the Gospel, he instructs those he has healed not to tell anyone about what he has done. Apparently he often worked among the crowds with near anonymity. That this is so is enforced by his question "Who do men say that the Son of man is?" and the answer the disciples give, "Some say John the Baptist, others say Elijah, and others Jeremiah or one of the prophets." Were it not for the attempt at secrecy, we should think this very strange; for all his fame, Jesus was not widely known in his own right.

"Who do *you* say that I am?" he asks the disciples. "You are the Christ, the Son of the living God," replies Peter. It is a significant confession, registering what may have been only a slowly maturing conviction on the apostles' part. In the boat, they had recognized him as the Son of God (Matthew 14:33); but we know that time sequences were often confused in the writing of the Gospels, and there is some reason to suspect that the episode in the boat may even have been at one time a postresurrection narrative akin to John 21:4–8. Matthew apparently construed Peter's confession as the first major recognition by the disciples of the true scope of Jesus' work and ministry: He is not merely a wonderful teacher and worker of miracles, he is the long-promised Savior of the people!

Again Jesus counsels the disciples not to tell anyone who he really is, as though the secret must not yet be disclosed. And, from this time on, he begins to prepare the disciples for the events of the passion week and beyond, which now loom palpably close.

Lord, what a moment it must have been for the disciples when they moved like this from one level of recognition to another. They were surely filled with exultation. I am intrigued with the notion that it might be like that with me also—that the quality of my whole life could be suddenly altered by a deepened awareness of the meaning of Christ to my existence. Let it be, I pray, through him who reveals himself to faithful disciples. Amen.

WEEK VII

"Blessed is he who comes in the name of the Lord. . . . Save now! Save now in the highest!" (Week VIII: Wednesday)

He prayed that the dreadful hour of testing might simply go away, if possible—that he might be wrong about the series of events he saw rapidly building to a climax. (Week XI: Tuesday)

Week VII: Sunday

16:21–28 LETTING GO OF LIFE IN ORDER TO HAVE IT

From here on out, the shadow of the cross falls implacably across Matthew's account of Jesus' ministry. And how quickly Peter falls from the sublimity of the new order to the fear and hesitance of the old! He has barely made the great confession that Jesus is the Messiah, the Son of the living God, when Jesus speaks of his impending death and Peter counters with an oath to say, "No, Lord, this shall never happen to you!" He can no more fit the two things together—Messiah and death—than the crowds of unbelievers could. Jesus has cured the sick, made the blind see and the deaf hear, restored the leprous, cast out demons, and raised the dead. How can one with such power speak of dying a shameful death?

Again, we remind ourselves, the true time sequence meant little to those who wrote our Gospels. Perhaps Jesus had not yet taught the disciples the profound sayings which Matthew gathered into the Sermon on the Mount—especially the part about not being anxious but leaving life to God (6:25–34)—so that Peter's lack of understanding is permissible. Or, if Jesus had already given the sayings to the disciples, then the matter of the cross retrieved them and underscored them with new meaning.

"Get behind me, Satan!" says Jesus, rebuking Peter as furiously as he had a short time earlier congratulated him on his insight. "You are not on the side of God, but of men." Or, as the Jerusalem Bible translates it, "The way you think is not God's way but man's."

If the early church described in the book of Acts had taken a motto from the sayings of Jesus, this might well have been the one. "The way you think is not God's way but man's." For they no longer thought in the usual terms of cost, probability of success, and failure. They were like a people on fire for God, turning the world upside down, because everything seemed possible to them under God.

The secret, as Jesus explained to the disciples, is not to worry about self. It is in trying to grasp life and keep what we have that we lose everything; it is in living recklessly for God that we find everything! In the tidal wave of the Kingdom, only those who swim wildly with the tide will be saved—and the tide is already rising.

I want to take risks, Lord, and live unencumbered by selfish concerns. I would like even to own no property, but to wander the world as a servant. But I cannot help feeling responsible for my family. What am I to do about them? How can I be fully committed to you while caring for daily matters like orthodontist bills and fixing my son's bicycle? Help me to know the answer to this, Lord, because it perplexes me a lot. Through Jesus, whose commitment makes me feel guilty. Amen.

Week VII: Monday

17:1–13 A FORETASTE OF THE NEW ORDER

This is an especially striking passage in the light of Matthew's theme that Jesus is the New Moses. The event apparently occurred during the Feast of Tabernacles, as Peter wanted to erect booths or tents for the three figures. The emphasis of Jewish thinking during this time was on the new age of the Messiah. The ascent of the mountain, the appearance of Moses and Elijah (who had been translated to heaven without dying), and the cloud representing the holy presence of God are all in keeping with this emphasis.

Jesus' face shines as Moses' did when he descended from Mount Sinai. The voice from the cloud, however, which is the same voice heard at Jesus' baptism in Matthew 3:17, announces that this is one greater than either Moses, who represents the Law, or Elijah, who represents the prophets. It is the beloved Son, which in Jewish thought is the closest identity a human being could have to God himself.

The entire event may be called an "eschatological theophany"—an appearance of God in a context suggestive of the way it will be in the Kingdom after the resurrection. The three disciples, who represent a kind of inner circle of authority not unlike that among the Qumran Essenes, are understandably frightened and excited by the scenario.

The presence of Elijah among the transfigured ones leads naturally to the disciples' question about the popular notion that he must return to earth before the age of the Messiah. Jesus indicates that the people of the age have already had their Elijah—John the Baptist—but failed to recognize him. And the reference to John is occasion for Jesus' reference to his own sufferings, which will be in dramatic contrast to the glory he has just shared in the transfiguration scene.

> *Mountains, light, the cloud—the symbolism of this passage is of height, loftiness, rarefication. It beckons me, Lord, from the tawdriness of my everyday concerns—from a cluttered desk, a messy laundry room, unpaid bills, a car in need of repair. Thank you for hallowing such moments, and for sending a light in my darkness.* Amen.

Week VII: Tuesday

17:14–20 WHEN FAITH IS TOO WEAK

This story must have been told for every lagging disciple in every age including our own. The situation in the life of the early church is not hard to imagine. After all the marvelous stories of Jesus' miracles of healing, and then of the disciples', especially in the book of Acts, some followers of the Way were distressed that they could not cast out demons, cure the sick, and raise the dead as their Lord and predecessors had. Did they not share the same power? Ah, says the Gospel, coming to their rescue, even the apostles failed on occasion because their faith was not strong enough.

We human beings are funny creatures. Faith transforms us. When we believe something strongly, we enter a new realm of possibility. I heard a man say that in an emergency his father had picked up the side of an automobile and held it while an injured person was removed from beneath the wreck; afterward he tried to lift it again and could not budge it. The crisis had propelled him into a new dimension of strength. Is it so hard to believe that miracles occur in the lives of those whose faith accepts miracles as natural?

> *Lord, moving mountains by faith is beyond my imagination. Maybe Jesus only exaggerated to make his point. I can believe in dramatic cures, telepathic messages, and superhuman strength. Help me to move from my present level of expectancy to one where such things are the rule and not the exception. Through Jesus, for whom miracles were a way of life.* Amen.

Week VII: Wednesday

17:22–27 A FISH STORY

Here, set against Jesus' prediction of his death and resurrection, this strange story. What can it mean? The intent is surely similar to that of the encounter between Jesus and the Pharisees in Matthew 22:15–22 about paying taxes to Caesar. The position of the early church seems consistently to have been pro-authority. Even though the government was corrupt and shared in the persecution of Christians, Christians were advised to pay their taxes, pray for their leaders, and live harmoniously in the temporal order. This passage involves the payment by Jewish Christians of the tax to maintain the temple in Jerusalem. After the Jews instituted new rules which deterred the Christians from participating in synagogue and temple worship, many Christians doubtless protested the temple tax assessments.

Jesus and his followers, who are giving their lives to God's work, should hardly be taxed to support a place dedicated to his worship. But, says Jesus in effect, we do not want to cause difficulty for those who merely enforce the rules, so we shall pay their tax. It is a rule of generosity for future generations, and much in keeping with the teaching of Matthew 5:41, "If a man in authority makes you go one mile, go with him two."

As for the fish story, which seems almost too fantastic to deserve a place in the Gospel, there is of course the possibility that it was symbolic and not realistic. We remember that the fish became a symbol for Christianity because the Greek word for fish, *ichthus,* was an anagram of the motto *Iesus Christos Theou Huios Soter*—"Jesus Christ, God's Son, Savior." Could the story have meant that the Christian community would pay the temple tax for its members? The early Christians, after all, did hold their goods in a common treasury.

> *It sometimes bothers me, Lord, to pay taxes to corrupt authorities. I feel that I could use the money much better for humane purposes. But Jesus never seemed to worry much about money; that wasn't what the Kingdom hinged on. Give me an open and generous spirit, I pray, that I may be more like him.* Amen.

Week VII: Thursday

18:1–14 GOD'S LITTLE ONES

This chapter constitutes another of the long discourses in Matthew which are collections of Jesus' teachings for the edification of the Christian community. To understand the full impact of this one, it is necessary to remember that one of the forces against which early Christianity had to contend was its own predecessor, Judaism. Throughout the Gospel, Matthew delineates the struggle between Jesus and the rabbinical system which was represented by the venerable rabbis who interpreted the Law and tradition. Much of Jesus' conflict with the scribes and Pharisees stemmed from the fact that his disciples were nonobservant Jews, neither learned in the Law nor committed to the traditions.

Now, in this brilliant passage, Matthew depicts Jesus as exalting not the aged figures of rabbis, growing more and more infirm as they master the arguments of earlier rabbis, but small children, who do not need the detailed refinements of the Law and tradition to mirror God's presence in the world. "Who is the greatest in the kingdom of heaven?" ask the disciples. And Jesus sets a child in their midst. "Unless you become like children, you will never enter the kingdom of heaven."

To the tradition-bound Jew, all of Jesus' followers are mere children, uneducated in the Law. Jesus passes from talking about actual children to these figurative children. "If anyone leads astray one of these little children who believe in me he would be better off thrown into the depths of the sea with a mill-stone hung round his neck!" (J. B. Phillips' translation).

Recall that, when Jesus denounced the cities that had refused his ministry, he said, "I thank thee, Father, Lord of heaven and earth, that thou hast hidden these things from the wise and understanding and revealed them to babes" (Matthew 11:25). It was a point Jesus made again and again in various ways. The Kingdom was a new creation; it could not be poured like new wine into old skins. It required fresh vigor and childlike imagination, untrammeled by too much devotion to mere tradition.

Perhaps Jesus anticipated criticism of the disciples and the Christian community. "Don't think too harshly of these little ones," he was cautioning in effect; "they have their guardian angels who look directly into the face of God. Of course they resemble sheep in their simple faith. But God has sent his Good Shepherd to find the sheep that the learned shepherds of Israel have disregarded. And there is great rejoicing whenever one of them is brought home to the Kingdom!"

Make me simple, Lord, as you are simple. Let my eye be sound and my entire body full of light. Calm my thoughts, that they fly not in a thousand directions. Still my impulses, that they may wait upon you as a sheep waits upon the help of its shepherd. Make me see your world fresh-washed and magical, like a child, and I shall glorify you this day. Amen.

Week VII: Friday

18:15–35 WHEN LITTLE ONES FALL OUT

How shall God's little ones deal with quarrels among themselves? Matthew here relates explicit teachings of Jesus on this subject. First there is patient exchange with the contentious person. Go to him or her and discuss the matter in question. If the person remains alienated, take one or two other Christians along and try again; perhaps he or she will be convinced upon hearing the facts from other perspectives. Should this not avail, then take the matter before the Christian community and let them deal with it. Perhaps the health of the entire organism is necessary to re-establish the health of the diseased tissue. But if the person remains obdurate even against the community, there is nothing left but to treat the person as an outsider.

The words spoken to Peter in the context of the great confession (Matthew 16:19) are repeated here: Decisions made in the community are decisions of the Kingdom as well. An ancient Jewish saying was, "Two that sit together occupied in the Law have the Presence among them." And, as the Christian community is formed by God's presence in the new creation, he is automatically involved in the decisions it makes.

Lest all of this seem too harsh, however, or the centrality of love in the community be lost, Matthew adds one more bit of teaching, about forgiveness. It is Peter, the head of the Christian community, who asks, "Lord, how often am I to forgive my brother if he goes on wronging me? As many as seven times?" Other Oriental laws of mercy said three times. Jesus replies, "I do not say seven times; I say seventy times seven." Such a number is no longer literal, of course; it speaks of such depths of concern and forgiveness as cannot be measured.

There follows a parable on the Kingdom to remind every member of the community that he or she is there only by the grace of God. In one sense, it is a gloss on the phrase in the Model Prayer "Forgive us our debts as we forgive our debtors." We were all so far in debt—the poor character in this story was in by a king's ransom!—that there was no hope of ever paying. For us to be hard or unforgiving toward anyone else, then, over what in comparison can never amount to more than a beggarly amount, a few coins, is absurd; it proves we have not truly appreciated the magnitude of God's gift to us, and cannot in fact consider ourselves part of the Kingdom.

Lord, what a deep well of the Spirit this presumes! It reminds me with terrifying vividness of the shallow level at which I daily live. Give me a renewed consciousness of my freedom from debt, that I may respond to others always with exhilaration and joy. Through Jesus, who forgave others even from his cross. Amen.

Week VII: Saturday

19:1–15 MARRIAGE MAKES ONE FLESH

Again Matthew takes up the greater-than-Moses theme, this time with regard to the law about marriage and divorce. Moses had said that a man could divorce his wife if he gave her a legal notification of dismissal. But Jesus, who said that he came to perfect the Law, not abolish it (Matthew 5:17–18), says that divorce is not permissible for any cause except unfaithfulness, regardless of Moses' saying. "It was because you knew so little of the meaning of love," says Jesus, "that Moses allowed you to divorce your wives! But that was not the original principle" (J. B. Phillips). In the creation, God ordained one wife for one husband; the two become one flesh. And in the new creation, it is clear, that is how Jesus intends it shall be.

In that case, say the disciples, it is better not to marry; marriage is too final a step to take. Not everyone is capable of making that decision, says Jesus; but whoever can ought to do so. Taken together with Paul's statement in 1 Corinthians 7:9, "It is better to marry than to be aflame with passion," this passage lays the foundation for clerical celibacy as it has been practiced through the ages.

Next, as if to underline the complexity of life when it must be regulated by law, Matthew turns once more to a picture of the children or little ones in their simplicity of lifestyle. Mothers have brought them to Jesus for him to lay hands on them and pray for them. The disciples, who characterize the insensitivity and male chauvinism of the age, and thus reveal much about the foregoing comments on marriage and divorce, try to drive them away. But Jesus stops them. He says again, "To such belongs the kingdom of heaven."

> *Lord, this hard teaching on marriage would not be necessary if we had only learned the lesson about forgiveness in the preceding parable. We are selfish and demanding of one another without being mindful of our flawed characters or the enormity of our indebtedness to you. Help me to live as if my wife were the person in the parable who owed so little and I were the one who owed so much—for I truly think that is the way it is. Through Jesus, who commended love above everything.* Amen.

WEEK VIII

Week VIII: Sunday

19:16–30 PROPERTY AND THE KINGDOM

The French philosopher-playwright Gabriel Marcel once wrote a book called *Being and Having*, the thesis of which was that it is very difficult to *be* and to *have things* at the same time. Having inevitably gets in the way of being and begins to crowd it out.

That is largely the point of this famous story. The nearly perfect young man has only one major flaw: He is possessed by his possessions. When Jesus tells him he must part with his wealth in order to become a disciple, he is very sad. He knows what a grasp his riches have on him.

In a sense this passage is an extension of Matthew 6:19–34, where Jesus warned against trying to serve both God and money and counseled the disciples not to be anxious about the morrow. It illustrates our inability, when we have considerable possessions, to extricate ourselves from them and make radical commitments.

Perhaps the man is meant to pose a contrast between the esteemed Jew who strictly observes the Law and the little ones of the Kingdom. He has obviously done no wrong. In fact, he is bent upon doing good works. Matthew emphasizes this by slightly altering the material used by Mark. Mark has the man say, "Good teacher, what must I do to inherit eternal life?" (Mark 10:17). In Matthew he says instead, "Teacher, what good deed must I do, to have eternal life?" In ordinary Jewish eyes, the man was perfectly righteous, one of the blessed.

But Jesus pointed out, in effect, that the righteousness of the Jews before the Law was not sufficient. The Law was unable to measure the intent of the heart. It could not disclose the degree to which the man really worshiped his possessions, not God. The Kingdom, on the other hand, calls for total allegiance—the kind given by the disciples who have left their fishing boats to follow Jesus.

In the new creation, says Jesus, those who have forsaken selfish values for the Kingdom will have their full reward. Around him in his "heavenly splendour," as the New English Bible translates it, the disciples will sit on twelve thrones. Those who have endured calumny from the pious Jews because they are untutored in the Law and tradition will rule over their learned detractors. And all the little ones will be repaid many times for their faithfulness.

Lord, I confess that this passage makes me uneasy. I am too much like the rich man, who wanted to keep his property and be a disciple too. Help me to renounce my dependence on material things, so that I am not possessed by my possessions. Through Jesus, who found freedom through prayer and fasting. Amen.

Week VIII: Monday

20: 1–16 EQUALITY IN THE KINGDOM

This passage, which appears only in Matthew and not in Mark or Luke, is brilliantly placed after the story of the rich man and the disciples' discussion with Jesus. It cuts in two directions. On one hand, it is a warning to the legalistic Jews that God, because he is God, will treat the little ones of the Kingdom, the latecomers, as well as he treats them. On the other hand, it may also be a warning to the disciples that they are not to expect special consideration because they left all to follow Jesus at an early point in the Kingdom's coming, but will share it fully with all the little ones who enter late.

The point is—and this is always hard for work-oriented people to grasp—that the Kingdom is God's and *he* decides who will enter it and what their rewards will be.

Society and family have always tried to instill in us the feeling that we are worth what we *do,* not what we are. As children we grow up estimating our own value by external measurements—how hard we have worked, what we have accomplished, how much money we have made, and how we have improved our surroundings. Those of us who have done well by society's standards enjoy a glow of satisfaction and pride; those who have not feel a sense of guilt, as if they have not succeeded in life.

But God, being God, is not bound to or deceived by our standards of measurement. He gives the Kingdom to whomever he wills, the way a generous householder rewards the negligent servants as well as the diligent ones.

This is an important reminder in a Gospel which was written primarily to encourage the early Christians to a life of righteousness and faithfulness. As Jesus said to Peter in Matthew 19:26, the range of possibilities with God does not always coincide with ours. He is God, and above all laws—even the law of averages and the law of expectancy!

> *Lord, this is far more hopeful to me than the last passage. I am not only a latecomer to the vineyard. I am terribly clumsy, and often step on tender plants or prune the wrong limbs. I also cherish the illusion that I am better than a lot of other workers. I am glad you are a God of mercy as well as a God of justice.* Amen.

Week VIII: Tuesday

20:17–34 THE WAY TO BE GREAT

A journalist who had once desired to be an artist was thrilled with the assignment to interview the great Picasso. They had had their meal at a sidewalk cafe in Montmartre, the fabled artists' quarter of Paris, and their coffee cups were empty. The journalist kept glancing toward the waiter, attempting to get his eye. He seemed very annoyed. Noticing this, Picasso disappeared behind a curtain, emerged with a carafe, and provided a fresh cup for the astonished writer.

"Whoever would be great among you," said Jesus, "must be your servant." It was an important word for the Christian community, which has always had as much trouble with personal pride as any institution comprised of human beings.

Part of the irony of the request of the disciples and their mother, in Matthew's narrative, lay in its timing. Jesus had just spoken of his humiliating death and was on his way to Jerusalem where it would take place. We do not know whether the other disciples were angry with James and John because of the inappropriateness of such a request at such a time or because they too wished the places of honor. Jesus' speech to them seems to indicate the latter reason.

If Matthew had known the story related in John 13:1–11, of Jesus' taking a towel and washing his disciples' feet, he would surely have told it in this Gospel, for it illustrates even more graphically than allusions to the cross the meaning of the passage. True greatness shows itself in humility, not in pride of rank or place. Whoever would be first must become a slave.

How easy it is, Lord, to get by in a society where rank and place are easily fixed. Then all we have to do is the proper thing. But the Kingdom sweeps away all such defenses and leaves no rule but love. We are all servants, for your sake. I can only pray, "Your kingdom come." Amen.

Week VIII: Wednesday

21:1–17 THE COMING OF THE KING

Rejoice greatly, O daughter of Zion!
  Shout aloud, O daughter of Jerusalem!
Lo, your king comes to you;
  triumphant and victorious is he,
humble and riding on an ass,
  on a colt the foal of an ass.
(Zechariah 9:9)

The last line of this poetic prophecy is known as a *parallelism*, and merely repeats in slightly altered form the last phrase of the line before it. Apparently some literal-minded translator did not understand this, and so altered the text as we have it in Matthew to picture an impossible thing: Jesus riding on two animals at once!

But the prophecy from Zechariah is an important background for comprehending the scene of Jesus' entry to Jerusalem at the beginning of the Passover week. No longer trying to keep his messiahship a secret, Jesus selects this image of the king riding a beast of burden as a way of announcing his mission. He comes as the one appointed by God to save his people.

As the crowd surges over the hill from Bethany and the Holy City comes into view, people along the way shout "Hosanna." The word is from Psalm 118:25–26 and is not a term of praise but a cry to "Save now!" The people do praise the Messiah by saying, "Blessed is he who comes in the name of the Lord." But the main shout that goes up from the crowds is "Save now! Save now in the highest!"

Jesus and the crowds apparently go straight to the temple, where Jesus overturns the tables of men who profiteer through exorbitant rates for currency exchange and through the sale of birds for sacrifice. The Gospel of John places the cleansing of the temple at the beginning of Jesus' ministry (John 2:13–22), and Mark chronicles it as belonging to the second day of the Passover week. But in Matthew's Gospel it is strategically located as Jesus' first act in this weeklong drama, perhaps underscoring his battle with the legalistic Jews. He cashiers those who traffic *legally* but *unspiritually* in the temple, and exalts it once again as a place of worship. In all the ancient prophecies, the temple had figured as the point of convergence for the new creation, with all nations flowing to it.

Similarly, the miracles of healing in the temple are symbolic of the new age, and the indignation of the chief priests and scribes to the cries of "Save now!" throws the conflict between old and new into sharp relief. Jesus has now seized the initiative. It is time for a culmination of the struggle between the old regime and the new.

Lord, save us now from unspiritual systems and uninspired leaders. Enter the sacred places of world finance, industry, education, and government where the poor are daily cheated and defrauded. Take our part, and help us to take the parts of others. Let every house become a house of prayer. Through him who has come, still comes, and is coming. Amen.

Week VIII: Thursday

21:18–22 THE LESSON OF THE FIG TREE

This magical story is hardly in keeping with the Jesus we have come to know in the Gospel. He does not go about performing miracles for his own sake or because he is angry. If he did, then he would in likelihood have yielded to the temptations described in Matthew 4. Moreover, fig trees do not normally produce fruit until early summer, and, even though the leaves were premature on this particular tree, it does not seem reasonable that Jesus would have cursed the tree for not bearing fruit out of season.

A clue to the meaning of the puzzling event may lie in verse 43 of this chapter, in the reference to "a nation that yields the proper fruit." The fig tree probably stood for Israel. It was considered the most important tree of the land, and was a symbol of fertility and prosperity. Several pictures of the wrath of God in the Old Testament referred to his destroying the fig trees.

Jesus' cursing of the tree, then, was probably a parabolic saying or even a parabolic action having to do with the failure of Israel. It may have occurred at some other time and been drawn into the chronology of Holy Week because of its dramatic picture of God's wrath against the nation. Israel had put forth the leaves of righteousness—the scribes and Pharisees had, that is—but had not really brought forth the fruit of righteousness; her heart did not truly belong to the Lord. Therefore God would curse the old Israel and she would never again have the chance to bear fruit.

Lord, forgive me for every time I have set forth leaves when I had no intention of bearing real fruit. Help me not only to be honest, but honestly to love you. Through Jesus, who was always what he appeared to be. Amen.

Week VIII: Friday

21:23–32 THE SON WHO PLEASES THE FATHER

It is Monday morning after the Great Entry on Sunday. When Jesus enters the temple, he is beset by the chief religious officers of the nation. "Who gave you the authority to act as you do?" they demand. The healings of the day before are still on their minds, but it was his act of riding into Jerusalem on the colt, announcing his messiahship, that has really jolted them. The cries of "Hosanna—save now!" probably ring yet in their ears. "What an upstart!" they must think. "How dare he come in here as though he were God's own anointed!"

They are shrewd old men. But Jesus gives them a taste of his own shrewdness. "Was John's baptism from God or from men?" They are political enough not to answer. So Jesus gives them a parable. Which is the father's delight, the son who promised a day's work and didn't give it or the son who said he wouldn't work but repented and did? They are practical fathers. There can be but one answer.

"Ah," says Jesus, drawing the noose, "the nonobservant Jews, whom you condemn, go into the Kingdom ahead of you, for they listened to John and repented. *You* are the sons who promised to go and did not."

How often, Lord, have I promised to enter the vineyard and did not. I meant to go, but the sun was hot or there were distractions on the way to the field. Now many less righteous than I go in ahead of me, because they acted promptly when they were asked to go. For-

give me, and let me go now, while there is yet time. Through Jesus, who pierces me to the heart with his stories. Amen.

Week VIII: Saturday

21:33–46 THE LANDOWNER'S SON

This remarkable parable is probably still a part of Jesus' answer to the question "By what authority are you doing these things?" His authority is that of a son—the final emissary sent from the landowner to claim the vineyard that was rightfully his.

As much as anything, the parable points to the violent death of Jesus only four days hence. The wicked squatters hurl the son outside the vineyard and there murder him. Jesus, as the writer of Hebrews is careful to point out in Hebrews 13:12, was crucified outside the city walls of Jerusalem.

But the disenfranchised son becomes the foundation for a new order. He is the stone rejected by the builders but reclaimed by the architect and established as the chief cornerstone of the building.

There is no messianic secret. Jesus' meanings are all too plain to the priests and Pharisees. They want to imprison him at once but are afraid of the crowds who cried, "Save now!"

Lord, I like to think I would have been on Jesus' side against these selfish, evil leaders. But I am not so sure. There is that in me which sides with the powers that be—with law and order and due process. So I confess the possibility that I would have acted wrongly, and ask your forgiveness. Through the Son who lost his life. Amen.

WEEK IX

Week IX: Sunday

22:1–14 THE WEDDING FEAST

Like the story of the landowner in Matthew 20:1–16, this parable is double-edged, so that it cuts both the self-righteous Jews and the false members of the Christian community.

First, the edge toward the observant Jews. From the beginning God, like the king in the parable, had given special invitations to the Jews. But they had not responded. Some were merely indifferent; others turned upon the servants who bore the king's message and brutally slew them. Finally there is no more time to send messages; the wedding feast is ready. Therefore the king redirects the invitation. This time it is to all the people in the streets, without regard to their backgrounds, stations in life, or anything else. These people pour into the dining hall until it is jammed with guests. Clearly this is a picture of the church or the visible kingdom. It is filled with people of many nations, who formerly have had no special relationship to the king.

But then comes the second edge of the story, the one directed toward the Christian community itself. The king enters the dining hall and finds a guest who has not even had the grace to dress for the occasion. The man is examined for this breach of etiquette and then cast out into the darkness. "Though many are invited," concludes the parable, "few are chosen."

The meaning for observant Jews is clear enough. But what does this portend for members of the Christian community? Taken in the context of Matthew's Gospel as a whole, it may be a warning to those who think they can be part of the banquet without conforming to the moral and ethical expectations of the host. Jesus, as the new Moses, expects his followers not only to fulfill the Law but to go beyond it. It would seem likely, then, that the king in the parable is not merely capricious in his behavior toward the guest without wedding clothes, but does what he does in righteous indignation at the disrespectful attitude shown by the guest.

Lord, I am tested by this parable. I like parties and banquets, and it appeals to me that the Kingdom is compared to a wedding feast. But I realize that I live in tattered garments—that my life is not so pure and gentle and self-denying as Matthew's Jesus asks. Help me to repent, and to find in Christ's righteousness a cloak for my own unseemliness. Amen.

Week IX: Monday

22:15–22 A CUNNING QUESTION AND A PIERCING ANSWER

It is not easy to deal with a question that is a trap and to emerge from it so victoriously as to leave the questioners dumfounded. Yet that it precisely what Jesus did in this instance.

The seriousness of the trap is underlined by the presence of the Herodians, supporters of Herod the Great, whom the Pharisees normally avoided. The fact that the Pharisees sent their disciples—an unusual case in the Gospels—probably means they avoided coming themselves. Because they considered Israel a theocracy and God their king, they felt religious scruples about the occupation of their country by foreigners and the payment of tribute money to a foreign emperor. Therefore they despised the Herodians, who curried favor with the Romans in order to maintain their local positions of influence, and would be opposed to any counsel from Jesus that it was lawful to pay taxes to Caesar. Moreover, if Jesus said that paying taxes to Caesar was lawful, they would surely spread the word and make Jesus unpopular with the crowds. The Herodians, on the other hand, would be unhappy if Jesus took the position that Roman taxation was unlawful, and would probably have him arrested on a charge of sedition. Either way, he was bound to lose.

But the clever questioners did not reckon with Jesus' resourcefulness. "Show me the money for the tax," he said. "Whose likeness and inscription is this?" It was Caesar's, of course. Every king or emperor, and some who only pretended to be, had coins struck in his image as a sign of his royalty. "Then give what is due to Caesar," said Jesus, "and give what is due to God."

It was a master stroke! Whatever bore the image of Caesar must belong to Caesar. But, by the same token, anything bearing God's image belonged to him. Man, made in the image of God, is not his own—and should be doing better things than trying to entrap good men with clever questions!

Lord, most of us prefer asking you hard questions to giving you our love and loyalty. How tawdry it is of us, and what joy we are missing. Break through our clever games and show us life as it ought to be. Through Jesus, who knew what is due to whom. Amen.

Week IX: Tuesday

22:23–33 THE GOD OF THE LIVING

How intense the opposition to Jesus grows! First came the Pharisees and Herodians, strange bedfellows, with their malicious question. Now come the Sadducees, who are opposed to the Pharisees in most matters but see Jesus as a threat to the stability of their relationship to the Romans. The Sadducees were the upper-class ruling party of Israel, who numbered among themselves not only many prominent and educated families but the chief priests as well. They were strong adherents to the Pentateuch, the first five books of the Old Testament, and denied that the other writings were scriptural.

Because they found no mention of a resurrection in the Pentateuch, the Sadducees refused to accept the resurrection of the dead as a religious teaching. The Pharisees argued with them constantly about this, adducing texts from both the Pentateuch and later scriptures which they insisted clearly taught the doctrine of resurrection. For example, they sometimes cited Deuteronomy

31:16, which says, "And the Lord said to Moses, 'Behold, you are about to sleep with your fathers; then this people will rise' "—but which goes on to say, "and play the harlot after the strange gods of the land." The Pharisees tried to ignore the second part of the verse.

The picture, then, is of a group of men whose only interest in resurrection was polemical coming to ask Jesus a trick question about a matter in which he was on the side of the Pharisees. They cite the case of seven brothers who obeyed the Mosaic law and, each in turn as the other died, married the same wife, who followed the seventh in death. "In the resurrection," they ask, not even believing in resurrection, "whose wife will she be?" We can imagine the prideful mirth playing at the corners of their mouths.

"You are wrong," says Jesus, in effect—there is no mincing in his manner—"because you don't know either the scriptures or the power of God. You assume that life in the resurrection is limited to the forms of your present life. But it isn't! In the resurrection we become as free and marvelous as angels! There is no more need for legal contracts and institutions such as Moses gave for our protection now."

But Jesus is not through with that. He enters the ground where so many Pharisees have contended with the Sadducees and lost—the Torah itself. "Haven't you read what God himself said," he asks—" 'I am the God of Abraham, and the God of Isaac, and the God of Jacob'? The verb is present tense. You admit that God is living. Then Abraham, Isaac, and Jacob must be living too!"

> *Lord, I cannot help feeling that there is something cheap about such arguments, even for Jesus. I wish he had not been compelled to enter into such fruitless debates. But I suppose that is life, isn't it? We have to contend with ignorance and absurdity and misguided people; otherwise we have no compassion on the multitudes and leave them totally to their own devices. Help me to be more patient in dealing with cranks, as Jesus was.* Amen.

Week IX: Wednesday

22:34–40 THE TWIN PILLARS OF RELIGION

Mark's Gospel makes it clear that the lawyer who asked the next question of Jesus did so in a friendly manner because he respected the way Jesus had handled the earlier questions (Mark 12:28–34). In all sincerity the man inquires, "Which is the great commandment in the law?"

Jesus replies with the commandment most familiar to every Jew because it was part of the *Shema*, the opening sentence of every Jewish worship service: "You shall love the Lord your God with all your heart, and with all your soul, and with all your mind" (see Deuteronomy 6:5). That is all the man asked, but Jesus is not content to stop there. The trouble with the scribes and Pharisees was that they did stop there. Their religion was entirely vertical and without compassion. Therefore it became a charade, a mere posturing for effect. How much so will be evident in the next chapter of Matthew's Gospel, which is devoted to Jesus' seven indictments of the scribes and Pharisees.

Because the love of God is hollow and pretentious without horizontal relationships, Jesus immediately connects another commandment to the first: "You shall love your neighbor as yourself" (Leviticus 19:18). The *Shema* must be said in this light, for the two commandments are the twin pillars supporting all the Law and the prophets. Take either of them away, and everything collapses.

> *Lord, I catch myself rejoicing that I am not so stiff-necked or hardhearted as the Pharisees, and I realize that is a bad sign. If I loved my neighbor as myself, I would sympathize with their human frailty and pray for their salvation. Forgive me for defining my neighbor in such a way as to make my loving easier, and grant that my understanding of religion may rest more solidly on genuine care for others. Through Jesus, whose love for you and his neighbor led him to a cross.* Amen.

Week IX: Thursday

22:41–46 MORE THAN THE SON OF DAVID

The Pharisees are apparently stunned to silence by Jesus' answer about the commandments, so Jesus follows with a question of his own. "Whose son is the Messiah?" he asks. It is a simple question. "David's," they answer, because "Son of David" is the most common messianic title. The scribes and Pharisees have heard the crowds calling Jesus Son of David, and know he is aware that they are thinking this.

"What about Psalm 110:1," says Jesus, "where David says, 'The Lord said to my Lord, sit at my right hand'?" The reference, it is agreed, is to the Messiah. "If David calls him Lord, then isn't he more than a mere son?"

If the hearers were stunned before, now they are awe-stricken. Have they heard correctly? Does Jesus claim to be more than a man? There will be no more badgering questions. The next questioner, in fact, will be the high priest who examines Jesus for blasphemy (Matthew 26:57–68).

This must have been a high moment, Lord—a daring moment. I appreciate the drama of it because I know its awful consequences. Help me to follow him whom you have named Lord, and who at the end claimed the title. Amen.

Week IX: Friday

23:1–12 THE TROUBLE WITH THE PHARISEES

We must recall again that as Matthew wrote his Gospel the Christian community was still struggling to establish its identity over against Judaism. This entire chapter constitutes another collection of sayings gathered under a special heading. There is no way of knowing for sure that all the sayings were given at once; probably they were not. Matthew has grouped them into an introduction, seven woes or indictments, and a conclusion.

The admonishment to do what the scribes and Pharisees say, but not what they do, is interesting. It is not the Law that is so bad, nor even the scribal additions to it, but the attitude with which the scribes and Pharisees approach them. They have set themselves up as an elite corps of men to make heavy burdens for others to bear.

Actually the Pharisees had existed for only a couple of centuries by Jesus' time. Their name meant "the Separated Ones." They dedicated themselves to obeying all the laws and regulations extrapolated by the scribes from the Torah—so many that they filled more than fifty volumes! Being a Pharisee was therefore a full-time job; one had to study and work constantly at perfecting himself.

As Jesus saw, such zealousness was often misplaced. Separation became a source of pride to many Pharisees, and they became unbearable tyrants toward others who were less perfect than they. Their sin was not their devotion to religion but their lack of charity toward others.

"They are self-centered," said Jesus, "and pretend to honor God when what they really do is honor themselves, for God takes no honor in uncharitable worship. They like to have the highest places at public events because they are regarded as holy men, and they enjoy being called Teacher because they can quote so many fussy laws. Don't ever aspire to that. Let the titles go. You have one Teacher, one Father, one Master—don't set up others."

The church, of course, has been as clever as the scribes at getting around this admonition. We have popes, bishops, archbishops, rectors, reverends, right reverends, pastors, associate pastors, canons, deacons, elders, deans, and a dozen other titles to which Christians can approvingly aspire. But Jesus counseled against being caught up in such peripheral matters. In words reminiscent of his counsel to the disciples when James and John wanted the places of honor in the Kingdom (Matthew 20:26–28), Jesus said that true greatness lies through service to others, not through self-exaltation.

Lord, it is hard to serve others without thought of reward, and to love when love is not returned. Yet Jesus has asked this of us, and has done as much himself. Help me to strive for this point of selflessness in my life, that I may enter the joy of the Kingdom. Amen.

Week IX: Saturday

23:13–39 THE SEVEN WOES

It is hard to imagine the Jesus of the Beatitudes giving vent to such invective as marks this long passage. As William Barclay says, "It is seldom in literature that we find so unsparing and sustained an indictment as we find in this chapter." But we must remember, to understand it, that the scribes and Pharisees, more than anyone else, were poisoning the spiritual wells of Israel. And they, more than anyone, were trying to block Jesus' ministry to the people. The last verses of this chapter indicate a man on the verge of tears in his frustration to minister to the holy city. Perhaps they are the best clue of all to the outrage he felt against the ever-present religious bigots who had stoned the prophets in earlier ages and would crucify him in this one.

The description of the scribes and Pharisees is devastating: They will not enter the Kingdom of heaven themselves and they keep others from entering; they scour the world to make disciples, and then make torments of the disciples' lives; they keep all the fine points of the Law and miss the most important ones; they make themselves appear holy but are filled with corruption; they speak of honoring the prophets but are as hungry to murder prophets as their fathers were.

No wonder the formula for the woes begins each time, "Woe to you, scribes and Pharisees, hypocrites!" There would be no more stinging indictment for persons who held religion in high esteem. The word hypocrite in Greek originally applied to an actor who carried a large mask in front of him as he played his part, one that could easily be seen by the whole audience. That was precisely the way Jesus pictured the Pharisees—they were men wearing oversized masks!

Lord, save us all from the burdens of other people's religious expectations, and save them from ours. Let us be content to meditate on our own faults and spend no time accusing others. And grant to each of us a sense of the positive meaning of faith, in order that we may not lose touch with you through expressions of negativism. Through Jesus, whose religion was so healthy-minded that he knew how to deal with scribes and Pharisees. Amen.

WEEK X

"Teach us the ways of him who prayed even for those who nailed him to a cross." (Week XII: Monday)

"O Lord, renew the sense of your presence among us, that your teachings may gain new purchase on our imaginations." (Week XII: Saturday)

Week X: Sunday

24:1–14 THE GOSPEL FOR THE WORLD

This chapter is another of Matthew's collections of teachings drawn from various times in Jesus' ministry and assembled because they all relate to a particular theme. The theme in this case is difficult times.

The first saying, verses 1–2, may have occurred on one of the first visits Jesus made to Jerusalem with the disciples, because we have the disciples coming to him in amazement, like gawking tourists, to point out the temple buildings. Although the temple was hardly large by contemporary standards, it probably appeared gigantic to these country visitors, and it was certainly magnificent, for it was constructed of white marble overlaid with gold. When Jesus said that not a stone of it would be left standing, he was apparently not referring to the destruction of the temple in A.D. 70, for Josephus said that the temple was then destroyed by fire. Possibly he was making a general statement about the failure of the religion of the scribes and Pharisees (remember the "woes" of chapter 23)—the temple, as the symbol of that religion, was doomed to eventual ruin.

The next saying, placed on the Mount of Olives, which was traditionally associated with the messianic age, is in answer to a question about signs of the *parousia*, or Second Coming, and the end of the age. Jesus describes the difficult early years of the church, when Christians were persecuted for their faith and there was much confusion in the world. Perhaps the most chilling part of the description is the warning that "men's love will grow cold." But the gospel will be preached to all the nations, and then—the time is not specified—the end will come.

Sometimes, Lord, I think this is the age when love has grown cold. People are so insecure and frustrated that they quarrel, cheat, and gouge one another without respect to either the morality or the love of Christ. It is a time of distress and unhappiness. Help me to be a reservoir of strength and gentleness to others this day, and to give my life in love as Jesus did. Amen.

Week X: Monday

24:15–31 A TIME OF CONFUSION

It would take far more space than we have here to begin to untangle the references of these verses, some of which are to the destruction of Jerusalem and some to the end of the age. The "desolating sacrilege" of verse 15 is clearly a reference to Daniel 9:27, 11:31, and 12:11, where the prophet reflected on the desecration of the temple by Antiochus Epiphanes, king of Syria, who erected an altar to Zeus there and sacrificed swine on it. Apparently Jesus is warning the Christians to flee from the city when a foreign ruler does this again, for it is a sign of the collapse of all things.

In a time of such confusion, there will naturally arise many false messiahs who assume, because they too can see the signs of the end, that they are God's intended leaders. Even some of the chosen community will be deceived by them. "But don't listen to them," says Jesus. "Remember what I have told you. When the Son of man really appears again, it will not be in a corner, in some limited way; he will be seen from east to west, like the lightning."

As for verse 28, it is apparently a proverb. The word for eagle may also be translated vulture, as most modern translators have shown. Taken thus, it probably applies to the appearance of false messiahs, who, like vultures, will gather over the body of civilization.

The whole universe is seen to collapse in the terrible Day of the Lord. But in the midst of the desolation will come the one who is to rule the new creation. His angels will fly all over the heavens, gathering the chosen together.

Lord, I get lost in all this business of signs and predictions. I am also bothered by those who don't see its poetic character, but insist on counting the days and weeks until the end. Help me to keep what is primary in all this, though—the vision of Christ as sufficient to all his little ones, whatever comes in the world—and not lose it with all of the unsettling language. Amen.

Week X: Tuesday

24:32–51 MORE SAYINGS OF THE END

There are obvious signs of the collapse of all things, says Jesus. The intelligent person learns to read such signs, the way he or she knows, when the fig tree puts out its leaves, that summer is near. But there is no way of knowing the exact time, so it is important to continue working and living as one normally does.

We know from Paul's writings that some Christians, expecting the imminent end of the world, simply quit working. Foreseeing this possibility, Jesus gave the parable of the servant who, when his master suddenly appears, is faithfully setting food before the other servants. The servant who says that because the master has been gone so long he will surely not arrive today, and therefore neglects his duties, will be punished with the hypocrites—and we remember that the formula for the seven woes of chapter 23 was "Woe to you, scribes and Pharisees, *hypocrites.*"

Lord, make us faithful servants to do the small things that are important in the daily affairs of people and save us from any tendency to resign our care for others. Through Jesus, who never asked to be waited upon. Amen.

Week X: Wednesday

25:1–13 THE JOY OF READINESS

It is possible that this parable is not about the return of Christ at all, but about the coming of the Kingdom to the Jews, and was attracted to its present textual position by its eschatological flavor. If this is so, then Israel was the bride of the story, and the ancient manuscripts may be correct which add "and the bride" at the end of verse 1.

The custom was for maidens to attend the bride, not the bridegroom, and then to accompany the two as the groom took the bride from her parents' house to his. If Israel was the apparent bride, then the maidens were the religious leaders responsible for seeing her delivered to the Messiah. Some of them, because of the hard intertestamental period and the failure of the Messiah to appear, had turned their thoughts to other things and simply were not prepared for the Kingdom when Jesus came among them with his message.

Verse 13 may have been at some point a textual addition, though not an unworthy one, for the theme of watchfulness is always applicable in spiritual matters.

> *Lord, we are all inclined to slothful spirits. Our sensibilities become dulled and we miss many opportunities each day of seeing your advent in our lives. Resensitize us, we pray, until we live on tiptoe, expecting you at every moment.* Amen.

Week X: Thursday

25:14–30 MISJUDGING THE MASTER

Once more we have a parable subject to two interpretations. Jesus very possibly told it with the Jewish religious leaders in mind: the scribes and Pharisees were the one-talent servants who had been mere niggardly guardians of what had been given them in the Law. But Matthew's placement indicates that the early church saw in the parable a challenge to faithful living in its own time, and indeed in that sense it is timeless.

The servant's error was his misreading of the master's nature. He had seen only half of that nature—the tendency of the master to be a zealous farmer, gathering in hay and grain even in places where it sprang up wild and had not been cultivated. He mistook this for miserliness, when in reality it indicated imagination, risk, and resourcefulness.

This certainly would have applied to the legalistic religious leaders of Jesus' day. They looked upon the religion God had given as something to be carefully guarded and restricted—hence their impossibly elaborated system of rules and taboos. They had completely overlooked the real dynamic of Judaism, which was able to produce John the Baptist, Jesus, and of course Christianity itself.

> *Lord, there is something in all of us that loves rules and prescriptions. We feel safer if we can take the measure of things and assign them to well-defined categories. But your Spirit is more than we are able to express in formulas and regulations. You transcend our definitions and dogmas; you elude our finest theologies. Help us not to be caught as the third servant was, with spirits timid and fearful. Let us ride the wild waves of the Kingdom's coming, like surfers joyous and unafraid, because we trust him who has gone before us.* Amen.

Week X: Friday

25:31–46 THE CENTRALITY OF THE "LITTLE ONES"

Few passages in Matthew's Gospel are more moving than this one. It represents the culmination of centuries of longing for justice; and, when justice is done, it is seen not in terms of mere legalistic righteousness, such as the scribes and Pharisees were interested in, but of care for all of God's little ones.

We tend, after centuries of habit, to read the saying as applicable to some distant future. But when the disciples first heard it, it was surely clear to them that the goats of the parable were the scribes and Pharisees, the strictly observant Jews, who had put heavy burdens on the common people and had not really cared about their salvation (compare Matthew 23:4). The sheep, on the other hand, were the little ones of the Kingdom. The Messiah-king identified with the little ones, and thus brought judgment on the others.

There is no sharper warning to religious people in any generation than this parable, for it reminds us of man's perennial tendency to regard the poor, the unattractive, and the powerless as outsiders in the human community; and such an attitude always carries its own judgment in God's created order.

> *Lord, I think of the person I most despise, and of the reasons for that. Is it wrong of me to make such judgments? Am I in effect pronouncing judgment on myself, because I have not loved as I was told to? I fear it is so. Forgive me—as I try to accept the person I despised.* Amen.

Week X: Saturday

26:1–13 A BEAUTIFUL ACT

Here, set between pieces of information about the gathering storm that will break over Jesus before the week is out, is a story of tender devotion which has, as Jesus predicted, been told all over the world.

Probably the action occurred in the evening, as it was in Bethany and Jesus spent his days in Jerusalem a few miles away. Jesus and the disciples were resting in the home of Simon the leper—apparently one of the persons Jesus had healed. John's Gospel indicates that the woman with the jar of ointment was Mary, the sister of Martha and Lazarus, who also lived in Bethany.

With her loving intuition, Mary perceived the tragic meaning of Jesus' predictions concerning his conflict with the authorities. With characteristic generosity, she came to him in Simon's home bearing the vessel of ointment which she had probably been saving for her own and her family's anointment after death. It was a very costly substance, worth as much as an average man might earn in a year. Either in sympathy or in loving protest of the way Jesus was about to spend himself, Mary poured the entire amount of ointment on his head, so that it ran profusely through his hair and into his clothing. The room was immediately filled with the sweet, thick odor of death.

The disciples, who had been sensitized to the needs of the poor, were outraged. (John's Gospel, written later, pins the blame for their outburst on Judas the traitor.) Why wasn't the ointment sold for the benefit of the poor, if she wanted to honor Jesus?

But Jesus commended the woman. She had seen something important: They were in the presence of the Lord of the new creation. There were other resources for the poor—and this example was never intended to gainsay the importance of caring for the poor. But Mary had prepared the King for his burial. Her recognition of the situation was greater than the disciples', and her deed would always be associated with the community's proclamation.

> *Lord, increase in me the capacity for spontaneous acts of generosity. Let me forget self and use my substance for others, as this woman did. I do not wish to forget the poor; but neither do I wish to lose the ability to do lavish, beautiful things for those around me. Through Jesus, who understood and approved.* Amen.

WEEK XI

Week XI: Sunday

26:14–25 THE PERFIDY OF JUDAS

Sometimes even strong men break under the pressure of relentless conflict. They are not innately bad or prone to misjudgment; it is just that something snaps and they do unpredictable things, things absurdly out of keeping with their usual character.

It may have been that way with Judas. Surely something in him had recommended him to Jesus as a disciple. But in the constant battle with the authorities in Jerusalem he reached a point where he couldn't take it any longer. Maybe he thought Jesus was wrong to speak of dying instead of fighting; or, as some have suggested, perhaps he thought he could provoke a revolution in which Jesus would emerge victorious.

At any rate, he agreed to deliver his master into the hands of the chief priests for thirty pieces of silver, which according to Exodus 21:32 was the price of a slave. Ironically, Judas enslaved himself and vilified his name forever in this transaction. The name Judas has ever since been synonymous with treachery and deceit.

How did Jesus know? There were surely many telltale signs in Judas' behavior. One of them, we now suspect from our knowledge of the Qumran materials, was his dipping his hand with Jesus into the bowl of bitter herbs which was part of the Passover meal. The rule in the Essene community at Qumran was that people dipped their hands in the bowl in hierarchic order; that is, in the sequence of their statuses. Judas' dipping his hand with Jesus suggests a breach of etiquette on his part—as though he suddenly felt equal with the Master.

> *Lord, there is Judas in me too. I bristle with self-importance and confidence in my own opinions. Sometimes I think I know better than you what I need or should do. At such times, I crowd the bowl by dipping as you dip. Forgive my terrible impertinence; help me to live humbly and devotedly, that I may not betray you.* Amen.

Week XI: Monday

26:26–35 THE FIRST SUPPER

A friend has suggested that the meal which Jesus ate with the disciples is improperly referred to as the Last Supper. Why shouldn't it be called instead the *First* Supper? It was, after all, the beginning of a tradition which has been so central to Christianity through the years as to make it the primary sacrament of the community.

But why, in light of this primacy in the community, did Matthew spend so little time describing it? In the Gospel of John it is accorded several chapters. Perhaps Matthew was more concerned with the actual enactment of the passion story than with its mere symbolization. All Christians knew the meaning of bread and wine. He was interested in the human drama being played out beyond the table, in Judas and Peter and Caiaphas and Pilate and all the others whose stories held so much significance for the entire community. Thus he hastens on from the bare fact of the Supper's institution to describe Peter's protestation of faithfulness —a protestation we know to be ill-fated.

Ironically, the hymn which Jesus and the disciples sang before going out was probably Psalm 118, which contains the words:

> With the Lord on my side I do not fear.
>   What can man do to me?
> The Lord is on my side to help me;
>   I shall look in triumph on those who hate me.
> It is better to take refuge in the Lord
>   than to put confidence in man.
> It is better to take refuge in the Lord
>   than to put confidence in princes. (6–9)

But Peter and the other disciples apparently forgot what they had sung.

Their guilt is my guilt, O Lord. I too betray you, in a thousand small betrayals. I disappoint children who have looked to me expectantly; I fail my elders, who desire my care and attention; I give less than my best to my friends, who had reason to hope for more. If they are your little ones, Lord, then I have fallen short of your wishes too. Forgive me and help me to do better. Through him who loved even those who let him down. Amen.

Week XI: Tuesday

26:36–46 PRAY TO BE SPARED THE TESTING

Professor David Daube has reminded us of a rule among the Jews that whenever one of the group celebrating the Passover fell asleep—not merely dozed but fell into deep sleep, so that he could not answer a question—it was the end of the celebration. This rule explains the puzzling way Jesus kept returning to the disciples as he prayed—he did not want the Passover celebration to come to an end.

There is great pathos in this picture of Jesus, deeply saddened by the betrayal of Judas and the impending events of the next few hours. It was entirely natural for him to seek comfort in prayer, for it had been his discipline at earlier times to spend many hours in prayer. Now the prayer had a cruciality about it that it had perhaps never had before.

What did Jesus pray at this time? He prayed that the dreadful hour of testing might simply go away, if possible—that he might be wrong about the series of events he saw rapidly building to a climax.

He also instructed the three disciples, Peter, James, and John, to pray a similar prayer for themselves. But of course they did not. They were tired and did not realize the seriousness of the hour, so they failed to pray as they were bidden. And with what enormous consequences! Jesus came out of Gethsemane refreshed in spirit and ready to endure the worst the authorities could do to him. If the disciples had prayed, they too might have been refreshed, and, instead of fleeing, they might have died by Jesus' side. It is a tremendous thing to ponder, isn't it? Prayer can actually get us into trouble; or it can keep us there if we are already in it!

Lord, too often my prayers are mere recitations of shopping lists. I do not use them as opportunities for listening to you and learning what I should be doing with my life. Therefore I live wastefully and in needless desperation. Help me to take prayer more seriously, and not to fall asleep. Through Jesus, who was crucified. Amen.

Week XI: Wednesday

26:47–56 NOT WITH SWORDS LOUD CLASHING

The irony of verse 25 is continued here as Judas calls Jesus Master and kisses him. It was considered impudent of a disciple to kiss his master before the master had first kissed him, and Judas once more demonstrated his feeling of equality with Jesus. In light of this, it is possible that Jesus' calling him "friend" was intended sarcastically, not seriously.

John 18:10 tells us that the unnamed disciple who drew his sword was Peter. The fact that a mob had followed the chief priests and elders to the site enhances the possibility that this action was very significant. It might easily have signaled the eruption of local warfare, for probably many in the crowd as well as in the entire city were prepared to follow Jesus in an armed rebellion.

There were surely in the early Christian community, too, many who felt that Christians should do more to defend themselves against imprisonment and persecution. Why not train secret militia to offset the power of the corrupt authorities?

The example of Jesus, and his words about not taking up the sword, have had great influence through the ages on the Christian attitude toward violence. In our own time, they were persuasive to

Mahatma Gandhi and Martin Luther King, Jr., both of whom influenced millions of oppressed people.

It is the royal demeanor of Jesus here that causes us to question his use of power for selfish purposes in the stories of the fish with money in its mouth (Matthew 17:27) and the withered fig tree (Matthew 21:18–22). Such tales are simply incongruent with the behavior of one who offered himself so gracefully to his own executioners.

Lord, we understand so little of the nature of power—that it finally harms those who would use it selfishly against others. We are always drawing our swords for this or that reason, and attacking the enemies without. Help us to know what enemies lurk within, and to submit ourselves to you for more perfect cleansing. Through him who resisted the impulse to summon angels in a frightening moment. Amen.

Week XI: Thursday

26:57–68 THE JUDGMENT OF THE OLD MEN

The Romans, as Matthew made abundantly clear, were only incidental accessories in the death of Jesus. It was the religious leaders of the Jews, from first to last, who resented his style of ministry, his popularity with the poor, and his way of besting them in argument. There is no mention in this chapter of a Roman soldier's having been present in the capture of Jesus, despite the danger the mob scene constituted to the civil peace. It was all the work of the Jewish authorities. And now the same authorities proceed with their council meeting to try Jesus.

As the Sanhedrin or Council of Elders had no power to impose the death penalty except in cases of Gentile violation of the sacred area of the temple, it is probable that they commenced by trying to find Jesus guilty of some seditious act which they could then report to the Roman procurator. But failing this, apparently because of confusion among the false witnesses, they finally established a religious accusation against him, that of blasphemy. When Jesus admitted to being the Son of God, the high priest, following a custom prescribed for such situations, tore his robes. The elders, shocked by the brazenness of the accused, declared that he deserved to die. Leviticus 24:16 prescribes death by stoning as the punishment for blaspheming. Perhaps because they lacked the authority to inflict the penalty they desired, the elders broke into a frenzy of petty retribution, spitting on Jesus, slapping him, and taunting him.

As Jesus had said about them, they were devoid of love, the absence of which turned their professed love of God into a demonic caricature of true religion. They acted out, in this wild scene, the very portrait of them he had painted.

> *Lord, was ever any scene more chilling than this? What terrible things men do in the name of religion, truth, and honor! Save me from participating in such assassinations. Let me suffer with the accused rather than be a party to such evil judgments—even when all that is involved is petty gossip and not a trial such as this. Through Jesus, who always befriends victims of injustice.* Amen.

Week XI: Friday

26:69–75 THE FALL OF THE ROCK

Why was the story of Peter's defection so much more important than those of the other disciples, who also ran away? Why, indeed, but that by the time the Gospels were written it was Peter who had clearly emerged as the most significant figure in the Christian community. Because he was the leader, the story of his faltering was all the more engaging to the community. It reminded them of the utter frailty of the human foundations of their movement. The man whom Jesus had called the Rock had proved unstable in a critical moment. He had slept when Jesus told him to watch and pray, and then he had lacked the courage to confess his relationship to Jesus in the very courtyard of the enemy!

Later, at Pentecost, Peter would be fired with courage and would excoriate the same elders for having crucified Jesus. He would become known for his dedication to the community, and legend would represent him as being crucified upside down because he did not deem himself worthy of dying as his Lord had.

Imagine what encouragement this biography would have been to frightened, hesitant Christians everywhere. Peter, the big fisherman, had once hesitated too. But then he had wept in repentance and become the rock Jesus called him to be. Surely every Christian can respond in the same positive manner to his or her own former acts of defection and become doubly responsible in the Kingdom!

> *I am grateful, Lord, for what the snatches of Peter's biography have meant to me in my own Christian pilgrimage. It is good to have someone imperfect to relate to, for there are times when I am discouraged by my own faithlessness and betrayal. Accept my repentant spirit for every time I have denied the impulse to witness to your presence, and help me to show fruits of that repentance as Peter did. Through him who stands forever in the dock as we struggle in the courtyard.* Amen.

Week XI: Saturday

27:1–10 THE REPENTANCE OF JUDAS

How difficult it is to call back a word or an action once directed against another human being. Judas learned this bitterly in the case of his betrayal of Jesus. Perhaps he thought Jesus would best the elders in a showdown. But when he learned that the elders had condemned Jesus and sent him to Pilate, the raw, ugly truth of what he had done hit him with sickening impact. Hurrying back to the chief priests, he tried to undo what he had done. Failing that, he hurled the blood money on the floor of the temple and left despondently. Whether he took his life that very morning, dying when Jesus did, or later, the record does not indicate. It only tells us that the money, because it was tainted by blood, was used to buy a burial site for strangers, fulfilling a prophecy from Zechariah 11:12–13 (not Jeremiah, as the manuscripts have it). Thus the memory of Judas would always be associated with strangers and outcasts—people who had no friends to bury them.

Lord, what a lonely position Judas was in. I pray now for all persons who contemplate suicide. Help them to know that somewhere, somehow, someone cares for them. Through Jesus, who was Judas' friend. Amen.

WEEK XII

Week XII: Sunday

27:11–26 A STRONG MAN BEFORE A WEAK MAN

"Are you the king of the Jews?" asked Pilate. It was an important question, legally at least. Apparently the chief priests and elders had translated the term Messiah that way for Pilate when they brought Jesus before him. Pilate was, after all, head of the Roman occupation, and would take the matter more seriously if he thought Jesus was after the throne of Herod; that would mean insurrection and trouble.

But Pilate was canny. He listened to the old men of Israel snapping off charges against Jesus, and he watched Jesus waiting silently before them. He knew that the old men did it all for envy—that they feared this strange young prophet with such deep ways.

Pilate was in a ticklish situation. He believed the man innocent. His wife had even had a dream about him, and warned Pilate not to have anything to do with him. But the situation was explosive. The elders could make trouble for him among the people and with his superiors in Rome.

So Pilate did the discreet, political thing—and earned infamy as a result. Now we class him with all those persons who consider career and influence above right moral action; and Jesus, who was willing to die for a righteous cause, is revered even by non-Christians throughout the world.

> *Lord, grant that I never lose touch with myself to the extent that I could wash my hands of anyone whose well-being depended on me—even someone I knew as fleetingly as Pilate knew Jesus. Let me be prepared instead to go to a cross of some kind, if necessary, in behalf of truth, honor, probity—the things that matter. Through Jesus, who would have acted differently if he had been in Pilate's place.* Amen.

Week XII: Monday

27:27–44 JESUS AND THE CARNIVAL

Bruegel the Elder once painted a crucifixion scene that captured the carnival-like qualities of that awful day. It is called *The Procession to Calvary.* It shows Jesus being led out of the city ahead of a mob of people who are excited by the smell of blood and violence. Someone is turning a somersault. A boy is pole-vaulting over a mud puddle. Two men are already on distant crosses. Jesus has fallen beneath his. In the lower left quadrant of the painting, a tug of war is going on between Simon of Cyrene's grim-faced wife and the soldiers who want Simon to help Jesus with the cross. Simon is in the middle, being held by his wife and pulled by the soldiers. Most of the people are utterly indifferent to the exhausted figure of Jesus. They are simply out for a good time.

Bruegel has seen what is apparent in this passage—the cruel and ugly side of humanity that takes pleasure in the pain of others or enjoys the defeat of a famous personality. It is not a pleasant thing to behold. In fact, it makes one ashamed that people could behave in such calloused ways.

But we remember that Jesus came as the Messiah of the new creation, and creation always means pain and suffering as order is wrought out of chaos. Here was the climactic moment in his struggle with the forces of evil, and evil was making its strongest play.

> *Lord, there is bloodlust in us that makes us take pleasure in other people's misfortune. Forgive this dark streak and turn us to tenderness; let mercy temper justice and love replace vengeance. Teach us the ways of him who prayed even for those who nailed him to a cross.* Amen.

Week XII: Tuesday

27:45–56 GIVING UP THE SPIRIT

When the crucifixion was over and the various stories about it were assembled, it was apparent that things were occurring at two different levels.

At one level, the carnival level, the crowds gaped at the spectacle of a man dying. Once, when Jesus was reciting Psalm 22, a psalm of both despair and victory, they thought they heard the name Elijah on his lips, and said he was calling the prophet. Elijah was believed to come to the aid of the righteous when they suffered. Someone ran to get a sponge and poured cheap wine on it and raised it on a stick to Jesus. The man may have meant well. But the others told him to wait and see if Elijah really would come to help the dying man. Then Jesus cried out with a loud voice—John says it was a cry of overcoming—and died.

At another level, according to Matthew, there were significant occurrences in nature. The sun was darkened from noon until three o'clock. There was an earthquake, and the curtain between the temple court and the Holy of Holies was ripped in two. The earthquake also opened many tombs, and dead persons came forth to walk through the city as predicted by Daniel 12:2. And the centurion and his men guarding Jesus were astonished and believed that he was indeed the Son of God.

The phrase in verse 53, "after his resurrection," suggests that this entire paragraph (verses 51–54) is out of sequence here, and really belongs after the resurrection. This would agree with the fact that Pilate appointed soldiers to guard the tomb of Jesus. But Mark, who does not mention the supernatural occurrences, says that the centurion confessed that Jesus was the Son of God when he watched him breathe his last on the cross.

Ernest Hemingway, the famous novelist, once wrote a brief play called *Today Is Friday*. It consists entirely of the conversation of two soldiers in a bar on the afternoon following the crucifixion. One line is repeated again and again. "He was good in there today," they say. "He was good in there today." It is the central impression made by the man on the middle cross. However confusing the record may be in other respects—about what actually happened at the cross and what at the tomb—there is no doubt about this. He died with faith and dignity. "He was good in there today."

It is an interesting and somewhat pathetic footnote that the women who had followed Jesus all the way from Galilee watched the grim proceedings from a distance. In their society they were all but powerless to intervene. We can only hope that if the priesthood and Sanhedrin had been open to female membership, mercy might have tempered the decisions reached by the men.

Lord, I am trying to recall the most terrible pain I have ever felt. It made me cry at the time. Remembering it now makes the suffering of Jesus more real. What a horrible death it was. How helpless the women must have felt as they watched! But what a miracle, Lord! That one death has been more curative of sick humanity than all the music ever played, all the gardens ever visited, and all the laws ever enacted! I can only thank you in the name of him who suffered. Amen.

Week XII: Wednesday

27:57–66 LAID IN A BORROWED TOMB

Joseph, according to the other Gospels, was a member of the Council of Elders (Mark 15:43) and did not give his consent to Jesus' death (Luke 23:50–51). If he was already a disciple at the time of Jesus' trial, it is possible that the meeting of the Council was called hastily and with only a select membership present. John 19:38–39 says that Joseph's relationship to Jesus was secret, and indicates that Nicodemus helped him remove the body and inter it.

Secret or not, it surely required considerable courage and devotion of Joseph to go to Pilate and request the body. Whether the disciples and the women lacked courage to do the same is beside the point; as strangers to the city, they would have had no place to bury Jesus, and a criminal's body was considered a defilement, especially on the Sabbath, which was almost upon them. At least the two Marys did not hesitate to be identified with Jesus, and came to mourn by the tomb.

We can only wonder what was really in the minds of the priests and Pharisees in requesting a guard for the tomb. Were they actually afraid of theft, or was it more than that they feared?

Lord, Jesus was laid in a borrowed crib when he was born and a borrowed tomb when he died. Truly he had no home, no place to lay his head. His life was a perfect example of the selflessness he preached. Now let him live in our hearts forever, for we owe him everything. Amen.

Week XII: Thursday

28:1–10 FALL DOWN AND WORSHIP!

This is the first instance we have of followers of Jesus other than the inner circle of disciples actually worshiping him. Before, they doubtless admired him, listened to him, puzzled over him, perhaps even loved him. But here Matthew says explicitly that the two Marys fell at his feet and worshiped. His resurrection identified him so completely with the power of God in establishing the new creation that the women did not hesitate to share with him the kind of adoration normally reserved for God the Father.

The four Gospels vary in the details of the resurrection narrative, but all are agreed on one thing: It was Mary Magdalene's devotion to Jesus that caused her to be at the tomb at daybreak on the first day of the week and led to her being the first of Jesus' followers to see him in his resurrected form.

Can it be then that love is the only prelude to true worship? It was love that kept Mary Magdalene near the cross in the hours of agony, that brought her to the sepulcher where Joseph and

Nicodemus buried Jesus, and that caused her to return at daybreak after the Sabbath. And it was love's vision of the risen Christ that led her to fall down to worship him.

Here was a perfect example of Jesus' teachings about the Kingdom of God. The scribes and Pharisees kept the Law with rigorous devotion. But that was not enough. Our righteousness must exceed that of the scribes and Pharisees, said Jesus—it must be characterized by love and forgiveness and joy. And Mary embodied the faith of the new order, because she loved so much.

Lord, how these women's lives must have been transformed from the events of Friday, when they watched from afar the gruesome execution of Jesus, to this remarkable Sunday morning in the garden where the tomb was. They were no longer on the periphery of things, helpless onlookers in a tragic drama; now they were at the center, touching the feet of the risen Lord, being sent to tell the others where to find him. Help us all to move from the one experience to the other. Let us fall down and worship because something extraordinary has happened to us. Through Jesus, who has been glorified through the resurrection. Amen.

Week XII: Friday

28:11–15 THE SOLDIERS TAKE A BRIBE

We can only be saddened by the guards' response to the miracle they had witnessed. How typical it is of people of every age. They had been present at the most wonderful event in history, yet resolved to treat it as a mere opportunity to make some cash and go on living as they had before.

Most of us, like these soldiers, regularly pass up chances to enter new dimensions of existence. We are so bent on earning a living or achieving status that we never even see the potential of great moments when they come to us. We miss the Kingdom that is in our midst, and fail to realize that the new creation waits at our very door to be born.

> *Lord, if I were only waiting at the tomb like the women, instead of rushing around trying to make a better living like the soldiers, you would appear to me more often. Save me, I pray, from my own spiritual sloth. Through Jesus, who is the Christ.* Amen.

Week XII: Saturday

28:16–20 THE NEW AGE OF THE SPIRIT

Matthew must have been running out of papyrus when he neared the end of his Gospel, for he condensed so much in this brief paragraph.

Jesus meets the eleven disciples, as is consistent with Matthew's emphasis throughout on his role as leader of the disciples, at a mountain in Galilee. We recall too the significance of mountains in the Gospel—especially the Sermon on the Mount and the Mount of Transfiguration. It is fitting that the one who is greater than Moses should give his final instructions from the mountain.

"By whose authority do you do these things?" the scribes and Pharisees had asked him. Now he says, "All authority in heaven and on earth has been given to me." The verb is perfect tense—it has already been accomplished. The disciples are to go to all the nations, as the coming of the magi and the healing of the Canaanite woman's daughter had prefigured, and make followers of all who believe. The baptism with which they baptize is not visibly different from John's baptism to fulfill all righteousness; but now it is in the name of the Son too, and of the Holy Spirit, for all of this is in and of the Spirit.

The disciples, moreover, are to teach those they baptize. They are to instruct them in all the things Matthew has tried to set down in his Gospel. The Kingdom is not to be a mere charismatic movement, strong on emotion and weak in doctrine. It is to have a firm and dynamic ethical foundation, going beyond the mere legal righteousness of the scribes and Pharisees. The Law of God is to truly flourish in the world.

And the most marvelous thing of all—the secret of the age of the Spirit—is that Jesus is now released from being in only one place at a time. Now he can appear freely to any disciple in any location at any moment when he chooses to disclose himself, and he will make himself known wherever disciples meet in his name. The child born in Bethlehem has become Lord of all creation!

O Lord, who taught and healed and broke bread with the disciples, teach, heal, and break bread with us. Renew the sense of your presence among us, that your teachings may gain new purchase on our imaginations. Let us live as those who have seen the hope of the ages consummated and know that you are indeed the Christ, the Son of the living God; and let us go and make disciples as you have commanded. For yours is the Kingdom and the power and the glory forever. Amen.

Mark

Drawings by
Richard Caffari

Contents

Introduction

The Gospel of Mark, it is agreed by most scholars, is the earliest of the four Gospels. Mark, or whoever the author was, is credited with having formed a new literary genre out of the various oral traditions about Jesus. As far as we know, no one had done it before.

I find this quite thrilling—to think, as I read the stories of Jesus' miracles and his conflicts with the scribes and Pharisees, and then as I meditate on their arrangement and on Mark's transitional comments, that here was a great creative mind at work trying to make theological sense of the varied traditions about Jesus and then to communicate the experience of this to thousands of readers, many of them a long, long way from where Jesus walked and lived in Galilee and Judea.

There are themes and counterthemes running through the book.

First, there is the idea of *power*. The Kingdom comes in power. Jesus does works of power. It is not a magical power, for he can do no mighty things in Nazareth, where they do not believe in his messiahship; it is the power of faith in God's promise to give the eternal Kingdom to his people. Nor is it a power to be used selfishly, for Jesus does not use it to save himself from the cross. It is a power deriving from being connected to God's will, a power producing great joy and good works in the world.

A second theme is *conflict*. Jesus has barely begun his ministry, in the Gospel of Mark, when the scribes and Pharisees begin to oppose him. Then John the Baptist is beheaded, and Jesus begins to see that his own ministry must end in violence. It is unavoidable, for evil is entrenched in the world and will not be overcome except at great cost. By chapter 3 of the Gospel, the Pharisees and Herodians, representing two very different spheres of interest, have been drawn into conspiracy to determine how to destroy Jesus. His existence is a threat to both religious authoritarianism and secular tyranny.

Growing out of the theme of conflict is the theme of *suffering*. The Jesus of Mark is set firmly over against any picture of a transcendent Messiah who does not experience both mental and physical anguish. From very early in the Gospel, he begins to show the disciples that he must die. When Peter chides him for this viewpoint, he calls Peter "Satan," for he knows that the temptation to avoid personal suffering can only end in denying the will of God. And Mark is insistent, in the language and imagery of the crucifixion and burial of Jesus, that he really died on the cross—that it was a limp and lifeless *corpse* that was removed and put in the tomb.

Finally, there is the theme of *misunderstanding*. The disciples constantly fail to comprehend at the deeper level what Jesus is saying about life and death and the Kingdom of God. He feeds the multitudes, and they immediately forget that he is the giver of bread. He explains that he must suffer and die, and they still expect him to be a triumphal king. He teaches them about watching for the Kingdom, and they fall asleep like ignorant fools. He tells them he will be raised up and go ahead of them into Galilee, and they tremble and are afraid to speak to anyone about what they have seen and heard.

Obviously the book is powerful for us today. Its message is every bit as contemporary as it was in the time of the early Christians. Power, conflict, suffering, misunderstanding—these are the stuff of our life, the matter of daily headlines, the subjects of our most vital concerns. The Gospel may have been written in the first century, but its importance to us is as fresh as this morning's newspaper.

I think you will find it as thrilling as I have if you will only take a few minutes every day to read it and ponder it, allowing the Spirit of God to actualize its meaning within your life.

I suggest that you have a certain time every day set aside to do this—perhaps before breakfast, or at your desk when you arrive at the office, or in the afternoon when you have tea, or even at the dinner table with your family.

Begin by reading the scripture passage indicated at the head of the page. Read it thoughtfully, letting the words and images seep into the pores of the mind. Then read the comments in this book, which will continue to focus your attention on the scripture. Finally, pray in your own mind the little prayer at the end of the day's commentary, adding whatever you will out of your own spirit and manner of expression.

You will find the habit agreeable, once it is established. And, more than that, you will find something happening to your life. There will be a new sense of confidence and power entering your daily affairs. You will be more conscious of the presence of God wherever you go. This old world will begin to look like his new world, and you—you will feel like a new person.

The secret will be that you are feeling his power in you. And the power, in turn, will make you more gracious with others. The old world will really become a new world, and his Kingdom will enjoy a greater reality than it ever has before!

JOHN KILLINGER

Nashville, 1978

WEEK I

The baptism of Jesus was a tender, intimate moment. God confided to his Son the pleasure he felt in him—and, by extension, in the new community of which he was a part. (Week I: Tuesday)

Week I: Sunday

MARK 1:1 A SCRIPT WITH TRUMPETS

What a world of meaning is packed into these few words: "The gospel of Jesus Christ, Son of God."

Some translations do not carry the words "Son of God." Numerous ancient manuscripts omit the phrase, and scholars admit they are uncertain about which ones to follow. But, even if the author did not originally include the words, they are by no means out of place in the manuscripts that have them. He did specifically identify Jesus as the Son of God five other times in the Gospel—in 1:11, 3:11, 5:7, 9:7, and 15:39. The story he was about to tell was clearly intended to be a narrative of the Son of God, the long-awaited Messiah of Israel.

We can hardly appreciate the meaning of "Christ" or "Son of God" today without remembering the context. For centuries little Israel had lain at the crossroads of the ancient world, constantly battered and plundered by larger powers. The people had dreamed of a great moment in history when God would dramatically reverse everything, bringing the old era to a close and inaugurating a new era in which he himself would rule the world from Jerusalem. Israel would become pre-eminent among the nations, and all roads would lead to its Holy City. But, as no one could ever look upon God himself, his Messiah or Christ would be his appointed one, and would be both the sign and the commander of this new age in human history.

Imagine, then, the startling, audacious character of Mark's announcement: Jesus, the Galilean who had been crucified, was the Christ! He was the "Son of God"—another messianic title well known in that day.

This is why Mark called what he was writing a "Gospel." The Greek word is *euangelion,* and means both "good news" and "proclamation." He was *proclaiming* this news, lifting it up for everyone to read and hear. If this were a play, the script would call for trumpets. "Jesus is the Christ, the Son of God." It is the greatest announcement in the world!

O Lord, my world is so diffused and routine. My consciousness is preoccupied with many things—with schedules and budgets and household duties. Help me really to hear this announcement of Mark's in all its significance, so that my life is altered by it. I must not miss it! Through Jesus, who is the Christ. Amen.

Week I: Monday

1:2–8 THE CALL TO A NEW BEGINNING

The quotation in verse 2 is actually from Malachi 3:1, not Isaiah. But Mark would not have been troubled by such a small error. He had something much bigger in mind—the preaching of the Kingdom of God!

John the Baptizer, the woolly, fiery-tongued prophet, was gathering a new community in the wilderness. This in itself was an important symbol, for Israelites still regarded the wilderness period of their history, when Moses led them out of Egypt, as their greatest era. Now, at a time when the land was fairly covered by populous settlements, John took to the wilderness again, calling people to a new beginning.

Spiritually, they were to join this new beginning through "baptism of repentance for the forgiveness of sins." The Greek and Hebrew words lying behind the concept of repentance suggest a "turning back" or "return," with a sense of sorrow for having gone away. Immersion, which was practiced in those days to initiate Gentiles into the Jewish religion, was offered as the ritual entrance into this new wilderness community. Even the Jews must come the same way, as Matthew 3:7–10 indicates.

Mark would play upon this wilderness theme again in chapters 6 and 8, in the stories of Jesus' feeding of the multitudes. In both cases the crowds were in the wilderness. To the early church during its years of persecution, the meaning of these passages must have been especially pointed. Christ feeds his people in the wilderness places of life.

In addition to the "baptism of repentance," John also preached the arrival of the Messiah, whose coming was popularly associated with the new community or Kingdom. "I have immersed you in water," he said, "but the One who is coming will immerse you in the Holy Spirit."

John did not want anyone to mistake him for the Messiah. "I am not worthy to untie his sandals," he said. It was the work of a slave to unfasten his master's footwear; but John did not feel even as worthy as a slave before the One who was coming.

Lord, I am no more worthy than John. But I want to be part of the community you are forming. Help me to turn from my preoccupation with other things—other gods—and be immersed in your spirit. There is nothing too lowly for me to do. Through Jesus, the One who came and is coming. Amen.

Week I: Tuesday

1:9–11 A TENDER MOMENT

Commentators have long puzzled over Jesus' baptism. If he was the Lord, the Messiah, then why should he have submitted to baptism in the same manner as all the others who came into the new community? Matthew's Gospel, written after Mark's, explained that it was fitting for Jesus "to fulfil all righteousness" (Matthew 3:15). The Gospel of John, written even later, seems to rationalize that it was in order for the Baptizer to see the Spirit descending on Jesus and thus to know that he was the Messiah (John 1:32–33).

There is a simple explanation if we follow only the account in Mark. John was forming the wilderness community through baptism. Jesus wanted to identify with that community, so he was baptized by John.

It was not a time of public recognition of the Messiah, according to Mark. Jesus was the only one who saw the heavens open and the Spirit descending like a dove, and he was the only one who heard the voice. It was a private vision, in keeping with the fact that Jesus was from the obscure town of Nazareth and that Mark would make much of the so-called "messianic secret," not revealing him to many persons as the Christ until shortly before the crucifixion. The "voice" was probably similar to that in rabbinic references to a *bat qôl,* which meant literally "the daughter of a voice" or echo of a voice. That is, it was not a public voice, heard by everyone, but an inner voice, heard only by the person to whom it was addressed.

The significance of the vision was a private one: It verified in Jesus' own spirit the calling of God to his ministry. The phrase "my beloved Son" may have been much more personal than simple identification with the Messiah role; as Professor C. E. B. Cranfield suggests, it confirmed Jesus' "already existing filial consciousness." It was a tender, intimate moment. God confided to his Son the pleasure he felt in him—and, by extension, in the new community of which he was part.

> *Lord, I am moved by this scene. I always get a lump in my throat when I behold parents watching their children being baptized. To think of your watching the baptism of Jesus is quite overwhelming. Thank you for the picture.* Amen.

Week I: Wednesday

1:12–13 AMONG THE WILD BEASTS

The Greek word for "led" or "drove out," *ek-ballei,* literally means "to throw or hurl out." It suggests a starkness or severity often associated with ancient Greek tragedy, when protagonists were cast out into lonely places without even the protection or assistance of a deity.

The wilderness, besides being associated with Israel's past glory, was also thought to be the habitat of demons. The length of the period may be an allusion to the forty years of Israel's desert wanderings (Deuteronomy 8:2, 16), or to the forty-day fasts of Moses (Exodus 34:28) and Elijah (1 Kings 19:8). It is a fairly common period of time in the Bible, hallowed by these and other precedents. It goes without saying that this was a time of prayer and meditation for the newly baptized Messiah, who, like the great heroes of legend, must undergo special testing of his worth and fidelity.

Among the outstanding saints and mystics of our tradition, it is well known that the experience of deep meditative prayer is often intimately related to temptation. The "dark night of the soul" spoken of by St. John of the Cross, for example, was not a period of apathy derived from godless existence; on the contrary, it was a terrifying span of restiveness encountered in the very midst of a spiritual journey. Psychologically, it may be described as the time of the soul's disengagement when it has progressed beyond dependence on man-centered images of God but has not yet attained final confidence in the divine as the imageless base of all reality. Several persons who have had this experience describe it as the most deeply disturbing period of their lives, because it is a period when faith is shaken to its very core.

Mark alone among the Gospel writers alludes to "the wild beasts." He may have done so in order to underscore the desolateness of the wilderness area, or because demons were widely believed to inhabit untamed animals. Even more exciting is the possibility that Mark saw this as a messianic touch; many prophecies, recalling Adam in Paradise, pictured the age of the Messiah as a time when the wild beasts will become tame and docile—when "the wolf shall dwell with the lamb, and the leopard shall lie down with the kid" (Isaiah 11:6).

Through his faithfulness in this time of trial, Jesus proved his worthiness as the Messiah. As a result, the very messengers of God came to his service.

Lord, I am anything but faithful. I have trouble glorifying you even where I am, which is a kind of paradise. What would I do if I were really in a wilderness? Forgive me, for I am unworthy of you and ashamed of myself. Help me to focus more and more on the King-

dom, that temptations of every kind may have less purchase upon me. Through Jesus, whose spirit was always obedient to you. Amen.

Week I: Thursday

1:14–15 TIME FOR A CHANGE

As we try to read between the lines of Mark's compressed narrative, we wonder if Jesus had already joined John the Baptizer in preaching along the Jordan River in Judea, and now moved north into Galilee as a consequence of John's arrest. At any rate, he appears in his home country, preaching the good news from God about the nearness of the Kingdom.

God had always, in theory, been King of Israel. But the people were unmindful of this, and the prophets had spoken of a day when he would take his kingship in full power and authority.

"That day is at hand," Jesus announced. "The time is fulfilled." In New Testament Greek there are two words for "time"—*chronos*, meaning clock or calendar time, or time in its usual linear sense, and *kairos*, meaning time that is ripe with significance. Here it is the latter word that is used. This is a special time. It is as though time itself were a pregnant woman and the moment had come for her to be delivered of an offspring.

The reaction to this news, Jesus announced, should be repentance, change of life, complete reorientation. It was the same message John had preached. To realize that the long-awaited Kingdom was upon the world should produce a sudden revolution in people's behavior. They would show their belief in the good news by acting as though at last it were really true.

Lord, how would I have responded to Jesus' announcement that the Kingdom was at hand? How do I respond now? For it is at hand, isn't it, growing silently in our midst even now, as Jesus taught his disciples? Grant that my repentance may be daily and that I may live a godly life unto salvation. In the name of Jesus, who preached the Kingdom as good news, not bad. Amen.

Week I: Friday

1:16–20 NO TIME TO LOSE

There are interesting parallels between this passage and 1 Kings 19:19–21, in which the prophet Elijah calls Elisha to be his follower: (1) Elijah had just spent forty days in the wilderness, where God had given him a mission to accomplish; (2) Elisha was plowing a field for his father when Elijah came by and "cast his mantle upon him"; (3) Elisha took long enough to kiss his mother and father good-bye, and to slay and cook a yoke of oxen to give the people; (4) then Elisha followed Elijah "and ministered to him."

With the impression of his ministry fresh and strong upon him, Jesus likewise felt the importance of securing helpers. He could not possibly preach to all the people alone.

It is noteworthy that he did not call unemployed folk to be his disciples. It is our tendency, when we want something done, to go to those whom we know to be unengaged or in a slack time. But not Jesus! He picked men who were at work, and offered them a higher task. "Come and be my disciples and you shall draw your nets on more important quarry." And immediately, Mark says, they went with him. James and John even left their father to become followers.

Mark liked the word "immediately." He used it eleven times in this chapter alone ("at once" in verses 28 and 43 of the Revised Standard Version is the same word in the Greek). Immediately this, immediately that. It is almost as if he wished to write the script for an old-time movie, with everything happening at double time.

Perhaps the word has theological significance in face of what Jesus was preaching about the *kairos* and the fullness of time.

With the Kingdom breaking in on everything, movement had to be swift. There was no time to lose!

I long for those days, Lord, when life was simple and people made commitments just like that! My life is so complicated. I long to be that resolute in my commitments too, but then I become enmeshed in the complexities of my existence and often feel that I have failed you. Teach me how to maintain my loyalty in the midst of complexity. In the name of Jesus, who was unswerving in his faithfulness. Amen.

Week I: Saturday

1:21–34 A DAY IN THE LIFE OF JESUS

We were told in verses 14 and 15 that Jesus came into Galilee *preaching the good news*. Now we are told about his *teaching* and *healing*. The three activities are inseparably linked in the Gospels, which suggests that the same ought to be true today as well.

Capernaum was a bustling town on the northwest side of the Sea of Galilee, and the synoptic Gospels agree that it was the headquarters for most of Jesus' ministry. This may be one reason he chose the fishermen as disciples, because their homes were apparently close by, as verse 29 would indicate.

Always faithful to the worthier traditions in the Jewish religion, Jesus went to the synagogue on the sabbath. There he astounded everyone with the wisdom of his teaching. Unlike the scribes, who were laymen devoted to studying the Law and developing its implications for daily life, he expounded the Law with great *élan* and authority. Where they cited footnotes and previous interpretations, he spoke directly and emphatically.

Then, as if to underline this authority, Mark records a miracle story. There was among those in the synagogue a man with an unclean spirit—a demon. The spirit, more perceptive than ordinary persons, recognized that here was no mere itinerant rabbi but the Messiah himself. He not only spoke about the Kingdom—he was the very sign of the Kingdom's presence!

When the spirit spoke through the unfortunate man, Jesus rebuked him. The Greek word *phimōthēti* in the speech of Jesus means "be muzzled" or "be silenced." This was probably a technical term used by magicians or exorcists of the age, but Mark surely employed it here on the lips of Jesus to enforce the concept of the messianic secret, because the people in the synagogue seem not to have become aware that this astonishing person was the Messiah himself. His fame spread quickly, but probably as a miracle-worker, not as the Messiah.

When Jesus returned to the house of Simon Peter and Andrew, the disciples, apparently prompted by what had happened in the synagogue, told him that Simon's mother-in-law was ill with a fever. He "lifted her up"—another technical term in stories of wonder-workers—and she began at once to wait on them at table. Jesus' power was so great that he eliminated not only the fever but its usual aftereffects of weakness and unsteadiness.

Finally, to indicate what the entire day was like, Mark tells about the multiple healings after sundown. The Jewish sabbath ended after sunset, and with it the restrictions against carrying people and traveling unnecessary distances. The whole city, apprised of the miracle-worker in its midst, had gathered at Simon's door. The ministry was off to a vigorous start!

> *Lord, help me to perceive how intimately healing is related to the presence of the Kingdom. Then let me submit myself for the complete healing of myself, that I may be a whole servant of the gospel. Finally, instruct me in ways to participate in the healing of others—in their spirits, their daily affairs, their environments, and even their bodies. Through Jesus, the worker of miracles.* Amen.

WEEK II

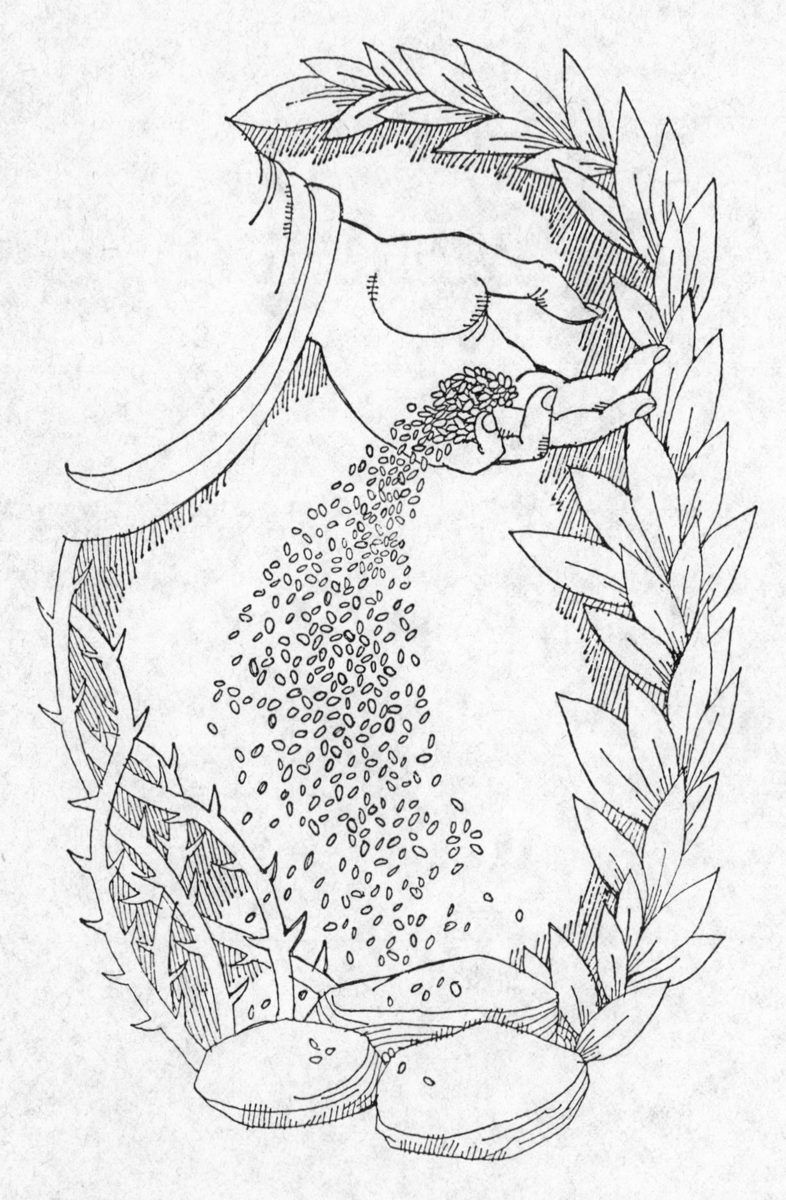

"Lord, you are a prodigious sower, scattering precious seed on all kinds of ground." (Week III: Thursday)

Week II: Sunday

1:35–39 THE CONSTANCY OF TEMPTATION

A problem we encounter in dealing with temptation is that it normally comes when we least expect it. Sometimes, as in this passage, it comes when we are in periods of great success and acceptance.

During his forty days in the wilderness, Jesus was tempted by Satan (verse 13). Now, in the early days of his public ministry, he was tempted again—but this time under very different circumstances.

He had met with tremendous popular acceptance in Capernaum. The phrase "and in the morning" (verse 35) does not necessarily link this day immediately to the one described in verses 21–34. Probably a number of days had elapsed, and support among the populace had been growing.

The temptation was to stay in Capernaum and secure his reputation there as a worker of miracles. But Jesus saw it for what it was—a temptation—and firmly resisted it. His mission was to go throughout the land announcing the arrival of the Kingdom. He must not be deterred by success in any one locale.

Characteristically, Jesus arrived at this decision in prayer. He had the same need that we have to be "alone with the Alone." It was there that Simon and the others—Mark pointedly does not call them disciples—found him to tell him that everyone was seeking him. But his head was clear. It was time to move on and proclaim the Kingdom in other places.

Lord, I am sorry to say that I seek you more when I fail than when I succeed; it is easier for me to know your leadership when I am lonely and afraid than when I am happy and things are going well. Help me to listen better in the good times, and in my thanksgiving to hear the still, small voice that directs my path. In the name of Jesus, who had integrity. Amen.

Week II: Monday

1:40–45 THE MESSIAH AND THE LEPER

Most of us have never known what it means to be an outcast and to have the outcast's mentality. Even at our worst we are still socially acceptable. People may have to make excuses for our behavior, but their world is not closed to us.

Here is a man for whom most of the world was closed. He had leprosy, one of the most dreaded diseases among primitive people. The Law forbade him normal contact with healthy people. He was required to remain always at a distance and to call out a warning of his uncleanness wherever he went.

What great faith he must have had in Jesus' power to heal him, to have transgressed this strict social rule and approached the Lord! He came and knelt, a practice generally reserved for royalty and great servants of God. "If you will," he said, "you can make me clean." What confidence he showed, both in Jesus' power and in his compassion!

Verse 41 is problematic. Scholars are agreed that the ancient manuscripts reading "moved with anger" are to be preferred to those that say "moved with pity." Some scribe, finding anger inappropriate in Jesus, probably changed the text to "pity." But why was Jesus angry? Was he incensed at the demonic influence that had made the man diseased in the first place? Was he angry with the man for crossing the social barrier? Or, in the light of verses 35–39, did he possibly resent the request for healing as another selfish intrusion on his mission of announcing the Kingdom?

We can only speculate as to the answer. But, whatever his feelings, Jesus did deal compassionately with the man. He touched him—a startling thing to do, for lepers brought defilement on anyone coming in direct contact with them—and made him whole. Then, concerned for the interference a reputation as a miracle-worker would mean to his preaching, Jesus strongly enjoined the man to silence and sent him to the priest for ritual cleansing and resocializing. Perhaps Jesus intended by this course to deflect public attention for the healing from himself to the priest. If so, the man's failure to obey destroyed this possibility, and soon the demand on Jesus as a wonder-worker was so strong in the cities that he retreated to the countryside.

Theologically, Mark may have set this story here to validate Jesus' messiahship again. Healing a leper, according to rabbinical literature, was nearly as difficult as raising the dead. And Jesus had done it with a touch and a word!

Lord, it is easy to understand why this man could not keep silent about what had happened to him. What is hard to understand is how I can keep silent about all that has been done for me. Is it because my senses are dulled by the enormity of my blessings? Teach me to see inwardly, that I may rejoice openly. Through Jesus, who overcomes defilement. Amen.

Week II: Tuesday

2:1–12 THE FORGIVENESS IS AMONG YOU

Here we enter a strange section of Mark's Gospel. Between verses 2:1 and 3:6 he tells five stories about Jesus' conflicts with the authorities. In these stories, Jesus suspends his emphasis on being silent about the works he does; in fact, he seems intent on being known through his works. This suggests that Mark had this body of stories intact from an earlier source—perhaps from Peter—and inserted it here in a text otherwise more of his own telling.

The first story is very dramatic. "At home" in Capernaum—probably in the home of Peter and Andrew—Jesus is teaching a crowd of people who not only fill the house but spill over into the street beyond. Four men come to the house bearing the pallet of a paralyzed friend. Unable to get in by the door, yet enthusiastic to bring their friend to Jesus, they go up the side stairs outside the house, tear a hole in the mud-and-wicker roof, and lower the friend on his pallet into the presence of Jesus.

It is a moving act of faith, and Jesus immediately greets it by saying, "My son, your sins are forgiven." Obviously he saw a relationship between the condition of the man's body and his need to be forgiven. Not that the man had done anything especially wrong. But being part of a world as broken as ours—a world where people are afflicted in body and spirit—is synonymous with needing forgiveness.

The scribes sitting in the crowd are visibly upset. They do not believe in forgiveness on earth—only at the last judgment. It is God's prerogative to forgive. For a mortal being to presume to exercise this role is blasphemy, and blasphemy is punishable by death. Perhaps this is why Mark included the story here—already the scribes are beginning to talk about the execution of Jesus.

Jesus, seeing the questioning in their eyes, answers it with a miracle they will find even more astonishing. He tells the man to rise, pick up his pallet, and go home; and the man does as ordered. They are all amazed and murmur praises to God, declaring that they have never seen anything like this. Apparently even the scribes take part in the outburst of the crowd.

In verse 10 Mark uses the title "Son of man" for Jesus. Although the phrase held the simple literal meaning of "man," Mark obviously employs it as a messianic title. The miracle, he says, is to convince those present—and, by extension, the reader—that Jesus is indeed God's Messiah and therefore has the power to forgive sins on earth before the last judgment. As the Kingdom is in our midst, he is saying, so is God's forgiveness.

> *Lord, I am prone to think of forgiveness in negative terms—as being let off for my failures and misdeeds. But here I see that it has a positive side too; it helps to create life and health. Enable me to rejoice in it and experience it as a sign of your Kingdom's presence in my life. Through Jesus, who has the power to forgive and heal.* Amen.

Week II: Wednesday

2:13–17 JESUS AND THE OUTSIDERS

Most of us are careful about whom we are seen with—especially if we wish to have some kind of public voice. It is unwise for statesmen to be seen associating with criminals, for ministers to be seen in the company of prostitutes, or for schoolteachers to be viewed with homosexuals and drug offenders.

We need to remember this to understand the importance of this conflict story in Mark. As the one proclaiming the long awaited Kingdom of God, Jesus daringly identifies himself with "the wrong people," thus risking the disapproval of the scribes and Pharisees who were the "solid citizens" of their time.

The Gospel of Matthew speaks of the man here called Levi as Matthew. Some biblical scholars think he is the same as James, also identified as a son of Alphaeus (Mark 3:18). The important point here, of course, is his occupation. He was one of Herod Antipas' customs collectors in Capernaum, the port through which northern travel around the Sea of Galilee ordinarily had to pass. Such petty tax officials were held in almost universal disdain as thieves and liars. The "sinners" of verses 15 and 16 may have been the "people of the land," who had not had the opportunity to study the Law as the scribes and Pharisees had and were therefore shunned by them. The word "Pharisee" meant "separated one," and was the name of a religious sect or party including people who set themselves aside for study of the Law and devotion to its applications. The scribes were only slightly less strict than the Pharisees, and appear to have taken the same positions in practically everything.

For Jesus to call Levi as a follower and to eat at his home with his associates was unthinkable to the scribes and Pharisees, not only because of the character of these people but also because the meal was certain to be ritually unclean. It was virtually impossible for such minor officials to avoid contamination in dealing with non-Jews; and they were notorious for failing to pay tithes on their own foodstuffs and for neglecting the rules about the proper cleansing of utensils and killing and preparing of food. Jesus had thus scandalized the Pharisees by his action.

Mark's point, again as in the preceding conflict story and the story of the leper (1:40–45), is that the Messiah is above contamination. Instead of the sinner's rendering him sinful, he makes the sinner whole!

Jesus underscores this with an analogy. It is right for people to avoid the sick, lest they too become infected. But the same rule does not apply to the doctor, who visits the sick to make them well. In the same manner, Jesus is above the ordinary rules governing righteous behavior; his mission is to restore righteousness to sinners. This is no condemnation of the righteous; it is only an explanation of Jesus' companionship with the unrighteous.

O Lord, who are the source of all rightness and goodness in this world, forgive me for expecting you always to be associated with the decent and honest people. Help me to imagine your consorting with the most unlikely persons in my community, so that I do not, like a Pharisee, cut myself off from those you love. Amen.

Week II: Thursday

2:18–22 SONS OF THE WEDDING

Each religion has its own characteristic tone. Hinduism, with its emphasis on reincarnation, is reverent of life. Confucianism, accenting filial piety, is conscientious. Zoroastrianism, with its perpetual struggle between light and dark, is filled with tension. Christianity, because of its emphasis on the Kingdom of God in our midst, should resound with joy and celebration!

This is the point of this conflict story involving a question raised by people about why Jesus' followers did not fast as the disciples of John and the disciples of the Pharisees did. "Why should they fast now?" Jesus asked them. They were celebrating the great eschatological wedding which God had promised for so long.

Fasting was not a legal requirement among Jews except on the Day of Atonement. Those who did so had some special reason. It is conjectured that John's followers were fasting because he had been taken away from them. This would explain Jesus' saying in verse 20 that his own disciples would fast when the bridegroom was taken away. The Greek word for "taken away" or "cut off" in this verse is probably a reference to Isaiah 53:8, which speaks of the Divine Servant's being "taken away" and "cut off out of the land of the living." It thus implies a violent death and is a reference to the crucifixion.

The small parables of the cloth patch and the new wine, like the allusion to the Great Wedding, emphasize the newness of the experience of the first Christians. People do not sew unbleached or unshrunk patches onto old clothes (the Greek distinguishes "outer garments," which people can see), for they will shrink when washed and pull away the threads joining them to the other material. Nor do people pour new, unfermented wine into brittle old skins, for the fermentation process will burst the old skins apart.

The point of both parables, placed in this grouping, seems to be that the disciples of Jesus should not be expected to be mournful and long-faced like their serious predecessors in Judaism, for what is happening to them is of another order. It is a time for celebration and dancing! We are, as the Greek says literally, "sons of the wedding."

> *Lord, I am accused by this passage, for I too am often gloomy and serious about my religion. I sense it more as duty and obligation than as joy and enthusiasm. Help me to be silent and wait upon your presence, and then to feel what Jesus was talking about. In his name I pray.* Amen.

Week II: Friday

2:23–28 THE MOST SCANDALOUS STATEMENT

As in the other conflict stories, the point here is that Jesus is the Lord of everything, including the Law. He could eat with people who were not ceremonially clean (verses 15–17), and he and his followers could pluck grain on the sabbath.

The Law permitted a person to take as much grain from a stranger's field as he could reap with his hands (Deuteronomy 23:25); but it also forbade reaping on the sabbath as one of their thirty-nine activities not permitted on the holy day (Exodus 34:21). The penalty for violating the sabbath was death by stoning, although violators were to be given one warning. This may have been a warning instance.

But Jesus answered with authority by citing the time when David and his men entered the tabernacle and persuaded Ahimelech the priest to allay their hunger with the holy bread consecrated for the use of priests and temple servants (1 Samuel 21:1–6). The Pharisees never spoke ill of David for this. And here before them, of course, was one greater than David, the Messiah himself.

"The sabbath was made for man," he reminded them, "not man for the sabbath." It was not an uncommon saying among rabbis at the time. But rabbis did not ordinarily behave with the freedom Jesus was demonstrating, and their teaching did not lead them to open conflict. It was the action, fully as much as the saying, that demoted Jesus' significance; he was indeed "lord even of the sabbath."

Professor Ernest Käsemann, in his famous book *Jesus Means Freedom*, says that this is the most scandalous remark Jesus ever made. It cut across in an instant the artificiality of a religion that had devolved into mere law-observance. And, in the end, it was the attitude voiced here that resulted in Jesus' crucifixion.

As a fast is stopped when a wedding is to take place, so even the Law gives way to the Messiah when he appears!

> *Lord, it is the old matter of the razor's edge again. How do I know when to obey the Law and when to follow the instincts I have in Christ? Help me, through prayer and devotion, to discern moments of obedience from moments of celebration, and to be true to you in both. In the name of Jesus, who is lord of both.* Amen.

Week II: Saturday

3:1–6 THE URGENCY TO DO GOOD

This is the last of the five conflict stories, and once more involves the sabbath, which lay at the heart of the Jewish legal system.

The rabbis permitted healing on the sabbath only in cases where persons' lives were in danger; otherwise, healing was regarded as work and a violation of sabbath law. As no reason is given that the man with the paralyzed hand could not have waited another day, we may assume that Jesus was openly challenging the injunction against sabbath healing.

In one sense, Mark makes the same point in all the stories. Jesus is encountering the scribal interpretations of the Law. He is the Messiah, and therefore Lord of the Law. He brings a new era, a new way of looking at everything.

In his eyes, it is important to do good for people whenever possible, and not to wait until another day because of a mere legal system. Doing good obviously takes precedence over doing nothing. Doing nothing, in fact, becomes tantamount to doing harm. As Jesus puts the question in verse 4, it is no wonder the scribes and Pharisees are silent; he has worded it in such a way that they must either agree with him or sound like inhuman monsters. He looks on them with anger (verse 5) because of the baseness of the position they maintain over against his ministry of teaching, preaching, and healing. Even though he understands the jeopardy his action will place him in, he heals the man.

The healing is done very openly. The words "Come here" in verse 3 imply "Come up here in the middle." The act is a purposeful demonstration of Jesus' messiahship.

Perhaps Mark counts the reprimand for reaping on the sabbath (2:24) as the single warning accorded sabbath violators before stoning them to death. If so, his conclusion in 3:6 is a natural ending for the story as well as for the entire section of conflict stories. Now the Pharisees go out to plot Jesus' death. They counsel with the followers of Herod Antipas, who held political jurisdiction over Jesus, and whose help would be important in securing his death under the Roman occupation. The die is cast.

Lord, give me the same kind of passion for doing good that Jesus had. Grant that selfish considerations may never deflect me from helping and caring for others, but let the exuberance of the Kingdom determine the character of all my behavior. Through Jesus, who would have healed my hand if I had been the man in the synagogue. Amen.

WEEK III

Week III: Sunday

3:7–12 THE SIMPLE FOLK RESPOND

Dmitri, in Dostoevsky's novel *The Brothers Karamazov,* says that God will be kept alive in the prisons even if he is allowed to die among intellectuals and respectable people. It is an age-old truth. Again and again in history it is the little people, the outcasts, the simple folk, who understand and respond to the call of God when he is most neglected in the finer circles.

After the five conflict stories which represent Jesus' failure with the religious leaders of his culture, Mark balances the account by depicting the enthusiastic response of the common people.

Jesus has withdrawn from Capernaum to more rural areas around the Sea of Galilee and great crowds follow him. They come from every part of the Holy Land except Samaria, which most Jews disregarded, and the Decapolis, or ten Greek cities, which were probably less Jewish than other parts of the country.

Typically, the people want only what Jesus can do for them and have little regard for his personal well being. There are so many of them and his ministry is so demanding that he has the disciples keep a boat handy for getting away for rest or safety.

It is the demons themselves—the agents of Satan—who recognize Jesus' real identity. They fall prostrate before him and cry out for mercy, probably in the screams of their poor victims.

And Jesus, true again to this strange theme in Mark's Gospel, orders them not to reveal his identity.

> *Lord, it is the simple part of me that comes after you, that will not stop coming after you. The other part chases many phantoms, dreams, illusions. Thank you for the simple part and its relentless return to life and health. In the name of Jesus, who casts out my demons.* Amen.

Week III: Monday

3:13–19a THE NEW ISRAEL

These verses assume a special force from what has preceded them. First, there were the five conflict stories, summarizing "religious" Israel's rejection of the Messiah. Then the Messiah turned to the common people, withdrawing to the seaside to teach and heal them. Now he goes up into the hills (the Greek actually suggests a mountain, which is always symbolic of an important action or event) and commissions twelve followers to be his special helpers. They too are common folk. Not one appears to have had any rabbinical training. And they are to be the pillars of the new Israel, as there had been twelve leaders of Israel in the days of tribalism.

Again, as in the calling of Peter and Andrew and James and John (1:16–20), the initiative comes from Jesus himself. In the Old Testament, God called the heroes of the faith. Now the Messiah, the one coming with the Kingdom, exercises this function.

Note the special dimensions of the call: The disciples are "to be with him, and to be sent out to preach and have authority to cast out demons." Normally the disciples of rabbis followed their masters in order to learn their teachings and to provide for them; their duties included securing food for the masters and, if they were traveling, to see that they had places to spend the night. But Jesus is no ordinary rabbi; he teaches "as one having authority." Therefore his disciples have a special assignment—to proclaim the Kingdom and extend the healing ministry of the Messiah.

Before anything else, though, they are "to be with him." It is a penetrating thought, isn't it? How many times we attempt to do the work of Christ without first being with him—without waiting in his presence to receive his spirit and power. But being with him —allowing him to be with us—is the only way we can really begin to do his work.

Lord, sometimes I am impetuous and rush out to do your work without having waited on you in prayer. At other times I neither wait on you nor rush out to do anything—I am simply useless, and the power to help others lies dormant and untapped within me. Help me both to wait and to go. Grant that my life may become a lovely rhythm between prayer and helpfulness. Through Jesus, who shares his authority. Amen.

Week III: Tuesday

3:19b–30 "THE OTHER SIDE"

Chaim Potok, in his beautiful novel *My Name Is Asher Lev,* tells the story of a young artist who is misunderstood by his family. Asher Lev's mother and father are Hasidic Jews—members of a rigidly orthodox sect whose pieties go far beyond the normal limits. When Asher Lev's great talent begins to develop, his family and friends in the synagogue are afraid of it. They say it is a gift from "the Other Side"—from Satan—and try to discourage him from pursuing it. Everything they fear or do not understand, in fact, they believe to come from "the Other Side."

Jesus encounters a similar response when he returns to Capernaum and the inordinate crowds that press continuously upon him and his newly appointed disciples.

First his family members leave home to take charge of him, thinking he is possessed by a demon. (The Greek words in verse 21 sometimes translated "his friends" are better interpreted "those of his household," and the expression "He is beside himself" is synonymous with "He has a demon.") Possibly they have heard the "official" interpretation of his work being spread by the scribes from Jerusalem.

The presence of the scribes from Jerusalem must be seen in the light of 3:6—it is probably part of the intensifying opposition of the Pharisees to Jesus' ministry. The scribes have come as a delegation to discredit his work. Clearly he acts with power; no one can deny that. Their only course, therefore, is to impugn the source of his power. So they go about telling everyone that he is possessed by Beelzebul—an obscure term perhaps meaning "Lord of the house" but apparently used as another name for Satan.

Jesus is forthright. He calls the lie-mongers to him and addresses them in parables. "Satan's work is to bind and destroy, to hurt and make sick," he says in effect. "I am freeing and healing. How can you say that is of Satan? It is clearly against him."

Verse 27 may be a reference to the temptation in the wilderness (1:12–13), when Jesus would have won a first victory over Satan. Having thus "bound" or inhibited the strong one, he is now proceeding to "plunder his house," setting the captives free.

Jesus' righteous anger flares at these enemies of the Kingdom. "Truly, I say to you," he says. The phrase is always an introduction to a strong statement. It literally is "Amen, I say to you," and appears to have been peculiar to the speech of Jesus, invoking God to guarantee whatever follows. It is thus equivalent to "Thus saith the Lord."

"All sins will be forgiven the sons of men, and whatever blasphemies they utter" (verse 28). This should be understood in the context of the frequency with which the rabbis were always saying that this or that sin would condemn a person to everlasting punishment.

"But whoever blasphemes against the Holy Spirit never has forgiveness, but is guilty of an eternal sin" (verse 29). That is, standing in the way of the Kingdom of God is *the* great sin. The rabbis themselves, who are always condemning others of serious transgressions, are the most guilty of all. If anyone is not to be forgiven, it is they.

> *This frightens me, Lord. Have I stood in the way of the Kingdom? Have I, by any word spoken, any deed done, any look of my countenance, discouraged others from believing? Have I stood in the way by being obtuse, unaware, unfeeling—by merely being there without joy and excitement? O God, forgive me. I know I am guilty. Through Jesus, who was right to be angry.* Amen.

Week III: Wednesday

3:31–35 THE REAL FAMILY

These verses must be read in connection with verse 21, with verses 22–30 as a long parenthesis between them. It is after the scribes have spread their slander everywhere that Jesus' mother and brothers arrive to take him home with them. If they lived in Nazareth, it would have been only a few miles distance to Capernaum and the rumors of the scribes' accusations would easily have reached them.

We should readily find sympathy for them. They have not been at the heart of the controversy all along. They are simple folk and would have a great natural respect for the opinions of the learned scribes. So when they come for Jesus, it is probably with heavy hearts. Their son and brother is sick, and they must take him home and care for him. Perhaps a lot of rest and a mother's supervision of meals will restore him to health and normalcy again.

Jesus' reply to those who tell him his family have come may seem callous to us if taken alone. But we must note that the Gospel writer does not bother to tell us what may have followed in the way of a reunion with them, and that his point here is to complete the narrative about the flare-up of opposition to Jesus' ministry.

Jesus is still talking about the Kingdom of the Spirit. "Who are my mother and my brothers?" he asked rhetorically. His eye sweeps the room, filled with the lame and the blind and the diseased he has healed, the simple folk who hang upon his teachings. "Here," he says. "Here are my mother and my brothers! Whoever does the will of God is my brother, and sister, and mother."

He has appointed the twelve to be the leaders of the new Israel. In this Kingdom, blood ties will not be the determining factor. The rabbis will not come in merely because they are sons of Abraham. Kinship will not secure a place for anyone. It is the followers—those who do the will of God—who will be Jesus' family.

Lord, I am deeply moved by this teaching. It speaks to me of the strange intimacy I enjoy with Jesus in times of devotion and commitment. But it also reminds me of the importance of doing your will and making the way of the Kingdom easier for others. Grant that I fail not, that the sense of intimacy may always be there. Amen.

Week III: Thursday

4:1–9 THE SEED OF THE KINGDOM

As there were five conflict stories (2:1–3:6), now Mark gives us five parables, which are not unrelated to the conflict stories. The conflict stories pictured Jesus' encounters with the scribes and Pharisees and ended with Mark's note about the Pharisees counseling with the Herodians about how to destroy Jesus. Then, after Jesus' calling of the twelve, the scribes accused him of being possessed by Beelzebul. Now the overall theme of the five parables is the working of God to bring the Kingdom to successful fruition in the world. As Mark arranges them, in other words, they are a message of assurance in the face of the difficulties posed by "authorities" and the unbelieving crowds.

We wonder about the fact that Jesus teaches this time from the boat. Is there special symbolism in this? In early Christian times, the church was often depicted in the image of a boat. The central portion of church buildings became known as the "nave," from *navis*, the Latin word for "ship." Did Mark have in mind not only Jesus teaching this way but the church broadcasting his parables to the crowds, to the world?

At any rate, the first parable is about the word of the Kingdom and the kinds of people who hear it or don't hear it.

The parable presupposes our knowing the Israelite method of sowing seed *before* the ground is plowed. This is the reason the seed is sown on the path and on the rocky ground. The path will later be plowed up. The rocky ground is ground where there is a thin layer of soil over a layer of limestone—a condition characteristic of land in Palestine.

Jesus' emphasis is probably not on the various kinds of ground but on the fact that *some* of the seed came to fruition and bore a rich harvest. Despite the opposition of scribes and Pharisees and despite the blindness of many of those who hear him, Jesus' announcement of the Kingdom will find lodging in some persons and spring up enormously.

The last verse, "He who has ears to hear, let him hear," is like a gauntlet thrown down to the present hearers. It leaves us with the question, "Will the Kingdom spring up in you?"

Lord, you are a prodigious sower, scattering precious seed on all kinds of ground. Prepare me, I pray, to receive more of the seed that falls on my life, and, nourishing it, to bring it to full measure for you. Through Jesus, who lived constantly with such matters. Amen.

Week III: Friday

4:10–12 THE REASON FOR PARABLES

We are accustomed in our day to think that *everyone* ought to hear the gospel and be persuaded of its truth. But there is a strong conviction in both the Old and New Testament writings to the effect that God would call certain persons to his Kingdom and not call others. It was perhaps a matter of preserving his sovereignty.

It is in this way of thinking that we are to understand these words of Jesus. Whereas we normally regard the parables as "earthly stories with heavenly meanings," told to illuminate some truth, they were apparently intended also to veil the truth from those God had not chosen. Professor Cranfield calls them "veiled revelations." They reveal and conceal at the same time.

This is in keeping with Isaiah 6:9–10:

> And he said, "Go, and say to this people:
> 'Hear and hear, but do not understand;
> see and see, but do not perceive.'

Make the heart of this people fat,
and their ears heavy,
and shut their eyes;
lest they see with their eyes,
and hear with their ears,
and understand with their hearts,
and turn and be healed."

In this sense, the parable is akin to the Old Testament riddle, an illuminating story or analogy which must be puzzled out before the hearer is edified. The riddle belonged to the Hebrew genre known as the *māshāl*, which in the Septuagint is translated by the Greek word *parabolē*, or parable.

"To you has been given the secret of the kingdom of God," Jesus says to the ones gathered with him and the twelve. The word "secret" in Greek is *mystērion*, a technical word from the so-called mystery religions to describe the very core of their belief and understanding. Saint Paul used the word several times in his letters. Here the implication is clear: Jesus himself is the Messiah, the bringer of the Kingdom, and his stories make sense only in the light of this understanding. Anyone who is not possessed of this mystery will hear only a clever saying or story, and is bound to misapply it.

Lord, help me to dwell with the "secret" you have given until it makes all of life clear to me; there is no other way I shall understand, even though I become renowned for my knowledge and praised for my speech. Through Jesus, in whom you continue to disclose the mystery. Amen.

Week III: Saturday

4:13–20 THE WORD IS THE SECRET

Here is a rare instance in the Gospels where Jesus is shown explaining a parable. Some scholars believe that the explanation is really a gloss added by a scribe or by the early church. It is not in keeping with Jesus' use of parables, they say, to provide an allegorical interpretation like this; his parables normally make a single point, and are not in the style of $A = B$, $C = D$, and so on.

But perhaps the scholars are reading this explanation the wrong way. There really is a single point to the story, even in the explanation. It is the sowing of the Word that finally results in the miraculous springing up of the Kingdom.

The word "word" is used eight times in seven verses. What could be more single-pointed than this? How could the explanation be given more focus? Some respond to the word in one way, others in another way. But it is the sowing of the word that is central to the parable.

This is what Jesus was about, what he was doing wherever he went. It is what the disciples' ministry was to be about. It is what the church in the ages has been about. It is what *we* are to be about.

Like the generous sower in the parable, we do not sow with an eye to where the seed may spring up and produce the Kingdom. We do not say, "I will avoid wasting seed here, for the birds will get it," or "I will not sow here; it is too close to the path."

Instead, we sow merrily wherever we go, knowing that others who come after us will plow the ground and nourish some of the seeds, confident that God himself will bring them to fruition in his own time.

It is a beautiful picture of how the Kingdom springs up in response to the broadcasting of the word about it.

> *O Lord, who have given the seed so abundantly, help me to sow less sparingly. I am so careful to measure what the response will be and where it will seem most affirmative. Teach me to share the news of the Kingdom wherever I go, so that it may spring up in the unlikeliest places. Through Jesus, whose wisdom is beyond question.* Amen.

WEEK IV

Week IV: Sunday

4:21–25 THE IMPORTANCE OF DILIGENCE

This saying of Jesus in verses 21 and 22 is apparently a reference to the messianic secret and the lowliness of his appearance. "It will not always be thus," he is assuring the disciples. "No one lights a lamp in order to put it under a vessel or under the bed. Nor has God begun the work of his Kingdom in me only to leave things as they are, in mystery and enigma. One day all the world will be able to see the light that shines in its midst!"

Therefore it is very important that we pay close attention to everything Jesus says—to ponder it and turn it over and over in our minds until its secrets are ours. For the more understanding we have garnered, the more we shall yet garner.

In this, the Kingdom is like the situation in oriental society, where the rich were always receiving gifts from others while the poor were buffeted and robbed even of what they had. If we have been careful to amass understanding from the teachings and deeds of the Master, it will act as a magnet to attract further understanding.

> *Lord, we have seen Jesus in his resurrection and understand about the light put on the stand. Yet he is still in secret to much of the world and has not yet really come to light. Let me therefore be diligent in studying his words. Teach me now to meditate on them day and night, that understanding may give way to a more direct apprehension of his real presence. For to know him is to know you.* Amen.

Week IV: Monday

4:26–29 THE MERRY FARMER

The picture here is not greatly different from that in the earlier parable of the seeds. Mark undoubtedly grouped it with the other parable because of their similarity.

The point seems to be about the joyous abandonment with which the farmer does his work, trusting God for the mysterious power by which it all gets accomplished. He broadcasts the seed, then goes about his daily routines. As the writer quaintly puts it, he sleeps and rises night and day. Then, without his knowing how, the grain appears. The earth seems to produce of itself, "first the blade, then the ear, then the full grain in the ear." It is a miracle.

But the farmer does not stop there. When the grain ripens, he takes his sickle, hones it, and goes into the field to cut the grain. Then he carries it to the threshing floor, where it is winnowed and separated, so that the kernels of grain may be ground into meal and used for baking.

The Kingdom of God is this way, said Jesus. The seed has been sown. Miraculously, it is springing up. When we see it, it is time to be like the merry farmer and take our sickles to the field. We should not spend our time asking what happened to make the seed take root, or how the growth of the ear occurred. Instead, we should be concerned for the harvest.

> *Lord, we are all scholars and scientists at heart. We prefer debating the secrets of photosynthesis and maturation to taking our sickles into the field and gathering the grain. Help us to learn from this parable. You have given the Kingdom. Let us go forth, as simple farmers, to do its work—even if we are scholars by profession. Through Jesus, who never disdained such tasks.* Amen.

Week IV: Tuesday

4:30–34 FROM HUMBLE BEGINNINGS

A friend of mine once showed me a necklace someone had given her. Hanging from the chain was a small charm made of clear plastic. Inside the charm was a small, round seed about the size of a poppy seed or a celery seed. It was in fact a mustard seed, said my friend, sent to her from the Holy Land.

In Palestine, the mustard seed was the subject of numerous proverbs because it was small—almost desperately small—and yet produced such a towering bush. Often the mustard plants around the Sea of Galilee rose to a height of ten feet or more and reached a circumference of as much as thirty feet.

So it will be, said Jesus, with the Kingdom of God. Its beginnings are humble—a prophet clad in the skins of beasts and a Messiah walking from town to town with a motley band of disciples. But from this unlikely seed will spring up an incredible growth, capable of sheltering believers from all nations and ages.

Are we discouraged by the smallness of the Christian efforts in our own day? Does the world's outlay for arms and military operations far exceed the church's gifts for missions? Do not despair. God guarantees his Kingdom to be like the mustard bush.

> *Lord, give me courage from this simple story. Bless the small beginnings of the gospel in my life, that they may spring up like this. And grant that my efforts for the Kingdom, however tiny and weak, may become a shelter for the soul of another. Through Jesus, who gives us the cross as a nesting place.* Amen.

Week IV: Wednesday

4:35–41 THE MASTER OF WIND AND SEA

To perceive the full significance of this wonderful story, we should bear in mind three things:

(1) God's creative power was often demonstrated with water, as in the account of Genesis 1:9–10, when he separated the waters from dry land.

(2) A tempest in the sea was frequently used as a sign of evil or demonic forces at work in the world (cf. Psalm 69:1–2).

(3) The church, in early Christian iconography, was often depicted as a boat.

D. E. Nineham notes two other interesting points from the Old Testament:

(1) The ability to sleep peacefully and undisturbed is a sign of complete trust in the watchfulness and protection of God (cf. Proverbs 3:23–24, Psalm 4:8, Job 11:18–19).

(2) During times of personal or national calamity, it was not uncommon for the people of Israel to accuse God of being asleep and to call upon him to awaken him (cf. Psalm 44:23–24, "Rouse thyself! Why sleepest thou, O Lord?").

What a rich story this must have been for the early church! At the end of a long day of teaching, Jesus told the disciples to take the boat across the lake. They took him along "just as he was"—that is, without getting out of the boat. Other boats put out alongside of them. Soon, one of the quick storms for which the Galilean lake is noted came up, and the boat Jesus was in apparently got separated from the others.

The disciples doubtless labored valiantly to save their small craft, but it was swiftly filling with water and was in danger of sinking. Jesus lay sleeping innocently on the helmsman's pillow in the stern of the boat. The disciples' words to him were a rude reproach: "Teacher," they called, "don't you care that we are perishing?!"

Jesus awoke and immediately spoke to the storm. "Be muzzled" is literally the expression he used—the same formula he had used to the demon in Mark 1:25, underlining the possibility that this should be read as an encounter with satanic forces.

Immediately the scene shifts. Mark is fond of contrasts, as in the darkness suddenly made bright by the lamp put on a stand (4:21–22), the earth that was bare and then produces grain (4:26–29), and the small mustard seed that in the next glimpse has become a gigantic bush with birds nesting in it (4:30–32). Here the scene of wildness and terror suddenly gives way to one of peace and calm. And in the tranquillity Jesus is asking, "Why are you afraid? Don't you believe?"

There is the real clue. Belief in the God who brings the Kingdom banishes fear. It enables one to sleep through storms—through misfortunes and persecutions—because then he knows that God is not really asleep but is in control of our ultimate destinies.

It is small wonder the disciples were "filled with awe"—they had seen one of the inner secrets of life!

Lord, I believe—almost. *I believe*—when conditions are favorable. *I believe*—when there is no storm. *Help my unbelief. Let my faith become an abiding trust, an anchor that holds deep and steady when the winds rise and the waves threaten me. Through Jesus, whose confidence did not wane even on the cross.* Amen.

Week IV: Thursday

5:1–13 AN ENCOUNTER WITH DEMONS

"Peace! Be still!" Jesus had said to the threatening waves. "Come out of the man, you unclean spirit!" he orders the demon in this passage.

Mark is clearly concerned to show the power of the Messiah to command both natural and supernatural forces. In each case it is a storm that is quelled, only in this instance it is a human storm, a psychological tempest.

The poor creature is obviously deranged—so badly, in fact, that he shrieks night and day, and does himself bodily injury on the stones. Completely desocialized, he lives in the caves along the lake, where the dead are buried. If he were not already regarded as demon-ridden, this would ensure his being thought so, for graves were considered the special haunts of devils, and ordinary people were contaminated merely from being there.

Jesus has no sooner alighted from the boat than the possessed man spies him, runs across the intervening distance, and falls down before him. Jesus immediately commands the demon to forsake the man. "What have you to do with me, Jesus, Son of the Most High God?" asks the demon. Like the waves of the sea, he recognizes the Messiah standing before him.

"What is your name?" asks Jesus.

"My name is Legion," replies the demon.

A Roman legion numbered from four to six thousand soldiers.

Apparently a veritable host of devils had taken command of the unfortunate man's soul.

Knowing they cannot win against the Son of God, the demons seek a compromise. They ask to be sent into the herd of swine milling nearby. It was not at all uncommon for unclean spirits, on being cast out, to wreak mischief as they went. Jesus grants the request, and at once the herd pours grunting and squealing over the precipice and into the sea, probably very near to the spot where Jesus, the disciples, and the man are standing.

It is a clear demonstration of the Messiah's unusual power, even over the forces of evil in the world.

> *Lord, there are demons in my life. Some have a name and some haven't. They make me hurt myself when I don't want to. They often make me feel antisocial and unlovable. I cry out night and day for peace within myself. Please, Lord, let Jesus overpower my demons too, and send them from me, that I may exult before you in quietness and joy. For his very name's sake.* Amen.

Week IV: Friday

5:14–20 THE HARDEST KIND OF WITNESS

Years ago there was a man in our town who had been a notorious alcoholic. A large person, he had often come home in a drunken rage and beaten his young wife nearly to death. Then he was converted in a revival meeting and instantly stopped drinking. He became an ardent worker in the church, and went all over the area telling the story of his miraculous transformation. His wife always went with him and sat there beaming as he told what Christ had done in his life. People who had known him were always amazed at the obvious change in him.

I once asked him how it felt to be the object of such amazement. He said he often wished that he could move away and start life over in a community where no one knew his past history, but that God wanted him to make his witness there among people who had known him.

It was the same with the man out of whom Jesus sent the demons. He wished to go with Jesus and the disciples—to leave the coast where he had been so mercilessly possessed and where he was known as a madman by all the people of the region. But Jesus sent him home to witness to those who knew him.

We must assume that Jesus spent some time with the man before embarking again—time enough at least for the herdsmen of the swine to go to a nearby city and spread the word of what had happened. Many people came out to see the strangers and the madman who lived in the caves.

The madman they beheld was of course quite different from the one they had occasionally glimpsed or heard tales about. No longer naked and rattling the remnants of chains that had bound him, or shrieking and clambering among the rocks, he sat docilely and fully clothed at the feet of the stranger in command, and talked lucidly with him.

Again and again, as the crowd grew, the wide-eyed herdsmen babbled out their tale of what had happened. Finally, in fear of anyone who talked to demons and had power over them, they begged Jesus to leave their territory. It was not because of the loss of the swine that they sent him away; it was because they did not wish to be in the vicinity of one who contended openly with the forces of evil; that could be dangerous.

The freed man knew instantly what it would be like to continue where he was. And, besides, he wanted to be with the one who had liberated him. But Jesus refused. "Go home to your friends," he said, "and tell them how God has had mercy on you." It was not a breach of the messianic secret of which we have spoken, for this was Gentile territory, not Jewish; and Luke 8:39 makes it clear that it was to God, not himself, that Jesus instructed the man to witness.

But, characteristically, the man spread the news about Jesus, not only about God, and soon the incident was known throughout the Gentile territory called the Decapolis. He "proclaimed" it, the Gospel says—the same word used for "preaching" throughout the New Testament.

Lord, it is hard to live with my past mistakes and problems. I want to forget them, to bury them out of sight, even to move away from them. But it glorifies you if my relationship to you has brought me beyond them to a new level of maturity and behavior. Help me to see this and to bear witness to your power in my daily existence. Through Jesus, who once landed on the shores of my life too. Amen.

Week IV: Saturday

5:21–34 A STORY WITHIN A STORY

Here is an interesting literary occurrence in the scriptures, a story that takes place within the telling of another story. Jesus is approached by a Jewish leader—a fact no early Christian would have taken lightly—and asked to heal his infant daughter. Then, as Jesus goes with him to his home, an incident occurs along the way.

Imagine the inner turmoil and distress of this poor woman. For twelve years her menstrual discharge has not ceased! She is not only anxious about her health and very probably weakened by the constancy of her condition; by tribal law, she is also regarded as being ceremonially unclean, so that no man can look upon her with favor. Her anxiety is evident in the fact that she has consulted many physicians and spent all her money or property on unsuccessful cures.

When the woman hears the reports of Jesus' great power, she thinks, "If only I can manage to touch him—or to touch the cloth of his robe as he passes—the power will cure me!"

It was not at all uncommon in those days to think of the power to heal as residing in inanimate objects such as trees or stones; therefore it was logical for her to assume that the personal power of Jesus would extend even to his clothing.

She touches him and lo! is healed in an instant—after these many, many years.

But Jesus is unwilling that the healing remain on a mere magical level. "Who touched my garments?" he asks. The disciples are amazed. There are crowds of people pressing around him, yet he is conscious of the healing power's having affected one person in particular.

The woman is transfixed. She has been cured, and realizes it. Her affliction of years has been banished in a moment. And now the strange man responsible for it is calling for her to confess who touched him. With obvious fear—perhaps she is afraid he will take back the cure—she falls down before him and tells her story.

"Daughter," says Jesus. It is a term of gentle affection. "Your faith has healed you. Go in peace." The word "peace," on the lips of Jesus, would have borne the meaning of the Hebrew *shalôm*, which means not only an absence of strife but genuine fullness of life. In this case, it would not be a mere formula for parting but a phrase bursting with promise.

> *How wonderful, Lord, if I could come as this woman came, and, touching your garment, be instantly transformed into wholeness of being! Help me to know it is possible. Give me faith like hers, and be there when I reach out.* Amen.

WEEK V

Anyone who has ever received Communion at a particularly desolate moment in his life or her life will recognize, in an instant, the inward truth of this passage. Jesus cares for his flock in the wilderness! (Week V: Thursday)

Week V: Sunday

5:35–43 A POWER TO RAISE THE DEAD

Here we resume the story of the Jewish leader's daughter, remembering that Jesus was on the way to their house when the woman touched his garment and was healed. The woman had consulted many physicians, none of whom could help her. And when Jesus approaches the synagogue-leader's house, his daughter's case likewise appears hopeless, for she has died. But Mark wants us to see that there is no limit to the power of the Messiah, for he can even raise the dead.

Professional mourning was customary in those days, and the people "weeping and wailing loudly" (verse 38) are probably hired mourners who had been standing by until the moment of death. If so, they are symbolic of our utter hopelessness in the face of death's inevitable advance.

Jesus reproaches them for their lamentations. "The child is not dead but sleeping," he says, indicating that her dying is not ultimate but a mere temporary state, an interruption in her living.

The mourners laugh at him. Do they not recognize death when they see it? Has any corpse ever come to life as they have bewailed its passing? His statement is ridiculous!

But Jesus puts them outside, probably with the anger with which Mark has characterized him in earlier passages (1:41, 3:5). He takes the child's father and mother, and the three disciples who have accompanied him, and goes in to where the child lies. Taking her hand, he speaks in Aramaic, the language spoken by most Jews in his day. *Talitha* is the femine form of "lamb" or "young one." It is a tender address, probably spoken quite softly. *Cumi* is the imperative "arise."

And *immediately*—how Mark likes that word!—she gets up and walks about the room, apparently in the manner characteristic of a twelve-year-old girl. Mark probably stresses the instantaneousness to emphasize the power of Jesus. Had she been only very ill or in a trance and then been revived by Jesus, she would have yet been too weak to rise. Jesus has demonstrated his authority as God's Messiah by performing the ultimate miracle: He has raised someone from the dead. It is a fitting climax to the series of stories Mark has narrated to show the Messiah's power.

Immediately—again the word!—the people, presumably both inside and outside the house, are "overcome with amazement." And why not? They have seen an epiphany, a revelation of the very power of God himself.

> *O Lord, our world, like the mourners, is inclined to laugh and scoff at any claim about raising the dead. Give us faith not to be drawn into this hopeless and joyless position. Let our constant nearness to Christ keep the memory of your power strong in our consciousness. In his name we pray.* Amen.

Week V: Monday

6:1–6 THE POWER OF UNBELIEF

We often hear about the power of belief. The titles of countless books and articles promise us that if we only have confidence in God, ourselves, and others, the world will become a paradise for us.

But here is an instance of the opposite's being true as well—when we lack belief, we limit even the power of God in our midst.

Jesus takes his disciples from their country to his country—to his home town of Nazareth. He teaches in the synagogue on the sabbath—and the tongues wag! "Where does he get such wisdom and power?" they say. "We know who he is. We have always known him. He is Jesus the builder, who worked here through his youth. We know his mother Mary, and his brothers and sisters as well. How can he be what he claims to be?"

So they take offense at him. It is a technical word in the Greek, akin to our word "scandal." Similar usages may be found in Romans 9:32–33, 1 Corinthians 1:23, and 1 Peter 2:6–8. Among the early Christians, it was the only way to explain why the Jews had rejected the long-awaited Messiah when he appeared: they were simply *scandalized* at the humbleness of his background and at his death on a cross.

Jesus' saying to the disciples about a prophet's receiving no honor from his own people echoes many similar statements from ancient times and foreshadows the experiences of many great persons since.

The sad part of the story is the limitation the people's unbelief puts upon their ability to participate in the benefits of the Kingdom's presence. It is not that Jesus' power is restrained; but there is no great believing hunger there, no enthusiasm of faith, to call it forth. It lies essentially dormant, and Jesus himself marvels at the obtuseness of the populace.

Think of the blind woman there who must remain the rest of her life in darkness, the leper who will never be clean, the invalid who will never walk. It is a terrible tragedy!

> *Lord, I am staggered by this passage. It reminds me of how I myself limit the benefits of your power in my life and the lives of those around me because I do not press daily for miraculous occurrences in my environment. It is not your fault that we are not whole, Lord, but mine. I am miserable at this realization. Forgive me and increase my belief. Through Christ, who works miracles.* Amen.

Week V: Tuesday

6:7–13 THE SENDING OF THE TWELVE

Even as the people in Jesus' home region failed to respond to his messiahship, he intensified efforts to prepare for the Kingdom by sending out his disciples.

They went in twos, an old biblical custom. They went simply, with no food, no bag, and no money—not even a coin in their belts or girdles. They were allowed sandals and a staff—the latter to ward off brigands along the way—but were not allowed so much as an extra undergarment.

They were instructed to claim hospitality in only one house in a village, and, when their work was done in that village, to move on. If people refused the message they preached and taught, they were not to argue or waste time trying to persuade them but were to observe the ancient Jewish formula of shaking the dust from their feet and moving on, thus declaring the place a heathen place and leaving the people responsible for their own fate.

The whole emphasis was on the urgency of the mission. Time was short. The word must be spread quickly. People must be warned to repent, preparing their hearts for the new era.

As agents of the Messiah, the disciples were also empowered to cast out demons and heal the sick. Wherever they went, it was as if static electricity were being discharged in advance of a great weather front. The Kingdom was arriving in Christ, and they were his emissaries.

> *Lord, what an ideal these early missionaries of the faith have left for successive generations! To go as they went, with nothing but the clothes on their backs, the sandals on their feet, and a staff for the way, challenges my desire for security and comfort in the service of Christ. Help me to see the correspondence between their faith and the lightness with which they traveled, and to adjust my needs accordingly. Through Jesus, in whom we have seen the Kingdom.* Amen.

Week V: Wednesday

6:14–29 VIOLENCE AND THE KINGDOM

This is the only story in Mark's Gospel in which the spotlight seems to be turned away from Jesus to someone else. But Mark surely has a purpose in telling it. Perhaps it is to underscore the violence that occurs in the collision between the present kingdoms of this world and the coming Kingdom of God. John the Baptizer is an early victim of the collision.

Herod of course is not the same Herod who tried to kill Jesus in the Massacre of the Innocents; this Herod was only sixteen years old when Jesus was born. Nor is he technically a king. Matthew and Luke correct this impression—probably a popular one—by calling him "tetrarch." He was the ranking Jewish ruler over

Galilee and Perea, though the Romans actually controlled the territories. It was his ambition to be a real king that finally led to his banishment by Emperor Caligula in A.D. 39.

John, as the fiery prophet of righteousness and repentance, had fearlessly denounced Herod for marrying his brother's wife despite the fact that, by Jewish law at least, Herodias had not been divorced from her first husband. Herod had imprisoned John, but had apparently become fond of visiting him in prison and talking with him. When Herodias, who was a scheming woman reminiscent of Jezebel in 1 Kings 21, wanted John killed, Herod refused and kept him safe from her in the prison.

What follows sounds like a tale from the Arabian Nights, but the excesses and immorality of the Herodian courts would attest to its credibility. Herodias' daughter Salome dances for Herod and his guests at a birthday banquet, and charms them so completely that Herod offers her anything she asks, up to half his "kingdom." She consults with her mother, who in spiteful vengeance directs her to ask for the head of John on a platter.

Apparently Jesus did not become famous in Galilee until after John's death. In fact, he may have returned to Galilee to fill the vacuum left there when John was killed.

Now, as his name is bruited about, speculations arise as to his real identity. Some think he is John come back to life. Others say he is Elijah, who was always popularly associated with the coming of the Kingdom. Still others guess that he is one of the other prophets.

Herod agrees with those who think he is John. This is in keeping with the uneasiness he must have felt over murdering the man he had found so fascinating. And Jesus' message, moreover, was an extension of the one John himself had preached.

For Mark, the whole episode is surely like the establishing of a theme in a piece of music. The sense of violence and conflict can only increase as the Kingdom waxes stronger. In the end, it will reach its crescendo in the death of the Messiah himself, for earthly powers will not take lightly this invasion of the realm they have held so selfishly and tenaciously through the centuries.

Lord, I cringe from such bloody violence as this—it is not in my nature to like it. I forget how many have died for the faith I claim, and for my very freedom to claim it. Heighten my awareness of the areas where belief still brings people into open conflict with the powers of this world, and give me the courage to be part of the battle. Through Jesus, who was crucified. Amen.

Week V: Thursday

6:30–44 BREAD IN THE WILDERNESS

This is an astonishing passage—and one of the most exciting in the Gospel when viewed in connection with the Christian liturgy of the Upper Room!

The disciples had returned from their missionary journeys. The experience had exhausted them. Jesus, always mindful of the importance of inner restoration, directed them to accompany him to a desert place across the lake (the word for "lonely" means "desert" or "wilderness"). But residents all along the lake saw them going and ran along to the spot toward which they moved, and so were there ahead of them. And Jesus, responding as always to enthusiasm for the Kingdom, began to teach them.

As the sun began to dip in the sky, the disciples became concerned about food. "It is time to send the people away," they said, "so they may secure food." "Feed them yourselves," replied Jesus. "With what?" they asked. It would have taken a great deal of money to buy enough. "Go to the boat and see what you have," he said. And they returned with five loaves of bread and two fish.

What happened next would be readily recognized by anyone who had partaken of a Christian Eucharist, for the pattern in the early church was very similar. The leader had the people be seated. He said the blessing for bread, broke it, and had his assistants distribute it among the people. They all "ate and were satisfied," and a dozen basketfuls of fragments were gathered up afterwards.

There were precedents for this miracle in Jewish history. Exodus 16 and Numbers 11 record God's feeding of the Israelites in the wilderness, with an emphasis on the abundance of the food provided. Second Kings 4:42–44 tells of Elisha's feeding a hundred men with the twenty loaves of barley and fresh grain brought by the man from Baalshalishah, and says that they all "ate and had some left." The story in Mark is thus set against the providence of God throughout Jewish history, and relates the Messiah to Moses and the prophets.

But it obviously goes beyond the precedents, for Jesus is much more special than Moses or Elisha. His presence as Host raises the feeding to the character of a Messianic Banquet, which had long been a feature of Jewish eschatological thought, and relates the Messianic Banquet to the Eucharist or Lord's Supper observed in all the churches of Christendom as a remembrance of his presence with the people.

How many times local congregations of Christians have found themselves in wilderness situations—poor, resourceless, destitute, separated from influential society—and have experienced a similar feast in the bread and wine of Communion! Merely curious readers or scholars may argue over whether the miracle of the feeding could actually have taken place, and how it might have done so. But anyone who has ever received Communion at a particularly desolate moment in his or her life will recognize in an instant the inward truth of the passage. Jesus cares for his flock in the wilderness!

> *Lord, there is no greater miracle in the world than the lifting of a heart, the resurrection of hope; and my heart soars at rereading this glorious passage. Indeed, my cup runneth over, and I cannot devour all that you give me in this lonely life. I can only say thank you, and bow my head before you. In the name of Jesus, whose Kingdom is forever.* Amen.

Week V: Friday

6:45–52 JESUS IN THE DARK HOURS

We can easily imagine the kind of situation in the early church for which Mark intended this narrative. Progress was not easy for the young church. Persecutions were frequent, causing defections from the membership. Congregations grew slowly in the face of almost overwhelming odds. It must have seemed as if the church were a helpless little boat on a large and stormy sea, unable to go forward and constantly threatened with imminent destruction.

In the very darkest hour when the storm is worst, between three and six in the morning, Jesus is pictured as coming to those in danger. He has a resurrectionlike appearance. They think he is a ghost, and are as frightened of him as they are of the storm.

"Take heart," says Jesus, "it is I; have no fear."

The Greek words for "it is I" mean, more literally, "I am." They are thus reminiscent of what God told Moses when Moses asked who he should say had sent him to the Israelites. Tell them, said God, "I AM WHO I AM." "Say this to the people of Israel, 'I AM has sent me to you'" (Exodus 3:15). This connection with the God of Moses is further enforced by the suggestion that Jesus "meant to pass by" the disciples; in the Septuagint or Greek version of the Old Testament, the same word for "pass by" is used in Exodus 33:18–23 and 1 Kings 19:11–12 to speak of God's glory passing by Moses and Elijah.

The ghostlike appearance of Jesus, coupled with this probable reference to God's glory passing by, assures us that this is a picture of the exalted Christ—the Christ who was raised from death by the power of God. We do not know why Mark pushed the story back into the biography of Jesus as he did, instead of offering it plainly as a postresurrection narrative, of something that occurred after the crucifixion. But the message is plain: Jesus the risen Lord comes to his people when they are in trouble and brings them hope and comfort!

Perhaps, though, we can guess why Mark situated the narrative here. The clue is in verse 52, which says that the disciples had not understood about the loaves—that they had missed the significance of the feeding episode which preceded this account. We have already noted that the feeding miracle was related to the Communion—that its real message was, "Jesus feeds his people in the wilderness." By linking the two episodes together as he has, Mark may have been saying something like this: "Jesus comes to his followers in their times of need and distress, causing the winds to subside and the waves to fall away; and the place where we find him doing this is in the Eucharist, for that is the sign of his presence."

Lord, help me to remember this vivid story whenever things seem to go tediously or severely for me. I know that if I pray and wait before you, I shall behold your glory passing by and shall become aware of Christ's presence in the ship with me. Then I shall neither despair nor be afraid. Amen.

Week V: Saturday

6:53–7:13 THE TRUE SPIRIT OF THE LAW

We may note two things in this passage: first, the contrast between the attitude of the common people who swarm to Jesus for healing and the attitude of the scribes and Pharisees from Jerusalem; and, second, the difference between the simple piety of Jesus and the intimidating legalism of the scribes and Pharisees. Mark is fond of pointing out the first, as we saw especially in chapter 2; and the second is a natural point of conflict whenever Jesus and the scribes and Pharisees are in the same vicinity.

Jesus' piety is observed in 6:56—the sick are content to touch the "fringe of his garment." This is the blue fringe or tassel commanded of every adult male in Numbers 15:37–41 and Deuteronomy 22:12. When God directed Moses to establish this tradition, he said, "It shall be to you a tassel to look upon and remember all the commandments of the Lord, to do them, not to follow after your own heart and your own eyes, which you are inclined to go after wantonly. So you shall remember and do all my commandments, and be holy to your God" (Numbers 15:39–40).

The encounter with the scribes and Pharisees which follows in Mark 7:1–13 turns on the very issue of commandments. Through the years, an extensive *oral* code of behavior has developed in addition to the Law of Moses. The Pharisees are its most zealous keepers, having separated themselves from ordinary pursuits for this demanding task. One major division of this oral tradition concerns the purification of both food and the person who eats it. For example, most Jews raised in this tradition dip their hands in water before eating.

Jesus' disciples are men from the borders of Palestine, where the population is not so rigidly Jewish and orthodox as the people nearer to Jerusalem. Primarily men of the sea, accustomed to having their hands in water much of the time, they have never bothered overmuch with ablution ceremonies; when there is food to eat, they simply pick it up and commence to eat.

The scribes and Pharisees immediately question this when they see it. If Jesus is the revered teacher they have heard that he is, why does he permit his disciples to eat with defiled hands?

Jesus neither condones nor defends the disciples' practice. Instead, he strikes forcibly at the weakness of the Pharisees' legalism. "Isaiah was right," he says. "You are hypocrites. You make a fine show of being holy and worshiping God, but your hearts are far from him. You distort the very idea of the commandments."

The illustration Jesus gives is a very penetrating one. A *Corban* was an offering made to God. In oral tradition, it became possible to set something apart from ordinary usage by declaring it to be Corban, or dedicated to God. The thing did not have to be actually given to God, only set aside for him. Hence a person who wished someone else not to have the advantage of something—say, some money—would simply declare it Corban, making it off-limits to others.

Jesus cites a hypothetical case, though one that was probably very common. A young man whose parents are financially dependent on him becomes weary of the relationship and declares his property Corban, thus blocking them from its benefits. Later, he repents of this attitude and goes to the scribes and Pharisees to see if he cannot get the Corban returned to ordinary usage. The scribes and Pharisees are inflexible—the property is now God's and cannot be used to benefit his parents.

Thus, says Jesus, the scribes and Pharisees actually prevent the son from fulfilling the *written* law about honoring his father and his mother. They "make void the word of God" through their traditions which are handed on by word of mouth from generation to generation.

> *Lord, deliver me from the small loyalties of habit or tradition that would keep me from larger loyalties of the spirit. Let me so incline myself to you that your presence in my life determines both what I think and what I do. Through Jesus, who understood the deeper meaning of freedom.* Amen.

WEEK VI

Week VI: Sunday

7:14–23 ATTACKING THE SOURCE OF EVIL

The issue here is defilement, profanation, rendering unrighteous. Mark has arranged the saying or parable of Jesus to follow the conflict with the scribes and Pharisees because it is a natural extension of the story. "It isn't what you put into your mouths," says Jesus, "—food that hasn't been ceremonially cleansed—that renders you ungodly, but what comes out of your mouths from the heart."

This establishes the real order of righteousness, which the scribes and Pharisees seemed to have forgotten. As all the Old Testament prophets had said, it is not careful attention to ceremonial regulations, burnt offerings, and the like that God desires, but basic human goodness, moral decency, and compassion for others.

As simple as the issue seems, it was nevertheless a matter of contention even within the early church itself, and has always remained so. The Apostle Paul was to battle legalism as a form of self-justification throughout his ministry to the churches in Asia Minor. The entire book of Romans is an eloquent protest against the false doctrine of works-righteousness, insisting that confidence in mere legalism brings death, while faith in Christ as the Messiah brings life and peace.

Nor are we free even today from the nagging presence of the pharisaical conscience that would translate our religion into a matter of fulfilling certain ritual or ceremonial obligations. These include such diverse things as not drinking alcoholic beverages, not taking drugs, not falling afoul of the law, attending Sunday school and church, paying one's tithe to the church, donating to local charities, avoiding relationships with persons of questionable character, and generally maintaining a posture of respectability in the community.

Such schematizations for salvation are noxious, for they end in our deceiving ourselves as the scribes and Pharisees did. Only full submission to the Kingdom of God, so that our hearts are turned to the light, will suffice to induce true holiness in us.

Lord, keep my mind and heart from petty rationalizations about my goodness or worth. My only hope for salvation is in you. Therefore let me be charitable with all persons, forgiving and anxious to love them, for in this only do I experience your Kingdom as a present reality. Amen.

Week VI: Monday

7:24–30 A WOMAN OUTWITS THE RABBI

Here is another healing story, only one made doubly interesting by the close reporting of the exchange between Jesus and the Syrophoenician woman. Jesus has apparently entered this boundary territory where the population is partly Jewish and partly foreign in order to seek some privacy. Yet, as Mark constantly observes with regard to the messianic secrecy, "he could not be hid."

Our sympathies are immediately drawn to the woman. She has a little daughter who is deathly ill. She hears of a Jewish miracle-worker who may be able to help her daughter. No matter that they are of different races or religious traditions—her daughter is in need. So she appears at the house where Jesus is trying to rest and beseeches him to cure her daughter.

Professor Nineham says: "The power of Jesus is not a general, but a particular spiritual power, and one that is associated with the Jewish race." Mark, he thinks, never presents Jesus as seeing himself as a universal Messiah; he is sent only to the house of Israel. This may indeed be the reason for Jesus' hesitation in this instance. But as to the larger truth of Nineham's conclusion, let us hold our opinion for a while.

At any rate, Jesus shockingly displays the Jewish ethnic attitude toward Gentiles. The word "dog," even though in this case it clearly means a house pet as distinguished from a cur in the street, is one of the strongest and most offensive epithets in an Easterner's vocabulary.

But the woman is clever. She is talking to a rabbi and knows that he would naturally be fond of verbal distinctions. Therefore she presses her case like a rabbi. "Yes, Lord," she says; "yet even the dogs under the table eat the children's crumbs." It is a small thing she asks, in effect—a mere crumb, something the children will not miss.

Jesus is surely delighted by her wit. "For this saying," he says, "you may go your way; the demon has left your daughter."

But it is more than the saying, of course. She has acknowledged that Jesus is the one who sets a feast before the children of Israel, a feast from which she hopes for a mere bite, a morsel. It is more faith than Jesus has met in the scribes and Pharisees. Therefore she deserves what she has won from him. And, when she arrives home, she finds it as he has said. Her daughter rests comfortably in bed, the illness gone.

Lord, I too am an outsider, a non-Jew. Thank you for the crumbs that have fallen my way. I am sorry that part of the Jewish nation failed you. Help me to be faithful for what I have seen and tasted. Through Jesus, who brought the feast. Amen.

Week VI: Tuesday

7:31–37 THE MIRACLE OF HEARING AND SPEAKING

This healing story has both an antecedent and a sequel. The antecedent is found in Isaiah 35:5–6, in a description of God's salvation of Israel:

> Then the eyes of the blind shall be opened,
> and the ears of the deaf unstopped;
> then shall the lame man leap like a hart,
> and the tongue of the dumb sing for joy.

The Greek word for "dumb" occurs only twice in the Greek Bible —in this passage from Isaiah and in the story in Mark. This strongly suggests the possibility that Mark used the story as a conscious gloss on the Old Testament prophecy.

The sequel to the story is in the elaborate baptismal rites practiced by the church during the centuries after Christianity became well established in the Roman world. The bishop or presiding officer conducting the baptism would spit upon his fingers, then touch his fingers to the candidate's ears, eyes, and mouth. The symbolism of this gesture obviously derived from Jesus' actions with the man who was deaf and had an impediment of speech. The action was meant to transform the person's abilities to hear the word of God and to speak in witness to his or her faith.

As the story is placed in the Gospel of Mark, it is undoubtedly related also to 6:52, which says that the disciples did not understand about the miraculous feeding in the wilderness, to 8:17–21, which discusses their lack of understanding, and to 8:22–26, in which Jesus makes a blind man to see. The whole section of Mark, indeed, is about being able to see, hear, and understand what is happening in Jesus the Messiah.

Jesus' method in this healing was not uncommon among wonder-workers in his day. What is more interesting, perhaps, is Mark's attention to his "looking up to heaven" and sighing before pronouncing the word of cure. The German scholar J. Schniewind says that the word for "sighed" is a particularly strong expression, and points out that it is the same word Paul uses in Romans 8:22–26 and 2 Corinthians 5:2–4 "for the inmost wrestling of the Christian." Apparently Jesus is contending with the whole host of demonic powers in performing this cure, and so not only looks to heaven but concentrates to the very depths of his being. This would be very much in keeping with Mark's consciousness of Isaiah's prophecy and how it had come to a head in the ministry of Jesus.

The astonishment of the disciples (verse 37) would also be consonant with this understanding. "He has done all things well" would mean "He has fulfilled everything"—even to making the deaf hear and the dumb speak!

Lord, in my case this may be the miracle of miracles—to make me truly hear what my ears hear and to liberate my tongue to give thanks and to speak generously of others. I ask you to do it again for me—and again and again, if necessary. For yours is the Kingdom in every age. Amen.

Week VI: Wednesday

8:1–10 THE SECOND GREAT FEEDING

This incident is obviously very similar to the one recorded in 6:30–44. Many scholars have supposed that the popularity of the story in oral tradition led to its development in variant forms, so that Mark had before him when he composed his Gospel two different accounts of the same miracle.

But there is no reason to suppose that Jesus did not perform two similar acts of feeding the multitudes—or more, for that matter. And Mark may well have intended us to understand something special from his arrangement of the two accounts.

Recall that in 7:24–30 he told the story of the non-Jewish woman who requested a miracle for her daughter. Then, in 7:31–37, he reported on the deaf mute who was healed in the region of the Decapolis, or Ten Cities, which was of mixed Jewish and Gentile population. The man may well have been a Gentile, as was the woman who asked for the crumbs from the table.

Until now, Mark has always been careful to record any geographical notes when Jesus moved from one place to another. Yet here there is no record of such a moving, leaving us to suppose that this feeding, the second, occurs in primarily Gentile territory.

Such a conclusion is supported by the opinion of Alan Richardson, who points out several interesting things in *The Miracle-Stories of the Gospels:* The five thousand were fed from five loaves (for the five books of the Law?), the four thousand from seven loaves (for the seventy nations into which the Gentile world was traditionally divided, for the Septuagint or Greek Old Testament, or for the seven deacons mentioned in Acts 6:3?). At the first feeding, twelve basketfuls of scraps are collected, suggesting the twelve tribes of Israel; at the second, there are seven basketfuls, for the same reasons as for the seven loaves. Moreover, the word for "basket" in the first story is *kophinos*, a distinctively Jewish type of basket, while the word in the second story is *spyris*, an ordinary kind of basket known throughout the Greco-Roman world.

So Mark may actually have in mind, moving as he does from the story of the Gentile woman and the account of the deaf mute, the universalizing of the gospel. In one instance, Jesus provided the Messianic Banquet for Jews; in the other, for the Gentiles. Thus, rather than providing a mere doublet account of the earlier miracle, Mark is saying in a rich and symbolic manner that the Kingdom of God is for all people. The prophecy that in Jerusalem all the nations of the world would be blessed is therefore singularly fulfilled in Christ, who is adequate to feed the multitudes.

We may note one further detail that confirms this interpretation: Jesus says of the people with him in the wilderness, "some of them have come a long way" (verse 3).

> *Lord, this is thrilling material! What a gifted interpreter Mark was, to weave these insights into such a provocative narrative! Thank you for his vision of Jesus feeding the nations. Lift my eyes to this vision whenever I come to the Communion table, that my own dedication may be more commensurate with the breadth and depth of its meaning. Through him who feeds us all.* Amen.

Week VI: Thursday

8:11–21 THE SIGNS WE ALREADY HAVE

I once knew a woman who could not quite believe that her husband loved her. He was very tender toward her and showed her every consideration. He provided her with a lovely home and continually showered her with manifestations of affection. But nothing—none of his gifts and none of his expressions of love—was ever enough for her. She constantly demanded new and more convincing proofs.

It was the same with the Pharisees in their attitude toward Jesus. Jesus had recently performed two stupendous miracles in feeding the multitudes, and, if the hints in Mark are reliable, lived in a constant situation of wonder-working. Yet the Pharisees came seeking a special sign, perhaps some apocalyptic token in the skies, such as halting the sun in its course or turning the moon to blood.

Jesus' deep sigh is a key to his disappointment and his resolution not to pander to such a desire for the merely sensational. He believed, of course, that only God could reveal the Kingdom, and would open the eyes of those he willed to perceive it. Thus, to gratify the request of the Pharisees would have been a useless display of his messianic power.

The disciples are another matter. They have been with Jesus for months now, and have been present at all the healings and feedings. Moreover, they were given to him by God. They, of all people, should understand who he is—that, as he says following a feeding miracle in the Gospel of John, "I am the bread of life" (John 6:35).

Yet, the disciples are represented as slow to perceive the deeper meaning of Jesus' presence among them. In the boat, he warns them of "the leaven of the Pharisees and the leaven of Herod," recalling the report in Mark 3:6 that the Pharisees and Herodians were conspiring together to destroy Jesus. Rabbis often used the word "leaven" as a metaphor for evil or pernicious influence. But the word triggers a different train of thought among the disciples. They have forgotten to bring any bread in the boat, even though it is a disciple's primary duty to care for the master's physical needs.

As they discuss the situation among themselves—probably with accusations flying about who should have remembered to bring the bread—Jesus interrupts them and chides them for their anxiety. He reminds them of the two feeding miracles. How many basketfuls of scraps had they gathered after the first? "Twelve." After the second? "Seven." And here in the boat with them is the breadmaker himself, the one whom the Fourth Gospel goes further to identify as the very Bread of Life! Why are they worried?

Have their eyes not seen what has passed before them, or their ears heard the sounds that were there to hear?

Jesus himself is the sign. His teachings, his healings, his gathering of a community and feeding it—what more can anyone ask as a sign of the Kingdom? What more, indeed?

Lord, every generation is the same. Doubt rises in us like the yeast in the dough. We continually ask for signs and wonders. Teach us instead to give thanks for the signs and wonders already surrounding us—for daily bread and changing seasons and tender care. Then we shall know the presence of Christ, and who it is that said, "I am the Bread of Life." Amen.

Week VI: Friday

8:22–26 THE MIRACLE THAT JESUS DID TWICE

This story is in some details very similar to the one in 7:31–37, which also followed a section of the Gospel that began with a feeding narrative. Interestingly, the first story was about the healing of a deaf man and this one is about the restoring of a blind man's sight—with Mark 8:18 *between* them, "Having eyes do you not see, and having ears do you not hear?"

Above and beyond recording the two incidents as bona fide healings by Jesus, the Evangelist obviously uses them in a symbolic sense as well. They clearly bespeak Jesus' power to make us hear and see with a spiritual insight we had been missing.

One of the most captivating details of this particular story is Jesus' asking whether the man sees anything. "I see men," he says, "but they look like trees walking about." The sight is not perfect. So Jesus again anoints his eyes with spittle, and this time the cure is complete.

This is the only instance in the New Testament of a healing that is incomplete the first time. It is so out of keeping with the usual preemptory character of Jesus' miracles, in fact, that it prompts us to consider its special meaning here.

Surely it is Mark's way of saying to those who have once been anointed with the vision of Christ but who still do not see all things clearly, "He will anoint you again, this time with perfect seeing."

Lord, I have seen part of the wonder and beauty of your Kingdom, but my cure has not been complete. I still struggle with imperfect ideas and an uncommitted will. Touch me again, through Jesus, and let me behold everything as I should. For his name's sake. Amen.

Week VI: Saturday

8:27–33 THE NECESSITY OF SUFFERING

It is at this point that Mark begins to build toward the climax of his Gospel in the narrative of the crucifixion and resurrection of Jesus. And he commences by defining in new terms the nature of the messiahship.

"Who do people say I am?" asks Jesus. The answer is identical to the information given in 6:14–16, introducing the story of John's death: Some say he is John the Baptizer returned to life; others, that he is Elijah; and still others, that he is another of the prophets.

For the first time, Jesus presses the disciples themselves to say who he is. Peter is spokesman for the others: "You are the Christ, the Messiah."

Now a strange thing. Jesus does not congratulate Peter, as Matthew's Gospel represents him as doing (Matthew 16:17–19). He merely warns them to tell no one about him. And the Greek word for "charged" in verse 30 normally means "rebuked." It is almost as if he were displeased with the answer.

Why?

Apparently we are still dealing with the question of how much the disciples can see and hear, as in 8:14–26. They have seen his wonders and they are satisfied that he is the Christ. But he knows their understanding is thin and tentative, that they are too simple to see yet that he must suffer great indignities at the hands of the Pharisees and Herodians who seek to destroy him.

At this point, then, he begins to instruct them about this, so that they may withstand when the time comes. He tells them plainly about his death and resurrection (though it is possible that the phrase "and after three days rise again" is a later addition to the text, for Peter at least appears not to hear this part of the message).

Peter takes him aside and chides him for such pessimistic talk. Jesus appears to ponder the matter a moment, looking at the other disciples. Does it flit through his mind, "Yes, Peter is right. Why should God's anointed suffer what I see coming to me?"

Then, in a flash, he rebukes Peter, seeing in his words such temptation as he felt in the wilderness at the beginning of his ministry: "Get behind me, Satan! For you are not on the side of God, but of men."

It is a blistering statement to make to a loyal friend who seeks only your welfare. But just as Jesus has seen Satan's power at work in the ill persons he has healed, now he sees him behind the kindness of Peter.

It is not merely Peter's understanding that is at stake; it is the whole battle with the demonic forces. The cross will not be only an unfortunate episode in which justice miscarries; it will be the last cruel effort Satan can make to avert the coming of God's Kingdom!

> *Lord, I sympathize with Peter. I too would have protested against such pessimism from the Master. But I often fail to see beyond the surface of life and realize the cosmic drama that is going on as you contend with evil and the demonic. Help me to look more sharply, and to be ready to die for the right. Through Jesus, who saw clearly.* Amen.

WEEK VII

"Lord, there are experiences like this [witnessing the transformation] for all of us who spend much time with you and earnestly seek your presence. If I have had none, it accuses me of being a lazy, undisciplined follower . . . and I stumble blindly through life." (Week VII: Monday)

Week VII: Sunday

8:34–9:1 THE PRICE OF DISCIPLESHIP

After telling the disciples plainly that he must suffer at the hands of the scribes and Pharisees, Jesus is pictured as calling in a multitude of people and warning them of the hardship they must face as his followers.

Doubtless he was moved by the violence that had come to John the Baptist and was seeing clearly now that a similar fate awaited him. It was in keeping with this presentiment of danger that he would have spoken such an ominous word to his growing crowd of adherents.

Admittedly, it seems unlikely that Jesus would have used precisely this language, alluding to the cross, for such a reference would have been without meaning in advance of his own crucifixion. More likely, the statement as we have it is an amalgam of an actual warning spoken by Jesus and the later awareness on the part of the Christian community of the way Jesus had died.

The phrase "and the gospel's" (verse 35) likewise argues for this assumption, as Mark's Evangel was probably written at a time when people were losing their lives in defense of the gospel.

At any rate, Jesus is depicted as a leader fully aware of the awful toll his people are about to pay in God's battle with the demonic forces. It is too late to back down, he says; the climax is inexorable. Any who try to forsake him will effectually lose all they have. (Judas, as it turns out, is unable to bear his act of betrayal and commits suicide.) But all those who pay with their lives will actually be saving their lives.

The last verse (9:1) testifies to the intensity to which Jesus sees matters as having come. Some of those standing near him, he says, will still be alive when the Kingdom has come in power.

This word has caused some scholars to think that Jesus was flatly mistaken in his apocalyptic vision of things; clearly, they argue, the Kingdom did not come in the sense that he expected.

But we must remember that Mark was writing this years afterwards. What did *he* think? Surely, if he thought Jesus' expectations had been misplaced, he would not have added this verse. He would simply have omitted it. But he did not. As far as he was concerned, Jesus had been right. The Kingdom *had* come in power. If we do not think it has, that is because the quality of our experience of Christ is not what his was. It is a test of what we see and understand!

> *Lord, I feel that my life is so drab and colorless, lived so far from a time when there were wars of faith and deeds of heroism. Help me to see with truth what cosmic battles are being waged in my own day and in the very environment where I live. Then let me make my commitment to follow Christ and fulfill it every hour, that I may not lose my soul in the mindless routine of days. For his name's sake.* Amen.

Week VII: Monday

9:2–13 A FORETASTE OF GLORY

This is surely another of the most striking passages in the Gospels. Mark doubtless had a purpose in placing it directly after Jesus' warning to his disciples that he must suffer, and they as well. It is essentially a picture of Jesus transformed as he would be in the resurrection. What could be more encouraging to the disciples after the warning?

Everything in the picture conspires to depict the arrival of God's Kingdom.

First, there is the transformation of Jesus' clothing. Popular thought about the end of time was filled with the idea that the final state of glorification would extend to the clothing one was wearing. First Enoch 62:15–16, for example, promised that God's people would be "clothed with garments of glory from the Lord of spirits"; Revelation 4:4 and 6:9–11 speak of the "white robes" of the saints.

Then there is the appearance of Elijah and Moses with Jesus. It was also popular expectation that famous figures from Israel's past would appear at the end to preside over the changes in the world. Elijah's name was most often mentioned in this regard. This is why many people in Palestine said that Jesus himself was Elijah risen from the dead—his miracles made them think of those associated with the great prophet.

Finally, there is the matter of the cloud. God's presence, his *Shekinah,* had since the days of the Exodus been intimately associated with the cloud. And now the voice from the cloud testifies to the sonship of Jesus! It is an endorsement to overshadow the promise of suffering that has gone before.

In the light of all this, Peter's desire to build booths or tabernacles and stay on the mountain is more than the mere human desire to prolong an exciting experience. It was widely believed that in the last days God would once more pitch his tent and dwell with Israel as he had in the time of the wilderness wanderings. Ezekiel 37:26b–27, for example, says: "I will bless them and multiply them, and will set my sanctuary in the midst of them for evermore. My dwelling place shall be with them; and I will be their God, and they shall be my people." The disciples thought the end had come indeed!

But suddenly it was over. It had been momentary—a vision out of time. Jesus was alone. His garments no longer shone. The voice was silent.

Thoughtfully the men descended the mountain. They were full of questions. Jesus warned them not to speak of this until after his resurrection. He must still "suffer many things and be treated with contempt." Yet through it all they would have this to remember. It was an unforgettable experience.

> *Lord, there are experiences like this for all of us who spend much time with you and earnestly seek your presence. If I have had none, it accuses me of being a lazy, undisciplined follower. Then my sufferings have no vision to enlighten or palliate them, and I stumble blindly through life. Help me to be faithful in my devotion. Through Christ, who was transfigured.* Amen.

Week VII: Tuesday

9:14–29 THE POWER OF BELIEF

This is the final exorcism story in the Gospel of Mark. Mark probably placed it here, following the transfiguration narrative, to emphasize that Jesus continues to walk among human needs even after his transformation or resurrection.

It is an absorbing story. Returning from their time in the mountain, Jesus and his three most intimate disciples find a crowd around the other disciples. In the crowd are a number of scribes, who are arguing with the discouraged disciples.

We do not learn the substance of the argument, but we can infer what it was. A man has brought his son, who is apparently a victim of epilepsy, hoping that Jesus will cure him. In Jesus' absence, the disciples themselves have attempted the healing but have not been successful. The scribes have probably accused them of following a false messiah, and an argument has risen out of this.

When Jesus hears the anguished father say that the disciples failed to heal his son, he flares up, apparently at the whole age in general and at the disciples in particular. (We must remember that these are the same disciples as those described in Mark 8:14–21, who could not see or comprehend.) "How long shall I be among you?" he asks rhetorically. "Will you be able to learn in time for my being taken away?"

But then his sympathies for the boy overtake his wrath. "How long has he been this way?" he asks the father.

"From infancy," replies the father. "If you can do anything, have pity on us and help us."

"If you can!" says Jesus. "All things are possible to him who believes."

Some have taken this saying of Jesus to underline the importance of a positive attitude in human affairs; if we only believe in the possibility of something, we are halfway to the goal. But, given the context of the entire Gospel, Jesus implies no such belief-in-general. It is belief in the Kingdom of God he means, and the Kingdom's presence in the very moment and location where he is speaking. If one accepts the arrival of the kingship of God in everything, there is no questioning—then all things *are* possible.

"I believe," cries the excited father; "help my unbelief." It is the word of a man who has leapt on a running vehicle and is partway aboard; he calls to one who is fully aboard to help him to make it all the way.

Jesus, seeing another crowd approaching (the matter is unclear —scholars think perhaps two original versions of the story were joined together, producing confusion about the crowd), immediately commands the demon to leave the boy. When it does, the boy is still, as though dead, until Jesus takes him by the hand and raises him up.

It is possible that the exorcism exhausted the boy, leaving him supine. And it is also possible that Mark implies even more—that, as in the story of Jairus' daughter in 5:35–43, who Jesus said was "not dead but sleeping"—this is a prefiguring of the resurrection of all believers. The latter interpretation seems especially likely in view of the transfiguration story, with its resurrection motif, preceding the passage.

Later, in private, the distraught followers ask why they lacked the power to cast out the demon. Apparently they had had some successes at exorcism when they were sent out on their mission in 6:7–13. "This kind," says Jesus, "cannot be driven out by anything but prayer."

This is curious, for no mention is made of Jesus' saying a prayer when he performs the exorcism. What it undoubtedly means is that utter belief in the Kingdom is necessary for this power, and that that kind of belief results only from hours of practicing the presence of God. There is an obvious rhythm in Jesus' own life and ministry; he withdraws to be with God alone, and then enters the crowds again to minister to the needy. Without the withdrawal, there can be no ministering.

This is a constant emphasis in the New Testament, as we see for example in Acts 8:18–19, where the sorcerer Simon tries to buy the "spirit" by which the disciples perform healings. The spirit cannot be bought; it come only through total surrender of self to God and his kingship. Then even demons and death become powerless before us.

Lord, this passage, like so many others, is frightening in what it demands of me. It asks nothing less than my total commitment, my unreserved belief. I am ashamed of my weak "cultural Christianity." Help me to give myself to you in prayer and love and excitement—and so to believe radically in your Kingdom. Through Jesus, who led the way in such belief. Amen.

Week VII: Wednesday

9: 30–37 WHAT IT MEANS TO SERVE GOD

These verses and the ones following them constitute a highly compressed section of the Gospel. The author has obviously brought together several sayings of Jesus that were originally delivered in different and perhaps unrelated contexts. In general, however, they all deal with his attempt to enlighten the disciples about the nature of his messiahship and the Kingdom of God.

First we are told that Jesus was traveling incognito through Galilee; he wished to use his time to make the disciples understand about the crucifixion and the resurrection. Since the death of John the Baptist, apparently, he had begun to see the probability of a violent end to his own life. Yet he wished his followers not to despair at this, for he expected God to vindicate his messiahship through the resurrection.

Typically, the disciples did not understand. But—and this is a warmly human note—"they were afraid to ask him" about the matter.

Mark seems to have seen a connection between the suffering of the Messiah and the passage which follows. The disciples had been arguing among themselves about who was the greatest. Jesus appears to have called the three "special" disciples to him and asked what they were discussing; but they were ashamed and said nothing. So Jesus called all twelve of the disciples together to give them an important lesson.

Being first among others, he said, is not something you either achieve or boast of; instead, it is something that happens when you forget yourself while serving others. "If anyone would be first, he must be last of all and servant of all."

Then, taking a little child—perhaps it was playing nearby or was borne in its mother's arms—he held it up before him. "Whoever receives one such child in my name," he said, "receives me." And furthermore, he added, it is the same as receiving God.

What a tremendous lesson in priorities it was! Being responsive to a child is to do the will of Jesus and of God. How different from trying to put oneself ahead and be the greatest!

> *Lord, there is so much I do not know about service. I talk about the poor, but I do not give them my goods. I talk about the hungry, but I do not feed them. I talk about the oppressed, but I do nothing to set them free. I talk about the little children, but I do not spend time with them. Forgive me, Lord, and help me to really love the children of the world—all of them.* Amen.

Week VII: Thursday

9:38–50 SOME HARD SAYINGS

Some scholars do not believe that verses 38–40 are a genuine part of the early Christian tradition because they conflict so obviously with the behavior of the Christians. If the incident really happened, then why were the Christians so exclusivist? Acts 19:13–17, which is about some Jewish exorcists who tried to use the name of Jesus, is clearly not sympathetic with such usage.

But such contradiction is all the more reason to accept the validity of this passage. Surely no scribe would have undertaken to add to the tradition something that contravened the actual practice of the church.

It is probably another case of Jesus' insight and understanding going so far beyond our own. In his perception of the way the Kingdom was breaking forth all around him, he was not worried about the presence of unauthorized wonder-workers who used his name. It is when we lack faith in the overpowering nature of the Kingdom that we begin to worry about the purity of our organization and its methods of operating.

Think of the guilt we bear for our prejudices regarding denominations and forms of church governance, modes of piety and patterns of worship. We have often behaved as if our own forms and methods were the only ones, and all the others were less than Christian. Yet Jesus was tolerant of those who used his name though they had never been with him, and said, "He that is not against us is for us."

The next verse is a non sequitur here, and is probably added because, like the ones before it, it speaks of "the name of Christ." It is a saying about the reward that will be had by anyone who does a good turn to any of Christ's followers. Those who bear Christ's name are often referred to as "little ones," and this serves as a bridge to the next idea, that woe will come to anyone who causes one of his followers to doubt or turn back from following. It would be better for that person, says Jesus, to have a great millstone—the kind turned by a donkey, not one of the small ones turned by hand—tied around his neck and be dropped in the sea. It would be a kinder judgment than the one he will receive.

The theme of judgment then becomes a pivot for the next series of verses—only this time it is the judgment which threatens the Christian himself. The "hell" that is spoken of is hardly an apt basis for a doctrine of eternal punishment. It is literally *Gehenna*, the name of the valley southwest of Jerusalem which had been desecrated by Josiah (2 Kings 23:10) and was afterward used as a place to burn refuse. It was thus a dump infested by maggots and characterized by smoldering fires, and had become identified in Enoch 27:2 and 4 Ezra 7:36 as a place of divine retribution.

It is better, said Jesus, to lose a part of your life quite dear to you than to be led astray by that part and so lose everything.

The phrase "salted with fire" is probably a reference to Leviticus 2:13 and other Old Testament passages indicating that Jewish sacrifices had to be accompanied by salt. The Christians in this time of persecution would be seen as human sacrifices purified by fire. The word "fire" would account for the author's placing this saying after the one before. Unrelated sayings were often connected this way in order to remember them by certain catchwords.

The last saying, verse 50, is added here for the same reason. This time the catchword is "salt." It is a plea for the Christians not to lose their saltiness—the Kingdom quality in their lives—and so become useless in the world.

Lord, the world is a hard place and the demands upon me as a Christian are great. I cannot meet them alone. Be with me and give me a sense of your presence at all times. Then I shall be able to withstand the pressures and care for your little ones. Amen.

Week VII: Friday

10:1–12 MARRIAGE AND THE HEART

Anyone who does not want to be married to the person he or she is married to can be the most miserable person in the world. He has a hard time thinking of the Kingdom of God.

In this passage, Jesus has left his seclusion in Galilee and emerged in Judea, not far from Jerusalem. The crowds are around him once more, and the Pharisees have resumed testing him. This time they ask a question about divorce: Is it in keeping with the Law?

"What did Moses command you?" asks Jesus. "Moses allowed a man to write a certificate of divorce," they said, "and to put his wife away."

The reference is to Deuteronomy 24:1–4, which speaks of a man's divorcing his wife if he finds "some indecency" in her. He is to give her a bill of divorce which she can then present as proof of her divorce should another man wish to marry her. One school of Jewish thought held that "some indecency" meant adultery; another school said it meant any cause of displeasure the husband felt toward the wife, such as unattractiveness or inability to cook.

When Jesus asks what Moses commanded, he may have in mind more than "What did Moses say about divorce?" The very first commandment was that the people were to have no gods before the Lord himself (Exodus 20:2–3). And Moses also commanded, "You shall not commit adultery" (Exodus 20:14).

The questioners immediately think of the commonly cited text permitting a man to divorce his wife. But Jesus evidently has a more rigorous text in mind. "That one," he says in effect, "was given merely for your hardness of heart. But God never intended for male and female relationships to end that way. He created a man and a woman. In marriage they become one flesh. What God has intended to be joined together, then, let no man put asunder."

Jesus' theology of the Kingdom of God is obviously at work here. If God is king in our lives, then our hearts are transformed so that we do not sit around worrying that we have a bad marriage and wondering how we can get out of it. The very thing that allowed Jesus to sit loose to the Law in the matter of the sabbath (2:27–28) now necessitates his sounding very rigorous about it. But the two responses are very compatible; both hinge on the fact of the Kingdom's presence.

> *Lord, when you are close to my consciousness, my whole world is beautiful. Then it is easy to fulfill the highest expectations for my life. Help me therefore not to dwell upon my problems but upon the fact of your presence, and I shall glorify you with joy. Through Jesus, who understood this perfectly.* Amen.

Week VII: Saturday

10:13–16 A KINGDOM OF CHILDREN

How much poorer we should be if this story had not been

preserved! And what an accusation it is of our pretentious, complicated lives as adult Christians!

Wise men have always spoken well of the open, receptive nature of children, and of the importance of our maintaining their best qualities in our maturer years. There is a lovely little tale from the annals of Zen Buddhism about the childlikeness of Ryokan, a celebrated Zen master. Once Ryokan was playing hide-and-seek with some farmers' children. When his turn came to hide, he secreted himself in a haystack, where he fell asleep. The children's mothers presently called them to dinner. On the following morning a farmer went to the haystack to get some food for his cattle and found Ryokan there. "Shhhh," said the Zen master, rubbing his eyes. "The children will find me."

Many authorities believe, however, that Mark's story is more than a benediction on childhood. It *is* a beautiful picture of the Kingdom of God as a kingdom of joyous, childlike persons, to be sure, but it may also be an early apologetic for accepting children in baptism. The phrase "do not hinder them" echoes a part of the liturgy of baptism, which asked the question "What hinders?" In Acts 8:36, the same question occurs with reference to the Ethiopian eunuch who wishes to be baptized. The fact that Jesus is described in verse 16 as "laying his hands upon them" also suggests liturgical meaning, for the laying-on of hands was a part of the baptismal ceremony.

Whether or not we see this additional meaning in the story, it is a rich and lovely little narrative. Jesus was rejected by most of the responsible Jews of his day, and he was often misunderstood by his own disciples. He could well hold up the happy, responsive children as examples of those who are truly of the Kingdom of God!

Lord, I try hard to uncomplicate my existence, but I seem unable to do it. Teach me the joy of the quiet and simple life, in which I accept the blessing of your presence the way a child accepts the presence of a dear friend. Then I shall gladden your heart by the renewed innocence of my spirit. Through Jesus, who lays hands upon me. Amen.

WEEK VIII

Week VIII: Sunday

10:17–31 SURRENDERING ALL IMPEDIMENTS

Here we have a striking example of someone who could not enter the Kingdom like a little child. It is a man who is wealthy and whose riches have become the basis of his security. A child will give up anything for something he or she desires, but this man cannot do it.

His approach to Jesus is almost obsequious—"Good Teacher"—and Jesus at once defers all goodness to God. Jesus is the Messiah, and the Kingdom comes with him; but, in Mark's theology, it is God who is the source of all power and goodness, not Jesus himself.

"You know the commandments," says Jesus. We are reminded of the earlier passage about divorce (10:2–12); "What did Moses command you?" Jesus had asked.

Indeed the man does know them, as every pious Jew may be expected to. And he has kept them faithfully. Again this is no surprise, for most Jews observed the commandments scrupulously.

So we come to the point. "Jesus looking upon him loved him." To love probably means here "to show affection." Jesus most likely puts a hand on the man's arm or places an arm around his shoulder. He cuts to the heart of the matter: "All right," he says, "there is one more thing. Go sell your property, give the proceeds to the poor, and come join my followers!"

The man is devastated! It is the one thing he cannot do. He is attached to his wealth. The sight of his walking away is one of the saddest pictures in all the scriptures.

Jesus and the disciples talk about it. The disciples are amazed, for like most people they take the ownership of property as a sign of God's blessing. But Jesus is undeterred by their attitude, and tries to make them understand. Entering the Kingdom is not easy. It requires complete confidence in God. If our dependence is in anything else, we must forsake that.

A similar point is made in numerous books that have appeared in recent years about Zen Buddhism and the skill of archery, or Zen and the game of golf, or Zen and the art of running. Zen, say the books, teaches one to abandon himself wholeheartedly to whatever he is doing, so that self-consciousness does not enter in to interfere with the achievement of what is aimed at. The archer learns to "think like an arrow." The golfer learns to treat the club as an extension of his person and connect totally with the ball. The runner enters into the running so completely that it becomes a mystical experience.

Jesus is simply being practical about discipleship. Whatever requires our attention outside the Kingdom will prevent our truly entering the Kingdom. It is like what he said in 9:43–48: If any part of our being interferes with our complete devotion to God, we are better off to cut that part away and hurl it into the flames.

Peter reminds Jesus that he and the disciples have left all. Yes, says Jesus, and the reward will be commensurate with the sacrifice. What is given up will be restored a hundredfold. The persecution endured now will be replaced with eternal life in the age to come, and the tables will be turned for many people.

The reference to persecution is undoubtedly a scribal addition to Jesus' remarks, included for the many Christians who after the death and resurrection of Jesus had to face severe punishment for their faith. But it is very much in keeping with the story of the rich man. He lost all because he would give up nothing; the early Christians found everything because they gave up all they had.

> *Lord, help me to look hard into my own life and desires and recognize the dependencies I have not surrendered. Are they my home? My family? My job? My education? They are all dear to me. But grant that I may love you so much that none of them stands between us, now or in the future. Through Jesus, who gave up all from the very beginning.* Amen.

Week VIII: Monday

10:32–34 JESUS GOES AHEAD OF US

This is the third and most specific of Mark's predictions of the passion of Jesus. It is the first time Jerusalem has been mentioned, but not the first time we have been aware of it. In Mark, the Holy City is ironically the center of the evil power in the world. It is from there that the scribes and Pharisees have come who have opposed Jesus and refused to understand him. Now, as he approaches the city, we feel a natural heightening of suspense and conflict. It is little wonder that the disciples are afraid. We can almost picture them cringing, as in a melodrama. They know that something terrible is about to happen.

What a powerful image Mark gave the early Christians though, with Jesus going ahead of his followers. This would surely have been a comforting picture to Christians who faced persecution and death for their faith. Jesus always precedes his disciples. Ministers, missionaries, and lay workers have often commented on this in their own experience. Wherever they have gone, into jungles, foreign cities, palaces, or ghettos, they have been anticipated by the presence of Christ. He is always there first.

Perhaps the most interesting feature of this prediction of the passion is the reference to Jesus' being delivered to the Gentiles—to the Romans—who will mock him, spit on him, scourge him, and kill him. This is a literal preview of events Mark later describes in 14:65 and 15:15. Whether Jesus predicted the very details of his trial and death or Mark added them after the fact is probably beside the point. The important thing in the narrative is his apprehension—and the disciples'—of his coming execution.

As for the resurrection—this must have been a dark mystery indeed to the disciples at this point. As Mark says very tersely in 14:50, when Jesus had been captured by the priests and their guards, "They all forsook him, and fled."

> *Lord, you go ahead of me into the strangest places. Often they are places where there is pain or conflict or misunderstanding, and I am afraid to follow you. Teach me faithfulness, that I may not abandon you, but may follow with courage and love. For you are with me, even to the end of the world.* Amen.

Week VIII: Tuesday

10:35–45 FOLLOWING A SERVANT LORD

How often we make the same mistake James and John made, of thinking that our religion exists for us. "We want you to do for us whatever we ask of you," they said to Jesus. Doesn't that sound like us? "Do for us whatever we ask."

Some of us even judge the efficacy of our religion by how dependable God is to do that. If he answers our prayers and gives us what we want, we think our belief is true and good. If he does not, we suppose there is error in our faith.

But Jesus turns the matter around for James and John. In the Kingdom of God, he says, it is not that way. We do not enter the Kingdom for our own advantage. In the Kingdom we are servants, not lords. In the world around us, it is true that the greatest men appear to be those who rule over others. But in the Kingdom the greatest are those who serve others.

Jesus himself is the primary example. He is the Messiah, the Son of man. Yet he came "not to be served but to serve, and to give his life as a ransom for many."

Can James and John drink the cup he will drink, or be baptized with the baptism he is facing? The references are two-pronged. On the surface, they allude to Jesus' impending death. At another level, they surely spoke to the New Testament church about the Lord's Supper and the ritual of baptism; to engage in either was a dangerous act, and might involve the participant in following Jesus to a premature dying, especially during times of heavy persecution.

Even if the two disciples can follow Jesus in this, he says, it is not his to say who will sit at the places of honor with him. The Kingdom is God's, and God must be the one to decide such matters.

We are back to the matter of entering the Kingdom like little children. In the world, people race and strain to get ahead of one another; they want to succeed, to take honors, to be "number one." But in the Kingdom it is enough to be a mere servant, to be the "slave of all." The joy comes not from place or position but from the presence of God in our midst.

What a tragedy and what a judgment it is—even in the church—that we still vie for honor and recognition. This is to live as the world lives, by the world's vision. It denotes our continued failure to understand, and our continued need of conversion.

O Lord, who walked humbly among us, teaching with patience yet suffering indignities and pain beyond the telling, help me, who am proud, ambitious, and selfish, to learn to be gentle, restrained, and self-emptying, even as you are. Amen.

Week VIII: Wednesday

10:46–52 THE GIFT OF SIGHT

This is an exciting story, enthusiastically told, and it also comes at an exciting point in the Gospel. It happens at Jericho, the ancient city east of Jerusalem, and thus signals Jesus' approach to the Holy City—he is now only fifteen miles from his final destination. After this, all action in the Gospel will occur in or near the great center of power, Zion itself.

We should recall all that Mark has had to say about the importance of *seeing,* especially in chapter 8, where Jesus accused the disciples of having eyes but not seeing (verse 18) and soon after restored a blind man's sight in Bethsaida (verses 22–26). There is surely special significance about the gift of sight at this particular moment, when Jesus is leaving Jericho and beginning the last brief segment of his journey to Jerusalem.

Even before he receives his sight, the man sees something of profound importance—he recognizes Jesus as the Son of David and Messiah of Israel.

It is a dramatic picture. A man whose eyes behold no light is sitting by the road, asking alms of passersby. He hears that Jesus of Nazareth is coming his way. Suddenly the ancient apocalyptic dream is triggered in him. The Messiah of God is approaching on this very road! The Kingdom of God is that near to him.

"Jesus, Son of David, have mercy on me!" he cries out. It is all he can do, for he is blind. His shouting must make intersection with the Kingdom. It is the only way he can enter in. Others rebuke him for making noise, but he will not stop. He must not! It is his only chance to intersect the Kingdom!

Jesus hears and stops. "Call him," he says. They interrupt the blind man's shouting. "He is calling for you," they say. Throwing aside his cloak, which would normally have been spread in the road to catch the coins of passersby but which he may have gathered around him when he began to call out to Jesus, the man leaps up and runs unseeingly in the direction of Jesus.

"What do you want me to do for you?" asks Jesus. It is the very same question, word for word, he has asked of James and John a short while before. Then, Jesus had said the requests was not for him to grant. Now, when the man says, "Master, let me receive my sight," Jesus bestows the favor.

The request is of a different order. It does not come from the disciples, who have been with Jesus for many months and still have not learned his ways very well. It comes from a poor, untutored blind man whose faith has leapt up to embrace the Kingdom. "Go your way," says Jesus; "your faith has made you well." The Greek word *sōzein*, "to make well," refers to salvation as well as to healing. The man has done well—he has intersected the Kingdom.

Immediately—how Mark loves that word!—he receives his sight and follows Jesus "on the way." He joins him in the final part of the great pilgrimage to Jerusalem, and will be among those who tear palm branches from the trees to spread in the road.

Jesus no longer cautions the one who is healed not to speak. There will be no more messianic secret. It is time to recognize the One who comes in God's name. The man who follows him in the way may now shout it all he wishes. The Son of David draws near the Holy City! The Kingdom is at hand!

Lord, remove my blindness too. Let my faith leap up as this man's did, and own your holy presence in my life. I too am only a beggar beside life's road, sitting helpless as the crowds pass by. But let me see you with the inner eye, and I shall confess you to all men and follow you in the way. For you are the Christ of God. Amen.

Week VIII: Thursday

11:1–11 JESUS ENTERS THE CITY

To understand the meaning of Jesus' entry into Jerusalem, it is necessary to know something of the Old Testament and the place it held in popular expectations for the Kingdom of God. Zechariah 9:9, for example, reads:

> Rejoice greatly, O daughter of Zion!
> Shout aloud, O daughter of Jerusalem!
> Lo, your king comes to you;
> triumphant and victorious is he,
> humble and riding on an ass,
> on a colt the foal of an ass.

When Jesus sent the two disciples for the colt, then, it was obviously with this prophecy in mind. And the fact that no one had ever sat on the colt before was in keeping with a general understanding that any animal to be used for sacred purpose should not have been used before for any other reason.

An even more important Old Testament association for the event is Psalm 118:19–29. This is the last of six psalms known as the Hallel psalms, and appears to have been derived from an occasion when a king came to the temple to offer thanks for a great victory in battle.

> Open to me the gates of righteousness [it says],
> that I may enter through them
> and give thanks to the Lord.
>
> [verse 19]

Note verse 22 of the psalm, which is widely quoted in the New Testament (for example, in Matthew 21:42, Acts 4:11, and 1 Peter 2:7):

The stone which the builders rejected
has become the chief cornerstone.

Doesn't this pick up a theme that has been dominant throughout Mark's Gospel—the rejection of Jesus by the scribes and Pharisees, the "builders" of Israel?

The psalm continues:

This is the Lord's doing;
it is marvelous in our eyes.
This is the day which the Lord has made;
let us rejoice and be glad in it.
Save us, we beseech thee, O Lord!
O Lord, we beseech thee, give us success!
[verses 23–25]

The words are perfectly attuned to the coming of the Messiah to the Holy City. Certainly his ministry has been "the Lord's doing." The "day which the Lord has made" is not just any day, but the Day of the Lord, the eschatological day of the Kingdom's arrival. And "Save us" in the Hebrew was *hoshianna* or *hosanna*, the cry of those along the way where Jesus passed.

Moreover, this psalm had come to be used always with the Jewish Feast of Dedication, commemorating the cleansing of the temple by Judas Maccabeus in 165 B.C., and had come to be associated with the waving of bundles of green branches actually called "hosannas" by the people. Verse 27b says:

Bind the festal procession with branches,
up to the horns of the altar!

So the people had adopted the practice of carrying and waving branches and grass stalks as part of the celebration.

When we note that Matthew 21:12–13 has Jesus' cleansing of the temple following directly upon the entry to Jerusalem (though Mark 11:12–19 postpones it to the following day), we are assured that this psalm and the "festal procession with branches" lay immediately behind this event.

Perhaps the most striking thing about Mark's account of the entry is the comparative quietness of it. It is not accompanied by the great crowds of Matthew's account and does not appear to upset the city officials. (The "many" of verse 8 may well be disciples.) Nor does Jesus create an immediate disturbance in the temple. He merely enters it, looks around, and retires to Bethany, two or three miles away, to spend the night. The greeting in verses 9 and 10 is derived from Psalm 118:26, "Blessed be he who enters in the name of the Lord!"; and, though it seems messianic in nature, it was probably spoken by a band of disciples, not, as in Matthew, by great crowds of people.

It is possible, despite the blind man's proclamation in Jericho, that the messianic secret is still operative here, or at least exerts a lingering effect. Mark probably saw this as an occasion of deep symbolic significance, though not one in which a great tumult was raised among the populace. Jesus chose the colt purposely and entered the city as a king, whether there were crowds present or not. It was a victorious moment in the spiritual sense, if not in the physical sense as well. The ministry had reached a climax, and Jesus had been utterly faithful to God. Now the scene was being set for the greatest drama of all.

Lord, I would like to have been there to watch Jesus' procession as it wound over the Mount of Olives and up into the Holy City itself. It is always exciting to observe history as it is being made. But it is far more important that I shall see the entry of the Son of God in the day when all history is consummated. Then the shouts will be deafening indeed. Prepare my heart for that moment, I pray, through him who rode upon the foal of an ass. Amen.

Week VIII: Friday

11:12–26 A JUDGMENT ON THE JEWISH RELIGION

Mark was fond of telling a story within a story, as we saw in 5:21–43, where Jesus healed the woman with a hemorrhage while on his way to raise the daughter of Jairus. Here we have the narrative of the cleansing of the temple inserted between two parts of the fig-tree story.

It is probably best to keep the two accounts together, especially when interpreting the report about the fig tree. This latter story is the only reference in any of the Gospels to a *destructive* miracle by Jesus, and, as such, occasions us no little difficulty. Mark plainly says that it was not the season for figs, making Jesus' action appear all the more egocentric and unreasonable, as if he were some swaggering tyrant who struck out at whatever failed to satisfy him. But if we examine the fig-tree narrative in the context of the temple cleansing, we may understand it more generously.

Many scholars think the story of the fig tree was originally a parable that got translated into a historical incident. Others believe it was given as an "acted parable," a symbolic action similar to the enacted parables of certain Old Testament prophets.

We know that the fig tree was often regarded as a symbol of the nation Israel. Luke 13:6–9 is a parable in which this connection is obvious.

It seems highly probable, then, that the story is set here at the beginning of the passion-week events as a symbol of Israel's failure. She had put out leaves that would indicate the presence of fruit—that is, her many rituals and observances. But in the encounter with the Messiah she was found wanting of fruit.

The temple narrative thus becomes part of the larger picture. The temple was swarming with pilgrims in the Passover season, and there was much trading in the birds and small animals for sacrifice, as well as in the exchange of foreign monies for the local currency. All of this was occurring in the outermost of four concentric courts of the temple, known as the "court of the Gentiles" because it was the one court into which non-Jews were permitted to come.

We must remember that in Mark's account this is only the second time Jesus has seen the temple, the first having been on the afternoon of the preceding day. Perhaps his piety, nurtured in the more rural districts, was incensed by what he saw that afternoon; thinking about it overnight, he returns the next day and in a spirit of righteous indignation attacks the money-changers and sacrifice-vendors in the outer court. Apparently he also invokes an old temple ordinance against carrying anything, even a staff, a purse, or a sandal, through the temple district (verse 16). In the fashion of a stern, unyielding prophet, he reminds the people that God's temple is to be a place of prayer, not of commerce and busyness.

The withering of the fig tree is thus a picture of what will happen to Jerusalem and the Jewish religion as a result of their falling away from true holiness; and Jesus' anger at the barren tree is directly related to his prophetic ire over the conditions in the Holy City.

To the conclusion of this episode Mark has appended comments on the effectiveness of faith and prayer. That faith overcomes obstacles was a common rabbinical teaching; and Jesus' sayings about the relationship of forgiving others to one's own forgiveness are woven throughout the Gospels. The point of the entire passage is not to be confused by these last verses; it is really centered on Jesus' arrival in Jerusalem and his conflict with the empty ritualism of the scribes and Pharisees. He has dealt with their hypocrisy throughout his ministry in the provinces; now he faces it directly in the very heart of their kingdom.

Lord, it is easy for me to side with Jesus in his indignation about the commerce and emptiness in the temple. What is harder for me is to hear a similar judgment against my own lack of spirituality. My existence is like the temple—profaned by economic considerations and the bustling activity of busy days. Forgive me, Lord, and make me *a place of prayer. Through him who saw to the heart of everything.* Amen.

Week VIII: Saturday

11:27–33 A QUESTION OF AUTHORITY

Mark sets here the first of several "conflict stories" between Jesus and the authorities that will end with Jesus' crucifixion. In this instance, the encounter appears to arise from the cleansing of the temple. The chief priests, scribes, and elders would doubtless represent the Sanhedrin, the high religious court of Israel, and, as it was in charge of the temple police, would be responding to a complaint about Jesus' behavior.

The question of authority is vital. Israel was in theory a

theocracy, with God as its head. The Jewish ruler (if we ignore the fact of Roman occupation) derived his authority from God. So did the Sanhedrin. The question asked of Jesus may have been designed to see whether he considered himself a prophet sent from God. It probably was not intended to test his messiahship.

Jesus' answer is typically rabbinical. He poses another question, about the authority of John the Baptist, who was generally accepted by the people as a true prophet. "Was John's authority to baptize from God or from men?"

The crafty old men see that they are bested. They cannot answer the question either way without committing themselves to an outcome with which they would be uncomfortable. So they do not answer, and Jesus refuses to continue the matter.

It is interesting to note that this first conflict story turns on a reference to John the Baptist. As we have seen in earlier passages, John's violent end seems to have brought Jesus to the first realization of his own probable death by violence. This story, set at the beginning of the passion week, thus provides a theme or leitmotif that will culminate in the crucifixion itself.

Lord, I confess that I am like these old men from the Sanhedrin. I too like to argue fine points of religious philosophy when I should be opening my heart to you. I listen to sermons and pick at their grammar while evading the deeper issues they are raising. Make me stop this play-acting, Lord, and be ready to meet you everywhere. Through Jesus, in whom we see you most clearly. Amen.

WEEK IX

Jesus was reminding his questioners of an even higher obligation. Their very lives were from God. His image was imprinted on every one of them. Their most sacred charge was to humble themselves before their Creator. (Week IX: Monday)

Week IX: Sunday

12:1–12 THE REJECTION OF THE OWNER'S SON

This allegorical parable had its source in Isaiah 5:1–30:

> Let me sing for my beloved
> a love song concerning his vineyard:
> My beloved had a vineyard
> on a very fertile hill.
> He digged it and cleared it of stones,
> and planted it with choice vines;
> he built a watchtower in the midst of it,
> and hewed out a wine vat in it;
> and he looked for it to yield grapes,
> but it yielded wild grapes.
>
> [verses 1–2]

The reference in both Isaiah 5 and the parable in Mark is to Israel. God had tenderly cared for this vineyard, and it had rich possibilities; but the grapes turned out to be small and bitter, a poor reward for his work.

The part of the parable original with Jesus is the story of the owner's repeated attempts to collect some of the vineyard's profits from the churlish tenants. Jesus' hearers would have readily identified with such a story. Israel had many foreign landowners in that day. It was easy to imagine a case in which the tenants, thinking the owner could do nothing to them at long distance, maltreated the slaves or servants who came from him. And there was indeed a law that if the only heir of a piece of property was killed, the property might belong to anyone who claimed it, with the occupants having first claim. So the death of the son was not an entirely fanciful idea.

The religious leaders of Jerusalem doubtless saw the point of the parable, as we are told in verse 12. The attempt to arrest Jesus could have been made only on the charge of identifying himself as the owner's son. Here he was, right in the center of the vineyard, and the tenants were plotting how to get rid of him. It was an ingeniously self-fulfilling prophecy.

Verse 9, about the owner's vengeance, is a reinforcement of the prophecy in Isaiah 5:

> And now I will tell you
> what I will do to my vineyard.
> I will remove its hedge,
> and it shall be devoured;
> I will break down its wall,
> and it shall be trampled down.
> I will make it a waste;
> it shall not be pruned or hoed,
> and briers and thorns shall grow up;
> I will also command the clouds
> that they rain no rain upon it.
> [verses 5–6]

The "others" referred to in verse 9 of the parable are doubtless the "little ones" who have accepted and entered the Kingdom of God.

The whole story turns on the rejection of the owner's son, and rejection becomes the linking word for verses 10 and 11. These verses are a direct quotation from Psalm 118:22–23, which we have seen plays a substantial part in Mark's understanding of the passion. The religious authorities have rejected the son, but—we must suppose that the point of view here is *after* the resurrection—he has now become the cornerstone of the building or the keystone of the archway (the Greek allows either interpretation).

Lord, I too am prone to think I own the things I use from day to day—my home, my clothes, my money, my body, my mind. Forgive my presumptuousness and lack of sensitivity. Help me to remember that all I have is a trust from you, and that every person I meet is potentially your messenger or your son. In the Son's own name. Amen.

Week IX: Monday

12:13–17 AN HONEST ANSWER TO A DISHONEST QUESTION

The anonymous "they" of this passage we assume again to be the religious leaders who were actively seeking to destroy Jesus. We can almost imagine the scene as they selected the cleverest men in their midst and commissioned them to "get" the Nazarene.

The approach of these clever ones was designed to elicit a self-incriminating answer from him.

Most Jews passionately resented having to pay the universal poll tax imposed by Caesar. Perhaps most galling of all was the fact that the tax must be paid in silver coins bearing the image of Tiberius Caesar himself, and not in the normal Jewish coinage, which bore no images. The laurel wreath above Caesar's head and the inscription *Tiberius Caesar Divi Augusti Filius Augustus Pontifex Maximus* proclaimed Caesar divine. This was an inestimable affront to the Jahweh-worshiping Hebrews.

If Jesus answered that it was right to pay taxes to Caesar, he would incur the wrath of the nationalistic populace, dashing any hopes of a future ministry among them. If on the other hand he said it was wrong to pay the taxes, he would be reported immediately to the Roman officials on the charge of sedition. Either way, they thought they had him handsomely.

They introduced the question in the adroitest of manners. "Teacher," they said in effect, "we know that you are straight in all you say. You do not try to bend the truth to curry favor with anyone. Now tell us honestly, should we pay taxes to Caesar?"

"Bring me a coin," said Jesus. He wanted a denarius, one of the silver coins used to pay the tax. "Now whose face is this?" he asked when they had brought it.

"Why, Caesar's," they said.

"Then give it to Caesar," said Jesus. "But give to God whatever belongs to him."

Behind this lay the common understanding that all coin of the realm—money bearing Caesar's name and face—literally belonged to Caesar. Others might use it temporarily, but in point of fact it was the emperor's.

So Jesus was actually saying, "Let Caesar have what is his." But at the same time he was reminding his questioners of an even higher obligation. Their very lives were from God. His image was imprinted on every one of them. Their most sacred charge was to humble themselves before their Creator.

And the implication was, of course, that they were doing exactly the opposite. They were harassing the Son who had come among them as Messiah.

Lord, how many times have I been indignant about some injustice in the world—something done to the poor or the powerless or the children—when I myself was less than sensitive to your presence or to your requirements of me. Help me to pay what is due in the world, but also to render to you what is due to you. Through Jesus, who lived in complete awareness of your lordship. Amen.

Week IX: Tuesday

12:18–27 THE GOD OF THE LIVING

This time it is the Sadducees Mark pits against Jesus, possibly to show how completely rejected he was by all the leading factions in Jerusalem. The Sadducees were a wealthy social class with strong traditionalist leanings, and the high priest was always chosen from among them. Doctrinally, they rejected the relatively "liberal" theology of the Pharisees, who were much closer to Jesus on teachings about eternal life, the Spirit of God, and even the Kingdom. They accepted only the Pentateuch, or first five books of the Old Testament, as binding on their beliefs, and discounted all further developments.

Hence they begin by citing Moses in Deuteronomy 25:5 and pose a question which seems to demolish the possibility of Moses' having believed in the resurrection. If a woman had seven husbands, as Moses' law would have ordered, whose wife would she be in eternity? It appears a clever question.

Jesus is cutting in his reply, and twice tells the Sadducees they are wrong. They fail to see that those who rise from the dead are like angels, who have no need of wives or progeny to be immortal. Moreover—and here Jesus turns their own pride in Moses upon them—Moses said in Exodus 3:6 ("the passage about the bush," the only way to distinguish location before chapters and verses were devised) that God said, "I am the God of Abraham, and the God of Isaac, and the God of Jacob." Not I *was* but I *am*. He is not the God of those who have died, but of those who live.

Professor C. E. B. Cranfield says: "The fact that in Moses' time God could still call himself the God of Abraham, Isaac and Jacob implies that at that time he still remembered and cared for them, and, since he is the living, almighty and faithful God, those whom he remembers and cares for must be alive. . . . The kernel of the argument is the faithfulness of God."

> *Lord, help me to escape the snares of my own wit and cleverness, that would entangle me in questions like those of the Pharisees and Sadducees. Let my meditation be upon you and your power, so that my mind sails like a silver ship through the dark waters, calm and steady in its sense of your presence. For you have the words of life.* Amen.

Week IX: Wednesday

12:28–34 THE HEART OF THE MATTER

In Eugène Ionesco's play *The Chairs*, an old man is preparing to give a summary of his philosophy. Out of his years of living, he has distilled his wisdom into a single speech, which he wishes everyone from the simple folk to the emperor to hear. He has even hired a professional orator to make the speech for him, lest any of it be lost through poor delivery. When the orator finally arrives on stage, the suspense is terrific. He stands with his back to the audience, composing himself. Then he turns and begins to deliver the old man's message.

"Mmm, mmm, mmm, gueue, gou, gu. Mmm, mmm, mmm, mmm."

He is a mute, and cannot pronounce a single syllable! It is the playwright's way of representing the void he believes to lie at the heart of existence. There is no meaning—only silence and absence.

How different is the positive note lying at the center of Jesus' life and belief. What is the central commandment? asked the scribe. And Jesus replied with this remarkable combination of answers, one from Deuteronomy 6:4–5 and the other from Leviticus 19:18. First we are to love God with everything in us; and then we are to love others as solicitously as we care for ourselves.

Trying to summarize the Law in a single saying was not uncommon in Jesus' time. Many rabbis attempted to formulate such a statement. Hillel, for example, had said several years earlier: "What you yourself hate, do not do to your fellow; this is the whole law; the rest is commentary; go and learn it."

That Jesus' summary was so much more positive is very revealing of the healthiness at the core of his being. In an instant, he had brought to focus the essential message of both the Law and the prophets, that God prefers loving-kindness to all religious rites and sacrifices.

When the scribe perceived the rightness of what Jesus had said and commented on it with true feeling, Jesus praised him. In effect, he said, "You are standing on the threshold of the Kingdom of God!"

Lord, what a simple thing love is. It is so much less complicated than great ethical philosophies or the many rules of ancient religions. It cuts through all the knotty, difficult problems as if they weren't there at all. Yet how hard it is too. I am not sure I am secure enough to love the way you love. I try, but then I falter and fail again. Help me, Lord, to be so sure of your presence at all times that I may love everyone in my world. For your Kingdom's sake. Amen.

Week IX: Thursday

12:35–44 SMALL CAN BE BEAUTIFUL

This passage seems almost to be an illustration of the last one, in which Jesus told one of the scribes that the love of God and love of one's neighbor are the heart of the Law.

First we have a short section (verses 35–37) about an argument with the scribes over whether the Messiah was the Son of David. Most scholars agree that these verses are all that remains—the mere ending—of a conflict story similar to the several we have recently encountered. If they are, the meaning must be left somewhat imprecise. Probably Jesus was insisting that the Messiah is God's son more than David's, and therefore of even greater importance than the Jewish leaders realized.

The next section (verses 38–40) is much clearer. Addressing the crowds who listened intently, Jesus issued a warning against mere legalistic religion.

The scribes were a symbol of legalism. They liked to parade around in their extremely long robes, which were supposed to represent great learning. They enjoyed receiving the deferential salutations of others in the streets, for the rule was that the less learned people greeted the more learned first. They had fostered a custom of taking the front seats in the synagogues, where all eyes could see them well each time. They took advantage of the piety and generosity of widows, who probably listened to them and supported them more readily than others. They used their prayers, which should have been sincerely addressed to God, as a means of gaining attention and admiration in public.

All of this is a caricature of true religion, Jesus was saying. Certainly they had not taken seriously the saying of the prophet Micah:

> He has showed you, O man, what is good;
> and what does the Lord require of you
> but to do justice, and to love kindness,
> and to walk humbly with your God?
> [Micah 6:8]

The last section of the passage (verses 41–44) offers a beautiful contrast to the ostentatious religion of the scribes. Jesus sat watching the treasury at the temple. The rich put in large gifts. A poor widow came and dropped in her two tiny coins. The Greek word for "coin" used here, *lepton*, means something extremely minute. These were not the silver coins with Caesar's image we met in Mark 12:15, but simple little coppers with no image at all. They were but a straw compared with what the rich gave.

"There you see," said Jesus, "a real example of giving. That poor woman has given more than all the rest, for she has put in everything she had." The woman obviously loved God with all her heart and mind and strength.

> *Lord, I am a calculator, and I live in a calculating world. I am always figuring what I can afford to give you or what I can afford to give others. Help me to be like this beautiful woman who asked what she could afford to keep and then gave everything.* Amen.

Week IX: Friday

13:1–13 AN INJUNCTION TO FAITHFULNESS

Chapter 13 of the Gospel of Mark is often called "the little Apocalypse," for it deals with the end of all history and how Christians are to behave until that moment. It is set at a turning point in the Gospel. Chapters 1–12 are the story of Jesus' ministry. Chapters 14–16 are the account of the crucifixion and resurrection. This chapter, then, forms a transition between the two parts of the Gospel. It also serves as a farewell discourse, much as chapters 13–17 of the Gospel of John do.

The discourse begins with a remark made by a disciple as he comes out of the temple. This is probably his first time to be in Jerusalem, and he is accordingly impressed by the size of the stones and buildings. "Look, Teacher," he says, "what wonderful stones and what enormous buildings!" Yes, says Jesus, but their end approaches; not one stone will be left atop another.

The discourse is resumed later on the hillside known as the Mount of Olives. Jesus and the four disciples—the first he called—are probably on their way out to Bethany. They may have stopped to pray among the stones on the hillside. The view of the temple is unobstructed; it rises beautifully and spectacularly on the opposite hill.

"When?" ask the disciples as they look back at it, pondering the prophecy of its destruction. "When will this be, and what will be the sign?"

It was common in those days to ask prophets what the sign of the last days would be. Jesus does not give them a single sign, but many. Others will come claiming to be Messiah. There will be wars and rumors of wars, earthquakes and famines. But these are only "the beginning of the sufferings."

The important thing, says Jesus, is not their knowledge of when the end is, but their behavior in the interim. They have much to bear for the gospel. There will be persecutions and imprisonments. The disciples will stand before rulers to give an account of their faith. Families will be torn apart as some stand up for the Kingdom, and Christians will be hated by others.

"But he who endures to the end will be saved." It is not knowing when that saves; it is being faithful.

> *Lord, it is even harder to be faithful now than it was then. Wars and disease and natural disasters have been relentless. Temples have risen and fallen. Styles have changed again and again. Give us courage to wait despite these things. Through him who knew that cleaving to you is everything.* Amen.

Week IX: Saturday

13:14–27 GREAT POWER AND GLORY

The ancient country of China has experienced many earthquakes through the centuries, some of them extremely devastating. In 1976 there was a quake that killed nearly 700,000 people. Chinese scientists have been experimenting with simple, readily available techniques for predicting imminent quakes. A pamphlet published in 1973 by the Earthquake Office in Tientsin advises peasants to expect a quake when cattle, sheep, or horses refuse to enter the corral, when rats run out of their hiding places, when chickens fly up into trees and pigs break out of their pens. There is no doubt that a heavy quake is one of the most frightening ordeals in the world.

In "the little Apocalypse," Jesus paints a similar picture of the great Day of the Lord. It is a time to flee to the mountains. The person who is on the housetop and comes down the side stairs should not even take time to run into the house. The person working in the fields should not take time to pick up the outer cloak he has laid aside while working. Hopefully it will not be in winter, when the wadis and river beds are running deep in water. Only God's mercy for the remnant of ancient Israel will prevent the utter destruction of everyone.

An unmistakable sign of the end, says Jesus, will be "the desolating sacrilege set up where it ought not to be." This is thought to be a reference to Daniel 9:27, 11:31, and 12:11, which describe the profanation of the Jewish temple by Antiochus Epiphanes in 168 B.C. At that time, Antiochus set up a statue of Zeus in the temple, causing outrage to Jewish minds. Mark may be thinking here of the establishment of the Antichrist in the temple—some power utterly devoted to the destruction of the old Judaic worship.

The heavens themselves will reflect the darkness on earth. Neither sun nor moon nor stars will give any light. It will be a time of horrible chaos.

Then—the imagery is from Daniel 7:13–14—"then they will see the Son of man coming in clouds with great power and glory." (Think of Christians through the ages praying the model prayer: "Thine is the kingdom and the power and the glory forever.") And, when it is all over, the Son of man will send forth his messengers to gather the saints from all directions, "from the ends of the earth to the ends of heaven."

This is the eternal hope of every Christian. After the wars and rumors of wars, after the quakes and famines, after all sufferings, the coming of the Son in power and glory. Then justice will reign forever.

Lord, this is frightening stuff. A person can really go overboard on it, especially if he or she is very imaginative. I don't know what to think about it. Should I be concerned about the end time, or shouldn't I? Speak to my heart of its meaning for me, that I may not miss an important truth merely because apocalyptic is a genre strange to our time. Through Jesus, to whom be power and glory forever and ever. Amen.

WEEK X

Week X: Sunday

13:28–37 THE IMPORTANCE OF WATCHING

There is not in this passage, as some have supposed, a contradiction of the passage preceding it, when Jesus seemed to be announcing "signs" of the end. Actually the signs he gave were of a very poetic or imaginative sort and did not remove the necessity of the disciples' watching for the end. And the signs were to occur before the end, leaving the time of the end itself unknown.

A characteristic prophetic note is the imminence with which the end should be anticipated. When the fig tree puts out its leaves—when the signs occur—the summer is near.

Therefore the true Christian posture is one of expectancy, of standing on tiptoe for the arrival of the great Day of the Lord. This does not mean letting all one's duties go, so that the world must take care of itself. On the contrary, it means a heightened attention to all responsibilities.

This is the point of the short parable in verse 34: When the master is away, the servants are to be at work, though one servant waits at the door and all are excited with the prospects of the master's imminent return. We are all to be about our jobs, but with a keen sense of watchfulness.

Verse 30 has been the subject of much speculation. Did Jesus really expect the end of all things to come in his own time? It is possible that he did. But he may also have meant that the *signs* of the end which he had been discussing would all appear before the present generation had died out. Certainly this was true. The temple was destroyed by the Romans in A.D. 70 and many people suffered calamities described by verses 5–23.

If this interpretation is correct, the weight of meaning for us is on the theme of continued watchfulness. The signs of the end have been fulfilled many times over. The end itself could therefore be at any time, and faithful servants will always be ready, regardless of how long we have already waited.

Lord, we forget that all time—past, present, and future—is forever now *to you. Help us to be in your pres-*

ence so much that it becomes now *to us as well, and we live on tiptoe, watching for your Kingdom. Through Jesus, who told us to watch.* Amen.

Week X: Monday

14:1–11 CONFLICTING PASSIONS

We have noted before Mark's technique of interrupting one story to tell another (cf. 5:22–43, 6:7–32, 11:12–25) with the result that the two become related. Here he has followed the technique with brilliant results.

He begins by talking about the Passover and the desire of the religious leaders to kill Jesus, switches to the story of the woman's anointing him, and then returns to the first matter by telling about the betrayal. What we have then, entwined in a single narrative, is the record of how two persons responded to Jesus under the gathering pressures of the Passover week.

The woman, whom John's Gospel identifies as Mary the sister of Martha and Lazarus, anoints Jesus with her own burial ointment. It is a costly gift—three hundred denarii was nearly a year's wages for a workman. Breaking the flask possibly symbolized her intention to use all of the ointment, saving none for herself. In Hellenistic times, also, flasks were often broken and left behind in persons' graves. This latter symbolism is highly suggestive here, as the anointing is clearly connected with Jesus' approaching death.

The word "Messiah" literally means "anointed one." The woman's behavior is clearly a confessional act. This is emphasized by the fact that she anoints Jesus' head, while Luke 7:38 and John 12:3 picture her anointing his feet. Anointing the head is a gesture akin to crowning.

Some of the persons present—Mark leaves them anonymous, while John identifies Judas—do not understand the ritual significance of the act. We remember Mark's constant emphasis on the disciples' failure to see and understand. They protest that it is a waste, that many poor persons could have used the money from the spilled perfume. But Jesus identifies the act with his going away from them. "You will not always have me," he says.

Judas' behavior is of an exactly opposite character. Instead of treating Jesus as the Messiah, he goes out and betrays him in an act of infamy. Wherever the gospel is preached, as Jesus said, the woman's beautiful story is told. And wherever Judas' name is mentioned, his deed of treachery is remembered. In fact, his very name has become synonymous with betrayal.

> *Lord there is both Judas and Mary in me. I betray you and I love you. I wish it were not so; I want only to love you. Forgive the dark side in me and help me, by exposing it constantly to your light, to reduce its power over me. For your name's sake.* Amen.

Week X: Tuesday

14:12–16 PREPARING FOR THE PASSOVER

As we have seen, the Gospel of Mark places strong emphasis on the eating of bread in the presence of Jesus. In chapter 6 the five thousand are fed. In chapter 7 the Syrophoenician woman asks for the crumbs that fall from the children's table. In chapter 8 the four thousand are fed. And, afterwards, the disciples are in the boat without bread and must be reminded that Jesus is able to give bread whenever he is present with them.

Now all of these allusions to the Eucharist come to a head in the passage about the Last Supper. It is reminiscent of the feeding stories in chapters 6 and 8. Once more the disciples come to inquire of Jesus about how to prepare for the meal.

Jesus has prearranged a place for the meal. The two disciples are to find a man carrying a water pitcher; he will take them to an upper room furnished for the occasion. In a country where only women carried water jars, the man would have been easy to find.

The meal itself is highly charged with symbolism, for it is a Passover meal, celebrating the escape of the Jewish people from bondage in Egypt. Jesus is to be the lamb for the New Passover.

As the blood of the first Passover lambs was smeared on the doorframes to keep the Jewish children safe, Jesus' blood will keep his followers from eternal harm. He later calls the cup of wine "my blood of the covenant" (verse 24).

The emphasis in this passage on *preparing* is a reminder of how much preparation had truly gone into getting ready for this hour. In a sense, the whole Gospel of Mark has led up to it. Not only the "bread" passages we have alluded to, but Jesus' entire ministry of preaching, teaching, and healing had been a prelude to this important occasion. Even the ministry and death of John the Baptist were part of the prologue to the Messianic Banquet which Jesus was now ready to eat with his disciples.

> *In the rush of my busy life, Lord, I often fail to reflect on what deep causes lie behind simple occurrences. Teach me to pause, and, pausing, to see your hand behind history, working out your loving will for our world. Through Jesus, who saw the importance of preparation.* Amen.

Week X: Wednesday

14:17–21 "LET A MAN EXAMINE HIMSELF"

What inward pain it must have been to Jesus to think that one of the twelve whom he had chosen as disciples was conspiring with the religious leaders to bring him to trial and possibly to death.

Mark must have sensed this, for the phrase "one of the twelve" is used twice to describe the betrayer (14:20, 43).

Twelve men whom he had called and taught . . . twelve men with whom he had traveled and worked and eaten and slept . . . twelve with whom he had prayed . . . and one of them would deliver him up to death.

But there are two levels of betrayal suggested by the passage. One is the level of ultimate betrayal—betrayal unto death. The other is less final. It is the level represented by the other disciples. We might call it the level of failing a friend. Before the night is out, each of the disciples will have betrayed Jesus this way. Through fear and cowardice and lack of understanding, they will all have failed him.

"Is it I?" they ask, one at a time.

This may have been a liturgical question in the early church. Paul had written to the Corinthians about the importance of self-examination before taking Communion. "Whoever . . . eats the bread or drinks the cup of the Lord in an unworthy manner," he said, "will be guilty of profaning the body and blood of the Lord. Let a man examine himself, and so eat of the bread and drink of the cup" (1 Corinthians 11:27–28).

Imagine a section of the liturgy that might have gone like this:

READER: And Jesus sat at the table, eating with his disciples.
PEOPLE: Disciples like us.
READER: And he said to them, "One of you will betray me."
PEOPLE: Who, Lord? One of us?
READER: One who is eating with me.
PEOPLE: Lord, is it I?

For which one of us can believe that he or she has never betrayed the Lord, that he or she does not betray him now, that he or she will not betray him tomorrow?

Lord, it is I. There is no question about it. I have failed to understand. I have missed the vision. I have not loved my neighbor. I have not glorified your name. O Lord, it is I, and I am ashamed. How can you forgive me? I have betrayed innocent blood. Amen.

Week X: Thursday

14:22–25 THE JEWEL OF THE LITURGY

It is remarkable how quickly our author tells the story of the table once he has gotten to it. It seems almost anticlimactic. First we had all those great stories about bread—bread in the wilderness, bread for a Syrophoenician woman, bread for the disciples in the boat—and now this. Four scant verses.

The reason, it has been suggested, is that these words are part of a solemn tradition Mark had inherited—like the words Paul wrote to the Corinthians about the Communion (1 Corinthians 11:23–26). They too were four scant verses.

These few words are like a precious jewel for which the goldsmith prepares an elaborate setting. The setting is much larger than the jewel. It carries images and stories designed to enhance the luster of the jewel. But it is the jewel that counts. Without it, the setting would be worthless. Here is a priceless treasure—the words of institution for the central rite of the Christian church—and their simple beauty dignifies everything around them.

What words of ours could enhance it further? It is one of the world's masterpieces. We can only read it or say it with awe.

> *Thank you, Lord, for the bread and cup of your presence. There is no worth in me, that I should eat or drink at your table. But you have loved me, and, in accepting that, I reflect your worthiness. Through Jesus, who died for me.* Amen.

Week X: Friday

14:26–31 A SAD PREDICTION

We can never overlook the importance of the psalms of Israel as a background for the final events in the life of Jesus. It is almost as if the bittersweet music of the nation were distilled into life through the upper room, the crucifixion, and the resurrection.

The hymn which Jesus and the disciples sang before leaving the Passover table to go to Gethsemane was almost certainly from the last of the great Hallel psalms. Quite possibly it was Psalm 118, which contains these words:

> It is better to take refuge in the Lord
> than to put confidence in man.

It is better to take refuge in the Lord
than to put confidence in princes.
[verses 8–9]

It may have been these very words that led Jesus to say to the disciples, "You will all fall away." The Greek word is derived from *skandalizein,* "to scandalize" or "to cause offense," and means "you will be offended." It is the same word used in Mark 6:3 of the people who heard Jesus teaching in his home synagogue at Nazareth. The corresponding noun, *skandalon,* means a trap or something that causes one to trip or fall; it appears in 1 Corinthians 1:23 to describe the response of the Jews who could not accept a crucified Messiah. The idea of tripping or falling because of something in the nature of the Messiah was obviously a common one in Christian usage. Mark is saying here that even the disciples were about to stumble in their understanding of the Messiah's suffering. Not seeing the importance of it, they would "fall away."

The word about the shepherd and the sheep is from Zechariah 13:7–9, where God says:

"Strike the shepherd, that the sheep may be scattered;
I will turn my hand against the little ones.
In the whole land, says the Lord,
two thirds shall be cut off and perish,
and one third shall be left alive.
And I will put this third into the fire,
and refine them as one refines silver,
and test them as gold is tested.
They will call on my name,
and I will answer them.
I will say, 'They are my people';
and they will say, 'The Lord is my God.' "

It will be a time of severe testing for the disciples and other followers of Jesus. Even his promise to be raised up and be reunited with them in Galilee, where they had their ministry together, will not allay their deep fears and confusion when he is smitten.

Typically, Peter does not understand. He thinks he knows himself. He would die with Jesus, he says, before he would fail his master.

Jesus knows better. Before the cock crows twice, announcing

the arrival of morning, Peter will have denied his Messiah three times.

It is better to take refuge in the Lord
than to put confidence in man.

Lord, this is one of the saddest facts of human life. I want to believe in others and trust their love, but I am often disappointed. Help me to forgive them, as Jesus forgave Peter, and to put my confidence in you, for your Kingdom and your promises are forever and ever. Amen.

Week X: Saturday

14:32–42 THE TESTING OF THE DISCIPLES

We have traditionally assumed that this well-known story is about Jesus' wrestling with the Father over the death he is to die—and of course it is. Jesus has come to the crossroads, as it were—to the last possible moment of escape—and he chooses the hard way, laying down his life as an act of ultimate obedience to the Father's plan. It is a beautiful and enduring picture of the greatest sacrifice in all of human history.

But as Professor Werner H. Kelber has noted in a compelling monograph, "At Gethsemane it is the disciples who undergo temptation!" Not Jesus, but the disciples.

Jesus prays that "the cup" might be removed from him—meaning the cup of suffering and death. But he submits to the will of the Father, seeing that there is no other way. It is for this hour that he was born and shaped.

Yet the disciples face "the cup" too. Jesus earlier asked James and John, when they wanted to sit at his side in the Kingdom, "Are you able to drink the cup that I drink?" (10:38). They had answered "Yes," and he replied that they would indeed drink it.

In Gethsemane, however, it becomes apparent that the disciples are not ready for the cup. Later they will drink it, as martyrs for the faith. But not now, when Jesus drinks his. They do not yet understand all things.

Three times Jesus leaves them to watch and pray. The language, the picture, the mood, are eschatological; that is, they suggest watching for the end of all things. Mark was surely aware of how close he was setting this story to the last words of "the little Apocalypse" of chapter 13, with its parable of the man going on a journey who puts his servants to work and charges his doorkeeper to stay awake and watch for him at any hour.

"Take heed, watch," Jesus had said, "for you do not know when the time will come. . . . And what I say to you I say to all: Watch" (13:33, 37).

"In both instances," says Kelber—in chapter 13 and here in the Gethsemane passage—"waking is virtue and sleeping is fault." The disciples are asleep when the Son of man comes in the night.

Do you see what a pointed message this was for Christians in the early centuries? They too were being tested for faithfulness. Like the disciples, they were often sleeping when they should have been watching, and so failed the Master. What about us? Is it not a message for us as well?

> *Forgive me, Lord. I do not maintain the sharp edge of watchfulness that is required of a Christian. The Kingdom comes around me and I do not even know it. The Son comes and stands beside me, and I snore in his presence. Help me to be more faithful, both for his sake and my own.* Amen.

WEEK XI

"What a thrill it is to imagine Jesus crying out in triumph as he died! Help me to be such a follower and practicer of your presence that I cry out when I am dying, not in pain but in victory, not in regret but in unspeakable joy!" (Week XII: Monday)

Week XI: Sunday

14:43–52 THE PERFIDY OF A FRIEND

"Even my bosom friend in whom I trusted," says Psalm 41:9, "who ate of my bread, has lifted his heel against me." Jesus had said that one of those close enough to dip bread with him in the dish would deliver him up.

Now it happens. Judas comes and plants a kiss on Jesus' cheek. It is not an unusual form of greeting between a disciple and his master, but it is nevertheless a token of affection. As such, it becomes in this case a symbol of treachery. Ever since, we have spoken of a "Judas kiss" as a sign of betrayal and perfidy.

The other disciples apparently try to make a stand. One, at least—identified in John 18:10 as Simon Peter—strikes out with a sword and cuts off the ear of the high priest's slave. But as Jesus reprimands his enemies for the manner in which they have seized him, coming in the evening with swords and clubs instead of capturing him among the crowds in the daytime, all of the disciples take flight.

"They all forsook him, and fled," says the witness. It is no wonder they all asked at the table, "Is it I?" Each knew there were limits to his faithfulness.

Verses 51–52 have long puzzled commentators. It has traditionally been assumed that the "young man" was Mark himself, but there is no evidence to support the view. If it had indeed been the author, he would surely have given a reason for his being clad only in a linen cloth on a cold spring night.

Some think the verses are a reference to Amos 2:16, in which God says of the day of his judgment against Israel that

> he who is stout of heart among the mighty
> shall flee away naked in that day.

At any rate, the picture is of Jesus' utter forsakenness. Everyone, even the hapless young man, flees into the darkness, leaving Jesus completely alone with his captors.

Lord, I am no better than they. I too have forsaken you in times of real testing. You have gone to your cross alone more than once. I am sorry. My heart trembles with emotion. Forgive me, I pray, and help me to be more stalwart if I have the privilege of being tried again. For I cannot live without you. Amen.

Week XI: Monday

14:53–65 NO LONGER A SECRET

This passage is a climax in Mark's narrative. From very early in the Gospel, Jesus' ministry has been depicted in terms of the conflict with Jerusalem. It has also been characterized as a *secret* ministry, probably in order to avoid a final contest until Jesus is ready for it.

Now he is ready—his hour has come—and the conflict reaches its fulfillment in the encounter with the high priest, who is the embodiment of the Jewish religious system.

The report of some witnesses that Jesus said he would destroy the temple and in three days build another is part of the whole drama, whether Jesus actually said it or not. The temple was the very symbol of Jerusalem. It was from there the scribes and Pharisees had come who showed up in the crowds when Jesus healed and taught in Galilee. When he came to Jerusalem, he went straight to the temple (11:11). The next day he purged the temple of the money-changers and pigeon-sellers (11:15–17), and cursed the fig tree that, like the temple and its religion, was not bearing fruit (11:12–14, 20–21). Sitting on the Mount of Olives, from which the temple could be seen rising clearly and majestically above the city, Jesus delivered "the little Apocalypse," which had as a fundamental feature the destruction of the temple (chapter 13). The temple stood as a tangible reminder of the failure of the old Israel. Its fall was therefore part and parcel of the Kingdom's arrival. At the precise moment of Jesus' death, Mark will observe that the veil in the temple has been split completely in two (15:38), symbolizing the demise of temple worship.

It is fitting, then, that the encounter with the high priest brings an end to the note of messianic secrecy. Suddenly all the stops are pulled out. There was a harbinger of this in 10:46–48, as Jesus passed through Jericho on the way to Jerusalem. The blind beggar Bartimaeus called out the name "Son of David," which was a messianic title. Now the messianic names flow freely. "Are you the Christ, the Son of the Blessed?" asks the high priest. "I am," says Jesus; "and you will see the Son of man sitting at the right hand of Power, and coming with the clouds of heaven." It is a total announcement of his messianic identity.

The high priest's reaction is the only possible one, given his stake in the conflict. Following the old custom in reaching a verdict of blasphemy, he tears his garment and asks the council of elders for their decision. They instantly find Jesus guilty and condemn him "as deserving death." They do not pronounce the death sentence themselves, possibly for fear of what Pilate, the Roman procurator, would say. But they decide that he *should* die, and begin to seek a way to accomplish it through the Romans.

Immediately they begin a kind of *danse macabre* around him, heaping indignities upon him. Some spit on him. Others drop a cloth over his head and strike him, defying him as a prophet to say who did it. The guards or servants of the high priest take him away, cuffing and shoving him as they go.

Jesus' final humiliation has begun. The disciples could not understand this, but he is the *suffering* servant of God.

> *Lord, a blind man realized that Jesus was Messiah. He saw what the religious leaders missed. That worries me, for I myself am a religious leader. Is there something about being a leader that makes me less sensitive to your presence? Help me to listen to the blind ones I know—the beggars, the children, the strangers I meet—and see Christ always anew through their eyes. For your Kingdom's sake.* Amen.

Week XI: Tuesday

14:66–72 THE FALL OF A LEADER

Again Mark has followed his favorite technique of starting a story, interrupting it with another, then completing the original narrative. In verses 53–54, he brought Peter into the courtyard of the high priest, following Jesus "at a distance." Then, in verses 55–65, he told of the encounter going on inside, between Jesus and the high priest. Now he resumes the story of Peter.

At the moment when Jesus on the inside is confessing his identity as the Son of God to the high priest, Peter on the outside is denying that he knows Jesus at all, or what any of this is really about. Again the conflict is couched in terms of Galilee versus Jerusalem. Jesus is called a Nazarene. Then the maid accuses Peter of being one of the Galileans. And finally the bystanders in the courtyard agree with her and call him a Galilean.

At this, Peter invokes a curse, swearing that he does not know Jesus. And instantly a cock crows somewhere for the second time, reminding Peter of Jesus' prediction of his denials. Peter breaks down and cries.

What was Mark's interest, we must ask, in this full account of Peter's denial of Jesus? Peter became a leader in the early church. In Acts 2, he is portrayed as standing courageously before the Jewish populace and preaching Jesus as the Messiah of God. In Acts 3:13, he even accuses others of *denying Jesus* in the presence of Pilate. But Mark consistently showed Peter's failure to understand and follow Jesus. In 8:31–33, when Jesus spoke of his suffering and death, Mark pictured Peter as protesting, and Jesus even identifying him as Satan! What point was Mark trying to make with his constant downgrading of the chief apostle?

Some scholars have recently suggested that Mark was probably encountering a tendency in the early church to de-emphasize the suffering of Jesus in favor of his triumphal resurrection. If so, Mark made Peter and the other disciples into models of misunderstanding in order to dramatize the unswerving way Jesus himself faced the humiliation of his trial and crucifixion.

Whether this theory is correct or not, Peter's failure and brokenness have always been a great inspiration to ordinary Christians. Here was the number-one apostle, the chief spokesman for the early church, floundering about like an unsure adolescent, denying his Master to preserve his own safety. If Peter could be forgiven and make the recovery he made, there is hope for every faltering Christian in the world!

Thank you, Lord, for the gift of tears in times of failure and frustration, for they bring relief and cleansing.

Help me to come to that point now. Let my denials of Christ move me to the abyss of deep reflection, and produce such a purging of my conflicting emotions that I may weep and begin anew in your service. For Jesus' sake. Amen.

Week XI: Wednesday

15:1–5 THE PROCURATOR AND THE KING

In this passage we come upon yet another messianic title, "King of the Jews." Apparently the chief priests and other Jewish leaders have attempted to frame the entire matter in terms designed to arouse the Roman governor. "King of the Jews" has overtones far more political than "Messiah" or "Son of man." Jesus is thus represented as a threat to civil peace and obedience.

For Mark, the term would also have been apt in light of earlier references in the Gospel. In 2:25–26, when reproached by the Pharisees because his disciples plucked grain on the sabbath, Jesus referred them to David, who, before coming into his kingdom, took the holy bread from the altar. And, in 10:46–48, the blind beggar in Jericho called Jesus "Son of David." An earlier discussion of Jesus and the temple is also to the point: Jewish thought since the prediction of 2 Samuel 7:11–14 that an heir of David would "build a house for my name" had associated the coming of Messiah with the building of a temple. So the phrase "King of the Jews" reflects all of these references at the same time that it has a certain seditious meaning to Pilate.

Pilate's residence was normally in Caesarea. He was probably in Jerusalem to keep an eye on the crowds during the Passover feast, and may have been staying in the fortress Antonia on the north side of the temple. If so, it was there that the Jewish leaders "delivered" Jesus to him with their accusations.

Historical references are less kind to Pilate's memory than the Gospels. A letter from Agrippa I to Caligula, for example, describes him as "inflexible, merciless, and obstinate." But Mark was doubtless concerned to put as benign a face on the Roman government as possible, for the Christians needed the favor of Rome merely to exist. Thus he pictured Pilate as unusually respectful of Jesus in this interview. Pilate is even said to have "wondered" at him—a word which in Greek has very religious undertones.

The cause of Pilate's "wonder" is apparently Jesus' silence before his accusers. The early Christians would have understood and appreciated this in the light of Isaiah 53:7:

> He was oppressed, and he was afflicted,
> yet he opened not his mouth;
> like a lamb that is led to the slaughter,
> and like a sheep that before its shearers is dumb,
> so he opened not his mouth.

Lord, royalty is a matter of inner bearing, not outer office. The truth of Jesus' kingship was never more evidenced in his miracles than it was in his behavior before his accusers. Grant that I, as your child, may learn the same bearing in the world. For your name's sake. Amen.

Week XI: Thursday

15:6–15 TWO SONS OF THE FATHER

"A man called Barabbas"—literally, in the Greek, "the one called Barabbas." Most textual scholars agree that this usage normally follows a given name, and that Barabbas' given name probably appeared in original manuscripts and was then expunged for some reason. In some early manuscripts of Matthew's Gospel, Barabbas' full name is shown as "Jesus Barabbas" (Matthew 27:16). Jesus was not an uncommon name in that time, and it is entirely possible that it was Barabbas'. It may well be, then, that subsequent Christian scribes piously deleted the name of their Lord when they found it attached to the insurrectionist who was released in the Messiah's place.

It is ironic, if it was true. Two Jesuses. And Barabbas is an Aramaic name meaning "Son of the father." Two Jesuses, two sons of the father. Did Pilate see the irony? Was it a clever act on his part to put the two before the Jewish crowd and offer to release whichever one they asked? Jesus the murderer or Jesus the Messiah. Which would they free?

The chief priests did their work among the crowd. Mark could imagine them, as he wrote, moving in and out like weasels, like creatures of evil, persuading the people to ask for Barabbas.

"And the King of the Jews?" asks Pilate. "What shall I do with him?"

"Crucify him," they cry. "Crucify him!"

So, as one Jesus is turned loose in the world as a murderer, the other is tied to a post and scourged, then delivered up to be crucified.

Scourging was a regular part of crucifixion. It was done with leather whips in which were embedded bits of bone and metal. It was a dreadful punishment in which the victim's flesh was horribly torn and disfigured.

> *Lord, how cruel are the instincts of some people. Little children can abuse their playmates so horribly. Parents can torture infants. Husbands and wives act spitefully toward one another. I confess that I cringe at this, Lord, but for the most part I manage to avoid it. I know it happens, but it is less painful if I can shut my eyes to it. In the name of Jesus who suffered unjustly, help me not to avoid instances of similar suffering today, but to pit myself against them with all my mind and heart and strength. It is one way of giving meaning to his terrible suffering.* Amen.

Week XI: Friday

15:16–20 THE MOCKERY

Sir James Frazer, in *The Golden Bough,* describes certain ancient rites in which there appear to be parallels to his scene of mockery and jest. In these rites a poor fool or a prisoner was usually dressed as the king, given a toy scepter and a bodyguard, and made the center of a mock court. Sometimes the rites were associated with a religious ceremony in which human sacrifice was made, though the "king" was not the one killed.

Whether such pagan rituals formed the background for the soldiers' behavior with Jesus can never be known. But he, of course, was both mocked as king and then sacrificed.

The entire battalion—from two hundred to six hundred men—was called out to witness the spectacle. Probably none of them knew anything of Jesus. They were young men from other parts of the empire. Some may have been sympathetic to the poor figure being treated so disrespectfully. Most of them probably took up the game with delight.

A purple soldier's cloak was thrown over his raw and bleeding back. A crown of thorns in the shape of the royal diadem was set upon his head. In mock gravity, the soldiers came to attention and saluted, arms outstretched. It was as if they were greeting Caesar with their usual "*Ave, Caesar Imperator!*" "Hail, King of the Jews!" they shouted, their voices filling the courtyard.

In despicable playfulness, as is liable to come over grown men in moments of distorted reality, they alternately struck him, spat upon him, and fell at his feet, pretending homage. Possibly all their individual rage and resentment against the excesses of cruelty in various commanders and caesars was given vent in this shameful ritual.

At last, their brutal hunger either sated or caught up in a bloodthirstiness that could be quenched by nothing less than the poor victim's death, they reclaimed the purple cloak, draped Jesus' own robe about him, and led him away to crucify him.

Through it all, apparently, he uttered no sound, but suffered in the same silence that had brought even the calloused heart of Pilate to "wonder" at him.

Lord, do I mock you too? When I claim you as King and then serve my own interests, is that a mockery? And when I wear your cross but do not have a thought for the Kingdom for days on end, what of that? Lord, I am as guilty as they. Restore me to full devotion, I pray, lest I end by mocking myself. For your dear name's sake. Amen.

Week XI: Saturday

15:21–25 THE SHAMEFUL DEATH

We can only marvel at the extreme compression of Mark's narrative of the crucifixion. It is clearly the point to which the entire Gospel has built. Yet it is admirably restrained and matter-of-fact in its reporting, probably indicating the existence of a strong oral tradition about the crucifixion which preceded the composition of the Gospel—a tradition that even Mark would have hesitated to embellish upon.

Alexander and Rufus were obviously well known to readers of the Gospel, so it is likely that Simon of Cyrene, the hapless fellow impressed into carrying Jesus' cross, afterwards became a Christian. He would also have been the most probable source for information about the crucifixion, assuming that the disciples were afraid to approach their dying master.

The part of the cross that was carried was the crossbeam itself, the upright or vertical section being already fastened in the ground at the place of crucifixion. The victim would have his hands nailed or strapped with rawhide thongs to the crossbeam; it would then be fastened atop or near the top of the upright. We assume that Jesus' scourging had disabled him so that he could not bear his own crossbeam, as the person to be crucified normally carried his own.

Giving wine and myrrh (or wine and frankincense, which would have had an analgesic effect) was a custom that seemed to fulfill the words of Proverbs 31:6:

> Give strong drink to him who is perishing,
> and wine to those in bitter distress.

Jesus' refusal to take it was probably part of his resolution to drink to the full the cup of suffering his Father had set before him.

When Jesus' body had been affixed to the upright cross, the soldiers began to cast lots for his simple clothes, as it was their prerogative to do. Part of the shame of public execution was the victim's nakedness, especially in a condition of such extremity that he could not control his own bodily functions.

It is little wonder that Christians have always cherished Psalm 22 for the haunting way it foreshadowed their Lord's death, including the dividing of his garments:

> Yea, dogs are round about me;
> a company of evildoers encircle me;
> they have pierced my hands and feet—
> I can count all my bones—
> they stare and gloat over me;
> they divide my garments among them,
> and for my raiments they cast lots.
> [verses 16–18]

It was the third hour, says Mark—about nine o'clock in the morning. The long hours of dying were ahead. Crucifixion was noted for the slowness with which death came to the victim.

> Golgotha, *Lord. The name is heavy, evil, forbidding. A place of death, blood, suffering, loneliness. Remind me, Lord. Let me never forget it. You paid too much in suffering for me to lose sight of it for a single day.* Amen.

WEEK XII

Week XII: Sunday

15:26–32 THE KING UPON HIS THRONE

When a criminal was led out to a public place for execution, he always bore or was preceded by a placard stating his name, place of origin, and offense. Whether Jesus' inscription carried the full information or was limited to the ironic title "King of the Jews" we have no way of knowing. It is possible that the soldiers decided, in the air of sport and excitement surrounding the mockery in the palace, to put nothing else on Jesus' placard.

The two robbers crucified with him also had placards, from which those who first told the story of the crucifixion learned their offenses.

But it was Jesus who drew all the attention. King of the Jews indeed! All day long the people passed by and ridiculed him. Apparently the charge against him before the council of elders had circulated widely—was it possibly written on his placard?—for everyone taunted him with it. "You who would destroy the temple and build it in three days, save yourself, and come down from the cross!"

The religious leaders were there too, bantering with one another about his plight. Possibly some of the scribes were ones Mark had mentioned as early as 2:6. Now they were witnessing the end of this popular wonder-worker they had opposed in Galilee.

"He saved others," they said, "but now he cannot save himself." The word for "save," *sōzein,* means "to give health to," though Mark would have understood it in its larger Christian meaning as well.

"Let this Messiah, this King of Israel, come down from the cross," they said, "and we will believe." They had seen other wonders he had done—the lame walking, lepers healed, the blind given their sight—but these had not convinced them. Their taunt here cannot be taken seriously. They did not want to believe, but merely continued to mock the one on the cross.

Even the robbers on the other crosses joined in the chorus of jests and indignities. First the passersby—then the chief priests and scribes—and now the robbers. The threefold development corresponds to Mark's other use of the tripartite division: three predictions of the passion, three failures of the disciples to watch and pray in Gethsemane, three denials by Peter, etc. And it makes Jesus' humiliation complete, that even his fellow victims should turn upon him.

The supreme irony, of course, is that Jesus *is* the King of the Jews, the scion of David, the one coming in the name of the Lord. Yet, as Mark understood, he is the suffering servant. He must remain silent before his accusers, and drink the awful cup to the dregs. Only thus can he truly fulfill the prophecies about him, that he is the King of an entirely new order of Kingdom.

> *Lord, words are poor, inadequate things to speak of your great suffering, of the shame and torment, the loneliness and agony. Help me to feel it now without words, to let its terrible weight descend on my soul like a medieval body press. Then I shall weep and praise your name, for you are a King like none other the world has ever known. May your Kingdom come, now and forever.* Amen.

Week XII: Monday

15:33–39 TRIUMPH OUT OF DARKNESS

The first verse of this passage had both Gentile and Hebrew precedent. One of the legends attached to the Ides of March, when Julius Caesar was murdered, was that the earth was then plunged into darkness from noon until nightfall. And, doubtless even more important to the Gospel writer, Amos 8:9 had predicted, concerning the great Day of the Lord:

> "And on that day," says the Lord God,
> "I will make the sun go down at noon,
> and darken the earth in broad daylight."

The sixth hour was at noon, and the darkness lasted until three o'clock.

At three, when Jesus had been on the cross six hours, he cried out "with a loud voice," saying, "My God, my God, why hast thou forsaken me?" It is remarkable, considering his condition before crucifixion and the ordeal of the crucifixion itself, that he was physically able to cry out this way. That alone commanded respect.

But the ejaculation of the words—as if in triumph?—helps us to interpret their meaning. They are the first line of Palsm 22, which is anything but a song of defeat. Although it begins with a complaint, it rallies into a paean of praise:

> All the ends of the earth shall remember
> and turn to the Lord;
> and all the families of the nations
> shall worship before him.
> For dominion belongs to the Lord,
> and he rules over the nations.
>
> [verses 27–28]

Jesus probably spoke only the first line of the psalm, but in his mind was this incomparable doxology. It was not defeat but victory that he saw from the cross.

If spoken in Hebrew, the words may have caused some to think he called out to Elijah. In the popular mind, Elijah was the great prophetic figure who came to the aid of persons in unusual distress, so this would have seemed proper.

The vinegar is thought to refer to the executioners' *posca*—a mixture of vinegar, water, and egg commonly drunk by Roman legionnaires. The Jews would not have been allowed to approach the dying man, so it was probably one of the soldiers who offered the drink on a sponge. The saying, "Wait, let us see whether Elijah will come to take him down," was possibly spoken originally by one of the Jews, but in the tradition got attached to the soldier extending the posca. At any rate, early Christians would have seen the action itself as fulfilling Psalm 69:21b—"and for my thirst they gave me vinegar to drink."

Two things happened as Jesus drew his last breath and died—the veil of the temple was rent and the centurion was converted. Each is of profound significance, though reported so tersely.

Mark saw the splitting of the veil—probably the one keeping the common people from the Holy of Holies (cf. Hebrews 9:11–12)—as the climax of Jesus' conflict with temple religion.

The temple was indeed "destroyed," and Jesus would build another, more spiritual temple in the community of believers.

If the rending of the veil had significance for Jewish readers, the conversion of the centurion had similar meaning for Gentile followers. (Remember Mark's turning from the Jewish feeding of the multitude in chapter 6 to the Gentile feeding in chapter 8!) Unlike the Jews, the centurion needed no special sign to believe. Facing him as he died, this man discerned from Jesus' appearance and his manner of dying that he was indeed the Son of God. He saw an epiphany in a corpse!

Lord, there is almost too much for me in this passage. It is crammed with both emotion and significance. What a thrill it is to imagine Jesus crying out in triumph as he died! Help me to be such a follower and practicer of your presence that I cry out when I am dying, not in pain but in victory, not in regret but in unspeakable joy! For thine is the Kingdom! Amen.

Week XII: Tuesday

15:40–41 THE WOMEN WHO SERVED HIM

This passage deserves considerable reflection in light of the human liberation movements in our time.

Curiously, it is the first time in the entire Gospel that Mark has mentioned the women who followed Jesus. He does it now to prepare for 15:47, and chapter 16, when the women are the sources of witness to the resurrected Jesus. But the women were obviously part of the entourage of disciples throughout much of the Galilean ministry, and had traveled with Jesus and the other disciples to Jerusalem for the confrontation with the religious leaders.

Magdala, the home of one Mary, was an area on the west side of the Sea of Galilee. The other Mary was apparently known to Mark's readers by her sons James "the small" and Joses, just as Simon of Cyrene was known to them by his sons Alexander and

Rufus (15:21). Matthew 27:56 identifies Salome likewise as "the mother of the sons of Zebedee."

The picture, in other words, is of mothers who raised their children in the faith and saw them become well-known figures in the early church. We cannot but wonder what the history of Christianity might have been had it not been for them and countless women like them, who, often nameless and unhonored, provided the stability of belief and progeny that enabled the church to perdure.

The fact that there were "many other women who came up with him to Jerusalem" suggests that there may even have been more women than men among Jesus' followers and that the staying power of the church in those trying years owed more to them than we are usually aware of.

Certainly the women's movement in our day has derived great impetus from Jesus' attitude toward women. Unlike many males of his time, he seems to have looked beyond gender in valuing other persons. His Kingdom has always transcended the world's way of distinguishing between Jew and Gentile, slave and free, male and female, for it regards all to be "one in Christ Jesus" (Galatians 3:28).

Lord, help me to be sensitive to persons who have not been given full status in the world. I want to appreciate their feelings and communicate with their needs, through him who reaches out to me in my own. Amen.

Week XII: Wednesday

15:42–47 THE BURIAL OF THE KING

There are certain problems about this text. If evening had fully come, as verse 42 says, the sabbath would already have begun, for it started at sundown and extended to the following sundown. Joseph could not have buried Jesus on the sabbath, for that was expressly forbidden by law.

And, if Jesus died on the Passover, as Mark has indicated all along, the strictures against burying the body would have been almost as great then as on a sabbath. Also, on either day, Joseph would have had difficulty purchasing the shroud we are told he purchased (verse 46).

We do not have more information about Joseph. The location of Arimathea is uncertain. That Joseph was "looking for the Kingdom of God" may mean only that he was a pious Jew, not necessarily that he was a believer. It was considered meritorious among the Jews to bury the dead on the day when they died, though the Romans often left bodies to decay upon their crosses for indefinite periods of time.

Two things seem to be clear:

(1) Mark was dealing with a fragment of tradition that did not fit precisely into the timetable of events as he was describing them.

(2) What Mark was really interested in was to underscore the fact that Jesus had *died*. The word for "body" in verse 45 should really be translated "corpse," as the Jerusalem Bible has it. Mark wanted his readers to understand that Jesus did not merely appear to die—his death was a cold, hard fact!

Sometimes those on crosses died slowly. Pilate was apparently surprised that Jesus had already expired. When he had sent a man to verify the fact, he consented to Joseph's burying the remains. Joseph bought a shroud, took down the corpse, rolled it in the shroud, and laid it in a tomb carved out of rock. Then he rolled the large disklike stone in front of the tomb. *Finis*. A real death, a real corpse, a real shroud, a real tomb, a real stone before it.

And one final touch—the two Marys watched the entombment from a distance. This note was necessary to inform us of how they would know which tomb Jesus was in when they went to anoint his body on the day after the sabbath.

> *Lord, death is an overpowering fact when it takes someone close to us. Until then, it may seem remote and unreal. But in that moment its reality is uncontestable. Help me to remember this passage when it comes to a person near to me. Then I shall know that Jesus has entered the heart of the same reality and reigns triumphant over it. In his glorious name.* Amen.

Week XII: Thursday

16:1–8 A QUERULOUS ENDING

In several very reliable ancient manuscripts, this is the final passage in Mark's Gospel. Almost all scholars agree that verses 9–20 were added by someone other than Mark, and that either Mark meant to conclude with verse 8 or he wrote another conclusion which was subsequently lost. As it is, we are left to suppose that verse 8 did complete his account and to ask what this passage means as the final word of the Gospel.

The two Marys and Salome, who we were told watched the crucifixion from a distance (15:40–41) and then followed Joseph of Arimathea to see where the corpse was laid (15:47), lose no time in returning to the tomb as soon as the sabbath ends and daylight returns. They come with spices to anoint the body. Approaching the tomb in the freshness of the early morning, one of the women asks, "Who will roll away the great stone for us?" It is a good question, for grave stones were normally from six to twelve inches thick and ranged from three to six feet in diameter. Even one of the smallest dimensions would require considerable power to roll it aside.

But at the very moment the question is asked the women look up and see that the stone is already rolled away. They step inside, where there is room for them to stand erect. The hollowed-out rock where the body should lie is empty. Instead of Jesus' body, they are startled to see a young man in a white robe sitting on the right, probably on a ledge formed beside the hollow space for the body.

"Do not be amazed," says the young man. "I know it is Jesus of Nazareth you seek—the one who was crucified. He has risen. You won't find him here. See, here is the place where his body was laid. He is going before you into Galilee. You must go and tell the disciples—and especially Peter. He will meet you in Galilee, as he promised."

The "young man" is obviously an angelic messenger. Some scholars think he was prefigured, in Mark's characteristic style of introducing persons ahead of time, by the anonymous "young man" in 14:51–52, who fled naked after the soldiers seized his linen cloth. The linen cloth, it is speculated, may symbolize the one Jesus left behind (in the hands of the enemy!) when he rose from the dead. The white robe of the young man in the tomb is clearly the garb of a heavenly being.

The words spoken by the young man should not be strange to the women, for they are precisely what Jesus has tried to explain to them all along—that he would be crucified, would return from the dead, and would meet them in Galilee.

Galilee is throughout Mark's Gospel the setting for the real ministry of Jesus, and is pitted against Jerusalem, the Holy-City-become-ominous-and-unholy. Jesus comes to Jerusalem only for the final stage of his conflict with the religious leaders, as if he were a knight invading a citadel of evil. His *parousia*, or return to the disciples, will be in Galilee, where the Kingdom was most evidenced among the "little ones" who accepted his ministry.

But the women still do not understand. Like the disciples, they cannot see and grasp what is happening. So they flee from the tomb in breathless fear and amazement. And, contrary to the beautiful image in Luke 24:1–12, where they return to tell the disciples that Jesus is risen, in Mark they remain silent and say nothing!

Period.

This is where the Gospel seems originally to have ended. Why? What could Mark's purpose have been? Why was he not interested in the resurrection appearances reported by the other Gospels and by Paul? Why this querulous ending in which the poor, frightened women say nothing?

Perhaps—we can only speculate—Mark wished to preserve a sense of absolute mystery about the nature of the resurrection and the risen Christ. Angels were often used in ancient literature as intermediaries between God and men to protect the privacy of God. The white-robed young man in this passage symbolizes the presence of a mystery without letting us see the mystery directly—which of course we could not do.

Jesus has risen. There is no doubt of that. Like the young man in 14:51–52, he has left the Romans holding only his grave clothes. The angel points to the bare hollowed place where the corpse lay, and it is empty.

What Jesus wants the women and disciples to do—including Peter, who has been such a failure—is to go back to the scene of his work with the multitudes, where they will see him again. They have learned that his messiahship lies through obedience, suffering, and death. Now they must practice the same manner in their discipleship by returning to Galilee, where the Kingdom comes through laboring among the people.

Seen this way, it is a powerful message to us as well as them. We are so prone to want visions of the resurrected Jesus in order to know he was truly who he claimed to be. What we are given instead is the word that the tomb was empty and that he sends us to the place of ministry to work for the Kingdom.

Lord, this affects me deeply—in some ways, much more deeply than the elaborate "appearance" stories of the early traditions. I feel the mystery that is involved, and the impossibility of its being represented in words and images. Jesus was raised, and has ever since been meeting us in Galilee—in the ghetto kitchens, hospital wards, schoolrooms, and other places of Kingdom service in the world. Help me not to be blind, Lord, the way the disciples often were in this book. Open my eyes and let me see Jesus as I work for him. For his name's sake. Amen.

Week XII: Friday

6:45–52 A DISPLACED RESURRECTION APPEARANCE

Yes, you have read this passage before. No, it is not a mistake that it is set here and you are directed to read it again. Actually, you see, it is what might be called a displaced resurrection appearance of Jesus. It is therefore appropriate to look at it again after Mark's ending at 16:8.

In ancient literature, the sea was often a symbol of chaos and evil, especially when it was stormy. The disciples were in the boat alone, distressed by the pitch of the waves, when Jesus came walking to them on the water.

They cried out, for they thought it was a *ghost*—an apparition of someone supposed to be dead. They were terrified—even more afraid than they had been of the storm.

"*Tharseite*," said Jesus—"Take heart" or "Have courage"—the same word spoken to Paul by the risen Christ the night after Paul was imprisoned by the soldiers (Acts 23:11)! "Take heart, it is I." Or, as we commented earlier on this verse, "Take heart, *I am*"—the same word given to Moses when Moses asked who God was—"I AM WHO I AM." And Jesus got into the boat with them and the winds ceased.

"And they were utterly astounded, for they did not understand about the loaves, but their hearts were hardened."

"The loaves," we said, refers to the first of the feeding miracles, when Jesus fed the five thousand (6:34–44)). But what didn't they understand? How it had been done? Or the fact that Jesus feeds his people in the wilderness? The latter, if we follow the symbolism of the feeding stories and of the entire Gospel. "Their hearts were hardened." Mark saw the disciples' failure to see and understand—a perpetual theme with him—as the work of Satan. Satan actually blinded their eyes, so that they could not see.

Now let us reflect once again on Mark 16:1–8, the original ending of the Gospel. Still the women did not understand, even though the angel reminded them of all that Jesus had said about his death, resurrection, and going ahead of them to Galilee.

Mark was not against using resurrection apearances to tell the story of Jesus—this selection from 6:45–52 indicates that. But he wanted us—his readers—to understand something he pictured the the disciples as never understanding, namely, that the real proof of the resurrection is not in the appearances to certain women and apostles, but in the bread we eat in the wilderness and the way Christ comes to ease our hearts when the nights are dark and the seas are stormy.

We can participate in the mystery of the resurrection in our own discipleship if only we have eyes to see and ears to hear. In this sense, the entire Gospel of Mark is but a gloss on the single verse of John 20:29, when the risen Jesus said to Thomas, "Have you believed because you have seen me? Blessed are those who have not seen and yet believe."

Lord, I believe. I have eaten the bread in the wilderness. I have sensed your presence at the height of the storm, and have felt my heart grow calm and my pulse steady. It is not necessary to see you with my eyes. A blind man knew you as you traveled from Jericho to Jerusalem. Help me to live always by this inner sight, and to serve you faithfully in the way. For yours is the Kingdom forever and ever. Amen.

Week XII: Saturday

16:9–20 THE TRADITION OF APPEARANCES

Here, as we have said, is some scribe's addition to the original ending of the Gospel. There is a tenth-century Armenian manuscript of the Gospel which attributes these verses to an elder or presbyter named Ariston, but we are not certain about the matter. Suffice it to say that the addition was made by the time of Irenaeus, who referred to it in the middle of the second century.

Whoever added the verses wanted the reader of the Gospel to be acquainted with the tradition of Jesus' postresurrection appearances. Probably he felt that these appearances really clinch the fact of the resurrection for most Christians. Moreover, some tradition such as this is necessary to bridge the gap between where Mark 16:8 leaves off and the story of the early church begins. If Mark 16:8 had been the last word, there would have been no church.

We are first told, in contradiction to 16:1–8, which said that Jesus had gone ahead of his followers to Galilee, that he appeared to Mary Magdalene (not to the other Mary and Salome), and that she, instead of keeping silent as in verse 8, came and told the other disciples who were grieving.

Then we are informed about the appearance to two of the followers as they walked in the country. Luke 24:13–35 identifies these as the men from Emmaus, who walked with Jesus and then recognized him in the breaking of bread.

Finally Jesus appeared to the eleven themselves, as they would not believe either Mary Magdalene or the two men from the country, and chided them "for their unbelief and hardness of heart."

The author of this section next provided a commissioning similar to that given by Jesus in Matthew 28:18–20. The disciples were to "go into all the world and preach the gospel to the whole creation."

Commentators believe that this kind of saying, while common among second-century Christians, would not actually have come from Jesus to the first disciples; otherwise Peter would not have needed his vision about the Gentiles in Acts 10:9–16, and the early church would not have required the Council of Jerusalem in Acts 15 to determine that the gospel should be extended to the nations. Many scholars are also convinced that the so-called "signs" of believers in verses 17–18—especially speaking in tongues, picking up serpents, and drinking poison—are later descriptions of the Christian experience based on instances of these occurrences in various congregations.

The ascension of Jesus in verse 19 is likewise traditional imagery, based perhaps on Psalm 110:1:

> The Lord says to my lord:
> "Sit at my right hand,
> till I make your enemies your footstool."

How much more powerful was Mark's original ending, which simply sent the disciples and other followers off to Galilee with the promise that he would meet them there. The effect was virtually the same as that described here in verse 20, with miraculous signs attending the preaching of the Kingdom. Mark's real message is not that Jesus is in heaven at God's right hand, but that he meets us in the highways and byways of life as we go about ministering to people in his name.

This is the greatest promise of all—and it is fulfilled every day of our lives, if we only have eyes to see.

Lord, your power is beyond description. You turn the world upside down and stand all our expectancies on their heads. But save me, I pray, from needing special signs of this power to know that you are alive and with me. Give me instead the gift of quiet reflection, of meditation in your presence, that I may truly see and understand where you are at work in the world I live in. And yours be the power and the glory forever and ever. Amen.

LUKE

Contents

Introduction

Most people, if pressed to say which of the four Gospels in the New Testament is their favorite, would probably answer that it is the Gospel of Luke. Matthew contains the Sermon on the Mount, with its beautifully phrased Beatitudes. Brief little Mark is full of miracle narratives and sayings about being able to "see" with one's eyes. John talks grandly of eternal life and the "many mansions" in the Father's house—passages of great comfort often read at funerals. But Luke, more than any other Gospel, is the Gospel of stories.

There are the popular Christmas stories about the angel's visits to Zechariah and Mary, the birth of the child in the stable, and the lowly shepherds who heard heavenly choirs singing "Glory to God in the highest." There is the unforgettable tale of the good Samaritan—probably the most haunting picture ever given to mankind of what it means to be a neighbor. There are the three ever popular stories of the lost sheep, the lost coin, and the lost boy. There is the sobering narrative of the rich man and Lazarus. And there is that long, inspiring resurrection story of Jesus' walk with the two disciples on the road to Emmaus.

It is hard to imagine the history of Christian faith and its preaching without these incredibly pictorial stories. Yet not one of them appears in any Gospel but Luke's.

There is something else unique about Luke. It is the only Gospel whose author wrote a sequel, a companion-volume about the history of the early church. That is what the Book of Acts is—a companion-volume to Luke. This means that Luke is the only Gospel whose language, structure, and theology we can interpret in the light of another book written by the same author. You may not have thought about it before, but this can be extremely important in trying to understand some of the more obscure sayings in an ancient manuscript. It is certainly very helpful in the case of Luke.

We know very little about Luke himself, as we know little of the other Gospel writers. Tradition holds that he was the doctor whom Paul mentioned in Colossians 4:14, Philemon 24, and 2 Timothy 4:11 as his traveling companion. There is no strong evidence against this tradition and the language of medical knowledge in both the Gospel and Acts would seem to corroborate it.

Luke's being a doctor might indeed account for the strong humanitarian flavor of his writings. More than any other Gospel, his emphasizes God's care for the crippled and rejected members of society. From the song of the angels to the poor, semireligious shepherds on the hillsides (Luke 2:8–20) to Jesus' promise of Paradise to the criminal next to him at the crucifixion (Luke 23:42–43); from the Master's announcement in Nazareth that his ministry was for the poor, sick, and oppressed (Luke 4:14–30) to his controversial decision to dine with Zacchaeus, the outcast tax collector (Luke 19:1–10), the unfailing orientation of the Gospel is toward the weak, the lost, and the despised.

Luke may also have been sympathetic toward the rejected people of Jesus' environment because he himself was a Gentile writing for a Gentile audience. Both the Gospel and Acts were addressed to a certain Theophilus, whom Luke called "most excellent," possibly indicating that he held a position of eminence in the Roman government.

Rome had taken a very hostile attitude toward Christians since A.D. 64, when Nero unjustly accused them of burning the city. Luke was probably attempting to present their case in a more favorable light by retelling their story from the beginning through the missionary advances made in the years after Jesus' death. He was concerned to show both that Christianity was the true fulfillment of Old Testament religion and that it was the contentious old Judaizers, not the members of the Christian movement, who were the real rabble-rousers and troublemakers. Jesus' Kingdom, Luke tried to demonstrate, was never meant to replace the rule of Caesar; it was a transcendent, spiritual Kingdom, aimed at restoring dignity and hope to the poor and neglected. The Jewish elders had misunderstood this and, against Pilate's wishes, had insisted on Jesus' crucifixion. Even as he had gone to his death, Jesus had warned the people of Jerusalem that their foolishness would bring reprisals from Rome (Luke 23:27–31).

Far from counseling sedition and revolution, Luke maintained, Jesus had spoken to the people of joy and devotion. If there is a single tonal theme uniting the entire Gospel and the Book of Acts, in fact, it is the note of great joy that came to the people with the birth of Jesus. Over and over again, Luke used the words *joy, great joy*, and *rejoicing*. The angels' song reverberates throughout his writing, as the very heavens themselves resound with excitement at what is taking place in Jesus' ministry and the work of the early church.

Perhaps this fact, together with the unforgettable stories we have alluded to, accounts for the perennial appeal exercised by the Gospel of Luke. In a day of instant communication, when we are continuously depressed by the news of a world in general distress, it is wonderful to be able to turn to a Gospel like this that begins with a miraculous birth during a tax enrollment and ends with the crucified Christ walking the roads with his disciples and making their disillusioned hearts burn again with hope.

If you yourself are ever bothered by disillusionment, there is nothing better you can do in the next twelve weeks than spend a few minutes a day reading through this Gospel, meditating on the commentary in this book, and then waiting quietly in prayer before God. It cannot fail to affect your attitude toward yourself, your disposition toward others, and your understanding of what it means to be a follower of Jesus.

I must emphasize the importance of *listening* as you read. It is not enough merely to race through the words, repeating them.

The meaning is often in the silences, the gaps between words and sentences. It is there that the "still, small voice" comes to speak to us, in accents known only to the heart. It is there that we hear the real note of joy, there that we feel the call to discipleship, there that the world is changed for us.

So wait and listen—and you will not be disappointed.

John Killinger

WEEK 1

Week 1: Sunday

Luke 1:1–4 A Definitive Account

"Every biographer and historian," says the essayist Northrup James, "attempts to write the best account yet. Drawing on all that has gone before him, yet adding that unique quality which he alone can give, he seeks to say the definitive word, the one that will marshal all the others into gleaming perspective. Even though additional writers may come after him, assaying the same task, his story, he hopes, will provide the unavoidable focus for theirs."

This must have been the feeling of Luke as he began his account of the life of Jesus and the early church. Many others, he said, had already written their accounts. But he wanted to write his, putting it together with his own unique touch.

Theophilus, to whom both the Gospel and the Book of Acts are addressed, may have been a well-to-do patron or benefactor of Luke, as suggested by the courteous form of address. His name, which means "beloved of God," could indicate that he was born of Christian parents and was younger than Luke. If this is the case, then the Gospel and Acts were written by Luke as an effort to lay before his young friend the salient facts of the early Christian movement as he had received them from both eyewitness reports and the writings of others who were ministers or servants of the Word. Theophilus had already heard reports of the origins and progress of the movement; but Luke wished him to have a very careful account and to "know the truth."

Lord, thank you for the men and women in the past who have cared enough for the truth to write reports about matters for those of us who would come after them. Help me to cherish their efforts and to ponder their accounts for the meaning they have in my own life. Then help me to love my children and their children and their children's children enough to pass on to them my own testimony on these things. For your kingdom's sake. Amen.

Week 1: Monday

Luke 1:5–25 Starting with the Temple

Luke significantly begins his Gospel in the temple. Mark began with the story of John along the banks of the Jordan River, and Matthew commenced with the genealogy of Jesus. But Luke is thinking of the account of the Christian movement he will write in the Book of Acts; with its center in Jerusalem, it will surge outward to the Greco-Roman world the way ripples travel outward from an epicenter. In other words, Luke sees with a *spatial* vision, even when writing history. Therefore he begins his account in the temple, which for centuries has been at the heart of God's dealings with Israel. A Gentile himself, he is interested in the way the gospel of the Kingdom has reached the nations. But the story necessarily starts in Jerusalem.

It begins with Zechariah, the elderly priest who was to father

John the Baptist. As a male member of the tribe of Aaron, Zechariah was entitled to offer sacrifice in the temple. But there were so many descendants of Aaron that they were divided into groups which served in the temple only two weeks each year. Within each group, lots were cast to decide which priest would be permitted to officiate. No priest was allowed to do this more than once in a lifetime, and even then many never had the opportunity. We can imagine Zechariah's excitement, therefore, when the lot fell to him "to enter the temple of the Lord and burn incense." He must have trembled in anticipation. He would burn the incense representing the prayers of the people while the crowds of people stood outside. It was a supreme honor—enough even to offset the sense of shame Zechariah had felt at having had no child.

Then it happened! As the prayers of the people were being offered, an angel appeared to Zechariah in the midst of the smoke from the incense. God would answer both the prayers of the people for deliverance and Zechariah's prayer for a son. The son's name would be John. He would take the ascetic vows of a Nazirite, and would go out "in the spirit and power of Elijah," who was regarded as the greatest of the prophets.

Zechariah could not believe it. Like so many of the Jews depicted later in the Gospel, he asked a sign of proof—and received a very personal one—he was struck speechless until the time of the birth! How the people must have talked that day when they went home about the priest who had seen a vision at the altar and was left dumb by the experience. But aren't all great mystical experiences finally unspeakable?

Lord, I have been speechless a few times in my life, but never like this. Lead me through prayer and contemplation to greater depths of spiritual experience, so that I talk less and hear more. Through him whose story is at the heart of this mystery. Amen.

Luke 1:26–38 The Greater Miracle

From the miracle of birth to the elderly, God now turns to the miracle of birth to an unmarried young woman. If John's birth was special, the Savior's birth must be even more special. He would be born as the offspring not of an old priest of the temple but of the Holy Spirit of God himself.

"Hail, Mary, full of grace," Jerome translated the Greek in the Latin Vulgate edition, and a tradition arose which venerated Mary as the receptacle of grace that could be dispensed to others. But the Revised Standard Version more properly translates, "Hail, O favored one, the Lord is with you!" It was indeed an incredible honor; she had been chosen to bear the Savior of the world.

Luke, with a touch of human understanding that is characteristic of him, shows us the puzzled, frightened side of Mary's reaction. She "was greatly troubled at the saying, and considered in her mind what sort of greeting this might be." The angel's answer to her thoughts was an assurance and a promise. It was the same promise the Jewish people had been concerned with for centuries—the promise of an eternal King to sit on the throne of David—and this time the promise involved Mary herself, as the mother of this King. Verse 35 is a beautifully reserved description of how the conception would occur. The birth would be the fulfillment of ages of national hope and expectation.

I like what Professor G. B. Caird of Oxford has written about this. For Luke, he says, the special sense in which Jesus was "the Son of the Most High" was only the starting point. "As the Gospel proceeds, we shall see Jesus taking this inherited notion and remodelling it in the crucible of his own experience. He spoke of God as 'my Father' and of himself as 'the Son,' not to expound a doctrine or to claim a rank but to express his own personal relationship to God, whom he knew intimately as only a son can know a father."

Meanwhile, Mary's final response to the angel was one of astonished modesty and humility: "Behold, I am the handmaid of the Lord; let it be to me according to your word."

Lord, this story is liable to seem fanciful and untrue in the kind of world we live in today. Yet you still send your word to those you favor, and your Holy Spirit upon those who are devout in their own spirits. Teach me to say, "Let it be to me according to your word," that I may know your will in my life, and submit to it in similar humility. In the name of him whose Kingdom is forever. Amen.

Week 1: Wednesday

Luke 1:39–56 The Blessedness of Believing

This is a remarkable passage, especially in view of the low general estate of women in New Testament times. With continuing sensitivity, Luke describes the gentle, feminine side of this mighty event that was taking place in the history of Israel and the world.

What Luke attempts to do is to relate the later ministry of the Lord to the entire context of prophecy and expectancy in Israel's long history. God is working behind the scenes, so to speak, to coordinate the events that will finally culminate in the birth, death, and resurrection of a Savior.

Mary, in all of this, personifies the faithful remnant in Israel who persist in believing in the promises of God. As Elizabeth says, "Blessed is she who believed that there would be a fulfilment of what was spoken to her from the Lord" (v. 45).

The song attributed to Mary is called the *Magnificat,* which is the first word in the song's Latin version. It is a psalm of thanksgiving, very much like many of the poems in the Book of Psalms. It speaks of God's covenant-faithfulness; as God has chosen Mary over all the highborn ladies of the age to be the mother of the Savior, he is now ready to exalt the low, the poor, and the hungry over the high, the rich, and the well fed. As the psalm concludes, this is no new promise, but the fulfillment of the one made to Abraham long ago.

Luke does not say it directly, but he implies that Mary remained with Elizabeth until Elizabeth delivered her child. It would have been the kinlike thing to do, and three months should have brought them just about to that time. What wonders we can imagine the two women sharing during this period!

Lord, fulfillment must have been hard for these people to wait on, and then hard to believe when it was almost upon them. Strengthen my faith in the promises you have given us, that I too may live in the blessedness of believing. Through Jesus, who is *the fulfillment.* Amen.

Week 1: Thursday

Luke 1:57–80 The Gracious Gift of God

Here, especially in verse 65, we are given a clue about where Luke got these stories that are not told in the other Gospels. They circulated among the people in the little hill communities near Judea, where John was born. Luke apparently heard them from Christians in this region.

Like the other stories, this one provides interesting personal details whose ultimate meanings reflect universal truths. Zechariah's and Elizabeth's neighbors came to rejoice with them at the birth of their son and to be present for his ritual circumcision. At the moment in the rite when the child is to receive his name, the neighbors and kinfolk, assuming that the boy will be named for his father, proceed in the father's silence to name him. But Elizabeth speaks up to say that his name will be John, meaning "gracious gift of God." It is an understandable gesture, given the parents' elderly status. But the friends and kin brush Elizabeth's answer aside, deferring to Zechariah. They fully expect a sign from him confirming that the child should bear his name.

Zechariah startles them—twice. Writing on a tablet, he indicates that the child will indeed be called John, not Zechariah. Then he startles them again by suddenly regaining his voice. He begins to speak, and his first words are expressions of praise to God. The neighbors and kinfolk are filled with fear. They know that something far beyond the usual is going on here. They are dealing not with man but with God.

Given the gift of prophesying, Zechariah delivers a poetic utterance praising God and predicting that John will be the forerunner of the Lord himself, preparing his ways by calling people to repentance and forgiveness of their sins.

Lord, a birth is a sacred occasion, and so is receiving a name. Make me more aware of the sacredness of my own life, and let me know it is a gift from you. Through him who calls us to new life in your will. Amen.

Week 1: Friday

Luke 2:1–20 News of a Great Joy

In this passage, Luke revels in a major theme of his Gospel—the joy that is associated with Jesus and the Kingdom. Gabriel had promised "joy and gladness" to Zechariah (Luke 1:14). The babe in Elizabeth's womb leaps for joy at the visit of Mary (Luke 1:44), and Mary's psalm rejoices in God (Luke 1:74). When the seventy disciples return from their preaching mission, they announce with joy that even the demons are subject to them (Luke 10:17). Jesus tells them to rejoice that their names are written in heaven (Luke 10:20). He himself rejoices in the Holy Spirit (Luke 10:21), and then declares to them, "Blessed are the eyes which see what you see!" (Luke 10:23). After Jesus healed the woman bent with an infirmity, "all the people rejoiced at all the glorious things that were done by him" (Luke 13:17). And of course there are the three stories of joy in chapter 15, about the finding of the lost coin, the lost sheep, and the lost boy. Who can ever forget the loving father's glad cry when his boy returns: "Bring quickly the best robe, and put it on him; and put a ring on his hand, and shoes on his feet; and bring the fatted calf and kill it, and let us eat and make merry; for this my son was dead, and is alive again; he was lost, and is found" (Luke 15:22–24)? More than any other New Testament writer, Luke is captivated by the notion of joy, and the Gospel resounds with it.

Here, of course, is the central occasion for joy—the coming of the Savior in human flesh to inaugurate the long-awaited Kingdom. Appropriately, he is identified by birth with the poor, who have no place to lay their heads, and with the religious pariahs—the shepherds—who are socially despised by the religious rulers of Israel.

And the religious outcasts see the shining glory of the Lord's presence and hear the voice of an angel. "I bring you good news of a great joy," says the angel, "which will come to all the people" (v. 10). When the announcement is made, the whole sky is suddenly filled with the music of heavenly choirs, praising God and promising peace among those "with whom he is pleased!"

Peace is more than the absence of war, in this case; it is the Hebrew *shalom*, meaning fullness and blessedness. As for what it means to please God, we have but to remember the words of Luke 3:22, which were heard at Jesus' baptism: "Thou art my beloved Son; with thee I am well pleased." Jesus pleased the Father by being obedient to a baptism for repentance and forgiveness of sins.

Characteristically for Luke, the shepherds, having learned the joyful news, in turn become its bearers. They went back to the hills, "glorifying and praising God for all they had heard and seen" (v. 20). The joy of the kingdom is that contagious!

Lord, I am heartily sorry for the lack of joy in my life. I am too frequently tired, depressed, and annoyed. My life should be a continual paean of praise, for I have both heard and seen the coming of your eternal Kingdom. Forgive my tediousness. Restore to me the passion of your salvation, and let me bear joyful witness to others of your transforming power. Through Jesus, who took his place among the poor and rejected of the world. Amen.

Week 1: Saturday

Luke 2:21–39 The Reward for Waiting

Luke, being a Gentile, was apparently somewhat confused about the Jewish legal requirements following the birth of a firstborn son. There were three such requirements. The first was circumcision, to be performed eight days after birth. The second was the payment of five shekels as a redemption offering, to be made at any time after the first month. And the third was the purification of the mother, performed after forty days, to restore her from uncleanness to the privilege of public worship. Luke seems to have mixed the second and third requirements in this passage—though it is possible that one trip to the temple would have sufficed for both.

The important thing is not the accuracy of his knowledge of Jewish legal customs, however, but the witness of the two old people in the temple to the special mission of Jesus as Savior of the people. Simeon's prophecy, composed largely of allusions to Isaiah 40–55, is remarkable for two things: it forecasts the universal mission of Jesus (he is to be "a light for revelation to the Gentiles") and it predicts the stormy, uneasy nature of the mission, including the pain that will pierce the soul of Mary herself when Jesus is crucified. Anna's speech, on the other hand, seems to have been one only of thanksgiving and witness to the redemption of the Jews.

There is something very tender about this vignette. I wonder how we would regard Anna today if she spent most of her time fasting and praying in church. Probably we would dismiss her as a harmless old woman whose devotion has gone a bit far. But in the Jewish culture of Jesus' day, aged people were highly regarded for their wisdom and spirituality, and the testimony of these two elderly souls who had waited all their lives to see God's redemption was a great benediction on the future Savior.

One question nags us: Why did Joseph and Mary marvel at what was said about Jesus? Could it be that their understanding of his mission was not full in the beginning—that it had to grow even as ours does?

Lord, I wonder if I really understand what it means that Jesus is the Savior of the world. It is such a large concept, and the world seems so resistant to being saved. Help me to fast and pray as Anna did—to lead a life of disciplined devotion—in order that I may comprehend more fully in all my being what my mind already knows about Jesus. For your Kingdom's sake. Amen.

WEEK 2

Week 2: Sunday

Luke 2:40–52 A Sign of the Future

How eagerly some parents observe their children's abilities and activities in order to determine what their life's work may eventually be! "Doctor, lawyer, merchant, chief" is an old game based on this eagerness to know the future. Today it has been replaced by aptitude tests and counseling services designed to point young people in the most appropriate directions.

In this passage, Luke reveals the early direction taken by Jesus. At the age of twelve, like every Jewish boy, he became *bar mitzvah*, a son of the Law. It was—and still is—one of the most important occasions in a Jewish male's life. Probably it was in celebration of this that Mary and Joseph took the boy on a pilgrimage to Jerusalem for the annual Passover festival. They would have been in the holy city for an entire week.

The fact that Jesus was not with his parents when they began the journey home, and that they traveled for an entire day while supposing him to be with kinfolk or acquaintances, gives us a fascinating insight into the nature of his social environment as a youth. We normally think of his family as though it were a nuclear family like our own. But it was actually a large, extended family, in which the young people moved freely among aunts, uncles, cousins, and friends. Therefore his parents assumed quite naturally that he was in the Galilean caravan as it moved slowly northward.

Jesus was, in fact, in the temple, revealing his leaning toward a future rabbinical life. He gravitated toward the learned teachers the way some youngsters today incline toward newspaper offices, laboratories, or mechanical contraptions. And his agility in discussing the Law utterly astounded the rabbis. It was confirmation both to them and to him that he would one day be known as a famous rabbi.

When his mother reprimanded him for being thoughtless of her and other members of the family, he replied with a significant answer—they should have known they might find him in his Father's house. It is an important identification. Already he understood his place as Son of God. How seriously he took this the world had yet to know.

Mary, says Luke, pondered all these things in her heart. Apparently she was the source of this story, and it became part of the oral legend of Jesus kept alive among the Christian communities in the Judean hills.

> *Lord, grant to the children I know the sense of direction and inner identity that Jesus had by the time he was* bar mitzvah. *And let Jesus himself stand at the center of where they are going with their lives. For his name's sake.* Amen.

Luke 3:1–14 No Hiding Place

Whatever image we may have of John the Baptist, it certainly isn't of a soft-soaper! He did not cajole the crowds with humor or sentimental language.

"You brood of vipers!" he called them—a nest of snakes. "Who warned you to flee from the wrath to come?" It is the picture of a family of snakes wriggling furiously to escape the advance of a raging fire or swirling flood. The wonder is that multitudes swarmed the river bank to hear so abusive a preacher.

But John had to be strong and decisive to fulfill the prophecy of Isaiah about the forerunner of the Messiah. Isaiah pictured him as predicting the leveling of mountains and raising of valleys, the straightening of crooked ways and the smoothing of rough paths. He saw the judgment that was coming on Israel and the world, and knew that there would be no hiding from that judgment. There would be no crevices or turns in the road where anyone might take refuge.

Many people recognized the authenticity of John's warning and asked what they must do to avert the disaster.

It is interesting that his answer is couched in terms of simple justice. People who have more property than they need are to divide with those who have none. Those who have food are to share with those who are hungry. Tax collectors are to do their duty but forego the often exorbitant fees they have been accustomed to extracting for personal use. Soldiers are to live simply and honestly, not using their positions to rob or to falsely accuse people of crimes and confiscate their property.

The injunctions are not different from those which Jesus will give later for citizens of the heavenly Kingdom. They imply a new orientation in life, a new spirit, so that God, not personal profit, becomes the center of the person's life.

And, interestingly, Luke sets his account of the great wilderness prophet into a universal context. He begins (v. 1) by locating John's ministry in the reign of Tiberius, the Roman emperor, and then names the local governor, tetrarch, and religious leaders. John's message of repentance and justice was not meant for the little land of Judah alone, but for the world!

Lord, am I part of the hills—or of the valleys? Do I have more than others? Then I too need to hear John's message and prepare the way of the Savior in my life by sharing what I have. Grant me the grace, imagination, and resoluteness acceptably to do this. In the name of the One who has come and is always coming. Amen.

Week 2: Tuesday

Luke 3:15–20 A Great Humility

Only persons with a special quality of inner assurance and self-identity are capable of true humility. I once knew such a person. He was a powerful man and controlled the affairs of many employees. Yet, in the presence of anyone who could do anything better than he could, he gracefully acknowledged the other person's ability. I once heard him, when accepting an honor, enthusiastically credit his superior in another city with the leadership and insight that were responsible for the honor.

John was obviously in touch with himself in this way. When people came to him asking if he were the Messiah, it must occasionally have been tempting to him to suggest that he was, or at least to wonder in his heart if indeed God was not preparing him for this great station. But he was apparently quite resolute on the matter, and pointed people instead to the One whose ministry would follow his.

"I baptize you with water," he said; but the One coming "will baptize you with the Holy Spirit and with fire" (v. 16).

As Luke was also the author of Acts, we cannot help associating this verse with the description of what occurred at Pentecost, when a sound "like the rush of a mighty wind" filled the house where the followers were, "tongues as of fire" rested on each of them, and the Holy Spirit welled up in them and they began to speak in other languages (Acts 2:1–4). John's followers had experienced baptism in water. So had Jesus' disciples. But the *real* baptism, the one that would be the sure sign of the Kingdom's presence, would be the baptism of the Spirit and the fire, and that was the baptism Christ would bring.

John the Baptist, as Karl Barth has said, was content to be a signpost pointing the way to Jesus.

Lord, make me a signpost too. Let the joy of my spirit and the helpfulness of my actions point others unmistakably to Jesus, who stands at the center of everything. Amen.

Week 2: Wednesday

Luke 3:21–38 A Great Moment

There is no tenderer moment in a parent's life than the one when his or her child undergoes a rite of initiation or passage. A baptism, a confirmation, first communion, *bar mitzvah*, graduation, marriage—each is a time of deep and satisfying emotion, combining reflection on the past and anticipation of the future.

It is surely no wonder that the Gospel traditions represented God as speaking his delight at the moment when Jesus, his "only begotten Son" (John 3:16, KJV), was baptized by the prophet John. It is beside the point whether Jesus needed to be baptized "for the forgiveness of sins" (Luke 3:3); the important thing is that by accepting baptism from John he identified himself with penitent Israel, the Israel whose hope was still in the Lord. It was a sign of expectancy and obedience. Luke's way of putting it, "when Jesus also had been baptized and was praying" (v. 21), implies that the

Holy Spirit came to him in the form of a dove after he left the riverbank and was alone in contemplation. This seems less dramatic and improbable than the picture we have in both Mark and Matthew, where the Spirit descended immediately upon Jesus' leaving the water. Whenever it happened, at any rate, the Spirit's physical appearance was accompanied by a voice from God saying, "Thou art my beloved Son; with thee I am well pleased."

This is an interesting combination of scriptural quotations. The first, "Thou art my beloved Son," is from Psalm 2:7. Psalm 2 is a hymn exalting the king whom God has set over the nations to rule "with a rod of iron" and dash his enemies to pieces "like a potter's vessel." The second phrase, "in thee I am well pleased," is probably from Isaiah 42:1, in which God is speaking of his servant who will redeem Israel through the ministry of suffering and "bring forth justice to the nations." So the two motifs are combined—exaltation and suffering—and set at the very beginning of Jesus' ministry.

Then Luke gives a long genealogy, relating Jesus to David, the great king of Israel, to Abraham, the father of the Jews, and eventually to Adam and thence to God himself. The justification for placing the list of names here is the phrase "the son of God," which may be linked back to the voice saying, "Thou art my beloved Son." And by relating Jesus to Adam, as well as to David and Abraham, Luke underlines again his proclamation of Jesus as a universal Savior, not merely the Savior of the Jews.

Lord, the early church must have been thrilled by this picture of the Savior being baptized and hearing your voice as the Spirit descended on him like a dove. Help me to feel a similar excitement now as I contemplate the scene. Arouse in me a new enthusiasm for your Kingdom and for the leadership of your Holy Spirit in my own life. Through him who became a suffering King. Amen.

Luke 4:1–13 Trial in the Wilderness

"Thou art my beloved Son," God had said when Jesus was baptized. "*If* you are the Son of God," the devil says in two of the temptations recorded here. It was a challenge to Jesus' understanding of his identity—an attempt to get him to forsake the role of suffering servant God intended the Savior to take.

Each temptation was extremely basic to human nature.

The first was for *bread.* Jesus had been fasting for nearly six weeks, and was very hungry. Perhaps in his imagination the rounded stones of the barren foothills where he was meditating began to look like loaves of bread—luscious, hot loaves of bread fresh from the oven. "Go ahead," the devil invited. "Turn this stone into bread. You are the Son of God, aren't you?"

Jesus' reply is directly from the words of Moses in Deuteronomy 8:2–3: "And you shall remember all the way which the Lord your God has led you these forty years in the wilderness, that he might humble you, testing you to know what was in your heart, whether you would keep his commandments, or not. And he humbled you and let you hunger and fed you with manna, which you did not know, nor did your fathers know; that he might make you know that man does not live by bread alone, but that man lives by everything that proceeds out of the mouth of the Lord." The Israelites had spent forty years in the wilderness; perhaps it was for a symbolic reason that Jesus spent forty days here. In any case, the point is clearly made: as important as bread may seem, humble obedience to God is even more important.

The second temptation was to *power* and *glory.* The devil promised to make Jesus a great king if he would only fall down and worship the prince of darkness. According to famed psychoanalyst Karen Horney, this too is a temptation familiar to all mankind. In varying degrees, we all yearn for recognition and authority. If we are neurotic, it is the most basic drive in our make-up.

Again Jesus' reply is from the words of Moses: "You shall fear the Lord your God; you shall serve him, and swear by his name. You shall not go after other gods . . . for the Lord your God . . . is a jealous God" (Deut. 6:13–15).

The third and final temptation was *to put God to the test.* Whisked up to the top of the pinnacle on the temple porch, which rose to a height of 450 feet above the Gehinnom Valley at the base of Jerusalem, Jesus was urged to leap down. Psalm 91, after all, promised protection to God's chosen one; he could not be hurt, if indeed he *was* the chosen one.

How often we are tempted to put God on trial in our lives! "God, if you truly care, do this." "If you are really there, do that." But Jesus responded firmly, again from Scripture: "You shall not put the Lord your God to the test" (Deut. 6:16). Testing is God's prerogative, not ours.

In all three temptations—for bread, for glory, and for religious certainty—Jesus responded with the need for absolute obedience to God. What an important passage this must have been to early Christians who, for one reason or another, were tempted to defect from the faith! It places temptations squarely in eternal perspective—enduring them now in the wilderness of life leads eventually to the Kingdom which God alone can give.

Lord, I have too often forgotten the meaning of real obedience. This age knows far more about being free than about obeying. Yet it misses the first principle of freedom—that freedom is lost the minute one fails to obey you. Help me to discover again how to be faithful to the heavenly vision, and thus to be truly free. Through Jesus, who fulfilled this paradox magnificently. Amen.

Week 2: Friday

Luke 4:14–30 The Design of Jesus' Ministry

Having flatly denied the devil's attempts to make him into a self-gratifying, power-hungry earthly king (Luke 4:1–13), Jesus now clearly denotes the kind of ministry he intends to pursue. It is to be a ministry to the poor and outcast, the blind and unaffirmed. And what happens when he announces his intentions signals the kind of reception he can expect from the religious Jews throughout the entire ministry.

Luke places the announcement of the servant ministry in a synagogue service in Nazareth. The synagogue was the heart of Jewish educational and religious life. A sabbath service in the synagogue usually consisted of a call to worship known as the *Shema* (Deut. 6:4–9), an assigned passage from the Law, a free passage from the prophets, a sermon, and assorted prayers. Any man in the synagogue, even a visitor, might be given a scroll and asked to read the Scripture or preach the sermon. The sermon was always preached from a seated position after the Scriptures had been read, and might be followed by questions from the audience.

On this occasion, Jesus was obviously invited to read the free selection from the prophets and then to provide the sermon. He chose Isaiah 61:1–2, which begins a long poem about the mission of God's mighty servant who is to restore Israel. When he announced that the long wait for the Scripture's fulfillment was at an end, the people were at first excited and pleased.

But then their doubts began to rear. This was Joseph's son talking. How could he hope to figure in the salvation of all Israel? Surely God would not use a hometown boy to save his people!

Some of the details of the conflict seem to be missing, and we must patch together what transpired. Apparently there was an exchange about the wonders Jesus had performed in Capernaum, another city to the north of Nazareth. But, as Mark informs us, he could do no mighty work in his hometown because of the people's disbelief (Mark 6:5–6).

Finally, in keeping with Luke's general emphasis on the worldwide mission of the Savior, Jesus went even further, and suggested that the Jews might entirely miss the great blessings of God. Israel had been full of widows in Elijah's day; yet Elijah went to the house of a widow in Sidon. Similarly, Israel had many lepers in Elisha's time; yet Elisha had given the blessing of God to a man from Syria.

The proud Jews could take no more! Touched to the quick, they rose up in anger and carried the brash young prophet out to throw him to his death, possibly on the charge that he had uttered blasphemy. Somehow, though—Luke does not trouble to be more specific—Jesus managed to walk through their midst and escape.

The tone of this entire passage is clearly an extension of that set by the temptation narrative. Jesus is faithful to the vision of God's will for his people, which calls for justice for the poor, the prisoners, the blind, and the oppressed. He will not swerve aside for anything—not to feed himself, not to gain personal glory, not to test God, and not to please the citizens of the town where he grew up!

Lord, how would I receive it if Jesus came into my life, as he did into these people's lives, upsetting the power balances and social structures within which I have learned to maneuver? I confess that I would probably feel as they did, and try to resist him. I know this means I am not fully converted to your Kingdom. Forgive me, Lord, and give me a humble spirit, that I may acquiesce in his vision and be saved. Amen.

Week 2: Saturday

Luke 4:31–44 Teaching and Preaching the Kingdom

In our day, we are prone to think of the teaching and preaching of the Kingdom primarily in terms of oral communication. Sometimes, as a professor of preaching in a theological seminary, I receive mail addressed to "The Professor of Speech."

But for Jesus, the Kingdom was coming in power, not mere talk. Therefore his teaching and preaching were interfused with miraculous acts of healing. When he announced in the synagogue at Nazareth (Luke 4:14–30) that he was anointed "to preach good news to the poor" and "to proclaim release to the captives and recovering of sight to the blind," he obviously had in mind far more than a mere announcement of the Kingdom's arrival. For him, teaching and preaching meant participating in the power of the new Kingdom! This passage (Luke 4:31–44), then, is the logical one to follow the declaration in 4:14–30. It shows the preacher of the Kingdom in action.

Luke seems to have taken over this particular collection of material almost verbatim from the Gospel of Mark (1:21–39), or from some source of stories available to both Mark and himself. About the only change he made in it is in the last verse (44), for which Mark reads, "And he went throughout all Galilee, preaching in their synagogues" (1:39). Luke does not mean to relocate the ministry by setting it in Judea, the territory to the south of Galilee. He uses the word Judea to denote all of Palestine (cf. Luke 1:5; 6:17; 7:17; 23:5).

The purpose of the selection in both Mark and Luke is to relate Jesus' healing ministry to the "authority" with which he taught and preached. When he spoke, it was not the carefully guarded speech of the scribes and Pharisees; it was the penetrating, free-moving discourse of one who was obviously in touch with his subject—and the miracles were simply further proof of this.

The demons recognized him as the true Son of God, and knew his coming shook their power and authority to the very depths. Their cries, as they left their victims, were filled with awe and respect: "You are the Son of God!" (v. 41). They realized that it was the beginning of the end for them. The scribes and Pharisees had never had any power over them. But they knew it was different with Jesus. He was "the Holy One of God," and his Kingdom's arrival meant the collapse of theirs.

Lord, I wonder if the demons did not show Jesus more respect than we often show him today. We sing "Oh, How I Love Jesus" and flash our bumper stickers with the message "Honk If You Love Jesus." Then we live as if he had not died for our sin and been raised as an eternal presence in our midst. It made more difference in the lives of the demons. They went away in hushed respect, forsaking even their dwelling places. Let him matter more to me, I pray, for his name's sake. Amen.

WEEK 3

Week 3: Sunday

Luke 5:1–11 An Astonishing Catch

What an encouraging story this must have been to the early church in times of frustration or despair!

The crowds had pressed Jesus right up to the water, trying to hear the Word of God about the Kingdom. As he talked, he saw the two boats come in empty from a night's fishing. The men in the boats tied up their vessels and began the arduous task of washing the leaves and algae out of their nets.

Getting into Simon Peter's boat, Jesus had him row out a short way from land and anchor there. Getting a little distance on the crowd in this manner, he was then able to sit down and teach from the boat. He probably did not preach uninterruptedly, as ministers usually do today, but answered questions as they came up, or even sat sometimes in silence, waiting for ideas to form into words or parables. And we can imagine Simon Peter, tired as he was from the night's fishing, waiting quietly in the boat and listening as Jesus talked.

Then, when he had finished speaking, Jesus turned his energies to his benefactor with the boat and the empty nets. "Launch out into the deep and let down your nets again," he said (v. 5, P). Simon started to protest, but thought better of it and obeyed. He and his men rowed out into the lake and dropped their nets again. How tired they must have been, and how useless this all seemed. But, to their utter amazement, the nets came in writhing and bulging with fish. There was such a catch that they had to signal the men in the other boat to come and help them, so the nets would not break, making them lose all the fish.

Peter's reaction is interesting. It was as if he had never before realized the holiness of the one he had heard teaching from his boat. Suddenly he was aware, and fell to his knees to worship. His words (v. 8) are reminiscent of those of Isaiah when he had a vision of God in the temple (Isa. 6:5). He had seen the Lord himself!

Jesus' words to Simon and the others were, "Do not be afraid"—further indication that they had recognized his holiness. They would be used in a special way in the Kingdom as fishers of men. So they obeyed their vision of his holiness by leaving their boats and homes to follow him.

Think how the early church would have heard this story. There must often have been periods when the Christians seemed to make no progress in converting the world regardless of how they had toiled. Then they would see this picture of Simon Peter, who became the head of the church, reluctantly rowing to deep water again and slowly letting out the great nets. They would envision the sudden churning of the waters as the nets were drawn up, with all the silver bellies flip-flopping in the air and spraying foam everywhere. What a lesson it was! They had but to listen for the voice and let down their nets at his bidding. He would give the church its increase.

Lord, I am often tired and lose faith when nothing seems to be happening in my life. Teach me to hear your voice at such times and to steer for the deep waters again. In the name of him who can keep the nets full. Amen.

Week 3: Monday

Luke 5:12–16 Release for a Captive

In the dialogue following his sermon at the synagogue in Nazareth, Jesus had alluded to Elisha's healing of the leper Naaman (Luke 4:27). Now he himself heals a man "full of leprosy."

Leprosy was one of the most dreaded diseases of that time, not only because of the way it wasted the body but because it isolated the victim socially and religiously. This man clearly became one of the "captives" referred to in Jesus' reading from Isaiah (Luke 4:18). According to Leviticus 13–14, which gave specific rules governing the leprous person, he was declared "unclean" by the priest and cast out from normal society.

Jesus is depicted as doing what most Jews would never do—he touched the leper, risking social and religious contamination for himself. But then the miracle occurred. Instead of his being contaminated by the leper, Jesus cleansed the man! He reversed the usual direction of effect, and opened a new future to the man!

Jesus' instruction to the man that he go to the priest and conform to the Levitical law and be pronounced well was probably for the man's sake socially—he would then be reintegrated into the normal fabric of Jewish society.

The verbs in the final sentences of the passage are interesting. They are all in the imperfect tense, denoting continuing activity. The word about Jesus *kept* going out; great crowds *kept* gathering to hear him and be healed; and he *kept* withdrawing and praying.

This is the picture we have seen in Matthew and Mark as well, of the dialectic between prayer and activity in Jesus' ministry. He constantly withdrew into solitary places to nourish his inner person through prayer and meditation. This, in turn, gave him unusual power in dealing with the great pressure of human needs and demands when he was among the crowds.

Lord, I am so guilty of forgetting this dialectic and trying to meet the demands of life without times of prayer and reflection. Please help me to see once and for all that I simply can't do it—that only the continued refreshment of your presence will enable me to deal adequately with the burden of busy days. Through Jesus, who fully understood this. Amen.

Week 3: Tuesday

Luke 5:17–26 A Characteristic Detail

The Pharisees were a special group of men who had separated themselves from normal pursuits in life to become guardians of the Law; hence their name, which means "the separated ones." The Law which they watched over was the Law of Moses plus the hair-splitting elaborations of each individual law within it; in other words, it was a very complex body of legalities. "Teachers of the law" was Luke's term for the scribes. These men specialized in interpretations of the Law, making them natural companions of the Pharisees.

The fact that Pharisees and teachers from all over Palestine had gathered to hear Jesus is an obvious sign of his growing fame and popularity.

As usual, Jesus seems to have been practicing a combined ministry of teaching and healing. Luke's word that "the power of the Lord was with him to heal" (v. 17) is one of the clearest indications in Scripture that this power was not always resident in Jesus himself but was a special gift from God. We can well imagine that the paralyzed man brought on a stretcher was not the only one who had come to Jesus borne by friends. But this one became the object of special attention because of the controversy with the scribes and Pharisees and the unusual manner of his entrance. Mark 2:4 pictures the man's friends removing part of the clay-and-wattle roof of a typical Palestinian home, but Luke provides the detail about removing the tiles (v. 19), indicating a Roman style of house.

The controversy arises over Jesus' first words to the paralyzed man, forgiving his sins. We are not certain why he spoke thus. Some commentators think he recognized the man's paralysis as a psychosomatic affliction; others, that he was underscoring the rootedness of illness and affliction in the presence of sin and evil in the world. I am inclined to the latter interpretation, and also believe that he ejaculated these words of forgiveness in celebration of the eagerness of the man's friends to bring him to Jesus by such an imaginative way. At any rate, the words released a torrent of questioning from the legalists present, who thought it blasphemous for any person to assume God's prerogative of pardoning iniquity.

Jesus' response is to show them something even more incredible—the restoration of the man's normal physical functioning. If they doubt his ability to forgive sin, then why is he given such power to perform visible miracles? They are all amazed and filled with awe, as if they have beheld sacred mysteries.

And Luke adds a characteristic detail omitted in Mark. He says the man who was healed went home "glorifying God." This is the note of joyous discovery that runs throughout the Gospel of Luke, from the announcement of the Savior's birth to the story of his resurrection.

Lord, I understand about Jesus' forgiving the man before healing him. I too am inwardly paralyzed by my sins and failures, and it is only as I feel your acceptance of me despite them that I begin to experience wholeness and joy. Then even my body feels better. Thank you, Lord. Hallelujah! Amen.

Luke 5:27–39 A New Mood of Rejoicing

At first glance, there appear to be two separate passages here, one about Levi and his friends, and the other about the question of fasting, amplified by the short parables of the garment and the wineskin. But one spirit pervades them both and makes a unity of them.

It has to do with the new kind of order that has come in Jesus. He is not a mere continuation of the old religious tradition represented by the scribes and Pharisees and their restrictive view of the Law. Instead, he brings an air of liberation, a fresh spirit of joy and celebration in life.

The people who have been cast away from the religious center because they could not keep the Law perfectly are brought back with joy (note the "great feast" in Levi's house), just as the prodigal son is received in the parable (Luke 15:20–24). And the disciples who follow the Master, themselves common, "unreligious" persons, likewise live joyfully instead of ascetically, celebrating their Lord's presence in their midst.

The brief parables of the garment and the wineskin, then, are metaphorical ways of saying that this exhilarating movement of Jesus cannot be merely appended to or enclosed in the traditional forms of religion; it is too dynamic, too volatile, and can only end by destroying the old way, as an unshrunken patch of cloth will do when sewn to a shrunken garment, or as active new wine will do when poured into old, dry skins.

Verse 39 appears only in Luke, and not in the parallel versions of Matthew and Mark. It seems to be a comment on those who find the old religion adequate—especially the scribes and Pharisees. They find the old wine to be good, so simply do not try the new wine. Jesus understood the difficulty of giving up old habits or traditions.

Lord, my problem is that I have allowed the "new" religion of Jesus and the disciples to become old in my life. My responses to you have become dull and routine, and I no longer have a continual sense of delight in my faith. Come as new wine in my life, tearing up old wine-skins; break me open to current joys in the Kingdom. For Jesus' sake—and mine. Amen.

Week 3: Thursday

Luke 6:1–11 The Priority of People over Traditions

This passage should be read as a continuation of Luke 5:27–39, for it is further commentary on what Jesus said there about the new mood of joy and excitement in the Kingdom. Fussiness about sabbath law was part of the strict religious tradition developed by the scribes and Pharisees. Jesus did not violate the Law of Moses, for he was a humble observer of divine law. But he certainly was not about to conform to the niggardly elaborations of that Law that had become such a web of bondage to observant Jews.

The first incident, plucking and eating grain on the sabbath, revolves about a regulation against milling corn on the holy day. It seems silly to us that rolling a few grains of wheat in one's hand to separate the kernels from the husks should be construed as milling or grinding, but that is the way the scribes and Pharisees had come to interpret it.

Jesus' answer to them on this score did not try to argue with the absurdity of their interpretation. Instead, it went to another "offense," one recorded in 1 Samuel 21:1–6 about David, who, with his men, had eaten the sacred bread of the Presence in the tabernacle. What this illustrated, as Jesus used it, was the priority of human need over any commandment. Thus the summation, "The Son of man is lord of the sabbath" (v. 5). It seems likely that Luke reported the phrase "Son of man" here as it was often used in the Old Testament (cf. Ps. 8:4), as merely a synonym for "man" and not as a messianic title. In other words, we do not have here a pronouncement about Jesus' lordship but a common-sense statement about the importance of human need when that need appears to contradict religious commandments.

The second incident, healing on the sabbath, defies the rule that a person could be doctored on the sabbath only if his life were in danger. Obviously this man's withered hand had not gotten that way overnight, and could await the following day for restoration. But again Jesus challenged the priority of the Law over human need by effecting the cure on the sabbath. What is more, he appears to have done it as an open affront to the legalists, because he invited the man to come and stand in the very center of the crowd as he performed the healing. It was a direct reflection of his declaration of ministry in Luke 4:16–30—healing the sick and releasing the captive were to have top priority in the Kingdom!

Verse 11 is a dark hint of what was to come. Those who cherished the old traditions could not bear to see them broken in this manner. They would eventually have their pound of flesh.

Lord, forbid that I should ever follow in the footsteps of the legalists by making any Christian *regulation more important than the people I meet in life. Fill my heart with such love and exultation that I shall never become defensive about mere traditions or habits of thinking. Through Jesus, who drew fresh dedication from everything.* Amen.

Week 3: Friday

Luke 6:12–19 The People of the New Spirit

Following his controversies with the religious leaders of Israel (Luke 5:17–6:11) and their rancorous discussion of what to do to him (Luke 6:11), Jesus appoints the twelve disciples who are to be the pillars of the new movement. The importance of the act is underlined by his spending the night praying in the hills. These are to be men whom God wants and who will be entrusted with the power to heal and to preach the Kingdom.

The number twelve is suggestive of the twelve tribes of Israel, indicating that the community of joyful celebrators gathered through the ministry of Jesus and the apostles would be the replacement for the moribund old Israel, which was too wrapped up in concerns for its regulations and traditions to fulfill the calling of God for a servant people to save the world.

With his newly appointed cabinet around him, Jesus then descends from the hills and meets the people "on a level place" to teach and heal them. This contrasts sharply with the picture in Matthew 5–7, where the "sermon" of Jesus is given on a mountain. Possibly the source from which both writers drew did not specify a place and each provided a different location from pure conjecture. Luke's basis for having the sermon on the plain would seem to be the pattern from Exodus 24, where Moses received the Law on the mountain but then descended before giving it to the people. Matthew, however, was concerned to represent Jesus as "a greater than Moses"; perhaps this led to his portraying Jesus as giving his sermon from the mountain instead of from the plain, indicating that he occupied a position higher than that of an intermediary, as Moses clearly was.

Regardless of what is intended by the place symbolism, Luke obviously emphasizes two things. First, the wide territory represented by the crowd that has gathered—it embraces all of Palestine and even the outlying districts of Tyre and Sidon. And, second, the continued connection of Jesus' activities with the program he announced in the synagogue in Nazareth (Luke 4:16–30)—he uses his power from God to effect healing for the sick and release for the captives.

Lord, Luke obviously intended to link Jesus' choice of his disciples with the ongoing work of healing and liberating people. How connected have these been in my own life? Have I too easily assumed that my discipleship has nothing to do with healing the hurts and illnesses of the people around me? Help me to ponder this and let you be Lord in my life the way you want to, not the way I think you should be. For your Kingdom's power. Amen.

Luke 6:20–31 A Sermon for the New Israel

Like Matthew's Sermon on the Mount (Matt. 5–7), Luke's Sermon on the Plain begins with the Beatitudes, describing the blessedness of those who are gathered up in the new Kingdom. This section forms a natural extension of Luke 4:16–30, in which Jesus defines his ministry as being to the poor, the sick, the outcast, and the oppressed. It is to these persons that the Kingdom belongs.

Thus the "woes" which follow in Luke's version (Matthew does not report any "woes" in the sermon) are most appropriate, for they are spoken rhetorically of all those who will miss the Kingdom because their riches, fine foods, present joys and respectability deafen them to the word of the gospel. Some commentators have conjectured that this section of "woes" was added to the text by the early church and was not really spoken by Jesus. But if we recall the extensive list of "woes" Jesus directed against the Pharisees in Matthew 23, we should not so readily question the authenticity of these "woes."

Matthew of course lists *nine* beatitudes, while Luke provides only four. And there is another notable difference in the two lists: Matthew has *spiritualized* his. That is, he has Jesus speak of "the poor in spirit" and those who "hunger and thirst after righteousness." Luke's Jesus, however, speaks of real poverty, real hunger, and real sorrow. The point he thus preserves is that God is going to look after the little ones of the earth; he is going to produce a great revolution in which the poor will receive what the rich have possessed. This is consistent with what John the Baptist predicted in Luke 3, that the high places would be brought low and the low places raised up, as well as with Jesus' sermon in the synagogue in Nazareth (Luke 4).

Running through this passage and the remainder of the sermon (vv. 32–49) is the note of intoxicating joy we have observed before in Luke. There will be great vexation among those who ignore the Kingdom's arrival, for they will lose everything. But the poor, the sick, and the oppressed will have reason for great rejoicing. They will eat and laugh at a great feast!

Lord, again I confess that my life is not joyful enough. Perhaps it is because I have too much, like the rich and the full in this section of "woes," or because I am shallow, like those who laugh now, or because I work too hard at being respected, like those who are well spoken of. These things crowd my mind and I cannot concentrate on you and the Kingdom. Forgive me, Lord, and lead me into a new level of consciousness where I shall know true blessedness. For your Kingdom is not only forever, but is here now. Amen.

WEEK 4

Week 4: Sunday

Luke 6:32–38 The Law of Love

This brief passage is Luke's equivalent of Paul's famous "love chapter," 1 Corinthians 13. It is set here in the Sermon on the Plain to indicate the absolute centrality of the loving spirit in the Kingdom of God.

To appreciate it fully, we must recall the ethic of the old Israel with which it contrasts. The heart of the Mosaic Law was the love of God and a careful adherence to the commandments. In practice, respect for the commandments had deteriorated into mere legalism—doing what was required of one and no more.

Jesus takes away nothing from loving God—in fact, on another occasion he says that loving God is the first commandment (Luke 10:25–28). But he seeks to avoid the spiritual and ethical impasse of the old legal system by describing those who are in the Kingdom as people who love and who therefore go beyond the requirements in their generous concern for others. They bless those who curse them, pray for those who abuse them, lend goods where there is little hope of return, and forgive those whom the Law would never forgive. In short, they are inwardly motivated to behave in a way that completely transcends the rule of law.

The genius of this way of life, of course, is that it rewards the person of the loving spirit with joy and peace that cannot be had on other terms. The person who keeps the Law faithfully may feel self-satisfied and righteous. But the one of the loving spirit feels something even better—an exuberance and sense of life akin to that of "the Most High" himself!

Lord, my mind has known the truths of these words for a long time, but I have forgotten them in my spirit. Rescue me, I pray, from the inadequacy of merely doing what is required, and give me the great joy of living selflessly, as you live. Through Jesus, who is a perfect example. Amen.

Week 4: Monday

Luke 6:39–49 Words for Disciples

Jesus had said that part of his ministry had to do with "recovering of sight to the blind" (Luke 4:18). While he meant this literally, it also had a great deal of figurative truth too, as we see from this passage. Being able to see matters clearly was regarded as essential in a disciple—otherwise Jesus' followers would produce the wrong kind of followers of their own.

If they had truly learned all they could from him, then they would produce good fruit, the way healthy trees do. They would be like a man who lays a solid foundation for his house, not like the one who is in haste to get his house up and so builds on the flat sandbar by the river without troubling to dig down and lay his foundation on the bedrock.

As Luke has arranged this material, it is an extended exhortation to thorough learning and discipleship, so that the follower of Jesus really becomes like his or her Master. Then the Kingdom will truly flourish in the world.

Lord, I am too prone to give you second-rate obedience instead of wholehearted discipleship. I am lazy about studying and learning what a follower of Jesus should know and practice in his or her life. I do not spend enough time each day in prayer and meditation. Help me to begin again and lay a better foundation before the floods of life come upon me and sweep away the little I have done. I want to see clearly and behave lovingly, for Jesus' sake. Amen.

Week 4: Tuesday

Luke 7:1–10 The Faith of a Foreigner

Luke has already ended his report of Jesus' Sermon on the Plain (Luke 6:20–49), but he may well have placed this story of the Roman centurion here as an illustration of the kind of life advocated by the sermon. The centurion is clearly a remarkable human being. Although technically an officer of the enemy occupation forces, he has behaved respectfully and lovingly toward the captive citizenry under his command. He has constructed a synagogue for their worship and educational needs, even though their religion differs vastly from his own, and has apparently shown his love for the people in other ways. When the elders from the synagogue come to bring Jesus to heal his slave who is very ill—probably a Jew who is a member of the synagogue—the centurion treats Jesus with the kind of respect normally reserved for kings and potentates. "I am not worthy of having you in my home," he says. "You can but say the word, and my servant will be healed." Beneath these humble words lay a great thoughtfulness. If Jesus were an orthodox Jew, entering the home of a foreigner would have been considered a defilement for him. The centurion probably expected that this was the case and wished to spare Jesus this transgression of his native custom.

"I tell you," exclaimed Jesus, "not even in Israel have I found such faith" (v. 9). The faith was obviously in Jesus' power to cure the man's slave. But it was also in a way of life which lay at the heart of Jesus' teaching. This centurion was a great example of the loving spirit of the Kingdom!

I saw a similar man once. He was a commanding officer in the U.S. Air Force. I went for a walk with him one day in Chieng Mai, a lovely town in Northern Thailand, and followed him into a Buddhist school and temple. He picked up the small children and loved them, and removed his shoes when he entered the temple, lest he offend an old man who sat watching us. Somehow he reminded me of the centurion in this passage. Jesus liked such people.

Lord, give me a loving spirit like this. Help me to see that the essence of true religion is in how I respond to the poor, weak, and oppressed of the world—not in how faultless I am about matters of religious dogma. Through Jesus, who lived this way himself. Amen.

Week 4: Wednesday

Luke 7:11–17 An Act of Compassion

This story of a dramatic resuscitation has rather clear theological import. Like Elijah in 1 Kings 17:17–24 and Elisha in 2 Kings 4:32–37, Jesus is seen as a prophet acting in the power of God to raise the dead. In this regard, the story serves as a preparation for the passage to follow, in which John the Baptist questions whether Jesus is the one "who is to come."

But Luke is obviously carried away in the telling by more than theological consideration. He is overwhelmed by the sheer human sentiment of it.

The picture is enough to bring tears to the eyes of the sternest of viewers. Jesus comes upon a funeral procession in a small town in Galilee. In the slow, mournful custom of the region, the procession winds through the narrow streets, led by the family, the professional weepers, and the coffin of the deceased. Apparently the poor widowed woman is in this case the only family member—all the others are friends. She will be left alone in the world—a terrible lot for an older woman in that culture—for she is burying her lone child.

It is a stark drama that greets Jesus as he arrives upon the scene—the mourning clothes, the loud wails of lamentation, the sight of the single woman accompanying the casket through the street. This is precisely the kind of setting he has said the Kingdom addresses.

"Do not weep," he comforts the mother.

He puts his hand upon the coffin—considered a defilement in traditional religion—and stops the procession.

"Get up, young man," he says. And the young man does.

It would be impossible to describe accurately the scene that follows. The people are jubilant—not merely because their friend's son has been raised from the dead, but because God has sent "a great prophet" into their midst! Small wonder that the "report concerning him" spreads like a windswept fire in dry grass to all the surrounding regions.

Lord, help me not to balk at the miracle of this story by asking if it really happened. Instead, let it speak movingly to my heart of the faith in which I am grasped, for there is truth that lies beyond the truth of my logical mind. Amen.

Luke 7:18–35 The Very Best Proof

In the narrative about the births of John and Jesus, Luke recorded how the baby John leaped for joy in his mother's womb when Mary came to visit Elizabeth (Luke 1:44). Here is a more realistic picture from adult life. Unlike Matthew, Luke reported no special recognition from John when Jesus was baptized. We are left to conjecture that the realization that Jesus was the promised Savior only began to dawn on John as he heard from his prison cell continued reports of the amazing ministry of Jesus.

When the men come from John seeking verification of Jesus' role, he gives them the best proof available. They observe as he heals the sick and restores the sight of the blind. "Go and tell John what you have seen with your own eyes," says Jesus—and he summarizes what they have beheld again in terms reminiscent of his declared program in Luke 4:16–30.

When the men have gone, Jesus ruminates about John and says what a great figure he has been. But he quickly adds that even the least of his followers who has seen the Kingdom is greater than John. It is Luke's way of emphasizing that John was the last of the old order and Jesus the beginning of the new.

Jesus' commendation of John apparently pleases many in the crowd who were disciples of John, but it raises murmurs of dissent among the scribes and Pharisees, who had been unwilling to accept the baptism of repentance. Noting the latter, Jesus muses about those who hold back and are unwilling to be caught up in a renewal movement. They are like children who hang about the marketplace—perhaps Jesus is watching some as he speaks—and complain that others will not do things their way. They did not like John because he was too strict and ascetic, and they do not like Jesus because he is too free and uninhibited in both his actions and his relationships.

The last word, "Yet wisdom is justified by all her children," is probably a proverb expressing a spirit of tolerance. We would say, "It takes all kinds to make a world."

Lord, I am often as fickle as the scribes and Pharisees, liking in one person what I dislike in another. Give me a heart of compassion, I pray, that I may accept even my enemies in prayer and thanksgiving. Through Jesus, who forgave from his cross. Amen.

Week 4: Friday

Luke 7:36-50 A Lesson in Joy

This passage may well be placed here as a further example of Jesus' knowledge of people and compassion for them. First there was the centurion whose slave was ill (Luke 7:1–10); then the widow whose son had died (Luke 7:11–17); then John the Baptist (Luke 7:18–23); then the crowds who heard Jesus speak about John (Luke 7:24–35). Now we see how Jesus treats a known prostitute and the Pharisee to whose home she comes.

We can only speculate, of course, but it was probably a daring thing for Simon the Pharisee to invite Jesus into his home, especially after the remark Jesus made in Luke 7:34 about his reputation as "a glutton and a drunkard, a friend of tax collectors and sinners!" The man should have known, as a strictly orthodox Jew who observed all the table commandments and house commandments, that he was asking for trouble. Still, we know from the fact that he did not provide the usual courtesies to Jesus—the foot bath, the kiss of greeting, the oil or perfume—that he was at least uncertain about his guest and how to receive him. Perhaps he invited him out of mere curiosity.

Apparently the men were reclining in the Roman manner, with their shoulders to the table and their feet behind them, and the woman simply approached Jesus in the courtyard or through an open door without his seeing her. Before she could get her flask of ointment open to anoint him, she began weeping, so that her tears fell upon his feet. Overcome by emotion, she loosened her long hair (as no proper woman would have done) and began wiping the tears with her hair.

Simon was inwardly outraged, and Jesus could doubtless see it in his face. Perhaps with genuine compassion for Simon, and not as a rebuke, Jesus told him the parable of the two debtors and then applied it to the present situation. The nameless woman was like the debtor who had been forgiven a king's ransom—she had much to celebrate and be grateful for. Simon, on the other hand, had had no such upheavals in his life. He was a man of careful behavior and suspicious nature. He did not know how to love and rejoice as she did.

We don't know the woman's motivation; it is not clear. There is a similar story in Mark 14:3–9 about a woman of Bethany who came into the house of Simon the leper and anointed Jesus' head in anticipation of his death and burial; John 12:1–8 identifies this as Mary, the sister of Lazarus, and again indicates it is for his burial, but changes the story to an anointing of the feet. Luke is possibly drawing on the same story, but uses it to proclaim Jesus' compassion, not his death and burial. In this version, he defends the woman against the unfriendly attitude of Simon the Pharisee and tells her that her sin—the behavior that has cut her off from "decent" society—is forgiven.

Thus Luke closes the five tales of compassion as he began them. In the first, Jesus commended a foreign centurion for having more faith than he had seen among the Israelites; in the last, he commends an obvious sinner, telling her, "Your faith has saved you." Luke's picture is clear—Jesus is forming the new Israel, the community of the redeemed, out of people summarily rejected by the legalists of the old Israel.

Thank you, Lord, for the grace of this story. I am more like Simon than the woman. Help me to see that my sin is as great as hers, and therefore my forgiveness even more to be prized. Through him who said we should celebrate whenever we have the bridegroom with us. Amen.

Luke 8:1–21 The Sower Goes Out

At this point in the Gospel, Luke represents Jesus as leaving the synagogue setting and moving more actively through the countryside, stopping in villages and cities along the way. He is like the sower in his parable, widely scattering seeds as he goes. He and the twelve are apparently supported by some wealthy women in their entourage who have been healed of various diseases and are now dedicating their lives to the Kingdom.

The phrase "preaching and bringing the good news of the kingdom of God" (v. 1) derives its significance from the "compassion" stories which have preceded it (Luke 7:1–50). The good news is that the Kingdom has come to foreign centurions, widows, prostitutes, lepers, cripples, and the blind and the deaf. Skipping the traditionally righteous, it is now offered to others.

Not all people are able to hear this good news, of course; some are like the hard ground and thorny soil of the parable, and the seed either doesn't take root at all or, if it does, does not come to proper fruition. But Jesus is comforted by the knowledge that some bearers will be like the good soil, in which the seed will reproduce itself a hundred times over. Hearing the good news, they will "hold it fast in an honest and good heart, and bring forth fruit with patience" (v. 15). In a different metaphor, they will trim their lamps and put them on stands in the great entry hall, so that anyone who comes into the house will know immediately that something has happened to their lives.

Be careful then, says Jesus, how you hear; because the person who truly hears all of this will be exceptionally well endowed, while those who don't hear will lose all they have.

At this point Jesus' mother and brothers come to see him. Mark sets this visit in the context of Jesus' conflicts with the scribes and Pharisees, concluding it with Jesus' words that "whoever does the will of God is my brother, and sister, and mother" (Mark 3:35). Matthew follows Mark in both the conflict setting and the wording (Matt. 12:46–50). Luke has apparently altered the saying—though not the meaning—in order to make it tie in with the preceding 20 verses, which are all, in one way or another, about hearing the Word and doing it. Whoever hears the Word he is preaching about the Kingdom for the poor and oppressed, he says, becomes part of his intimate family.

Lord, thank you for the Word of the Kingdom that makes us part of the family of Jesus. Let me continue to hear the Word afresh in every season of my life, that it may never cease to spring up and produce its fruit in my thoughts and actions. In the family's name. Amen.

WEEK 5

Week 5: Sunday

Luke 8:22–39 The Lord of All

Two events, the calming of the sea and the healing of the Gerasene man, are combined in today's reading because Luke probably saw them as having significance in relation to each other. Together, they constitute an excursion in Jesus' ministry. He crosses the sea of Galilee to the country around Gerasa, on the eastern coast of the sea, and then, after healing the Gerasene man, returns to the Galilean side of the sea (v. 40), probably near Capernaum.

The point of it all is that Jesus shows his mastery of both the sea and the demons in the land beyond the sea. In other words, he is master everywhere in the world, not only in Galilee and Judea. Luke's Gospel, we remember, is always careful to exhibit the universal lordship of Christ, and even though the material in this section appears to be derived from Mark (4:35–5:20), he would have welcomed stories that make this point.

The Jews were never a seagoing people, and the sea was to them a symbol of chaos and disorder. In the Book of Genesis, when God created the world, he separated the dry land from the waters; and the Book of Revelation speaks of a new heaven and a new earth in which there is no more sea (Rev. 21:1). To the Jewish mind, the sea with its raging storms represented the last refusal of nature to be tamed.

When Jesus rebuked the wind and waves, producing immediate calm, it was a sign of his absolute mastery of the world. To the question, "Who then is this?" there could be but one answer: He was God's appointed one, with the power of God himself.

The story of the healing on the coasts of Gerasa contains the same kind of cosmic symbolism. The name of the unclean spirit who is devastating the poor man is given as Legion. A legion was a Roman division of six thousand men. Undoubtedly the spirit's name implied that a vast number of demons were residing in the man—far more than afflicted a person in any other biblical story. For Jesus to conquer thousands of demons at once, and on a foreign shore, clearly spelled his universal power.

When we remember Luke's feeling for the "foreign" mission of the church throughout the Book of Acts, we know what special interest he must have had in the witnessing of the cured man to the people of his own region. It would have been important preparation for the later establishment of a Christian colony there.

It is a wonder, Lord, when I think of it, that the power of Jesus not only crossed the Galilean Sea to reach the demon-ridden man of Gerasa, but crossed an ocean to touch my life in America. Teach me to live more constantly in awe of this power and mystery, that I, like the Gerasene, may share my awareness of it with others. For the sake of the Kingdom. Amen.

Luke 8:40–56 A Daughter of the Opposition

There must have been some human drama behind this story that did not get told in the Gospel, for Jairus was the president of the local synagogue, probably in Capernaum, at a time when the religious leaders were beginning to crystallize their opposition to Jesus. Jairus was probably torn between his political position and his personal need for Jesus' power to cure his daughter. Luke heightens the pathos of the story over Mark's account by adding that the girl was his *only* daughter. We can imagine what may have gone on in Jairus's mind before he finally succumbed to his love for his daughter and rushed out to beg Jesus to come and save her. The fact that he fell down before Jesus is an indication of the desperation he felt when he finally sought the Master's help.

The story is interrupted midway, as it is also in Mark's Gospel, by the story of the woman who touched Jesus in the crowd and was healed. Her condition has been identified today as menorrhagia, an unceasing menstrual flow. According to Levitical law, this made her continuously unclean, just as if she had leprosy or some other terrible disease. It was therefore rather daring of her to touch Jesus, for the Law forbade her touching anyone. This may account for her having done so stealthily, and also for Jesus' having discerned her touch among all the flutter of hands and bodies pressing against him in the crowd—her condition was a spiritual offense, in one sense at least, and produced a noticeable effect when brought into contact with the holiness of the Son of God. Again, as in the case of the leper whom Jesus touched in Luke 5:12–13, instead of his being infected by the unclean person, power went out from him to heal the unclean one.

The miraculousness of the healing is underscored by the information that the woman had suffered thus for twelve years "and could not be healed by any one" (v. 43). The best manuscripts available show that Luke omitted the phrase in Mark 5:26 that she "had suffered much under many physicians" who had taken all her money. This is a bit humorous when we remember that Luke himself was probably a physician; perhaps he was protecting the reputation of his fraternity! At any rate, Jesus stressed to the woman when she had come forward publicly that it was her faith in the Kingdom that had done this for her. She was to go in peace—*shalom*—which means gracious fullness.

Meanwhile, word came to Jairus from his house that it was too late, his daughter had died. He repeated the message to Jesus, releasing him from the responsibility of going further. But Jesus challenged the synagogue leader to have as much faith as the poor unclean woman who had worked her way through the crowd to touch him. "Only believe in the arrival of the Kingdom," he said in effect, "and she shall be well." Taking the inner circle of disciples and the girl's parents with him, and brushing aside the scoffers, he entered where the girl was, took her by the hand, and lifted her up as though he had wakened her from a mere nap. We can imagine the great joy that filled the household. "Bring her something to eat," said Jesus. "She's hungry."

Thank you, Lord, for these marvelous vignettes from the life of Jesus. What knowledge of people he had, and what compassion, what power! Let me have faith like this woman's, that, if I will but reach out to touch him, life-giving power will flow into me. Lord, I believe; help thou my unbelief. Amen.

Week 5: Tuesday

Luke 9:1–17 The Roles of the Disciples

This passage serves as a pivot between the first part of Luke's Gospel and the preparation of the disciples to go to Jerusalem and experience the passion there. It is essentially a picture of how the disciples helped in the ministry of Jesus and how he sustained them as a community.

The missionary thrust of verses 1–6 is obviously different from that of Luke 8:1–3, in which Jesus and a large company of followers moved together in an itinerant ministry financed by some wealthy women. Now the disciples are sent out in twos, in order to cover a wider territory, and are given orders to take nothing along for the journey but to move decisively from place to place, depending on the hospitality of friends where they can. When people are unreceptive to their preaching of the Kingdom and performing acts of healing, they are to use the ancient Jewish ritual of shaking Gentile dust from their feet when they reentered the Holy Land, and shake the dust of unbelievers from their sandals. The disciples represent, after all, the new Israel of God.

The hubbub that was raised around the country by this intensive, all-out mission attracted the attention of Herod, who had put John the Baptist to death. Now his uneasy conscience made him wonder if the flurry of new religious fervor caused by Jesus and the disciples was the work of John come back to life. The terse statement that Herod "sought to see him" (v. 9) is a foreshadowing of his meeting with Jesus during the Passover in Jerusalem (Luke 23:8).

The return of the disciples from their barnstorming ministry is the occasion for Jesus to draw aside with them, doubtless to hear reports of their activities and lead them in seeking spiritual refreshment. When the crowds follow them, Jesus continues to preach the Kingdom to them and to heal their infirmities. Then, in the "lonely place," Jesus feeds all of them in a meal obviously symbolic of the Eucharist or Communion. The quality of this messianic banquet is hinted in the fact that "all ate and were satisfied," and that afterwards there were twelve baskets of fragments remaining. The early church could not fail to see the significance of this narrative: Jesus always feeds his people amply in the wilderness places of life!

It is interesting to note that the disciples, who have had such a responsible role in preaching and healing during the recent missionary thrust, now have liturgical responsibilities for the meal. Jesus tells them to give the people something to eat, and orders them to arrange the crowd in orderly groups of "about fifty each." And, finally, it is the disciples who set the food before the people. They are the agents of Christ at the table as well as in the pulpit or by the sickbed.

Lord, the church itself is one of your greatest miracles—the long line of preachers, teachers, healers, pastors, and others who do your will in ministering to the peoples of the world; and the many lay persons who witness and pray and support the work in every way. Thank you for the meal that sustains us all in every place and condition, and for the presence of Christ at the table. Amen.

Week 5: Wednesday

Luke 9:18–36 A New Stage of Understanding

Jesus had been teaching his disciples for many months now, and had even sent them out on their own to preach and heal. It was time to raise their understanding of his mission to a new level. He himself had doubtless begun to see the future more clearly since John's violent death at the hands of Herod.

The conversation began on the reports the disciples brought back from their missionary journeys. Who were the people saying that Jesus was? Accustomed to thinking of the future in terms of the past, they had said that he must surely be John or Elijah or another prophet already dead.

Next, Jesus pressed them to see what their own thinking had become. Peter spoke for the group. They had come to the conclusion that he must be "the Christ of God." Matthew 16:17–19 says that Jesus congratulated Peter on this answer, but Luke merely says that he warned them not to use this title openly, lest it provoke an official reaction before he was ready.

Then, building on what the disciples understood thus far, Jesus proceeded to teach them three things about the near future: (1)

he must suffer and die after being rejected by the religious leadership of Israel; (2) they too must suffer, some of them possibly to the point of death; (3) God would give them victory, symbolized in the resurrection of Jesus himself. Because of these three facts, they must not hesitate to deny themselves and follow him.

There can be little doubt that Luke used the next story about the transfiguration as an illustration to the disciples of what Jesus' resurrection would be like. Alone with him in prayer, they beheld him in strangely altered form. His face was different and his clothing became dazzlingly radiant, as in biblical descriptions of angels. Moreover, he was conversing with Moses and Elijah, the two most popular figures of the Old Testament. They were discussing Jesus' "departure"—actually, in the Greek, his *exodus.* As Moses had led the Israelites out of Egypt to form a new nation, Jesus was about to lead his followers into a new Kingdom. Clearly, God was giving the disciples a picture of the transcendent Christ to verify Jesus' prediction that he would be raised up shortly after being slain.

God himself appeared to the disciples in the form of a cloud, and they heard him speak, saying, "This is my Son, my Chosen; listen to him!" Then the cloud was gone, and so were Moses and Elijah. It was a rare mystical experience, and it would later help them to perceive what was happening after the crucifixion.

Lord, I wonder how many experiences like this I miss because I do not spend my nights and days in prayer as the disciples did. Teach me to apply myself to acts of devotion, that the mysteries of the faith may become more palpable in my own life. Through him who has shown us the way. Amen.

Luke 9:37–50 A Tinge of Disappointment

The new level of understanding among some of the disciples appears to have been unmatched among others. When Jesus, James, John, and Peter came down from their mountainside experience, a man came to Jesus who had been feeling great frustration with the other disciples. They had been unable to heal his only son of the epileptic convulsions that frequently seized him.

Jesus cured the boy, but not before erupting angrily at the failure of the disciples to trust completely enough in the Kingdom's presence to do the work themselves. His anxiety is clearly the product of the urgency he now felt. The time was short, and they must be able to carry on when he was gone.

How little they understood is emphasized by the argument that soon broke out among them about which of them was the greatest. Jesus had only recently spoken of his own suffering role; now they were contending about their honor and glory. Jesus gave them an object lesson they would never forget. Setting a little child beside him—was it the one he had just cured of epilepsy?—he told them that there was no such traditional status in the Kingdom. Anyone who in his name was kind to a child was great in the eyes of God. God did not reckon worth as the rulers of society did.

The phrase "in my name" evidently spurred John to comment that they had seen a stranger using Jesus' name to perform exorcisms, and that they had forbade this unauthorized use of the Master's name. But Jesus was not concerned about this individual—it was the religious leaders who would never have used his name that really troubled him. His appraisal of the situation was more far-sighted than that of his disciples.

Lord, I too am prone to worry about my greatness. Since I was a child, I have needed recognition and praise. Now I call it "stroking." Forgive me for this smallness, Lord, and lead me into deeper faith and commitment, that my dearest joy may be in serving your little ones, not in receiving the admiration of others. Through Jesus, who died humbly at the hands of those who lived proudly. Amen.

Luke 9:51–10:24 The Fall of Satan

At this point, Luke pictures Jesus as turning toward Jerusalem and the final encounter with the religious leaders there. But the trip is anything but direct, and really seems to be a kind of suspense vehicle within which Luke can impart many of Jesus' teachings.

The trip from Galilee to Jerusalem normally took travelers through Samaria. The Samaritans and Jews had long been at odds, one side claiming that the holy center of life was in Mt. Gerizim and the other that it was in Jerusalem. Jesus' intention of climaxing his ministry in Jerusalem therefore provoked the hostilities of the Samaritans in one village, and this in turn stirred the wrath of James and John. As Elijah had called down fire from heaven (2 Kings 1:9–16), they wanted to do so now, proving the authenticity of their mission for God. But Jesus had rejected such temptations of power early in his ministry (Luke 4:1–13), and now rebuked the disciples for entertaining such a notion.

The commitment to the Kingdom required of followers is revealed in Luke 9:57–62. What was happening was of such intense consequence that there was no room for self-consideration or even for the traditional proprieties of life. The nearest analogy would be that of a military call-up; in a moment of national crisis, there is no time for personal errands.

The urgency of this particular phase of Jesus' mission is also shown in the appointment of the "seventy others"—to distinguish them from the disciples and perhaps from the messengers in Luke 9:51–52. Luke alone records this appointment of the seventy. It is possible that he saw in the symbolism of the number, which according to rabbinic reckoning was the number of the Gentile nations, a forecast of the spread of the gospel into all the world, as he later recorded in the Book of Acts.

The instructions to the seventy were similar to those given the disciples in Luke 9:1–6—they were to go out like persons on an urgent mission, making no advance preparations for their work and carrying nothing that would encumber them as they journeyed. They were not to trouble themselves about orthodox matters of eating and drinking, but to take whatever was offered them, regardless of the proprieties (10:8). Their message was simple: "The Kingdom is near you." This would alert the truly devoted persons but would probably infuriate others. Against the latter, the disciples were to shake the dust off their feet. Their villages would fare poorly when the day of the Lord came in all its terror.

The seventy returned from their mission in great joy—one of Luke's dominant themes—reporting that even the demons had been powerless before them. Jesus' response was to tell them of a vision he had had, of Satan plunging from heaven. Hebrew thought had always pictured Satan as located in heaven, where he acted as a kind of prosecuting lawyer against the godly (cf. Job 1 and Zech. 3:1–5). Jesus in this vision foresaw Satan's complete defeat and expulsion from heaven, so that he could no longer trouble the sons and daughters of men. A great victory was in the offing. This was, and still is, the good news of the Kingdom.

"You have been allowed to participate in unusual power," said Jesus. "But don't rejoice in this. Rejoice rather that your names are written in heaven—that God has foreordained that you would be part of the community he is saving!"

Exultant in the Spirit, Jesus prayed and gave thanks that God had given his Kingdom to simple people like these messengers, and not to the religious masters of the land. They were so fresh, so jubilant, so willing to accept at face value what God was doing! Their lives were not complicated by vain philosophies and the vanities of learning.

In the same mood, he reflected that only God could choose the one who would be his Son. The old men of Israel, with all their knowledge, could not do it. Only God. And, now that God had chosen Jesus, only Jesus truly knew and understood the Father as a Son would—only Jesus and those to whom he imparted the knowledge.

Turning to the disciples, who had seen so much with him, he spoke again of the joy of the Kingdom. "Blessed are the eyes which see what you see!" How many prophets and kings of Israel had wanted to see it, and could not. Old Simeon in the temple had seen it (Luke 2:25–32), and now they were seeing it. There would never be anything in the history of the world more wonderful to see!

Lord, when I shut my eyes and concentrate, I can see it too. The lion lying down with the lamb. The armaments of the world beaten into plowshares. The hungry fed. The poor walking through the city like rulers. The sun shining pleasantly on little children of all races at play together. The strong with their arms around the weak. Satan has fallen, Lord, and is falling, and will one day fall for good. The Kingdom is near us. Let it convert me to the very depths of my being, and let me witness to its presence. Through him you have chosen as Son. Amen.

Week 5: Saturday

Luke 10:25–37 The Real Way to Life

This magnificent story has been told and retold around the world, and has doubtless, in its artless simplicity, converted the attitudes of millions of people about what obeying the Law of God really means.

The lawyer—a scribe—probably asked his question about eternal life more to test Jesus than to get a true answer. He got far more than he bargained for. In Mark's Gospel (12:28–32), it is Jesus himself who summarizes the Law by combining two Old Testament passages (Deut. 6:5 and Lev. 19:18). But Luke recognized this as a combination already made by the rabbis of the time, so that the questioner would have his own ready answer to the question he raised. The dramatic difference between Jesus and the lawyer really lay not between the laws they knew but in how they applied them.

When the lawyer had gotten no more from Jesus than to have his question turned on him, he began to niggle, raising a question this time about his own quotation. "Who is my neighbor?" Again, Jesus wanted to make him answer his own question, but not before posing it in such a manner that he could not escape seeing the inner meaning of the Law.

The dramatis personae of the parable are interesting: a priest and a Levite, both central members of the religious elite of Israel, and a Samaritan, one of the people whom Jews regarded with hostility and prejudice. Luke may have located the story here because of the unfavorable mention of Samaritans a few verses earlier, in Luke 9:51–56. He may also have had in mind the movement of the gospel outward from Judea to Samaria and "the end of the earth" (Acts 1:8).

The man who was beaten was heading away from Jerusalem, toward Jericho. The fact that the priest and Levite both "passed by on the other side" indicates that they were going in the opposite direction, toward Jerusalem, possibly to serve their turns in the temple. As the poor victim was half-dead, there was no way they could be certain without touching him that he had not already died, and to do that would have defiled them according to ceremonial law. They obeyed the Law but missed the whole point of it.

The unorthodox Samaritan, on the other hand, really fulfilled the Law while not even being concerned to obey it. He "had compassion" on the poor man, bound up his wounds, and walked to the nearest inn while the beaten man rode on his beast. There he covered all the man's expenses until he was well enough to travel home. The lawyer could not but admit that the Samaritan was the real neighbor to the man, not the priest and Levite.

When we think about it, we realize that Jesus' entire ministry is summarized in the action of the Samaritan. From the very outset, he chose to have compassion on the poor and oppressed rather than to conform to the hundreds of rules and regulations governing the lives of the scribes and Pharisees.

Lord, I have always admired Samaritans—people who live on the edge of respectable society, yet respond magnanimously to the needs of others. Help me to live more generously and spontaneously myself, that I may better understand the heart of Jesus. In his name. Amen.

WEEK 6

Week 6: Sunday

Luke 10:38–42 The Most Important Thing

The village Jesus is here reported to have entered is doubtless Bethany, which we know from John 11:1 to have been the home of Mary, Martha and Lazarus. In terms of Luke's travel narrative it is highly unlikely that Jesus would have been in Bethany at this point, as it lay barely outside Jerusalem. What Luke has obviously done, then, is to place the story here, omitting the name of Bethany, because he sees a direct relationship between this little narrative and the parable of the Samaritan that has immediately preceded it. This helps us to identify more precisely Luke's own interpretation of the story.

In a way, the story is a gloss or comment on the parable of the Samaritan. Martha, who is anxious to serve Jesus properly, is really a Christian version of the priest and Levite in the parable. That is, she is deeply concerned to fulfill the law of proprieties. Mary, on the other hand, has the soul of the Samaritan. She is more concerned to respond in love than to conform to the rules or duties of the household.

It is surely unfair to brand the Marthas of the world unfavorably because of this passage—in her way, Martha was trying as hard as Mary was to be a compassionate host. Our homes, churches, and other institutions would soon be in pitiable shape if it were not for the selfless service of the caretaking persons.

Jesus' point—and Luke's—was more specific than that; namely, that the *first* obligation of a person is to give responsive love or compassion. When following the rules is put first, the most needful part—the love—is often missed or omitted.

We should be actively involved in society for God—but not before we have taken time to pray and worship. We should work zealously for the church—but not put it before the people who lie outside the membership of the church. We should strive to improve human conditions for the poor, the weak, and the sick—but not without first truly caring for them as persons.

Lord, it is so much easier to feel self-righteous when I am Martha than when I am Mary. When I wait before you in a mood of worship, or when I respond in generous sympathy to the personality of another, I don't even think to value my action. Then I experience true joy. Help me to be more like Mary, without forgetting the value of Martha. Amen.

Week 6: Monday

Luke 11:1–13 The Spirit of Prayer

It is helpful, if we wish to know how Luke felt about this material he was recording on prayer, to remember how prayer is treated throughout the Book of Acts. Never in Acts does any Christian pray for anything for himself. Almost invariably, prayer is for the Kingdom and other persons. It is for the sick, the imprisoned, the unconverted. If the Christian does appear to be at all at the center of his or her praying, it is only to know the will of God for a life of service and self-emptying.

Seen in this light, the present passage is quickly understood to center on the Kingdom. "Thy kingdom come" is the central petition of the model prayer Jesus gives the disciples. All the other phrases derive from this one. As Kingdom people, we ask little for ourselves—only daily bread, not expensive feasts and clothes and property. The emphasis on *daily* bread reminds us of God's provision of manna to the Israelites during their wilderness years; like them, we are a pilgrim people. Our other concerns are to be compassionate and forgiving, as befits those who in the Kingdom are forgiven and accepted, and not to be tested so severely that we abandon the faith. Temptation is not here to be regarded in terms of the nettling little sins of everyday existence, such as the desire for foods we shouldn't eat, the wish for money, or sexual fantasies. It has to do with temptation as Jesus experienced it in the wilderness (Luke 4:1–13), which, if we yield to it, causes us to fall away from our vision of the Kingdom.

Luke's version of the model prayer is considerably briefer than the one in Matthew 6:9–13, and scholars are confident that it is the more original of the two. Matthew's version has merely added liturgical phrases that do not significantly alter the meaning.

Aside from the rhythm of "Our Father who art in heaven," Luke's simpler "Father, hallowed be thy name" is surely preferable as being more in keeping with Jesus' ways and teachings. Professor G. B. Caird says in his commentary: "Any Jew could have prayed, 'Our Father, who art in heaven . . . ,' using the formal and exclusively religious *Abinu*. But when Jesus prayed, he used the word *Abba* with which a child addressed his human father. He transformed the Fatherhood of God from a theological doctrine into an intense and intimate experience; and he taught his disciples to pray with the same family intimacy."

After giving the disciples a form of prayer based on the intimacy between children and their father, Jesus proceeded to speak of the Father's willingness to hear their prayers and respond to them. He will surely be as attentive as a friend who hears us knocking for help in the night, or as earthly fathers who try to give their children the foods they ask for.

Verses 8–10 clearly recommend the importance of praying for our needs, even though God already knows what we require, just as children make requests of their earthly fathers. But verse 13 is equally clear that the gift which Christians are to seek in their praying is the Holy Spirit (Matt. 7:11 reads "good things").

The overall emphasis of the passage, then, is a spiritual one, in keeping with the coming of the Kingdom and the submission of the one praying to the will of the Father. This is borne out again and again in the Book of Acts.

Lord, too much of my praying has not been of a spiritual nature. I have often sought little gifts that would make life more attractive for me, ignoring the fact that the one thing that can change all my life for the better is to submit myself to you and your Kingdom. Then I would know joy indeed, even as the disciples did. Teach me to pray as they prayed, yielding myself to your Holy Spirit. Through Jesus, who was obedient unto death. Amen.

Week 6: Tuesday

Luke 11:14–36 The Sign of Jonah

If we are inclined today to despair over the shallowness of popular Christianity, we need only read this passage to know that things have not changed greatly since Jesus' own time.

First, there were people who doubted the miracles he was performing. Some even attributed his miraculous cures to Beelzebub, "the prince of demons." Jesus dealt forcefully with these persons. Would Satan work against himself, he asked, by casting out his own agents? The people should ask their own magicians and sorcerers, he said; they would tell them how difficult it was to perform true exorcisms! What the people should see was that "the finger of God" (Exod. 8:19) was at work in their midst—then they would realize how near the Kingdom was.

Satan, said Jesus, was like a strong man guarding his citadel. But Jesus had entered the fortress and was plundering the strong man's treasures. Surely the people could see that if they only looked.

Verses 24–26 appear to be a warning to those who had been cleansed of demons. They were like houses which required occupancy. Unless they were filled with the Spirit of God after their exorcisms, they were in danger of being reinvaded, not by one demon, but this time by seven! The same is surely true of people today. The initial excitement of religious attachment is not enough to maintain them—they must be filled with God's Spirit or end in darkness and despair worse than they knew in the beginning.

As Jesus was talking, a woman in the crowd called out an extravagant word of praise roughly equivalent to "Your mother must really be proud of you." But Jesus turned off this word as a bit of mere sentimentality. What is important, he said, is to hear and keep God's word.

Reflecting on those who kept asking for some kind of uncontestable "sign from heaven" (v. 16), Jesus then said that no sign would be given such an evil generation except the sign of Jonah the preacher. Jonah had gone to wicked Nineveh and preached the need for repentance, and Nineveh had repented in sackcloth and ashes. Here was Jesus in a similar role, preaching the coming of the Kingdom. That should be enough, if the people of his day were truly spiritual. But as they were not, the people of Nineveh and the queen of the South would rise in the day of judgment and accuse the Israelites, for they had repented without special signs.

Verses 33–36 are a collection of sayings on the theme of light. Israel had been called to be a light to the nations, but had covered the light she had. The eye, when it is good, causes the whole body to respond to the light; but, when it is bad, it results in the body's being swathed in darkness. The last two verses, which are difficult for all commentators, seem to recommend the results of really being able to see—which is the problem with most of the people in the crowd; they cannot see.

Lord, preserve me from being either too negative or too sentimental about religious faith. Let me watch and listen attentively, that I may discern your Spirit's presence in my life. And grant that I may respond by living in the way of the Kingdom. Through him who showed us the way. Amen.

Week 6: Wednesday

Luke 11:37–12:12 Warnings against Hypocrisy

Here are several sayings of Jesus grouped around the general theme of hypocrisy and truth.

First are a number of scathing remarks about Pharisees and scribes, roughly paralleling those found in Matthew 23. It is unlikely that Jesus ever delivered one long tirade against the Pharisees and scribes, as this arrangement suggests; probably the sayings were grouped thus after having been spoken on several different occasions.

The primary thrust of all the rebukes or "woes" is that the highly orthodox Jews paid much attention to inconsequential matters of the Law while neglecting the important matters—a charge in keeping with other teachings of Jesus, such as the parable of the good Samaritan (Luke 10:25–37), which, we recall, was spoken to a scribe.

They fastidiously scoured the outside of the cup, while completely neglecting the inside, which was more important. They went beyond the expectations of the Law, which said that general agricultural products were to be tithed, and paid a tenth even on their tiny herb gardens which were not worth bothering about; yet they completely ignored the question of justice for the poor and the matter of loving God. They were like unmarked graves, onto which unwary persons might stumble, defiling themselves by coming in contact with the dead. They constructed enormous burdens for the common people to bear, and then refused to help them at all. Having held the key to salvation, they themselves refused to enter the door and, moreover, blocked the way so that others could not go in.

Clearly, they were obstructing the work of the Holy Spirit and would not be forgiven for this (Luke 12:10).

The disciples were warned to beware of the same kind of hypocrisy in their own lives. They would be tempted, when brought before the courts and tribunals, to lie and put on falsehoods in order to save themselves. But Jesus warned them not to join the hypocrites in this manner; they should not fear those who had only the power to hurt their bodies, but the One who had power to punish them by cutting himself off from them forever. The God who cared even for the cheap, insignificant little sparrows could certainly be trusted to care about what happened to them when they suffered for the faith. He would instruct them through his Holy Spirit how to respond in times of crisis when they were hailed before officials of the government.

Lord, the love of your Kingdom converts our natures, so that we no longer higgle over little things that are of small consequence in the lives and affairs of people, but devote our energies to the larger issues, such as feeding the hungry, clothing and sheltering the poor, and healing the sick and tormented of heart. Help me to become an ambassador of your joy, disdaining the cost to myself. Through Jesus, in whom your light shines purely. Amen.

Week 6: Thursday

Luke 12:13–34 A Warning in a Parable

Diogenes is said to have given away all of his possessions except a shard of pottery which he used for drinking. Then he saw a small boy cupping his hands to drink from a stream, and threw away the shard.

Wise people have always realized that possessions can encumber a life until it is barely fit for living. Jesus constantly warned the disciples of the tendency in all of us to enslave ourselves to what we have.

The man who came to him asking for a judgment did so because Mosaic Law was always being interpreted by rabbis. But Jesus refused to accept the problem as a mere civil problem that could be solved by a judge's decision. Instead, he threw the burden back on the man himself, pointing out the importance of caring less about money and property.

The parable of the rich man is still a striking vehicle of truth for people who are careful about providing fiscally for their futures yet absurdly heedless of their spiritual conditions. One wonders what would become of the capitalist way of life and an economy that depends on Detroit and Madison Avenue if many persons took the story as seriously as it deserves.

Considering Jesus' teachings to the disciples about trusting God to provide their daily needs—the model is still that of the Israelites being fed each day in the wilderness—it is no wonder that Luke later pictures the early church as a fellowship of voluntary poverty, sharing from a common treasury. It raises an unavoidable question about our stewardship in the church today. Some churches hold more property than many business corporations in their cities, and have their most serious congregational squabbles over the maintenance of buildings. It is hard to believe that they have really considered the ravens or the lilies.

Lord, there is an incipient greed in me that is hard to kill. I have always felt insecure in the world, and thus want money and property as a hedge against poverty and distress. I am often the very rich man of whom Jesus spoke. Teach me so to apply my heart and thoughts to your Kingdom that I shall cease to be afraid—indeed, that I shall want nothing but the simple everyday things with which you have already supplied us so amply. Through Jesus, who left a great spiritual legacy but no property at all. Amen.

Luke 12:35–48 Living for the Master

The picture here is of genuine enthusiasm in the Master's service. "Girding the loins" was a way of getting ready for action—the long robes of the time were tucked up into the girdle or belt so they would not impede hard work or fast movement. Having the lamps burning also implied readiness, for the wicks must be trimmed and the lamps filled with oil. The disciples were to be like eager servants waiting up in the night for the master's return from a wedding feast. On returning and finding them so devoted, he would be so happy that he would reverse the normal roles, tuck his own robes into his girdle, and serve *them* at the table.

Possibly Luke knew the tradition on which John 13:2–10 is based, about Jesus' taking a towel and serving his disciples. But the symbolism of the feast and waiting is not completely clear. Was Jesus going away for the feast and then returning to the disciples? Is this a picture of the Parousia, or Second Coming? Peter's question in verse 41 is well put, but the answer seems enigmatic. In a way, the lessons apply to both the disciples and the crowds, including the scribes and Pharisees. Doubtless, too, the church saw meaning in them for itself.

It seems probable that Jesus saw the signs of a dark time coming for Israel, and therefore expected an imminent arrival for the great day of the Lord. In the face of this, he warned his followers to be faithfully obeying God's will at all times, so that no sudden cataclysm would take them unawares and result in spiritual disaster. As the special recipients of Christ's teachings, they would be held more accountable than others.

Lord, I tremble to think how accountable I am. You have given me so many insights into the nature of your Kingdom and your desire for my life. Yet I am daily out of harmony with those insights. Help me to be motivated in new ways to fulfill your expectancies for me, that I may rejoice in the coming of my Servant-Master. In his name I pray. Amen.

Week 6: Saturday

Luke 12:49–13:9 A Fire in the Earth

It is sometimes argued that Jesus and John the Baptist saw the coming of the Kingdom differently; but here is proof that Jesus, like John before him, viewed it as an occasion of extreme stress and suffering for many.

The "baptism" he said he must be baptized with was his death (cf. Mark 10:38). Apparently he saw that as only the beginning of the apocalyptic horror. His very dying would divide households and nations. It was a true word. We know that throughout history, especially in pagan countries, sons' or daughters' becoming Christians has led to expulsion from their families. There are nations throughout Africa and Asia where this still occurs. It is true, moreover, even in our own country, that radical devotion to Christ produces dissension in family groups—most of us prefer to take our faith in moderation!

The signs of the coming of this difficult time, Jesus told the crowds, were all around them. They considered themselves good weather prophets—a small cloud drifting in from the Mediterranean was enough to cause them to forecast rain. They should be more sensitive to the changing of the times, and should be actively trying to appease God, as one would try to appease a person suing him, even on the way to the magistrate's house!

Some people in the crowd raised a question about some Galileans whom Pilate had had killed in Jerusalem—were they terrible sinners, that this happened to them? People are always ready to speculate about retributive justice for those who have suffered. There may also have been some slur implied in referring to the unfortunate Galileans, as Judeans usually regarded them as inferior. "No," replied Jesus; and he shot back with an illustration of tragedy involving Judeans themselves, when a tower collapsed, killing a dozen and a half of them. They were no worse than other Jerusalemites, said Jesus. Pointing to cases like this was useless. What he meant, said Jesus, was that they were *all* in for terrible times unless they repented. God's action was going to destroy an entire nation.

The parable of the fig tree was exactly to the point. The fig tree was often regarded as a symbol of Israel—as her fig trees prospered, she was thought to prosper. Here the tree was unproductive. It took nourishment from the soil of the vineyard without repaying its owner with fruit—precisely as all the prophets had seen Israel doing. The owner instructed his foreman to destroy the tree, but the foreman begged a year's extension for it. He would dig around it, adding manure, to see if that would not cause the tree to produce fruit; if it did not, then it would be cut down and burned for fuel. The ministries of John and Jesus were probably the last chance Israel would have—if they could not turn the people to the way of the Kingdom, then the nation was finished.

Lord, it is so easy for me to be judgmental about Israel and to say the people got exactly what they deserved. What is not easy is to see how true Jesus' words are for me in my moral and spiritual life as well—that I become as complacent and useless as the ancient Jews were. Help me to return to true worship in my life, and to feed others with the fruits of my devotion, lest I too be destroyed by fire. Through him who was baptized in the flames. Amen.

WEEK 7

Week 7: Sunday

Luke 13:10–21 The Sabbath and the Kingdom

How often have we seen people like this poor deformed woman in the crowd and wished we could do something for them! We can imagine their wretchedness, their inconvenience, their pain and discomfort, and our compassion has rushed out to them.

This is how it was when Jesus saw the woman who could not straighten up. He was teaching in the synagogue, not healing. But when he saw her, he instinctively called out to her and healed her. It was an impulsive act of love.

The behavior of the synagogue leader may also have been instinctive. He was accustomed to rules and regulations, and rules and regulations dictated that no work was to be done on the sabbath. This meant the work of doctors as well as the work of farmers, builders, and housewives. Note that his words were directed not to Jesus himself—perhaps he was afraid of this man of power—but to the people. "Not today!" he said. "Not today! There are six days of the week when work may be done. Come back on one of them." He appears to have been a typical slave to routine and bureaucracy.

Jesus knew that the leader spoke thus because of all the others who would complain if the sabbath rules were not kept. Therefore he addressed him in the plural, denouncing the leaders, as he often spoke of the scribes and Pharisees, as hypocrites. "You take care of your animals on the sabbath," he said in effect. "Isn't this poor woman worth more than they are? She is a daughter of Abraham and has been afflicted this way for years. Your animals have been restricted and gone without water a mere twelve hours or so. Isn't it inconsistent to bend the rules for them and not for this woman?"

At this, the people rejoiced—one of Luke's favorite verbs—and his recalling that rejoicing led him to report Jesus' sayings about the Kingdom. Both sayings are about the enormous growth of the Kingdom. It is like the great tree that springs from the tiny mustard seed, making room for the birds of many nations to rest on its branches; and it is like the small lump of leaven in a bowl of batter, that makes the dough swell and regenerate until it is several times its original size. This was truly a cause for joy!

Lord, I have to sympathize with the poor synagogue leader. He was trying to do his job. How our jobs become our masters and make us do things it would not be in our natures to do if we weren't ruled by them! Help me, I pray, to keep my job in perspective, that I may not allow it to diminish my freedom as a person or dehumanize me in my relationship to your world. Through Jesus, who reshaped the roles he had to play and left them resilient and human. Amen.

Week 7: Monday

Luke 13:22–35 The Master and His House

The person who asked Jesus the question in verse 23 was merely being curious. Speculating about when the end would be and how many would be saved had long been the pastime of the idle and pseudoreligious. But Jesus characteristically formed his answer in such a way as to involve the questioner in a life-or-death situation. Brushing aside the question of "how many?" he pointed to the importance of entering the Kingdom when one has the opportunity. Otherwise the person may find himself or herself on the outside and unable to get in through a superficial acquaintance with the Master.

The picture Jesus gave was one of eternal disappointment—of looking in and seeing the great patriarchs of Israel sitting at the heavenly banquet not with them but with outsiders, people from all the other nations. Jesus had already demonstrated this in his ministry by dining with prostitutes and tax collectors—sinners before the Law. But in the Kingdom even the hated Gentiles would go in before the unbelieving Israelites.

It was appropriate that some Pharisees should come "at that very hour" to warn him of Herod's enmity, for such a picture of the Kingdom was the very thing that would provoke the violence of the crucifixion. But Jesus' response was cool and self-governed; he would not be hurried to the climax of his ministry in Jerusalem. When he was ready, he would go, but not before. No earthly sovereign was going to diminish the sovereign authority of the One who was Lord in the Kingdom!

Verses 34–35 are a word of lamentation about the failure of Israel to respond to the good news of the Kingdom. The gathering of Jerusalem's children from the four corners of the world had been a constant dream of Hebrew prophecy (see Isa. 60:4 and Zech. 10:6–10). But the children would not come when he preached the vision of the Kingdom to them. Therefore their nation and temple would lie desolate and forsaken, like ruins caressed by the winds of time.

The last sentence of the passage may be a promise that Jesus would not show up in Jerusalem until the Passover, when the people would shout "Hosanna!" at his entry (Luke 19:37–38). Or it may be a more apocalyptic saying, meaning that the people would not recognize him for who he truly was until the final triumph of the Kingdom. Then they would be like the unfortunate Jews in verses 26–30, who reminded the Master of the house that they had eaten and drunk in his presence and had even heard him teaching in their streets, but had not entered his house in time for the feast.

Lord, these apocalyptic pictures and sayings are frightening to me. They raise deep-seated anxieties about separation and abandonment. They speak of the severity that is the other side of your goodness, and the anguish that is the other side of the joy in your Kingdom. I pray that they will keep alive in me a genuine feeling for the urgency of preaching the gospel to everyone who has not yet heard with inward truth, and for doing *the gospel in my own life.* Amen.

Week 7: Tuesday

Luke 14:1–24 Some Table Talk

"They were watching him." How carefully Jesus was being scrutinized by the scribes and Pharisees, who hoped to entrap him and dispose of him. We could almost conclude that the invitation to dine with this prominent Pharisee was no more than a convenient arrangement to have Jesus where they could observe his every movement.

The man with dropsy was there, either as a guest or as an unbidden onlooker, like the woman who anointed Jesus' feet in Luke 7:36–50. What would the man of great compassion do? He put the burden on the Pharisees—what did they say? They were silent. If they said no, it was not permitted to heal on the sabbath, they would appear inhumane. If they said yes, it was all right, they would be contradicting their laws. So Jesus healed the man and once more (as in Luke 13:11–17) appealed to the humanitarian instincts in them of putting persons ahead of animals.

The next portion of the passage indicates that Jesus was watching his adversaries as closely as they were watching him. What he saw was their jealousy about the seating arrangements—each was anxious to have a place above the others. Always take the low place, Jesus advised them; it is better to be called up than put down.

Jesus also noticed that the host had carefully invited his best friends, kinfolk, and most prominent acquaintances to the meal. That is a mistake, he cautioned; one ought rather to invite the poor, the maimed, the blind, the outcast, who cannot possibly repay the favor. Then God will repay at the time of the resurrection. The Pharisee had been socially sagacious but had completely missed the way of the Kingdom.

It is possible that the early church read in these last verses a lesson to itself, not to strive to have only the finest citizens at the Lord's table; for the Lord himself had announced that the joy of the gospel is for the poor, the blind, and the oppressed (Luke 4:14–30).

And this is precisely the point of the parable in verses 16–24. The parable is given in response to the pious remark of one of the dinner guests. (We have seen a similar stylistic device in Luke 11:27–28, where Jesus reacted to a sentimental saying by a woman in the crowd.) Doubtless the man supposed himself to be included in the heavenly banquet. But Jesus used the occasion to point out again, as he did consistently in all his ministry, that everyone would be surprised when he or she saw the guests at that banquet. They would be the very persons the good Jews were ignoring, while the religious leaders themselves would not taste a morsel!

Lord, the politics of the Kingdom and the politics of this world are often at odds with each other. Help me always to seek the way of the Kingdom in my affairs, that I may rejoice with those who will enjoy the heavenly feast with you. Through Jesus, who watches me as I watch him. Amen.

Luke 14:25–35 Facing the Hard Realities

Despite his continuous conflict with religious leaders wherever he went, Jesus was still extremely popular and had an immense following among the common folk. Yet he was bothered by their lack of comprehension. They did not seem to appreciate the danger of his mission, either to him or to themselves. Therefore he turned on them and attempted to make them face the truth. Discipleship would not be easy, he warned; in fact, it would demand every ounce of loyalty they could summon.

Hating one's father and mother did not mean to the Jewish mind precisely what it means to us. As G. B. Caird has put it, "The semitic mind is comfortable only with extremes—light and darkness, truth and falsehood, love and hate—primary colours with no half-shades of compromise in between. The semitic way of saying 'I prefer this to that' is 'I like this and hate that' (cf. Gen. 29:30–31, Deut. 21:15–17)." What Jesus said, thus, was that their families must take second place, not first; first was for the Kingdom. He himself, we recall, when his mother and brothers came to see him, said, "My mother and my brothers are those who hear the word of God and do it" (Luke 8:21).

Being a disciple, he told them in a daring metaphor, is like bearing your own cross—committing yourself to the gallows, to execution, to death among strangers.

Count the cost, he warned. Even a builder does that before erecting a tower. A king does it before engaging in war. Any reasonable person does it. Therefore disciples should do it too—they ought not to begin a discipleship they cannot complete.

To be a disciple but unable to follow Jesus through times of stress and danger is to lack the real quality of discipleship. It is like being salt that does not have the real power of salt. Such salt is worthless. It is salt in name only, and people throw it out and have done with it.

Lord, these are bracing words. They sting my conscience like nettles, like thousands of needles of fire. What kind of disciple am I? Could I follow to the death, or am I only a disciple of convenience? How selfishly I have heard the gospel. Forgive me, O suffering One, and help me to increase the measure of my devotion, lest I betray you in a moment of forgetfulness or an hour of pressure. Amen.

Week 7: Thursday

Luke 15:1–10 The Kingdom of Joy

Here we come to what is for many the heart of Luke's Gospel. No other Gospel writer has recorded all three of the beautiful parables of this chapter. (Matthew 18:12–14 gives the parable of the lost sheep.) More than any other stories, perhaps, they represent what God was working out through Jesus' ministry.

The setting recorded by Luke is not unlike the one in which Jesus was frequently pictured—teaching and healing the poor, the blind, and the outcast, with the scribes and Pharisees looking on to criticize. This time, as on other occasions, they were complaining about the unsanctified company Jesus kept. They themselves would never have had dealings with such people; they considered contact with them to be defiling and degrading. And Jesus was *eating* with such persons—engaging with them at what Orientals would consider a most intimate level!

It was to answer the criticisms of the religious Jews that Jesus told these rare stories—the parables of the lost sheep, the lost coin, and the lost boy. Each would have been readily understood by those who heard them.

The essential note in each story is the note of joy. The shepherd tracks his errant sheep out in the wilderness where it has wandered, and "lays it on his shoulders, rejoicing." When he comes back, he calls to his friends, saying, "Rejoice with me." Even so, says Jesus, "there will be more joy in heaven" over the sinner who repents. The woman loses a single coin, a silver drachma, worth slightly more than a day's wages in ancient Palestine. Probably it has fallen among the straws or rushes on her earthen floor and is difficult to find in her dark, almost windowless house. She lights a lamp, sifts through the straws, and even sweeps the house, in search of the coin. At last her eye falls on it. She calls her friends together, saying, "Rejoice with me." In the same manner, says Jesus, "there is joy before the angels of God" when a lost sinner is recovered.

The angel who announced the birth of Jesus to the shepherds on the hillside said that he brought them "good news of a great joy" which would come to all the people (Luke 2:10). When Jesus announced the design of his ministry in the synagogue in Nazareth (4:14–30), he identified it with the poor and broken and neglected of the world. Here, in these parables, Luke has drawn these themes together in a climactic fashion. The Kingdom of God is a Kingdom of joy!

Thank you, Lord, for the unmitigated joy of your Kingdom. How wonderful it is to be part of a Kingdom in which everyone has been brought in with rejoicing. Help me to ponder this today, and to realize what it means for my relations with others in the Kingdom. Through Jesus, who led the search for all of us. Amen.

Week 7: Friday

Luke 15:11–32 The Two Lost Sons

There is only one way to the Father, English theologian P. T. Forsyth once wrote—through the far country! Each of us, to appreciate the love and generosity of God, must at some point experience disillusionment with self and the world, come to the point of despair, and then return to the Father in penitence, only to discover that he has been waiting all along with open arms to welcome us.

That is the genius of this story—or part of it, for it is truly one of the most remarkable stories ever told, and certainly one of the best loved. It is rich in human insights—how often two brothers will be so different, one happy and adventurous, the other grudging and insecure. Most of us can readily see ourselves in one or the other. And the picture of God as a father—warm, tolerant, compassionate, forgiving, rejoicing—is surely one of the most compelling we have ever known. It is a perfect story—literary, economical in detail, universal in application, and full of human warmth and understanding.

We do not know why the younger son wanted to go away—perhaps his scrupulous elder brother was getting on his nerves. But he requested and got, according to an ancient tradition of property settlement, his share of the family estate. Off he went to the far country, where he lived like a prince until his money ran out and the country entered a period of famine. At last, in sheer desperation, he found himself in the utterly degrading position of caring for a Gentile master's pigs. Staring at the pods of the carob tree, a kind of nutrient bean fed to cattle and swine, he thought how hungry he was and what good food there was at his father's house, even for the hired servants.

Composing a contrite speech, he arose and returned home. His father, apparently watching the road with a parent's wistful gaze, saw him at a distance, ran out, and embraced and kissed him, despite his obviously broken condition. The boy tried to recite his speech, but was interrupted by the father, who gave bristling commands to the servants to come and care for his son. "The fatted calf" which was ordered slain was a specially grown calf reserved for the most honored guests in the home. It was time to rejoice and celebrate!

That was a story in itself. But Jesus' point in telling it was not served by that episode alone. He wanted the scribes and Pharisees to see themselves in the other episode, when the self-righteous elder brother discovered the party his father was giving for the son who had returned. There was no compassion or joy at all in the elder brother—only a feeling of resentment that this upstart boy, who had earned no place in the home, had come back and was being treated so royally. Perhaps the elder brother would not have minded if the father had taken the boy at his own bargain and hired him as a menial; but to restore him to full sonship and give a feast in his honor was an outrageous affront to his sense of justice. He would have no part of it but complained that *he* had never had such special treatment though he had lived soberly and responsibly these many years.

The point is, the father had the right to decide as he wished in the matter. Near-Eastern fathers were supreme in their households. And he had welcomed his son back. It was too bad the elder son was such a selfish calculating type and could not enter the merriment; he was cutting off his nose, as the phrase goes, to spite his own face. It would have been more fitting, from a human, compassionate standpoint, if he could have joined in the rejoicing with his father and the servants. After all, it was as if a dead man had come back to life again! In the end, the son who had stayed home proved to be more lost to the father's heart than the one who had wandered off.

Lord, there is a streak of the elder brother in me. I too watch what others are receiving, and measure their good fortune by my own. I am grudging when they come off better than I, when I should rejoice for them and enjoy their parties. Help me to feel your presence so strongly in my daily life that I realize there is nothing richer to be had. Then I can truly find joy in everyone's success. Through Jesus, whose stories contain the most remarkable insights. Amen.

Week 7: Saturday

Luke 16:1–13 The Clever Steward

This parable of the steward seems out of place following the three stories of chapter 15. Contextually, it may seem to follow more appropriately after chapter 14, with its warnings about the radical demands on those who would enter the Kingdom. This passage too is directed toward the disciples, though we learn in verse 14 that the Pharisees were listening in.

The point of the parable is the shrewdness with which ordinary business persons act when confronted with a crisis situation, and an exhortation to the disciples to act similarly in the face of their nation's spiritual crisis.

The steward was probably a middle manager who oversaw his employer's tenant farms. When word of his improper handling of affairs reached the employer, the employer gave him notice of dismissal. Quickly taking stock of himself at his present stage of life, the steward decided he was too old to work in the fields and too proud to beg in the streets. So he decided to do something to cushion his fall. Before his employment fully expired, he went to his employer's tenants. The rent on one tenant's property had been fixed at a hundred measures of olive oil, part of which probably went to the steward himself. Using his authority to fix rents, the steward made a good friend of the man by reducing the rent by half. Going to another tenant, he followed the same tactic. Probably there were still others not mentioned for the sake of the parable's economy. The steward was cleverly making friends who would take him in when his employment terminated.

Some commentators believe the master of verse 8 to be Jesus himself, speaking well of the steward. This seems unlikely, as we have no other parable in which the Gospel writer switches to third-person description in this manner to have Jesus comment on his story. It is more likely, given the second half of the verse, that the master here is the same one referred to in verses 3 and 5, namely, the steward's employer. As a businessman, he might have regretted the steward's lack of trustworthiness, yet he could not but admire his ingenuity and praise him for it. The second half of the verse, then, is Jesus' comment: these businessmen are often wiser than the followers of God!

It is possible that the original parable ended here, with verse 8, and that the additional sayings were gathered to it because Luke or some earlier author saw a connection between them and the parable. The phrase "unrighteous mammon" was often used by rabbis to denote money that was legally obtained but not spiritually approved. Interest money or usury often fell under this category. The Law permitted people to take interest on money or property loaned to the poor, even though it was understood that God might not really approve such unmerciful behavior. Verse 9 draws the conclusion from the parable that, like the steward, we should take every opportunity to create friendships with our money or profits, thus earning an eternal merit. Verses 10–12 then suggest that if we do not behave in this manner with the world's goods, God can surely not entrust to us the greater spiritual riches of his Kingdom. We should remember that it is Luke, in Acts 2:44–45, who records that the early Christians sold all their possessions and held what little wealth they had in common, and then, in Acts 5:1–11, tells the story of Ananias and Sapphira, who lost their lives for dealing selfishly and untruthfully with the Christian community.

The final verse, verse 13, links the whole business again to the call to radical commitment in chapter 14, because it restates the importance of wholehearted allegiance. If we love God, we will use our money for spiritual purposes. But, if we love money, we cannot use God to further our business situations. He will not be a party to our selfish designs.

Lord, this is an ingenious story—so daring and imaginative. It invades the world of profit and loss to illustrate for us the great importance of living creatively for your Kingdom. Teach me to think prudently, as this steward did, and to use all my resources and energy in behalf of those who matter to you. Through Jesus, who served you completely. Amen.

WEEK 8

Week 8: Sunday

Luke 16:14–31 The Evidence of the Heart

To read this passage correctly, we must see it in the context of the preceding verses, the story of the clever steward (Luke 16: 1–8), which Luke says was spoken to the disciples. The Pharisees, listening in, scoffed at Jesus for teaching thus. Luke points out that they loved money, and the records do indicate that they often used their superior knowledge of the Law to financial advantage, thereby establishing themselves as the upper class in Israel.

Jesus' response to the Pharisees was pointed: They might know how to justify themselves legally before men, but God would not be fooled, for he knew what was in their hearts. Even though the Kingdom was being preached and those who entered it did so "violently" (that is, by repentance and conversion, which constituted a radical personal readjustment), the Law was not really altered by it. Every part of it would stand despite all the scribes' and Pharisees' clever attempts to manipulate it to their advantage. Even though they had figured out ways to divorce their wives legally, they would find themselves guilty of adultery.

To show how God judges by the heart, Jesus then told the parable of the rich man and Lazarus. Among the Pharisees, the rich man would have been highly regarded. He was enormously wealthy, as indicated by the purple and fine linen clothes and the daily feasts. And there is absolutely no indication that he was not a highly respectable citizen. But God knew him differently, for God saw how he neglected the care of the poor man who lay in sickness and need at his gate. So when the rich man died, he found himself in utter destitution. Now it was the poor man who was well off and the rich man who was crying for mercy—mercy he had never shown the beggar at his gate.

For the first time we are shown some evidence that the man can think of someone other than himself. He worries about his five brothers, who apparently are also wealthy and oblivious of the needs of the poor. Unless they are warned, they too will come to a similar fate. Curiously, the man asks that Lazarus go to warn his brothers—even though his presence at the rich man's gate had not been sufficient warning for him! But Abraham says no. The Scriptures should be enough warning for anybody—they repeatedly describe what God expects of his people.

The message should have been a powerful one to the Pharisees, who were always asking for "signs." They would not behave differently, Jesus said, even if someone returned from the dead to warn them. Their hearts were not right with God. They simply twisted the Scriptures to suit their purposes, and they must answer for it.

Lord, how could it be any clearer? Your will for me is to use all that I have for your little ones. No law or rationalization can protect my selfish interest from your condemnation. When I withhold anything, I keep it from Christ. Have mercy on me, O Lord, and teach me to give myself completely. Amen.

Luke 17:1–10 A Miscellany of Sayings

Here Luke recorded an assortment of Jesus' sayings that bear on discipleship—perhaps because the previous chapter dealt partly with that subject.

The first saying (vv. 1–2) is about causing "little ones" to sin. Matthew 18:6–7 and Mark 9:42 both clearly show that "little ones" to them meant disciples, so that is the probable meaning here. It is a tender appellation, much in keeping with the picture of the lost sheep, lost coin, and lost boy of chapter 15. As to what kind of temptations would lead a little one to sin, we can only conjecture. Perhaps in line with the meaning of temptation in the narrative of Jesus' wilderness experience (Luke 4:1–13) and the use of the word in the model prayer (Luke 11:4), it has to do with forsaking the Kingdom of God, falling away from the faith. Woe to the man or woman who causes any follower to shrink back from the life of the Kingdom!

The second saying, verses 3–4, is about forgiving a brother or sister in Christ. Seven times a day, like Matthew's "seventy times seven" (18:22), is a figure of speech implying endless patience and forbearance, qualities which are expected of disciples who have themselves been forgiven enormous debts (cf. Luke 7:40–47).

The third saying, verses 5–6, regards the power of faith. The reason for Jesus' reference to the sycamore tree may be its reputation for an extremely large and intricate root system, making it especially difficult to dislodge.

The fourth saying, verses 7–10, is not commonly known or preached upon today, but it is an extremely rich one for contemplation. It may originally have been spoken for the Pharisees, though it applies equally well to disciples of that or any age. Its point is that as servants of God we should never expect special attention for duties we have performed. Instead, we should maintain attitudes of humility, knowing that no works can ever make us worthy of the grace and presence of our Lord.

O God, the irony of this scripture is that, unworthy as I am, you have prepared a table for me and invited me to eat and drink. I am overwhelmed by your grace and what the banquet has cost you. I only hope that the dedication of my life will reveal in a small way how enormously grateful I am. Through your Son Jesus, who provides the bread and the wine. Amen.

Week 8: Tuesday

Luke 17:11–19 The Grateful Foreigner

Gratitude has always been closely allied to realizing the presence of God. People who are negative and ungrateful can be counted upon to be insensitive to the mystery on which their lives really border. If they only knew—only realized—how near God is to them, it would make all the difference in the world for them!

This little story puts the rate of thoughtful, grateful persons at one in ten. There were ten lepers—ten outcasts obviously of different nationalities, brought together by their common affliction. That is a lesson in itself, if we think about it. Being a leper was hard. It wasn't only the disease that was bad—the social penalty for having it was an additional hardship. Lepers had to maintain a distance between themselves and all other persons, even the members of their families. Hence, to have leprosy was to be cut off from all normal relationships in life. It was only as those who suffered from the disease associated with others in the same fix that they maintained any consistent human contact.

We note that these ten lepers "stood at a distance" when they called on Jesus for help. It must have been a pathetic sight, and we have seen throughout the Gospel of Luke how compassionate Jesus was. He had only to see them to wish to help them. "Go and show yourselves to the priests," he told them. This was in keeping with Leviticus 13:9–17, which gave explicit instructions for those having leprosy and wishing a clean bill of health. In

Luke 5:12–14, Jesus healed a leper and then sent him to the priest. Here, the lepers were ordered to go to the priest in the faith that they would be whole. As they were on their way—the Jews probably to Jerusalem and the Samaritan to Mt. Gerizim—the leprosy left them.

One of the ten, the Samaritan, when he found himself whole again, returned to thank Jesus. He was "praising God with a loud voice," says Luke. Jesus spoke words tinged with irony when he saw the man return. "Where are the others?" he asked. "Were there not ten? Where are the Jews? Is this Samaritan the only one who is grateful for what has happened?" (v. 18, P).

The implication is probably wider than the healing incident and the story of gratitude versus ingratitude. To Luke, the narrative was probably a harbinger of the times recorded in Acts, when the recognition of the Kingdom would often fare better among the Samaritans and Gentiles than in Israel itself.

Lord, teach me to seek your face each morning and evening, that I may daily live in sensitivity to the countless gifts surrounding me—gifts I perceive only when I am aware of your presence in my life. Through Jesus, who always lived this way. Amen.

Week 8: Wednesday

Luke 17:20–18:8 The Great Day at the End

These sayings are all related to the End of all things, which was a subject of much speculation among the ancient Jews. They remind us that the coming of the Kingdom had a negative side for those who would be unfavorably judged by its arrival; while it meant joy and fullness to the poor, blind, sick, and oppressed, it meant sudden terror and destruction to others.

First the Pharisees asked Jesus when the Kingdom was coming. They probably wanted to know what would be the signs of the

End. To them, Jesus replied that the Kingdom was already among them, in their very midst. They were seeing the works of the Kingdom wherever Jesus went. They should be repenting and entering the Kingdom.

Then Jesus addressed the disciples about the End. What he had to say to them was not really inconsistent with what he told the Pharisees—it was merely said from a different perspective. They knew the Kingdom was among them; but he talked to them about how it would be in the final hours of the present world order.

They should not be anxious about the coming of the End, thinking that every report of a local catastrophe was evidence of the End. If the End should come, they would know it; the Son of man will appear everywhere, like lightning flashing from horizon to horizon. Before that, he must suffer and die. But, when the day comes for him to be revealed, everything will happen suddenly, as the floods came when Noah entered the ark and Sodom was destroyed by fire when Lot left it.

There will be no time, in the End, to make any preparation or retrieve anything left behind. The person on the housetop cannot run down the side stairs and enter the house for his belongings, or the one in the field return to the head of the row to fetch the coat he left there (cf. Mark 13:16).

As in times of natural calamity, some persons will appear to be absurdly singled out for destruction while others are untouched. Two people will be asleep in the same bed (there is no warrant in the Greek for the KJV's "two *men* in one bed"), and one will be taken while the other is not. Two women will be standing side by side at the same grist mill, gossiping as they work, and one will be swept away while the other remains. Such a picture intensifies the sense of divine power involved—human intervention will be futile when the End occurs.

The disciples wanted to know where the End will come. The answer is somber—the vultures will gather where the corpse lies. Israel is a charnel house, full of death and putrefaction. The vultures have an uncanny way of finding their prey.

Finally, Jesus told a parable encouraging the disciples to pray constantly for the End to come. As the judge eventually gave in to the persistent woman, so God would one day accede to their prayers. Revelation 5:6–14, which pictures the day of "the Lamb who was slain" and is now worthy to receive power and glory, speaks of the golden bowls of incense which the angels take from the altar of God and which are "the prayers of the saints." The praying of God's people will hasten the day when everything will be reordered and renewed.

Lord, it will surely help to shape my daily existence if I pray sincerely for the day of the Lamb to come. My very being will strain toward that great event. Grant therefore that these images may remain vivid in my mind, both consciously and unconsciously, and that I may truly pray, "Thy Kingdom come." In the name of the Lamb himself. Amen.

Week 8: Thursday

Luke 18:9–14 The Braggart and the Beggar

The essence of this poignant little story derives from the Pharisee's failure to realize that he stood in the presence of God. Had he known that—had he felt even an inkling of it—it would surely have caused him to fall prostrate upon the ground, tearing his garments and bewailing his unworthiness as the humble tax collector did. But his religion itself blinded him to the possibility of the Lord's *shekinah* or unspeakable presence. He was so busy congratulating himself for fulfilling all the rules for piety—he fasted even when it was not required and paid tithes even on the smaller things in his possession though the Law did not require it—that he had no real thought for the awesome activity in which he was engaged, speaking to the Almighty God of Hosts. Ironically, he saw the tax collector prostrating himself and suffering the remorse of sin, and instead of being reminded of his own need of forgiveness, he idly added to his prayers that he was grateful not to be like that poor fellow over there.

How aptly this story fitted many of the Pharisees Jesus encountered in his ministry—they too counted their days of fasting and were scrupulous in their tithing, but missed the real secret of spirituality, which is to dwell sensitively in the presence of the living God. It was no wonder that Jesus said the Kingdom would be taken from them and given to prostitutes and tax collectors. At least the latter would have some feeling for the majesty of God when they came before him!

Lord, save me from pretentiousness and self-deception when I pray. Let the sublime mystery of your presence radically humble my spirit, bringing me into a new alignment with the world around me. For you are the living God, and greatly to be feared. Amen.

Week 8: Friday

Luke 18:15–30 The Sadness of a Ruler

There is an obvious contrast in this passage between the carefree innocence of the children and the sad, responsible nature of the ruler. Luke, like Mark, has set them side by side in order to point up this difference. The poor and oppressed are able to hear the good news of the Kingdom because they have nothing to lose and everything to gain. They are like the children. But there are others, like this ruler, who find it difficult to enter the Kingdom because it will mean surrendering their trust in earthly possessions. Thus the good news that means joy to some means sadness to others.

The ruler was probably a leader of a synagogue, not a ruler in the sense of being a king or potentate. Matthew includes the information that he was young (Matt. 19:20). He was apparently a very impressive young man, possibly a Pharisee who had kept the Law fastidiously, yet had a lot of money.

The tip-off to his attitude, in Luke's version, is the way he addresses Jesus as "good." Jesus does not actually try to deny his own personal goodness but to relocate the young man's sense of values. Beside God, there is no goodness—not even in the serious, self-disciplined ruler. The Law is good to follow as a moral guide to life, but it is not God and does not impart eternal life.

Jesus' demand that the man sell all his possessions—perhaps some farms, some town property, and many herds of sheep or camels—and give the money to the poor is designed to jar his dependency from his earthly power and respectability so that he may instead begin to place it on God. It is the fact that this dependency on worldly values has sunk such deep roots in him over the years that leads to his sadness. Perhaps he realizes the greater good he is missing, but cannot shake his need for power and property.

We do not know Peter's motivation for reminding Jesus that he and his friends had left all they had to follow Jesus. Perhaps it was a bit of self-congratulation. Or perhaps he saw Jesus look wistfully after the young man as the man went away, and wanted to speak a consoling word, such as, "Don't feel too bad, Master. Not everyone responds that way. Look at us—we left everything to come with you." And out of his reverie Jesus replies, in effect, "You're right—and everyone who has left anything will have more than he left, both now and in the age to come, when the Son of man is revealed."

Lord, I have more than I need to live. Grant that I may feel you so intimately present to me that I shall not be dependent on what I have, but may become more generous with it, sharing with those who have less. In Jesus' name. Amen.

Week 8: Saturday

Luke 18:31–43 What a Blind Man Sees

Luke now concludes the long section of teachings, begun in 9:51, during which Jesus and the disciples were supposed to be moving constantly toward Jerusalem. Before the section began, Peter had confessed that Jesus was "the Christ of God" (Luke 9:20), and Jesus had taken Peter, James, and John into the mountain with him, where they had witnessed a prefiguring of his resurrection (Luke 9:28–36). Jesus now reminds the twelve again that he must suffer and die, but they are not able to understand any of what he is talking about.

It is ironic, then, that the person who greets him as Son of David while he passes through Jericho is a blind man. The disciples, who have been with Jesus for months, and whose eyes are perfectly good, cannot "see" what Jesus tries to tell them. But the blind man "sees" perfectly well who Jesus is, and will not be silenced by those who try to stifle his outcry.

This is the only time in the Gospel when this messianic title is used. It is as if God had revealed the secret of the messiahship to a man who could not behold a sunset or look into the faces of people passing him in the road. And how appropriate it was that he should be the one to announce the Savior's approach to the Holy City, for Jesus had said at the beginning of his ministry that the coming of the Kingdom meant restoration of sight to the blind (Luke 4:18).

Jesus restored the man's vision. But he would never again see with more genuine perception than he had shown in recognizing the One who was drawing near to Jerusalem.

Lord, many things pass within the angles of my vision. Yet I fear that I do not see with enough true perception. Sight does not often enough become insight. Help me to listen better and watch more intently in your presence, that I may learn to see as this blind man did. Through Jesus, who is able to restore sight to the sightless. Amen.

WEEK 9

Week 9: Sunday

Luke 19:1–10 An Outstanding Sinner

This is the only time in the New Testament we encounter the title of "chief tax collector." Apparently Zacchaeus was in charge of all collections for the Roman government in the city of Jericho. This meant that he was free to keep part of all the money collected by the other tax officials in the city and perhaps in the entire region, and it accounts for the fact that he was very rich.

It also means that Zacchaeus was probably doubly despised by the orthodox Jews in the area. Any tax collector was considered unclean and sinful because it was necessary for him to enter the "unclean" houses of Gentiles and common people of the land, where strict food ceremonials were not practiced, and because he dealt in Roman coinage bearing the image of Caesar. But a *chief* tax collector, by the same token, must have been regarded almost as a chief of sinners!

Luke may have seen added significance, then, in placing this story where he did, as Jesus was right on the verge of entering Jerusalem for his passion. Certainly it emphasizes once more the point that has been made all along in the Gospel, that the Kingdom of God is coming to those who were not expected to have any part in it. This is the special meaning of verses 9–10, which emphasize that Zacchaeus, even though an outcast from orthodox Judaism, is nevertheless a son and heir of Abraham, and a participant in the promise that was made to Abraham.

The human drama of the story has always made it a favorite with preachers and hearers alike. Here was a wealthy publican, his curiosity piqued by the large crowds and the rumors about Jesus, climbing a tree in order to see the Master. And the Master stopped the procession right under that very tree, bade Zacchaeus to come down, and went home with him. Zacchaeus, says Luke, was joyful. This doubtless infuriated the religious leaders of the town, and fitted perfectly with other stories they had heard about Jesus' carelessness regarding the rules of piety.

But Zacchaeus himself was so moved by his visit with the Master that his entire economic behavior was drastically changed. He went far beyond the law in Leviticus 6:5, which required that anything falsely taken from another be restored in full plus one-fifth as penalty—he would make restitution at the rate of 400 percent! Besides that, he would immediately give half of his wealth to the poor.

This was surely a great object lesson for any wealthy persons who became Christians in the early centuries—they could see that sharing with the poor and living in honest simplicity were part of the ethics of the Kingdom. And the story contrasts markedly with the narrative about the wealthy young synagogue ruler in Luke 18:18–25, who could not readjust his priorities enough to give to the poor and enter the Kingdom.

Lord, I understand Zacchaeus's great joy at receiving Jesus in his home. Help me to receive him daily, that my spirit too may be utterly converted to charity. For his name's sake. Amen.

Luke 19:11–28 A Double Parable

This version of the parable of the talents is somewhat more complicated than Matthew's (25:14–30) because it combines the theme of the servants' trustworthiness with the punishment of the citizens who opposed the king's rule. In Matthew, the parable was obviously directed against the Pharisees, who had received various gifts in trust from God but had unimaginatively buried them in the ground to protect them from loss or injury in the marketplace; the Kingdom would be taken from them and given to others.

But Luke has a different application in mind, as he indicates in verse 11. He wishes to use the parable as a comment both on Jesus' absence and on the expectation of many disciples that the Kingdom would come immediately. And the story cuts two ways—to those who are appointed servants of the Lord and to those who have strongly opposed his rule all along.

As for the servants, it is probable that Luke sees these as representing the servants of Jesus—possibly even the disciples themselves—and not the Pharisees. While Jesus is away (clearly he is the nobleman) receiving his kingship, they are to act wisely and resourcefully with the small sums of money he gives them. (In Matthew the sums were much greater; here they are clearly to be used as a test.) When he does return as a king, the Lord will call them to account and reward the faithful ones with the rulership of cities, while depriving the unfaithful ones of everything.

The unruly citizens in this parable are probably the scribes and Pharisees and any other persons who for any reason have refused the Kingdom. There was a historical precedent which may have formed the basis for this part of the parable. When Herod the Great died in 4 B.C., his son Archelaus went to Rome to ask Augustus Caesar to appoint him King of Judea, and a deputation of fifty Jewish citizens followed him to oppose the appointment. Augustus did appoint Archelaus, and, though history is silent about whether he exercised reprisals against his opponents, it is almost unthinkable that he did not. The harshness of verse 27 would suggest that he did, if the parable owed anything to the story of Archelaus, because it does not seem characteristic of the Jesus of Luke's Gospel. At any rate, the story promises an unhappy end for those who stand in the way of Jesus' coming rulership.

Lord, is it ever possible that I stand in the way of your Kingdom? I fear it, not out of any intentional opposition, but because I am not as thoroughly committed to your will as I ought to be. Forgive me, and help me to be converted to your way, that the Kingdom may come more swiftly. In Jesus' name. Amen.

Week 9: Tuesday

Luke 19:29–44 A Time of Joy and Sadness

To appreciate fully Jesus' use of the donkey or ass's foal here, we must remember the stress ancient societies placed on dramatic action. Prophets often used symbolic, nonverbal actions to signify important moments or "messages." For months now, Jesus had been on his way toward Jerusalem, warning his disciples repeatedly that the final conflict with the authorities would occur there. His concern to dramatize his entrance, therefore, was most appropriate. He was entering the city as a king on a peaceful mission, even though certain parties would bitterly oppose him, just as the citizens refused the reign of the newly appointed king in the parable of Luke 19:11–27.

The approach to the city drew great shouts of joy and acclamation from the multitude of Jesus' followers. Their praise was "for all the mighty works that they had seen" (v. 37). The words they used were from Psalm 118:26—words probably spoken originally as a priestly blessing on a king coming to the temple after great victory in the field. Luke is therefore correct in the spirit, if not the letter, when he inserts the word "King" in verse 38, as neither

Mark (11:1–10) nor Matthew (21:1–9) does. Jesus had won a victory in the field and had come to Jerusalem for the final contest.

The disciples' enthusiasm could not be restrained. As we deduce from Luke 19:11, many of them apparently thought the Kingdom was about to come in all its glory. Typically, the Pharisees did not see things the same way. Either they considered the disciples' words blasphemous or they were afraid the Romans would regard them as seditious and take reprisals against all the Jews; so they demanded that Jesus silence the elated crowd. But Jesus knew how natural the disciples' excitement was. They had indeed seen vast evidence of the Kingdom's arrival, and they expected the arrival to be consummated soon. If they were muzzled, said Jesus, nature itself would have to cry out. The time was at that point of fullness.

Still, Jesus himself did not quite share the crowd's elation. He understood better than they what was transpiring. Therefore, staring at the city either from atop the Mount of Olives, looking straight across at the walls, or from the valley, looking up at the imposing profile rising above him, Jesus began to weep over the people's fate. They had refused the Kingdom. There was only one course open to them—they would be overrun by the Roman army during a time of rebellion. The Romans would push dirt ramparts up to the great walls, rush in over them, slay the inhabitants of the city, and then systematically lay the city in ruins—all because the people did not recognize the time of their "visitation."

Lord, how many times have I missed a visitation in my own life because I did not stop to watch for you and recognize your approach? How many times have I failed to see you in a beggar, a mourner, or a child? How often have I been preoccupied with self and selfish values when you bade me leave them all to follow you? I am sad too, Lord, the way Jesus was sad over the city. I really want to know you when you come. Grant that I may be more sensitive to your comings and goings. Through him who always knew. Amen.

Week 9: Wednesday

Luke 19:45–20:8 Intensifying the Conflict

The Gospel of Mark locates the cleansing of the temple on the day *following* Jesus' entry into Jerusalem (11:12–17). Matthew (21:12–13) and Luke both place it together with the entry, indicating that they regarded it as a significant overture to the week of conflict with the priests, scribes, and Pharisees that led finally to the crucifixion. It was an act of authority that clearly provoked the wrath of the religious leaders of the nation.

It is ironic, when we think about it. Throughout his ministry, Jesus was dogged by pietistic scribes and Pharisees who complained that Jesus and his disciples were not strict enough in their observance of religious rules and practices. Now, in this passage, Jesus is seen doing exactly the same to them. He reminds them that Isaiah 56:7 said the Lord's house was to be a place of prayer and chides them for having turned it into a thieves' warren by overcharging the pilgrims who come to Jerusalem.

Luke curiously abridges the account of the cleansing in Mark, omitting the fact that Jesus drove out those who were buying as well as those who were selling. He also neglects to draw the direct line Mark drew between the purging of the temple and the severe displeasure this provoked among the priests and scribes.

But the fact of the priests' and scribes' displeasure is there, and that is the important thing. They were seeking ways to destroy this strong, resourceful enemy of their system, just as the devotees of any system will try to crush the opponents of that system. The one thing blocking their way was the people, for Jesus was an exceedingly popular figure. They had to be careful, and so proceeded during the next several days to try to entrap him with clever questions.

One of these questions concerned his authority to do the works he did. They probably expected Jesus to assert that he was the Messiah sent from God. If he did, they would run to the Roman governor and charge him with sedition, for Messiah-fever always ran high in Passover season and the Romans were especially wary then of any possible uprising in the populace.

But Jesus was cagey. He returned a question for a question. Whence was *John's* authority—his baptism—from heaven or from human sources? The questioners were stupefied. If they said "from heaven," it would validate Jesus' own ministry. If they said "from men," then the people would react angrily, because they held John in great esteem. Lacking the moral courage to grasp either horn of this well-posed dilemma, they simply refrained from answering.

"If you won't give me an answer," said Jesus in effect, "then you won't have one from me."

Lord, why is it we resent anybody who does not fit into our systems? What compels us to oppose, harass, and even destroy him or her? I admit it is that way with me too. Help me to live so in your presence that I shall be more compassionate and tolerant. Through Jesus, who bids me enter the Kingdom. Amen.

Week 9: Thursday

Luke 20:9–18 The Coming of the Son and Heir

As citizens of occupied territory, Palestinians were doubtless very familiar with the absentee landlord practice. Many farms and vineyards in their country were owned by people who lived in Asia Minor, or even in Rome, and were worked by local tenants who did pretty much as they liked. We can imagine the consternation some of these tenants felt from time to time when a representative from the owner appeared and demanded an accounting of the property's management. Sometimes representatives were assaulted and killed just as this parable describes.

The story was very apt, as all Jesus' parables were, for the hearers could readily see the scene Jesus was setting. The hook in it, of course, was the line about the owner's sending his son to the tenants, who summarily rejected him, as they had the earlier emissaries, and killed him. It was true in real life that if the owners of property died or were killed, the tenants living on the property had first legal claim on it. Jesus was accusing the religious establishment of Israel of wanting to be rid of him in order that there would be no impediment to their assuming complete proprietary rights to their nation's life and spirit. But God was not some powerless owner residing at an impossible distance from Israel; he would come and destroy the tenants, and give the vineyard to other tenants.

The expression "God forbid!" appears only in Luke and not in the other Gospels. It is probably a reaction which interprets Jesus' prophecy as a prediction that Jerusalem itself would be destroyed.

The quotation about the rejected stone in verse 17 is from Psalm 118:22–23, and was apparently a favorite text among early Christians, who associated it with the Resurrection. Luke quotes it again in Acts 4:11, in the sermon of Peter before the high priests, scribes, and elders. The last verse of our passage is clear enough: anyone (such as the wicked tenants) who falls afoul of the One who is the cornerstone is found to be broken by the encounter!

Interestingly, Mark's account of the parable (12:1–12) has the son's death occurring inside the vineyard. But both Matthew (21:33–46) and Luke have altered the wording to have the death take place outside. We assume that this was to make the parable conform to the fact that Jesus was crucified outside the walls of the city (Heb. 13:12).

Lord, for me the terrible thing about this story is the realization that my life is your vineyard too, and that I have often turned away your servants and your beloved Son from taking control of it. Forgive me for my rudeness and possessiveness, and help me in the future gladly to surrender whatever you wish from your vineyard. For it is rightfully yours and your Son's. Amen.

Luke 20:19–26 The Things That Belong to God

Jesus' parable of the vineyard (Luke 20:1–18) could not but have reminded his Jewish audience of Isaiah's comparison of Israel to a vineyard (5:1–7), so there was no doubt in the minds of the religious leaders that he had indeed "told this parable against them." They would have liked to seize him immediately and silence him for good, but were still afraid of his popular following. If the people created a tumult, it might provoke the Romans, who would then fulfill Jesus' prophecies about the destruction of the city. So it was necessary for the leaders to bide their time and carefully gather evidence to present to Pilate, the Roman governor, when they finally arrested Jesus and took him before the authorities.

Verses 21–22 are an example of their clever data-gathering. The question they asked turned on the annual poll tax which Jewish citizens must pay to the Roman government, and pay in silver denarii bearing Caesar's image. If Jesus gave a popular answer, that it was morally wrong for worshipers of God to handle money extolling the divinity of Caesar and to pay for the support of a heathen government, then his enemies could instantly bring him before Pilate on the charge of sedition. If, on the other hand, he approved the payment of the tax, it would cause a great rift among his followers and weaken his popular support. Either way, he must lose. But it is evident from the way the question was posed ("We know that you . . . truly teach the way of God") that the questioners really wanted him to take the popular antigovernment stand, giving them the political ammunition they needed.

Coolly and shrewdly Jesus returned an answer that acceded to neither of their desires (vv. 24–25,P). "Whose image and inscription are on the coin?" he asked. "Caesar's," they answered. "Then it is Caesar's," he said. "Give it to him." Technically, it *was* Caesar's—all coinage issued by an emperor remained legally his, although used by his subjects. But there was another part of the answer: "Give what belongs to God to him as well."

At a stroke, Jesus had not only ingeniously eluded the trap set for him, but had reaffirmed the nature of the Kingdom he was preaching. It was not to be a Kingdom in rivalry with earthly kingdoms, commandeering their thrones and taking possession of their coinage. Jesus had settled that when he rejected the temptation to have power and glory from all the nations of the world (Luke 4:5–8). His was a Kingdom of another dimension, to be won through suffering and death. It is no wonder that his enemies marveled at his answer and became silent.

Lord, Caesar's kingdom bothers me a lot. I spend much of my energy worrying about taxes and reports and making ends meet. I think that if I spent more time contemplating your Kingdom I would have more energy for dealing with Caesar, as Jesus obviously did. I am going to try to do that, with your help. Amen.

Week 9: Saturday

Luke 20:27–44 The Lord of the Living

I once heard a rabbi shock a group of Christian ministers by announcing to them that Jesus took many of his teachings from the Pharisees. When pressed for an explanation, he pointed out that the Pharisees were the liberal thinkers of their day, as opposed to the far more conservative Sadducees, and that Jesus agreed with their teachings on such important matters as the resurrection of the dead and the existence of angels and demons.

The rabbi was right, at least up to a point. The Pharisees, like Jesus, did hold certain theological beliefs which developed late in the history of Judaism and did not find expression in the Torah or Law of Israel. The Sadducees, on the other hand, held rigidly to the Torah and refused to admit any doctrine not expressly contained there. Thus they came to ridicule Jesus' teachings about resurrection by citing a law in Deuteronomy 25:5–6 decreeing that a man should marry his brother's widow in order to guarantee progeny to the family. By imagining an almost absurd instance in which the law would apply, they produced a ridiculous picture of a woman with seven husbands in the resurrection.

Jesus first attempted to correct their vision of resurrected life. Its quality, he said, is quite different from that of this life. In the resurrection, human beings are freed from mundane necessities. They are like the angels, and have no worry about progeny to carry on their names. (Was Jesus also giving the Sadducees a lesson about angels?)

Then he turned on them their own trick of reading the Torah quite literally. Citing Exodus 3:6, when God told Moses, "I am the God of your father, the God of Abraham, the God of Isaac, and the God of Jacob," Jesus observed that there must be a resurrection, else these men could not be living and God could not truly be their God; for God had indeed put it in the present tense, "I *am* the God of your father. . . ."

Some of the scribes, whose business it was to deal in the minutiae of the Law, were obviously much impressed by such an answer. They themselves may have been Pharisees rather than Sadducees. Jesus had proven himself more than a match for any of them.

When they fell silent, he asked them a question. How could they, in the face of Psalm 110:1, where David called the Messiah "Lord," think of the Messiah as David's "son"? The point was, they expected the Messiah, as David's offspring, to have an earthly kingdom like David's. But Jesus was not only David's son, he was his Lord as well, and his Kingdom would transcend the kingdom of David.

Lord, something in me tends to reject subtle arguments that have to do with religion. Is that wrong? I don't want to be fuzzy-minded about my beliefs, but, on the other hand, I don't want to be fussy-minded either. Help me to steer a proper course between wholehearted devotion and sensible belief. In Jesus' name. Amen.

WEEK 10

Week 10: Sunday

Luke 20:45–21:4 A Model for Living

Everywhere in Jerusalem, and especially around the temple, Jesus and the disciples would have seen the figures of the scribes moving through the streets in their long robes with tassels that touched the ground. After the encounter with them recorded in Luke 20:39–44, Jesus commented on these ubiquitous figures to the disciples. They liked to be noticed, he said. They loved the special greetings of "Rabbi" or "Master" which others gave them in the marketplaces and they liked the seats of honor at banquets. Rabbinical writings in fact gave very precise regulations for the seating of scribes, so that the oldest and most authoritative had the greatest places. But in matter of fact, said Jesus, for all their respectability, they used their positions of influence and knowledge of the Law to bilk poor, trusting widows out of their inheritances. And their long prayers, often delivered in public places, were mostly hollow pretense, aimed only at increasing their level of honor among the populace.

How much more appropriate in God's eyes was the behavior of the poor widow Jesus happened to see placing her two small coins in the offering chest at the temple. The coins were not worth much by most people's standards—they were the small Jewish "coppers" which bore no image of Caesar—but they were obviously worth a great deal to the woman, whose appearance marked her as one in very meager circumstances.

In God's eyes, indicated Jesus, she had given more than all the self-important religious people, even though they probably made a great display of dropping their silver denarii into the offering chests. For God looks on the heart of a person, not on the elaborate piety developed for outward show.

Lord, thank you for simple people who are able to love you in simple but profound ways. They help to correct the vision of those of us who are more complicated and less natural. Help me to be more like them. In the name of Jesus, who also gave all that he had. Amen.

Week 10: Monday

Luke 21:5–19 Patterns of Suffering and Hope

Each of the so-called Synoptic Gospels contains a lengthy section of apocalyptic sayings—predictions of Jesus concerning a time of great destruction before the end of the old order and the beginning of the new. In Matthew it is chapter 24. In Mark it is chapter 13. In Luke it is this chapter, chapter 21. Both Matthew and Luke repeat certain material which appeared earlier in Mark. But Luke alone has added material from another source, blending it with the sayings from Mark to form a new apocalypse.

One of the most interesting facts about Luke's finished product is the way he has made the sayings parallel descriptions of Jesus' trial, crucifixion, and resurrection in chapters 22–24. Scholars have long noted the way Luke has developed very intricate parallelisms throughout the Gospel and the Book of Acts as well. But this particular section is greatly illuminated by noting the parallels. Here are some of them:

Chapter 21	*Chapters 22–24*
False Messiahs (v. 8)	Jesus the true Messiah (24:26)
The disciples in prison and before kings and governors (v. 12)	Jesus captured (22:54) and taken before Herod and Pilate (23:1–25)
The disciples betrayed by friends and relatives (v. 16)	Jesus betrayed by Judas (22:47–48)
The disciples hated (v. 17)	Jesus hated (22:63; 23:18, 35–39)
Assurance of God's protection (v. 18)	Jesus' faith in God's protection (23:46)
Endurance demanded of disciples (v. 19)	Jesus shows endurance (22:7–23:46)
Fulfillment of Old Testament (v. 22)	Fulfillment of Old Testament (22:37; 24:44–46)
Jesus' sorrow for those who have children or expect them (v. 23)	Jesus says the childless are blessed (23:28–29)
The times of the Gentiles (v. 24)	The gospel proclaimed to the Gentiles (24:47)
Signs in the sun (v. 25)	Darkness in the sun (23:44–45)
The coming of the Son of man in glory (v. 27)	The glory of the Son of man at the resurrection (24:26, 46)
Redemption (v. 27)	Jesus, the one to redeem Israel (24:21)

Luke appears to have been saying that the suffering of the disciples would essentially parallel that of Jesus himself, and that they must therefore brace themselves to endure the calamities and hardships as Jesus endured the trial and crucifixion. If they were faithful as he was faithful, they would then share in the glory and triumph of the One who had been resurrected from the dead. And, through it all, the God who raised up Jesus would prove more than adequate to their needs, giving them words to say at their trials and preserving them from harm.

Lord, the pattern of Jesus' suffering, death, and resurrection has been extremely meaningful to me whenever my own spirit has suffered in the human condition. I know there is hope in your power to bring good out of evil and light out of darkness. Grant that I may be more dedicated to spreading the good news of this hope. In Jesus' name. Amen.

Luke 21:20–38 When the Summer Is Near

Continuing to weave together verses from Mark and from his other source, Luke here provides a program sketch of how things will happen in the end. First, Jerusalem will be overrun by enemies. Then the whole of nature will erupt and shake the world powers. And finally the Son of man will come in power and glory, bringing redemption for his people.

Jesus frequently alluded to the destruction of Jerusalem. Some scholars think Luke added realistic touches to his description of this destruction when he wrote the Gospel after the actual fall of Jerusalem in A.D. 70. But Jesus' words are similar to those describing the destruction of the city in 586 B.C. and not to the description of the fall in A.D. 70 as depicted by the historian Josephus. He simply foresaw a time of great tribulation for the city that had rejected him. The "times of the Gentiles" (v. 24) seems to allude to chapters 11–12 of the book of Daniel, which describe the clashing of great Gentile armies before the End comes.

Verses 25–26 tell of the age of great natural calamities which will afflict even the Gentile world. The "roaring of the sea and the waves" suggests the temporary eruption of primeval chaos, as the waters which God tamed in the Genesis story of creation rise out of their boundaries and threaten to swallow the land again.

But, in all the disruption and horror, the Son of man will return, "coming in a cloud with power and great glory" (v. 27). Therefore the followers of Jesus should not fear, but should look about them alertly, for their redemption is drawing near. The calamities are like the leaves the fig tree puts out as a sign summer is approaching—they are harbingers of the End.

Verse 32 is admittedly difficult to interpret today. Some think that Jesus firmly expected a precipitous arrival of the End, even before the disciples had died. It seems unlikely, however, that Luke, writing after the fall of Jerusalem, should not have altered this verse when he saw the End being delayed. It is more likely, in the interweaving of sources about the destruction of Jerusalem and the end of the ages, that this particular saying originally applied to the prediction of Jerusalem's fall, not to the End and the return of the Son of man.

The important practical consideration, as verses 34–36 observe, is to live joyously in expectancy of the Kingdom, so that when the time of the End comes, it does not catch us unawares. Having hearts "weighed down with dissipation and drunkenness and cares of this life" is the opposite of living in the mood of ecstasy Luke has so frequently depicted as being appropriate to the Kingdom.

One more note: The other Gospels say that Jesus was spending his nights in the home of Mary, Martha, and Lazarus in the small town of Bethany, about three miles from Jerusalem. Luke says (v. 37) that he was lodging on Mount Olivet. Actually, one must climb Olivet and go beyond it to get to Bethany. Luke may have phrased it this way to impart more meaning to Olivet, as it is both the place of Jesus' retreat to the Garden of Gethsemane (Luke 22:39) and the scene of his ascension (Acts 1:12).

I am often weighed down, O Lord, by the cares of this life. My spirit is depressed by news of violence and greed and upheaval in the world. Sometimes it seems as if the ancient chaos has broken out again. Grant me the faith to watch through it all, living expectantly for the Son of man, who has already been revealed in history. Amen.

Week 10: Wednesday

Luke 22:1–6 A Wicked Agreement

As the day of Passover approached, the Messiah-fever in Jerusalem probably ran higher than ever. The town was garrisoned with soldiers to keep the peace. Jesus was besting the scribes and Pharisees in every discussion in the temple. Excitement was mounting.

The chief priests and scribes were feeling desperate. They knew they must do something—but what? They could not simply arrest Jesus in the daytime. He was far too popular, and there might be reprisals from the crowds. And at night, with the vast throngs milling about the city, it was probably impossible to find him. Until—

Judas became their answer. Judas Iscariot, the dark one, whose life has been largely swallowed up in mystery, except for the perfidy of his betrayal. Why did he do it? The question has been asked thousands of times. There are several possible conclusions. Some think, as John 12:6 indicates, that he had embezzled money from the disciples' common treasury, and needed to cover up his small crime with a larger one. Others believe he was a Zealot, a member of a party of fierce nationalists, and hoped to produce a bloody revolution when Jesus was captured. Still others defend him by suggesting that he may have been merely impatient with Jesus and hoped that the confrontation in the garden would provoke the immediate arrival of the Kingdom. Jesus had, after all, repeatedly spoken of the necessity of his being delivered up and crucified. Perhaps Judas understood this better than the others.

Luke did not trouble with such human alternatives. In his view, the betrayal had theological significance. Judas turned Jesus over to his enemies because Satan had entered into him. Unable to deflect Jesus from his goal of the Kingdom (Luke 4:1–13), Satan found one of the disciples of softer metal, and was working through him to prevent the preaching of the Kingdom.

It was done for money—thirty pieces of silver, says Matthew 26:15, the price of a slave in the Old Testament. After all Jesus' talk about riches—the story of the rich man and Lazarus (Luke 16:19–31), the encounter with the rich ruler who was sad because he could not give up his wealth for the Kingdom (Luke 18:18–30), the joyous meeting with Zacchaeus, the chief tax collector who gave so much of his property to the poor (Luke 19:1–10), the commendation of the poor widow who gave all she had to the temple treasury (Luke 21:1–4)—Judas defected for money. Luke was a doctor. He probably knew many people and had had occasion to witness their actions and emotions in intimate moments. He knew how often economic considerations are the fulcrum on which a person's whole life turns. Again and again, in the Book of Acts, he would note how the greed for money and property was an acid destroying people's lives. It is no wonder that Satan got to one of the disciples through this age-old door.

Lord, I am suddenly fearful of this door in my own life. How ready am I to put economic considerations above everything else—above personal friendships, family values, even my dedication to your Kingdom? I blush, Lord, and pray for forgiveness. Envelop me in your presence until I am safe from Satan's temptings. Through Jesus, who withstood all trials. Amen.

Week 10: Thursday

Luke 22:7–23 Eating the Passover

There was no meal in the entire year more important to Hebrews than the Passover meal. It was like our Fourth of July, Thanksgiving, and Christmas all rolled into one. It was a sacred meal, for it symbolized the birth of the Jewish nation, when a group of slaves in Egypt killed lambs and smeared their blood on the door lintels, so that the death angel spared the Hebrew children when slaying the sons of the Egyptians. But it was also a social meal, the highlight of family life and joy. Even today, it is among Jews a time for remembering the trials and victories of the past, a time for fun and festivity, and a time for considering the hope for the future.

It is much in keeping with Luke's picture of the human, compassionate Jesus that he shows him wanting to eat the Passover one last time with the disciples before he suffered. Other Gospels possibly make more of the theological significance of the Last Supper. Luke obviously sees the human depths of it.

Normally, one ate this meal with members of his family. But we remember that, in his commitment to the Kingdom, Jesus had said that his followers had become his family (Luke 8:19–21). Similarly, he had told the disciples that he must come first with them, even before their fathers and mothers and wives and children and brothers and sisters (Luke 14:25–26). Thus they had established a precedent to be remembered always in the Christian fellowship, especially at the time of communion—that the followers of the Lord are a special family together, transcending even the relationships among family members.

It seems strange that Luke has reversed the order of the bread and the cup, putting the sharing of the cup ahead of the breaking of the bread. A similar order is suggested, however, in 1 Corinthians 10:16–21 and in a second-century book of teachings for the church called the *Didachē*. It may be that both orders existed side by side in the early church. The symbolism of this one would actually be more precise than the one given in Mark 14:22–25 and 1 Corinthians 11:23–27, because Jesus' blood was spilled before his body was taken down in broken form.

Verses 21–23 refer of course to the betrayal by Judas. But the key words are in verse 22: "as it has been determined." Luke was invariably concerned to point out that everything that happened in Jesus' life and suffering had been prophesied and foreordained by God. Even the betrayal itself was assimilated into the divine plan and purpose.

Lord, I think of my mother-in-law eating her last Thanksgiving meal with us, and knowing it was her last. How much it meant to her! And how much this Passover meal must have meant to Jesus, who loved Israel as no man except the Son of God could have loved her. How the joy and sadness must have mingled in his heart that night! Help me to remember this strong personal emotion when I receive the cup and the bread and join with him in the prayer for the great banquet to come in the Kingdom. Amen.

Luke 22:24–38 The Way of the Kingdom

There is a kind of sadness in these verses. Jesus has been with the disciples for months, instructing them, sharing himself with them, modeling ministry for them. Yet they are still like children who cannot understand.

They are still like the scribes and Pharisees, who love to have the best places at the table (Luke 11:43; 20:46), and they fall to arguing about it, possibly after a bit too much wine to drink. Jesus reminds them that the Kingdom ideal is to serve, not to be served. As Father Louis Evely has reminded us, we come to the table to serve him, but he always puts on the apron and serves us.

If the disciples will maintain this posture of obedient service, then they will become the pillars of the new Israel, the leaders of the twelve tribes of the blessed! But they will not do so without interruption. First, they will all fall away—even Simon Peter, who thinks he is ready to go to prison and the grave for his Master. As Satan entered Judas, he has also demanded to try Peter. But Jesus has prayed for him, and Satan will not be able to keep him.

Verses 35–38 are a word of warning to the disciples. When Jesus sent them out before, they were able to live off the hospitality of others wherever they went. But shortly, when Jesus has been crucified and his name maligned throughout the land, they will find the going much harder. Doors will then be shut to them that were open before. They will find it necessary to carry provisions, and even to go about armed for self-protection. Jesus will be known as a transgressor, a criminal, and they will be labeled as his accomplices. Taking him quite literally, the disciples produce two swords. "It is enough," he says—meaning probably to let the matter go, they have said enough about it.

Lord, I want to serve you. But my spirit is unruly, especially when those I am to wait upon are slick and arrogant and undeserving. Then I want to be a ruler, not a servant. Help me to remember you in the

Passion, and humbly take my place beside you. For it is the way of the Kingdom. Amen.

Week 10: Saturday

Luke 22:39–46 The Custom of Praying

Luke alone, among the Gospel writers, records that it was Jesus' *custom* to go to the Mount of Olives to pray. Were it not for this, we might suppose that this experience on the night of the Passover was an isolated incident. But apparently it was not. Each evening throughout the week, as Jesus and the disciples returned from the temple to the place of their lodging, they stopped here to commune with God, to feel the presence that recomposed their minds and restored their energies.

Mark in his Gospel (14:26–42) was more interested in the disciples' failure to understand the cruciality of the hour and to pray than he was in the agony of Jesus. But not so Luke! Unlike both Mark and Matthew, he does not record how Jesus three times returned and found the disciples asleep when they should have been praying. Instead, he describes, as they do not, the manner of Jesus' personal anguish—how a heavenly messenger appeared to strengthen him in his praying, as one would be joined in a mighty task by an ethereal stranger, and how the very pores of his body exuded drops of blood because of the enormous stress and intensity of the prayer.

Luke wished us to see, without question, the terrible human struggle going on in Jesus as the devil made a last mighty effort to deter him from purchasing a Kingdom through his own suffering and death.

Lord, I am grateful for this warm, poignant picture of Jesus struggling through prayer with the destiny he knew was coming. It enables me to enter my own times of crisis-praying with more courage and confidence, for I see that the important outcome is not release from suffering but submission to your will. Amen.

WEEK 11

Week 11: Sunday

Luke 22:47–53 The Power of Darkness

Professor Harry Levin of Harvard University once wrote a book called *The Power of Blackness.* It was a critical study of the fiction of Hawthorne, Melville, and Poe, designed to reveal how the inordinate power of their writing derived at least in part from their ability to tap the dark side of events and the world. The phrase with which Luke ended this passage is similar to Professor Levin's title, for Luke, even more than Professor Levin, appreciated the way evil forces are at work in the world we live in.

Here, the evil triumph comes as the culmination of many battles with Jesus throughout his ministry. The devil never managed to touch Jesus himself in a vulnerable spot, but he had reached to the heart of Judas, one of his disciples. And he was using the religious establishment of Jerusalem—the chief priests, scribes, and Pharisees—as a veritable phalanx to move against Jesus. Here they were, massed together with torches, knives, and clubs, closing in on the Master at his place of prayer. Judas had been with him when he stopped there on preceding evenings, and so knew precisely where to lead the others to capture him.

The disciples had already alluded to the two swords they had among them (Luke 22:38). They are ready to defend their Master, and one (we know from John 18:10 that it is Simon Peter) even strikes off the ear of one of the enemy. But Jesus has already decreed that his Kingdom is not to be won as an ordinary kingdom and, healing the severed ear, bids the disciples not to offer resistance. He is, after all, no common criminal, that they should come for him with staves and swords. Their matter with him must be tried in the courts, not on the field of battle.

Perhaps the saddest note of all is in verses 47–48. It was the custom for rabbis and their followers to greet each other with a kiss. But Jesus, knowing what Judas had conspired to do, was unwilling to have him add to his perfidy the hypocrisy of a kiss.

It was indeed the enemies' hour—and Satan's. But Jesus' hour would come.

Lord, it has been said that the brave man murders with a sword, the coward with a kiss. How many times, I wonder, have I betrayed you with a kiss, saying the pious word, pretending a righteous gesture, acting as if I were on your side, when in fact I was weakly committed to you, if at all. Give me the courage to be honest in the expression of my feelings; and, even more, give me the grace to love you devotedly. Through Jesus, who refused a kiss that wasn't meant. Amen.

Week 11: Monday

Luke 22:54–65 A Bitter Reminder

In Mark's account of this part of the Gospel, Jesus was taken immediately before the Sanhedrin for trial, and Peter's denial occurred in the courtyard outside while the trial was going on. Luke's account, which is more probable, has Jesus being held in the courtyard of the high priest's house until morning, when he was brought to the Sanhedrin. This means that Peter was very close to where Jesus was being mocked and beaten by the soldiers—perhaps only a few yards away, in full view of it all—and that Jesus could hear each of his denials.

The courtyard would not have been large—perhaps sixty by seventy feet. The fire would have been lit for warmth as well as light, for the early spring nights are frosty in Israel. Peter showed a certain courage in entering the courtyard and then in staying after the scrutiny of a maid first identified him as one of Jesus' followers. But the courage did not run deep enough. Three times he denied that he had been with Jesus. And then, the third time, before the words had died on his lips, the cock crowed. Jesus, who all through the night had been the object of ridicule and mistreatment by men who were holding him for the dawn, heard it too, and looked at Peter. Their eyes met, and Peter remembered.

What could he do? He remembered all the good days together—how proud he had been to be the first of the disciples during the months of triumph and popularity—"and he went out and wept bitterly."

Lord, this is the saddest passage. I know how Peter felt in the courtyard—and how he felt when he realized he had betrayed a friend who loved him. But thank you for the story. It reminds us that we can return to faithfulness even after we have disappointed you. Help me to be faithful. Through Jesus, who prays for his own. Amen.

Week 11: Tuesday

Luke 22:66–71 Jesus and the Old Men

The assembly of elders was comprised of priests, scribes, Pharisees, and Sadducees, representing the main power blocs in Jewish life. As in other occupied countries, the Roman government allowed the local assembly to transact most of the business affecting their nations's internal affairs.

We can picture the assembly as it met on that fateful morning. The members were not all evil men. Many were persons of deep conscience and moral conviction. They were like the members of any court or tribunal, who must live with their own personal, business, and family problems at the same time that they take the bench and make decisions affecting others. They simply did not know all the facts in the case, and did not fully understand what they were doing.

They wanted to hear only one thing from Jesus—did he think he was the Messiah? "Why should I tell you?" Jesus replied, in effect. "If I did, you would not believe me. And if I question you—if I pose the evidence for you and ask you about it, as I have in the past—you will not answer, but merely become silent."

But he did tell them one thing—that from then on the Son of man would be seated at God's right hand, enthroned in power. His hour of glory had come. Satan's dominion would be shaken.

"Are you the Son of God, then"—the Messiah? they asked. Mark says that he replied, "I am" (Mark 14:62). But both Matthew and Luke have altered the account to read "You have said so" (Matt. 26:64) or "You say that I am" (Luke 22:70), as though Jesus were simply resigning the matter, and implying, "Think what you will."

At any rate, the elders accepted this as an admission of his claim to be the Messiah and bound him over to Pilate's jurisdiction. Their own charge against him was theological, that he was guilty of blasphemy; but the charge on which they would present him to Pilate was political, that he was guilty of sedition.

We can only wonder how many of the council members felt uneasy at going along with the majority in this condemnation. We know from Luke 23:50–51 that at least one, Joseph of Arimathea, was not in agreement with the decision. How many of them suspected that they had been pressured into a verdict wanted by a few leaders, and wished they had had no part in it?

To be human, O Lord, is to be involved in a network of complicity and guilt from which there is never complete extrication. We all make decisions—sometimes wrong ones—affecting the lives and destinies of others. Help me to be sensitive to this, and always to have the courage to act honestly and compassionately in matters involving others. Through Jesus, who suffered the greatest injustice at the hands of "good" men. Amen.

Week 11: Wednesday

Luke 23:1–12 A Basis for Friendship

It is unlikely that the assembly of elders had the power to order the death penalty for Jesus. Even if they had it, however, they probably preferred that the Roman governor be the one to pass sentence in a case so volatile as this one. So all of them—those opposed to the decision as well as those for it—came clattering into Pilate's hall to hear the matter prosecuted there.

The three accusations in verse 2 are all related to the charge of sedition—Jesus was stirring up the people, he had advised the crowds not to pay the annual poll tax, and he proclaimed himself to be a Messiah-King. The first two charges were absolutely false. Jesus had consistently refused to excite the populace about his messiahship, and had attempted to keep it secret. The agents for the chief priests and scribes had tried to get him to say that the people should not pay taxes to Caesar, but he had not been caught in their trap (Luke 20:20–26). And we have seen in Luke 22:66–71 how the assembly drew from him the admission—if indeed it was an admission—that he was the Messiah. But the Sanhedrin was not after truth in this matter, but action. It translated everything into a language it believed would move Pilate to do as they wished.

Pilate attempted to understand the matter as well as he could. "Are you the King of the Jews?" he asked Jesus. "Are you trying to start an insurrection in Jerusalem?" Jesus remained quiet and dignified, knowing that no direct answer from him would avail against the entire council of old men. Pilate said he seemed innocent enough to him. But the Sanhedrin declared that he was going throughout the country, from Galilee to Judea, stirring up the populace.

The mention of Galilee gave Pilate the out he needed. Learning that Jesus was indeed a Galilean, he declared that Herod should have jurisdiction in the matter, for Herod was the tetrarch of Galilee. It would be a good move, Pilate thought, to cement relations that had not been good in the past. It would please Herod—perhaps win him over.

Herod, we recall, had long been interested in Jesus. He had wondered if he were John the Baptist come back to life (Luke 9:7–9), and had tried to see him. Now his curiosity would be fulfilled!

But Jesus was no more talkative before Herod than he had been before the Sanhedrin or Pilate. So, after some mockery and buffoonery at Jesus' expense, Herod's soldiers arrayed Jesus in a fancy robe, as if he were indeed a king, and sent him back to Pilate. The occasion became the basis for a new friendship between the two rulers, and we can imagine their talking about Jesus at some subsequent banquet.

Verse 10 is a vivid parenthesis depicting the venomous activity of some of the council members—they were a rabble of accusers, spitting and hissing like a nest of vipers!

Lord, I pray for every innocent person who must bear this kind of treatment today from authorities in the law or government. Give him or her the grace to behave with inner composure as Jesus did, that the indignities may not wound deeply. And hasten the full coming of your Kingdom, that all people may dwell together as brothers and sisters with mutual respect. Amen.

Luke 23:13–25 The Master and a Murderer

The goddess Justice is usually pictured wearing a blindfold. This is meant to emphasize her impartiality in rendering judgments. But our experiences in life suggest that it might also be interpreted as a sign of her ineptness, her blindness to the facts that would really make for justice.

The story of Barabbas's release fits the latter interpretation better than the former. Ironically, Barabbas was in prison for precisely the same charges as those for which the priests and elders had arraigned Jesus before Pilate—sedition and insurrection. Yet, despite Jesus' innocence of the charges, they shouted vehemently for Barabbas's release and Jesus' crucifixion!

Verse 17, which has been omitted from the RSV translation because it is missing from the oldest, most reliable texts of the Gospel of Luke, is necessary to explain Pilate's action. The Romans, as a mark of favor to the Jews, had a practice of releasing a political prisoner of their choice during the festival time (cf. Mark 15:6). Therefore, when Pilate said that he had found Jesus innocent of the charges made against him, and that Herod, one of their own rulers, had found him innocent as well, and would consequently release him, they all set up a clamor to have Barabbas released but to have Jesus put to death.

If we had only Luke's account to reckon from, we would wonder what had happened among the populace to destroy the favor in which they had so recently held Jesus. But Mark 15:11 informs us that "the chief priests stirred up the crowd" to have Pilate release Barabbas instead of Jesus. We can imagine, when Luke says "they were urgent, demanding with loud cries" that Jesus should be crucified, that the priests and elders were among those crying the loudest. Clever people that they were, they incited the crowd to do their evil work for them.

Lord, it is a fearful responsibility to be a leader of any kind. I pray for those who have roles of leadership today, especially in the world community. Grant to them a fierce respect for human rights and justice, so that they always put the good of others ahead of their own self-interest. In Jesus' name. Amen.

Week 11: Friday

Luke 23:26–31 The Crying of the Women

Simon of Cyrene is one of those special people who, by happening to be at a particular place in a given moment, are cast by unexpected circumstances into the spotlight of history. We know almost nothing about him—he may have been a Jewish pilgrim arriving in Jerusalem after taking the Passover with relatives or friends in the country, or he may have been a one-time inhabitant of Cyrene now living near Jerusalem—but he has since become the subject of hundreds of paintings, poems, and sermons. The cross the soldiers ordered him to carry behind Jesus was the cross bar—not an entire cross—which would be hoisted and affixed to an upright pole or a kind of scaffolding at the scene of execution.

The women who followed with the crowd had commenced the funeral custom of loud public mourning even in advance of Jesus' death. Apparently they were not the same women who had accompanied him as disciples (Luke 8:1–3), but local residents, as he called them "daughters of Jerusalem." Jesus was not angry with them; he merely used their wailing as the basis for a prophetic warning about the future destruction of the city by the Romans. It was considered accursed for a women to remain barren and have no children. But Jesus reversed that popular standard, saying that in the day of catastrophe it would be the barren ones who would be thought blessed, for they would not have to witness the cruel slaughter of their children. If a miscarriage of justice such as one resulting in Jesus' death could occur under present relatively calm conditions, what would happen in that time of national disaster?

Of course, Jesus was right. Descriptions of the sacking and destruction of a city under seige are among the most horrifying accounts in all history, and the Roman demolition of Jerusalem would have offered no exception. The people of Jerusalem bought no favor with anyone by their failure to rise up in support of Jesus. Evil simply increased its hold on them until, a few years later, their beloved city was mercilessly destroyed.

Lord, I understand the feelings of the women of Jerusalem. They were helpless against the will of those in power. Teach me to listen to the voices of those who are powerless, that I may more often know what justice is. Through Jesus, who is on the side of the little ones. Amen.

Week 11: Saturday

Luke 23:32–43 Paradise in the Wilderness

For centuries, preachers have delivered series of sermons on such topics as "Faces Around the Cross," "Attitudes at Calvary," and "Choosing Sides at the Foot of the Cross." It is no wonder, for there is a marvelous spectrum of points of view and ways of behaving represented in this single passage of scripture.

First, there is the way of Jesus himself—regal, quietly confident, and forgiving of those who did not understand how Satan was using them as pawns and dupes in his last great bid for supremacy. It is one thing to be a king when the sun is shining and everything is going in your favor; it is quite another thing when everything is going against you, as it seemed to be for Jesus.

Then there was the way of the crowd. They stood "watching," says Luke. They were not sure what would happen. Suppose he really were the Messiah—would the Kingdom come as he hung upon the cross? Perhaps some among the crowd had shouted for the crucifixion hoping that it might be so.

And there was the way of the rulers—the priests and scribes and other elders of the city. They scoffed at Jesus, trying to convince the people once and for all that he was no messiah. "There are many reports of his saving others," they say—"all the way from Galilee to here in the temple. He healed and raised people from the dead. All right, if he is truly the Messiah, let him help himself now. That will prove his case."

What they didn't see, of course, and had never been able to see, was that his whole messiahship was of another order, a wholly unselfish order, than the one they envisioned for Israel. From the beginning, he had rejected the devil's offer of an easy kingdom and popularity for himself. His Kingdom was for the outcasts—the poor, infirm, blind, and oppressed. It was for the captive, like the poor criminal dying beside him, who asked to be remembered.

Even among the criminals crucified with Jesus there were two attitudes. One was like that of the rulers—rude, impertinent, mocking. But the other was that of a sober man who, even in the extremity of his dying, did not lose touch with the facts before him. Jesus was no criminal as they were. He was being put to death as "The King of the Jews"—a title both true and satirical at the same time.

"Remember me," asked the man, "when you come in your kingly power" (v. 42,P).

What did he know about Jesus? How much did he understand about the Kingdom? Clearly, at least, he understood more than the rulers of Israel who were crucifying Jesus—he understood that the Kingdom was for prostitutes and tax collectors, lost sheep and wayward sons, Samaritan pilgrims and penitent thieves—he understood that it was for him!

And Jesus, with the note of authority that had always characterized his ministry, said to him, "Today"—not tomorrow or at some future date when the Kingdom has fully come—"today you will be with me in Paradise." Paradise. The Aramaic word he used was from an old Persian word, *pardes,* meaning "garden." To the Jewish mind, it spoke both of the Garden of Eden and of the heavenly abode of God, where no evil existed but all was made innocent again in the divine presence. The criminal who believed would go from the cross to the Kingdom, from the wilderness to the garden, that very day.

Lord, how easy it is to sit here and take the right side in this story as I read it. But how hard it often is to take the right side when you are being crucified in the world today. Often I take the wrong side and only recognize afterwards that it was you being put to death in that legislative bill, in that election referendum, in that zoning decision, in that school classroom, in that dispute I overheard in the grocery store. Make me far more sensitive, Lord, to the way you are treated in the world around me, that I may not end up on the side of the mockers. Amen.

WEEK 12

Week 12: Sunday

Luke 23:44–49 Signs, Portents, and Sadness

Ancient peoples—and some not so ancient—believed that signs in nature often corroborated certain key events in human life and history. Passages in Amos (8:9) and Joel (2:10, 31; 3:15) connected such signs with the Day of the Lord. However literally or figuratively one wishes to construe verse 44, there could be no more fitting natural symbol for the death of the Messiah than that the sun, the center of the universe, blushed and hid its face at the shame of what was done.

The curtain alluded to in verse 45 was the great veil separating the outer part of the temple, where daily worship was performed, from the inner part, or Holy of Holies, where only the high priest entered and offered sacrifice once each year, on the Day of Atonement. Great fear was attached to this yearly entrance, for God's presence was believed to be concentrated especially in the Holy of Holies. A rope was even tied around the high priest's ankle, so that, in the event he suffered a heart attack and died there, becoming accursed, his body could be retrieved by the priests and people waiting outside. The legend among the Christians that the curtain had been torn in two was a dramatic symbol of the end of the priestly system or religion and the new freedom of all persons, including the unclean, to enter into the presence of God.

Jesus' final words, like so many others he spoke from the cross, are from the Psalms, and remind us once more of the importance of steeping ourselves in the great devotional literature of our faith. They are from Psalm 31:5, and are set in a context expressing strong assurance in God's care and delivery for the person beset by suffering.

> Yea, thou art my rock and my fortress;
> for thy name's sake lead me and guide me,
> take me out of the net which is hidden for me,
> for thou art my refuge.
> Into thy hand I commit my spirit;
> thou hast redeemed me, O Lord, faithful God.
> Psalm 31:3–5

Mark 15:39 says that the centurion, when Jesus had died, declared that he was truly the Son of God. Apparently it suited Luke's purposes of apologetic better to interpret his remark as a testimony to Jesus' innocence. This would have been important to a Roman audience, as it confirmed what Pilate, the Roman governor, had already decided (Luke 23:4, 13–16).

Luke alone records the information in verse 48 about the crowd's returning home in a mood of lamentation and penitence. Taken together with verse 35, which says they were "watching" the crucifixion in an attitude unlike that of the rulers, who scoffed and mocked, it indicates that the people were generally convinced that injustice had prevailed and Jesus was a good man. Even if they were not sure he was the Messiah, they knew a prophet and wonder-worker had been put to death that day.

And there is a mellow sadness in verse 49, which says that all of those who had followed him from Galilee "stood at a distance" and saw everything that happened. If Jesus could have spoken to them from the cross, perhaps he would have quoted to them the last verse of Psalm 31—verse 5—which he had cited in dying. It says:

> Be strong, and let your heart take courage,
> all you who wait for the Lord!
> Psalm 31:24

Lord, sometimes I wish the curtain in the temple were still there. It is such a responsibility to have your holy presence meeting me everywhere I turn. You are there in my morning shower, in the meal I eat, in the person I speak to, in the game I play with the children, in the way I do my work. Give me courage, Lord, not only to wait for you, but to meet you where you already are! In Jesus' name. Amen.

Week 12: Monday

Luke 23:50–56 An Act of Restitution

How many times in life the only thing we can do is to try in some small way to make amends for the wrong that has been done to another—to put an arm around the student who has been unfairly treated by fellow students or a teacher, to invite to dinner an employee who has been unjustly fired, to treat generously the victim of racial prejudice or social inequity. It does not undo the wrong or compensate in any way for the sacrilege committed. But it is all we can do, in our feeble manner, to reach out and say, "I am sorry, I wish it hadn't happened."

This is essentially what Joseph of Arimathea did in caring for the body of Jesus. Matthew 27:57 and John 19:38 say that Joseph was "a disciple of Jesus." Luke is more concerned to stress his humanitarian quality, his honest resistance to the Sanhedrin's "purpose and deed," and his basic Jewish hope in the Kingdom of

God. His act took some courage in the face of Pharisaic piety and the laws about touching the dead, who were considered unclean, and in Jesus' case, accursed as well. The tomb may have been his own, in which case the devotion shown would be similar to that of the woman in Mark 14:3–9 who anointed Jesus' head with her own expensive burial perfume. It was his way of saying he was sorry, that Jesus had not deserved such treatment as he had received.

While Joseph was taking the body to the tomb, the Galilean women followed—perhaps they performed traditional mourning rites along the way—and saw where it was buried. Then, returning to the marketplace, they purchased spices and ointments for anointing the body, and retired to their lodging places as the sun was setting, to wait through the sabbath day and come again to the tomb.

Lord, what a long day it must have been through which the women waited! I pray for all of those who wait now for their return to the grave where a loved one has just been buried. The hours drag for them too. Let them discover in this heavy time the hope that we have through him who was laid in a borrowed tomb, yet could not be held by death. Amen.

Week 12: Tuesday

Luke 24:1–12 A Throwaway Scene

The Gospel of Mark's account of the empty tomb contains some significant differences from Luke's: It has a single messenger at the tomb (Mark 16:5), not two (Luke 24:4); the messenger tells the women that Jesus has gone ahead of them to Galilee (Mark 16:7), instead of reminding them of what Jesus said to them in Galilee (Luke 24:6–7); the women are afraid and tell no one what they have found (Mark 16:8), instead of telling the others what they have seen and not being believed (Luke 24:10–11).

It accorded with Mark's themes and theology to end his Gospel with the women's fear and silence. But how does Luke's interpretation of this final event fit into his overall message? As Mark's narrative of the life and ministry of Jesus focused on its strange power and the disciples' inability to grasp its meaning, Luke's has centered on the theme of the great joy that has come to those who received the Kingdom. Thus this passage serves as a mere prelude to the joy experienced by the disciples from Emmaus when Jesus eats with them (Luke 24:28–32) and by the followers when they realize what has taken place (Luke 24:52). In dramatic terms, it is a "throwaway" scene—one that sacrifices any particular significance of its own to the building of plot and intrigue further on in the play.

The women find the tomb empty and are reminded that Jesus told them he must die but would not be held by the grave. Then they go to report this to all the other followers—but are not believed. It is the negative moment from which the joyous, positive ones will soon follow.

Lord, help me to recognize the throwaway scenes in my own life—those whose significance lies in what is about to happen—and thus to give thanks for those otherwise negative or less exciting times and wait in humble expectancy for what will be revealed. Through Jesus, who sanctifies all time, even the time when little seems to occur. Amen.

Week 12: Wednesday

Luke 24:13–35 A Remarkable Visitor

Luke alone, of the Gospel writers, has preserved this lovely story of the two disciples who were returning home in dejection and then were left in elation when they realized who had visited with them along the way. Very probably they had been among Jesus' acquaintances who had "stood at a distance" and observed the crucifixion (Luke 23:49). As traveling would have been forbidden after sundown on the day of crucifixion, because that was the beginning of the sabbath, they would have had to remain in Jerusalem over the sabbath. They were walking homeward the day after when Jesus approached them on the road and began walking with them.

We have normally thought of the two disciples as being two men, for the Greek word in verse 25 is masculine in form and is translated "O fools" (KJV) or "O foolish men" (RSV). But there is nothing in the Greek form to forbid the possibility that the two disciples were a man and a woman. In fact, considering the fact that they lived together, it seems probable that they were.

At any rate, Jesus gave the two persons an extended lesson in Old Testament prophecy. He showed them that the entire pattern of Hebrew thought should have pointed the Jews to understand Israel's mission in terms of suffering and servanthood; if they had only seen this, they would not have been put off by his death, for only by suffering could he enter the kind of glory God intended for him.

It would have been meaningful to early Christians that the two followers recognized Jesus in the breaking of bread *after* the long lesson in Old Testament prophecies. This pattern was not unlike that of their own worship—first having the Scriptures explained and then meeting the risen Lord in the eucharistic meal.

Jesus' vanishing out of their sight is in keeping with the nature of beatific visions. Our earthly psyches are too fragile to sustain such visitations for very long. We must return to our normal mode of existence. But our awareness of life is greatly heightened by such rare experiences.

Verse 32 speaks of the unusual sense of joy the two disciples felt even before they recognized who their strange visitor was, and it was in this mood of ecstasy that they retraced their way to Jerusalem that very hour—in the dark!—and found the eleven to tell them what had happened. The eleven were not entirely surprised, for Simon Peter had already had a similar visitation and reported it.

The Resurrection clearly meant one thing: Jesus was no longer confined by normal restrictions of time and space in which mortal lives are framed, but was free to appear wherever and whenever he pleased, to this disciple and that, in this place and another.

How often, Lord, you probably walk with me in my way and I do not recognize you. Forgive me for my lack of perception, and help me, through careful study of the Scriptures and a life of prayerful reflection, to discern your presence more regularly. Your only limits are the ones I impose upon you. Amen.

Week 12: Thursday

Luke 24:36–43 The Spirit Who Ate Fish

We are like the disciples in this passage. Our views about reality are largely set by the society around us and what it has taught us to expect. Therefore, even if Jesus were to appear to us as he did to the disciples, we would believe him to be an hallucination of some kind, not a real flesh-and-blood person.

It was especially important, in the early church, to emphasize that the resurrected Jesus was truly corporeal and not a mere phantom. There was a heretical form of the faith, called Docetism, which maintained that Christ's spirit came into his flesh at birth and forsook it at death. This was counter to the teaching of full incarnationism, which maintained that Jesus was resurrected in body, not merely in spirit. Luke was here trying to enforce correct belief. The Gospel of John, which is believed to have been written as a defense against the Docetists, contains similar stories emphasizing the true bodily nature of the resurrected Jesus (cf. John 20:24–29; 21:1–14).

Jesus invited the disciples to touch him and handle him—to know him nonverbally. It was a marvelous invitation, for it is quite possible that our deepest "knowings" are tactile rather than aural or intellectual. Ashley Montagu, in his classic study *Touching*, says that the act of touching and being touched when we are infants is the most important assurance we ever have of our parents' love and our well-being in life. Jesus wanted the disciples to be satisfied in the most basic way possible that it was really he who stood before them. He even took fish and ate it to show them he was no ghost. He was a vital, living person.

The phrase Luke used in verse 41, "they still disbelieved for joy," is characteristic of his thrust in the Gospel. This that had come to pass was simply too great to believe! Nothing in the disciples' experience of life had fully prepared them for it. They could only shake their heads in wonder at the outcome.

Lord, I become excited merely reading about the disciples' great joy. How could the church become so lethargic and apathetic in the wake of such a report? Help me to be open to the same "disbelief of joy" in my own life. Through him who is the cause for such joy, Jesus our Lord. Amen.

Week 12: Friday

Luke 24:44–49 The Charging of Witnesses

The disciples took seriously Jesus' charge to be witnesses to all they had seen and heard of his ministry, death, and resurrection. Later, as recorded in Acts 10:39–41, Peter declared to Cornelius, the man who sought his help for the Gentiles: "We are witnesses to all that he did both in the country of the Jews and in Jerusalem. They put him to death by hanging him on a tree; but God raised him on the third day and made him manifest; not to all the people but to us who were chosen by God as witnesses, who ate and drank with him after he rose from the dead."

The Old Testament is full of references to witnesses. Usually the word had a legal sense, as of those who testified to the truth of a matter. But perhaps the most significant ancient prototype for the Christian witness is to be found in Isaiah 43:10—

> "You are my witnesses," says the Lord,
> "and my servant whom I have chosen,
> that you may know and believe me
> and understand that I am He."

This entire chapter of Isaiah is set in the councils of heaven, which operate as a law court for the nations. The prophet describes God's intention of saving Israel and gathering up her offspring from the east, west, north, and south, that they may testify that he is God.

Jesus' disciples were commissioned to be witnesses of the new Israel, the spiritual community God would gather from the four corners of the world. They would begin in Jerusalem, but eventually their message would go out to all the nations. The "promise" of the Father was of a great people, as had been pledged to Abraham centuries before (Gen. 12:1–3), and the fulfilling of the promise would bring the "great joy" of which the angels had spoken to the shepherds when Christ was born (Luke 2:10–11).

Ironically, perhaps, the Greek word translated "witness" is *martus,* from which we derive the word *martyr.* In making their faithful witness, many of the disciples would suffer or lose their lives, for the evil one would not give up his world without a struggle. But the joy was never diminished by this. It was like a lamp whose wick was always trimmed and made to burn even brighter by slander and persecution.

Lord, in my way I am a witness too, for I have heard and seen things of the Kingdom. Make me daily more conscious of this, that I may give my testimony to others. Clothe me with power as you did the disciples, and use me in the fulfilling of your promise. Through Jesus, who will be Lord of lords and King of kings. Amen.

Week 12: Saturday

Luke 24:50–53 The Blessing and the Joy

Before Moses died at the edge of the promised land, he raised his hands and pronounced a blessing over the tribes of Israel (Deut. 33). Near the end of the blessing, he said these words:

> Happy are you, O Israel! Who is like you,
> a people saved by the Lord,
> the shield of your help,
> and the sword of your triumph!
>
> Deuteronomy 33:29

Jesus may have spoken similar words to the disciples when he blessed them before leaving them. He had gone with them on the road as far as Bethany, which took them over the Mount of Olives where they had been praying the night Judas led the enemy to him. Some ancient manuscripts add to verse 51 the words "and was carried up into heaven," which would accord well with references in Acts to his ascension (Acts 1:2, 9–11). But Luke may originally have omitted such a reference here, preferring to picture Jesus as being on the road to somewhere. Indeed, that is where the disciples would often find him as they traveled with the gospel—he would appear to them in this place and that, as he had to the ones going to Emmaus, and strengthen them for the task he had given them.

However it was, he blessed them and left them, and they returned to Jerusalem to worship in the temple and wait for the outpouring of God's power. Mark, it will be recalled, represented Jesus as ordering the disciples immediately to Galilee (Mark 16:7), where they would see him. Jerusalem, in Mark, stands for all that is evil and arrayed against Jesus; Jesus abandons it for the place where his ministry was successful. But Luke sees a different symbolism in the city—he remembers the prophecies that picture it as the center of God's renewing activity in the world (cf. Isa. 35:8–10).

Therefore he has the disciples return to the city and the temple, where the stage is set for the descent of the Spirit in Acts 2 and the beginnings of a vast missionary enterprise that will eventually carry the gospel into all the world.

The Gospel ends on the note that has been so characteristic of it all along—on the "great joy" of those who have seen what God is doing and have become a part of it. It has been a Gospel of angels' songs, great feasts, stories of glad returns, excitement about healings and resurrections, and the ecstasy of those who have recognized the arrival of the Kingdom of God. No wonder the last words are that they "were continually in the temple blessing God!"

Lord, this whole Gospel has accused me of being far less joyous and excited about your Kingdom than I have every right to be. Teach me to set my days in the light of your presence, that they may become storehouses of delight, and to see the world as the arena of your great victory, that I may hope even in the face of despair. Through Jesus, who blesses me and helps me to worship. Amen.

JOHN

Contents

Introduction

The Gospel of John, almost every one agrees, is special. It is different from the other Gospels. Even the most casual reader senses its uniqueness.

Its picture of Jesus is more exalted than that in other Gospels. There is no narrative of a humble birth, as there is in Matthew and Luke—instead, the prologue speaks of the pre-existence of Christ. There is no "Messianic secret" as in Mark—Jesus is openly and uncontestably the Son of God. There is no prayer of submission in the garden—Jesus goes to the cross triumphantly, calling it the hour of his glorification.

There are no parables in John. Instead, there are numerous "signs" and wonders, often followed by long discourses in which Jesus reveals great eternal truths. In some of these discourses are the famous "I am" statements of John—"I am the bread of life," "I am the light of the world," "I am the resurrection and the life," etc.—that help to characterize Jesus as superior to Judaism and all other religions.

There is much more material in John about the Last Supper—especially about what Jesus said to his disciples at the Supper. The comforting words about life after death, often read at Christian funerals, are part of this material not found in any other Gospel.

The Gospel of John is more sacramental than Matthew, Mark, or Luke. It does not speak directly of the church or allude in specific terms to the sacraments, but its entire background is the

Beloved Community, and it refers repeatedly to water, bread, and wine. It is the only Gospel in whose passion account Jesus' side is wounded, producing water as well as blood, thus suggesting the interrelationship of baptism and communion.

In John, there are allusions to the Holy Spirit not found in the other Gospels. The Spirit will lead disciples into truth, says Jesus (16:13). The Spirit will also be present to comfort and guide disciples when Jesus is no longer present with them in the flesh (14:26).

And, last but certainly not least, John is characterized, far more than the other Gospels, by an emphasis on eternal life. At times, in the Gospel, the phrase seems to refer to life after death. At other times it clearly pertains to life in this world. Taking all the passages together, they speak of a kind of life, known to the disciples of Jesus but not known generally in the world, in which believers are transcendent over all powers that afflict them in this life, up to and including death itself.

The internal evidence of the Gospel suggests that John was not written to convert outsiders but to support the faith of those who already believed. Just as Jesus sent the disciples of John the Baptist back to him in prison to say, "Look around you at all the evidence of my being the Christ," so the entire Gospel of John is composed to remind believers, some of whom may have been in prison as the Baptist was, that their faith was not misplaced.

What an important Gospel it is for our own day!

We too, like the early Christians, live in a world of conflicting loyalties and petty deities where the figure of Jesus should be more exalted. It is necessary to remember his humanity—he was one of us in every way—but it is also important to remember his glorification. This is the only way we can keep the great unrest of our time in proper perspective and not be overwhelmed by it.

We too need to be more aware of signs and wonders—to see what God is achieving in the world around us. Even in the churches there is often a reticence about miraculous events, visions, and healings. God's people languish in their faith because it receives too little mutual confirmation.

We too are hungry for comfort about death and the afterlife. We have allowed scientists and skeptics to erode our belief in the soul's survival, and consequently fear death as much as pagans do.

There is a connection, as the Gospel suggests, between this erosion and our low view of the church and its sacraments today. If we had a stronger sense of community with other believers, and a greater reverence for the sacramental aspects of the community's life, we would not have lost our confidence in Christ and the life beyond death.

By the same token, we need reminding of the Spirit's presence to lead us into truth. We are constantly bombarded by the media. There is more information and less truth around today than at any other time in the history of the world. Most of us don't know what we really believe. If we could only lay hold on the Spirit—or be laid hold of!—it would give us meaning and direction in a confusing world.

Finally, we desperately need, as the early Christians did, a sense of eternal life. Not only for assurance of the future, but for living today. Christians have lost the sense of triumph that is able to turn darkness into victory. We have forgotten how to live joyfully. But here is a Gospel that says to us, as Jesus said to Mary at the tomb of her brother, "Stop your weeping!" For it exalts One who is the Resurrection and the Life, the Living Water, the Bread of Life, the Beautiful Shepherd, the Door of the Sheep, the True Vine.

These things are written, says the author, "that you may believe that Jesus is the Christ, the Son of God, and that believing you may have life in his name" (20:31).

The Gospel does not identify its author by name. Tradition says he was John, the son of Zebedee, and probably also the "beloved disciple" mentioned in 13:23, 19:26, and 21:20.

For many years, this tradition was questioned. Scholars doubted the historicity of the Gospel because it differed so much from the other Gospels. They claimed to see Hellenistic ideas in it, and believed the prologue (1:1–18) was derived from Platonic philosophy. Many thought, because of references to Jesus' flesh and incarnation, that it was written to combat a form of heresy known as docetism, which taught that Jesus only *appeared* to become flesh.

Since the discovery of the Qumran scrolls in 1947, however, all these speculations have had to be revised. Comparable materials from a Jewish community in the second century A.D. indicate that John was indeed a Jewish Gospel, not a Greek Gospel. It is, in fact, probably more intensely Jewish than the other Gospels. And, while the author may have taken some swipes at docetism, the real intent of the Gospel was to encourage Christians who were under pressure from non-Christian Jews to convert to Judaism. This is why the

Gospel frequently refers to "the Jews" and not to "scribes and Pharisees" as the other Gospels do. The author was not refighting Jesus' battle with the self-righteous Pharisees; he was fighting the present battle against Judaizers who sought to destroy the faith of Christ's "little ones," including many Jews who had been converted.

There are some evidences that the Gospel had more than one author. The prologue is written in poetic form and uses theological terms such as Word *(Logos)*, grace *(charis)*, and fullness *(pleroma)*, not found again in the Gospel. There are apparent inconsistencies in the order of material in the Gospel. In 14:31, for example, Jesus concludes his remarks to the disciples at the Last Supper and gives the order to depart; yet these words are followed by three more chapters of discourse, and he and the disciples do not go out until 18:1. In 20:30–31, the author clearly draws the Gospel to a close; but this is followed by another chapter with yet another conclusion. This chapter (21) is different in stylistic details from previous chapters. And, in addition to all of this, there are certain repetitions of sayings in the discourses which seem to indicate the inclusion in the Gospel of two different traditions of the same sayings.

Although this may sound puzzling, it is all very easily explained. John the Apostle, the son of Zebedee, the beloved disciple, doubtless became the leader of a band of Christians, as did most of the Apostles. He delivered his image of Christ and Christ's teaching to his own disciples, probably over a period of several decades. Eventually either he or one of his disciples wrote down an account of the ministry and teachings of Jesus. The author may have known early versions of the other Gospels, and so may have chosen to stress materials different from the ones they emphasized. Then, at some later date, another disciple undertook to edit the original Gospel of John, adding to it other materials he had received from the tradition as John delivered it.

So John, whether or not he actually wrote every word of the Gospel himself, is in reality the author of the book attributed to him. It was his vision of Jesus, his knowledge of actual details, that made this remarkable Gospel possible. The Gospel was as fully his as any book is its author's today when editors, typesetters, and proofreaders have finished with it.

As the scholars for a period took John away from us—or at least cast doubts on the value of his reports—now they have given him back to us. It is a wonderful and timely gift. We have never stood more in need of what this Gospel has to teach!

You are in for a special treat if you read the Gospel faithfully each day, studying and meditating on the passages as indicated in this guide, and then waiting quietly in prayer for the meanings brought to you by the Spirit. You will find, as others have already discovered through the centuries, that it is in some ways the most spiritual of all the Gospels, and that the risen Christ who comes to his disciples in the upper room (20:19–29) will come to you as well. I know. It happened to me as I worked on these pages.

JOHN KILLINGER

WEEK 1

Week 1: Sunday

John 1:1–18 Jesus Is the Light

Word, light, power, grace, truth, glory, fullness. Like the overture to a musical play, the prologue of John's Gospel gives hints of all the themes to be developed later. It is a tremendous introduction—one of the greatest poems ever written. Frederick Buechner once called it "a hymn to perform surgery with, a heart-transplanting voice."

John knew he was writing nothing less than the story of a new creation. His words "In the beginning" instantly recall the opening of the Book of Genesis. The other Gospels—the Synoptics—emphasized the continuity between the ancient prophets and Jesus. John went further; for him, Jesus was the Word that existed before the creation of the world itself!

The good news in John is that this exalted, pre-existent Word became a human being. Let those who believed the flesh is evil think again—the Word was not ashamed to enter it. The redemption of the world would not be accomplished by divine fiat, but would come from within creation itself. Again and again, John underscores the humanity of Jesus. Even though Jesus is the eternal Word, the creative spirit of all life, he grows tired, shows anger, weeps, loves, becomes hungry and thirsty, and suffers on the cross.

Ancient Jewish writings—notably Job, Proverbs, the Wisdom of Solomon, Baruch, and Sirach or Ecclesiasticus—portrayed a spirit called Wisdom that comes from God, dwells among human beings to bring them to the light, then returns to God after being rejected in the world. John sees this spirit of wisdom in Jesus, who is the "true light," yet is rejected even by his own people, "the Jews."

The brightest note in the prologue, after the coming of the eternal Word, is that some have accepted the light and become children of God. These are born, as John says, "not of blood nor of the will of the flesh nor of the will of man, but of God" (v. 13).

These words are a key to the purpose of the entire Gospel. After A.D. 70, when the temple was destroyed, Judaism became stricter in the synagogues. A reformulation of the so-called Eighteen Benedictions resulted in the last benediction's becoming a curse on all heretics, aimed especially at Jewish Christians. Christians who attended the synagogue had either to leave or curse themselves publicly. We can imagine the dilemma this posed. Jewish Christians had grown up worshiping in the synagogues. Now they must choose between Christ and their familiar places of worship.

The Gospel of John was written primarily to encourage Christians—particularly these Jewish Christians—not to renounce their faith in order to be accepted in the synagogues. The Jewish people were born of flesh and blood—"of the will of man." But the children of the light are born of God. Moses, who never saw God, conveyed the Law. But Jesus, who not only saw God but came from the very bosom of God, brought grace and truth.

What more ultimate word could be spoken? Jesus was the very essence of the covenant God had made with his people in the beginning of their relationship. He was *word*, *light*, *power*, *grace*, *truth*, *glory*, and *fullness*. He fulfilled every promise God had ever made to the children of Israel.

O God, this is indeed a hymn for performing brain surgery! I feel that my mind is being carried beyond its limits, and I am shown mysteries too great for me to comprehend. I can only bow my head and worship you, content in the knowledge that your light will lead me to salvation, through Jesus Christ, the same yesterday, today, and forever. Amen.

Week 1: Monday

John 1:19–28 The Testimony of John

It is apparent from various evidences in the Gospels that there was rivalry between the disciples of John the Baptist and the disciples of Jesus. This may seem ridiculous to us, but imagine their situation. In an ancient country where communication was poor, they followed itinerant rabbis whose paths seldom crossed. Isolated and limited in perspective, each group of followers respected its own leader as the most important figure in the world. Even after the deaths of John and Jesus, a spirit of competitiveness continued to exist among their disciples.

The author of the Gospel wished to clarify the matter at once. The Jews sent a delegation from Jerusalem, he said, to ask John the meaning of what he was doing. The delegates were priests and Levites, persons intimately acquainted with ceremonial law, including the ritual of baptism. "Who are you?" they asked. John said, "I am not the Christ." The language here is significant. Literally, the Gospel says that John "confessed, he did not deny, but confessed" that he was not the messiah. In other words, John vehemently denied that he was the messiah.

The words John used, "I am not the Christ" *(egō ouk eimi ho christos)*, besides being emphatic, foreshadow a series of "I am" *(egō eimi)* phrases used by Jesus later in the Gospel—"I am the bread of life," "I am the light of the world," "I am the door of the sheep," etc. Surely no disciples of John the Baptist could miss the point—their master strongly denied that he was the Savior of Israel.

"If you are not the messiah," the delegation wished to know, "who are you? Are you Elijah or the prophet?" Baptism was an eschatological symbol—a sign of the end of all things. Popular belief said Elijah would return at the end of history (Mal. 4:5) or that some other prophet would be present to lead the people (Deut. 18:15). Again John uttered denials. "Then who are you?" pressed his questioners. The answer was appropriately modest: "I am a mere voice in the wilderness, crying, 'Make a straight road for the Lord'" (v. 23, P). John was citing a prophecy in Isaiah 40:3. The image was not uncommon in ancient times—kings and emperors often sent slaves in advance to secure the road on which they would travel.

There was only one question left to ask: "Then why are you baptizing at all, if you are not Christ or Elijah or the prophet?" (v. 25, P) That is, if John was not the one officially inaugurating the end of all things, what could be the significance of his baptizing?

John did not hesitate. "I baptize with water," he said. "But among you, in your very midst, stands one unknown to you who will come with another kind of baptism. And I am not worthy to loosen the thong of his sandal" (vv. 26–27, P).

The implication is that Jesus was among those standing on the river bank as John was baptizing. What drama there was in John's words! The real messiah was there, mingling with the crowd of onlookers, and they didn't know who he was.

There was a rabbinical saying at the time that a disciple might perform for his teacher any duty a slave might do for his master except one. He could not loosen his teacher's sandals. The Gospel was explicit: John saw himself as a disciple of Jesus!

O Lord, I, who am not even as worthy as John, beg to be your disciple. Grant that I may never get in your way, so that people see me when they should be seeing you. Baptize me in your Holy Spirit, I pray, that all my thoughts and deeds may glorify you, this day and forever. Amen.

Week 1: Tuesday

John 1:29–34 The Witness of the Spirit

Mark 1:9, Matthew 3:13, and Luke 3:21–22 all represent Jesus as receiving John's baptism. The account in the Fourth Gospel, however, tactfully avoids any scene in which Jesus is baptized. The author has been trying to emphasize John the Baptist's secondary role, and surely sees no point in confusing the issue by referring to the baptism.

Besides, the Christ of this Gospel is too exalted to receive baptism at John's hands. He is the pre-existent Word (1:1–3, 30). He and the Father are one (17:11, 20–23). When he prays, it is not for strength but to let the people know his relationship to the Father (11:42). He does not suffer in Gethsemane as the Jesus of the

Synoptic Gospels does. He is the transcendent Christ, the ruler of the cosmos; it would not be appropriate for John to baptize him.

In the Synoptic tradition, John recognized Jesus as the messiah after the baptism, when the Spirit descended on him like a dove (Mark 1:10; Matt. 3:16; Luke 3:22). Here, John purports to have witnessed the Spirit, but does not link it to Jesus' having been baptized. Apparently the descent occurred at some past time, so that John knew Jesus' real identity when the priests and Levites from Jerusalem came to see him.

It is not clear whether the priests and Levites are still present on this second day when John makes his pronouncements about Jesus; but this does not really matter, for they have served their purpose in the drama by permitting John to clarify his relationship to Jesus.

John makes three statements about Jesus: (1) Jesus is the Lamb of God, who takes away the sin of the world; (2) even though Jesus comes later than John, he existed before John and ranks above him; (3) the Spirit has descended on Jesus, and he is the one who baptizes with the Holy Spirit.

What is meant by the phrase "the Lamb of God"? Some scholars believe it refers to the apocalyptic lamb spoken of in Revelation 7:17 and 17:14, which is an object of terror and will destroy evil in the world. Others see it as the Suffering Servant of Isaiah 52–53, who gives his life for the people of God, or as the paschal lamb, whose blood was smeared on the door posts of the Israelites to save their children from the death-angel (Exod. 12:22). The latter interpretation fits especially well with the sacramentalism of the Fourth Gospel, which has Jesus condemned to death at noon on the day before Passover (19:14), the very hour when the priests began to slay the paschal lambs in the temple. But all of the interpretations are fitting, and it is possible that the author, with his great literary imagination, used the phrase for precisely this reason.

O Lamb of God, I worship you. I praise your name for this rich image of your saving power, and for the Holy Spirit with which you baptize your true followers. Help me to witness faithfully to your coming in my life, as John the Baptist witnessed to your coming in his. For you are indeed the Son of God. Amen.

Week 1: Wednesday

John 1:35–42 A Transference of Disciples

The Gospel presents three days in the life of John the Baptist. On the first, John witnesses to the priests and Levites from Jerusalem (1:19–28). On the second, he points to Jesus as the Lamb of God who takes away the sin of the world (1:29–34). On the third, John again calls Jesus the Lamb of God; and, this time, two disciples who hear John's witness leave John to follow Jesus.

This is the only Gospel that represents any of Jesus' disciples as having originally been disciples of John the Baptist. The other Gospels depict the calling of Andrew, Simon, James, and John at the seashore in Galilee. Many scholars are inclined to believe John's version is more accurate, or that the calling in Galilee occurred after the one in Judea, and the disciples had gone home to fish for a while. This would explain the apparent abruptness of the calling in the Synoptics.

In the case of one of the disciples who left John to follow Jesus, we are not told his name. Speculation suggests it may be John, the beloved disciple, who is mentioned again in 13:23, 19:26, and 21:20.

The scene is quiet but powerful. The two disciples walk away from John and follow Jesus. Jesus looks back, sees them, and asks, "What are you looking for?" It is a question he might ask any of us. The disciples reply by calling him "rabbi," which means "my great one" or "teacher." It is a title the author of the Fourth Gospel is fond of, for it accords well with the emphasis in the prologue on Jesus as the Wisdom of God. The disciples ask where Jesus is staying. He says, "Come and see." They come, and end by staying the entire day with him, because it is "about the tenth hour."

There is uncertainty about whether John's Gospel reckons time from midnight or 6:00 A.M. Probably it is from 6:00 A.M., making the hour 4:00 P.M. This means that the sabbath was upon them and they were unable to travel any distance before the next sunset.

The first thing Andrew does when he leaves Jesus is to go to his brother Simon and tell him they have found the messiah. Simon is to figure much more prominently in the early Christian movement than Andrew, but Simon might not have met Jesus at all if it had not been for Andrew. "We have found the Messiah" could be the most important message ever spoken by a disciple of Jesus, whether in their age or ours.

Jesus changes Simon's name to Cephas (Aramaic *Kēphâ*), which in Greek is *Petros*. The word means "rock," and probably expresses something Jesus sees in Simon's character or physique. In Matthew 16:18 Jesus infers that he calls Simon "rock" because he intends to build his church on him. The Fourth Gospel does not explain the renaming, but we recall that an act of renaming in the Old Testament (e.g., Abram to Abraham or Jacob to Israel) presaged some mighty use of the person renamed.

O God of Abraham and Israel, of Andrew and Simon Peter, what would you like to call me? What name might evoke the gift I am able to give you? Teach it to me as I pray, and let us have it between us as our secret, that I may hear you when you call me in the night, and respond, "Here am I, Lord." Through Jesus, my great one. Amen.

Week 1: Thursday

John 1:43–51 A Puzzling Disciple

There is something odd about this passage—none of the other Gospels mentions Nathanael as a disciple of Jesus. His name does not appear in the lists of disciples in Matthew 10:1–4, Mark 3:13–19, and Luke 6:12–16. John mentions it again in 21:2, with the information that Nathanael lived in Cana of Galilee. But otherwise he is a man of mystery!

The name *Nathanael* means "God has given." This has led some scholars to speculate that it is another name for Matthew, which means "gift of Yahweh." Others think he is to be identified with Bartholomew, for Bartholomew's name normally follows Philip's in listings of the disciples. Still others link him with Simon the Cananean, wrongly deducing that to be from Cana is to be a Cananean. The early church Fathers concluded that Nathanael did not become one of the Twelve, and so was never listed among them.

Given the custom of having two names, it is possible that Nathanael may have been included in the Synoptic lists under another name. We simply don't know. What is important in this vignette, however, is not whether Nathanael became one of the Twelve but the exchange he had with Jesus.

As Andrew had found his brother Simon and brought him to Jesus, Philip told his friend Nathanael he had met the one of whom Moses and the prophets had spoken. His name was Jesus. He was the son of Joseph of Nazareth. Nathanael's reaction was a jest, possibly because he came from the same region: "Can anything good come out of Nazareth?" (v. 46) Philip's words were the same ones Jesus had spoken to Andrew and the other disciple first called: "Come and see."

As Nathanael approached, Jesus said, "Behold a true Israelite, one without any guile" (v. 47, P). "How do you know me?" asked Nathanael. "Before Philip called you," answered Jesus, "when you were under the fig tree, I saw you" (v. 48).

On the surface, this is a light-hearted exchange. But John often packs even the simplest scene with deep significance. Nathanael probably represents the *real* Israel, that responds to God's redemptive activity without malice or deviousness. We recall that John was writing especially for Jewish Christians who were being tempted to revert to Judaism; they would have recognized the import of Jesus' hailing Nathanael as "a true Israelite," implying a contrast with the Jews who did not come to Jesus to see whether he was the messiah. The fig tree too is significant. In the Old Testament, the fig tree was often a symbol of a prosperous Israel. Jesus' remark about "a true Israelite" may have been prompted by his seeing Nathanael beneath a fig tree; or, on the other hand, the reference to a fig tree may have been designed to underscore the kind of Israelite Nathanael would become as a result of his coming to Jesus!

Nathanael's response was beautiful. First, he addressed Jesus as rabbi or teacher. Then he called him Son of God. And finally he named him King of Israel, which involves a play on the fact that Jesus had called Nathanael "a true Israelite." The order of progression from rabbi to Son of God to King of Israel is not anticlimactic, as it first appears, but climactic. When Nathanael called Jesus Son of God, it was more than calling him rabbi. And when he called him King of Israel it was more than a theological confession, it was a personal commitment. It was tantamount to saying, "You will be Son of God in *my* life, King of *this* Israelite."

Jesus' response to Nathanael was to tell him that the best was yet to come. If Nathanael had believed on the basis of their simple encounter, his heart would swell at all he would behold in months to come. What he would see would be utterly convincing—as if angels danced from heaven to earth and back again above the head of this man he had taken as his king!

O God, this is an inspiring passage. Help me to take Jesus as my king, that I too may be "a true Israelite." And, as I pray and meditate in the weeks ahead, let me "see" with spiritual eyes this confirming vision of Christ with the angels dancing above his head. For yours is the kingdom and the power and the glory forever. Amen.

Week 1: Friday

John 2:1–12 The Best Wine of All

Once more we are into material not represented in any other Gospel. This is extraordinary when we consider that John says it is the first miracle or sign performed by Jesus. Surely the disciples would never forget such a miracle, and it would figure prominently in all the traditions of the early church. The question naturally arises, did John see significance in this miracle that the other Gospel authors did not see, or was he imagining a story in order to illustrate a truth?

The beginning of the story makes us suspicious: "On the third day there was a marriage." On the third day from what? The answer is not clear. Some exegetes think it is the third day after Jesus' appearance at the place where John the Baptist was baptizing (1:29–34); others, that it is the third day after the calling of Philip and Nathanael (1:43–51). It has even been suggested that the third day is a reference to the resurrection, which occurred on the third day after Jesus' death. If this is true, then the mention of the third day is intended to signal a "spiritual" message to follow, having to do with a quality of life brought about by Jesus' resurrection. The possibility that this interpretation may be correct is enhanced by the fact that Jesus refers in verse 4 to his "hour"—a usage which in John always alludes to the hour of crucifixion and glorification (cf. 7:30, 8:20, 12:23, 12:27, 13:1, 17:1).

An Eastern wedding was a joyous occasion, often lasting seven days. It began with the friends of the bridegroom escorting the bride to the home of the groom, where there would be a great wedding feast. Friends and family members came from miles away. As Cana was only a few miles from Nazareth (some geographers identify it with a village two miles away, others with a village nine miles away), it is probable that Jesus' mother was related to the bride or the groom. At any rate, she and Jesus and his disciples came—including, presumably, Nathanael, whose home was in Cana.

At some point in the festivities—possibly after three or four days—the wine ran out. Jesus' mother came to him and said, "They have no wine." Jesus said, literally, "What is it to me and you, woman? For it is not yet my hour" (v. 4). The part played by Jesus' mother in urging him to perform the miracle has led some interpreters to believe that she felt responsible for the shortage. The wine at most weddings was furnished by the guests. Perhaps Jesus and his friends came with his mother, bringing no extra wine, and their presence caused the supply to give out.

It is doubtless significant that the miracle involved six stone jars that held water for the Jewish rites of purification. The number six meant incompleteness to the Jews, as the number seven meant completeness. If we assume that the wine had sacramental meaning—as a symbol of the Christian Eucharist or communion—we see the contrast between the inadequacy of the old religion and the fullness of the new. The steward of the feast—probably a friend of the bridegroom—pronounced the new wine even better than the wine they had already had, though it was customary to have the best wine served first at a feast.

In verse 11, John says this was the first of Jesus' signs (there will be many more in the Gospel) that "manifested his glory." "Glory" is a special word in the Gospel, and is usually related to the hour of Jesus' death. In the crucifixion, he will be lifted up for all to see (3:14) and the Father will glorify him (17:1).

Each of us must decide individually whether the author of the Gospel intended the story literally or symbolically. But, either way, it is impossible to miss a certain symbolic level in the passage. Early Christians could hardly have heard the account read in their presence without finding eucharistic meaning in it. Jesus is the one who gives the new wine of the kingdom. Wedding feasts were often used as a sign of the eschatological banquet—the great ingathering of God at the end of time. And Nathanael, the true Israelite (1:43–51), must surely have seen this.

O Lord, the old wine of my life has failed me. I thirst for the new wine of your presence and power. Come into my daily affairs, I pray, and give me a banqueting spirit. Transform the inadequate forms of religion in my life into wellsprings of faith and joy. For your wine is above all wines, and your kingdom beyond compare. Amen.

Week 1: Saturday

John 2:13–22 Talking about Temples

In the Synoptic Gospels, this scene occurs during the final days of Jesus' ministry and is instrumental in provoking the scribes and Pharisees to seek his death (Matt. 21:12–17; Mark 11:15–19; Luke 19:45–48). In John, Jesus visits Jerusalem not once but many times, and the cleansing of the temple comes at the beginning of his public ministry.

There may be significance in the placement of the story near the account of the wedding in Cana. At the wedding feast, Jesus demonstrated the superiority of the new order over the old. Here he moves from talking about the old temple to speaking of the new temple of his body, which would be raised up in three days.

We remember that the Gospel was written to encourage Christian Jews not to return to Judaism in order to continue worshiping in the synagogues. This passage had obvious meaning for such persons, because, in effect, it relocated "holy space" for them. Sacred space was no longer in a temple or in synagogues; Jesus had transcended all of this in his death and resurrection.

The cleansing of the temple precincts—the outer courts where birds and animals were sold and currencies were exchanged—became a mere launching point for the conversation with "the Jews," which is the weightier part of the passage. Those who sold birds and animals for sacrifices represented the old order of atonement, which the Epistle to the Hebrews would declare to be superseded by Jesus. Those exchanging money did so because the temple tax of half a shekel could not be paid in Greek or Roman coinage, which bore the images of pagan gods and emperors; they simply traded acceptable Tyrian coins for the other money, making a profit on each exchange. By fashioning a whip, probably from the rushes used to bed down the animals, and driving out the sellers and exchangers, Jesus was establishing himself in the tradition of the prophet Jeremiah. Jeremiah cried, "Has this house, which is called by my name, become a den of robbers in your eyes?" (Jer.

7:11), and threatened that God would destroy the temple in Jerusalem as he had the one in Shiloh.

The quotation "Zeal for thy house will consume me" is from Psalm 69. The context of the citation is interesting:

> I have become a stranger to my brethren,
> an alien to my mother's sons.
> For zeal for thy house has consumed me,
> and the insults of those who insult thee
> have fallen on me (vv. 8–9).

Taken alone, the phrase would indicate that Jesus did what he did because he was overwhelmed by feeling for the house of God. In its fuller context, the saying has another meaning—that his concern for the purity of the old religion, represented by the temple, has led to his disfavor among others, so that he receives the insults of those who were by their behavior insulting God.

In the conflict with "the Jews" (the Synoptics speak of chief priests, scribes, and elders), Jesus spoke with a double meaning. They asked for a sign of his authority—a miracle to attest to his messiahship. He answered with a dare: "Destroy this temple, and in three days I will raise it up" (v. 19). They assumed he referred to the temple from whose grounds he had driven the sellers and money-changers. In fact, he was referring to his own body.

Again there is a possible connection to the passage about the wedding feast at Cana. It too took place "on the third day" and was suggestive of the fullness of life to come through Jesus' resurrection.

It is little wonder, when Jesus had been raised from the dead, that his disciples remembered all these things and reconsidered them in the context of resurrection-faith. Then such incidents made sense to them in new and dynamic ways.

Lord, the old temple of my life is cluttered with things that dishonor you. Come in your cleansing presence, I pray, and drive them out. Resacralize my heart as a dwelling place for your Holy Spirit, and I shall praise you in word and deed, for yours is the glory forever. Amen.

WEEK 2

Week 2: Sunday

John 2:23–25 A Wary Jesus

The Gospel of John emphasizes a few signs or miracles of Jesus to the exclusion of many others described in the Synoptic Gospels. Here the others are at least mentioned. But we also receive an insight into the importance of the signs in John. They are significant for their spiritual teachings, not as proofs of Jesus' authority. Jesus himself disdains those who believe in him merely because they have seen some unusual act of power. This fits well with the saying in 20:29, "Blessed are those who have not seen and yet believe." The premium is on understanding, not on excitation by signs and miracles.

Verses 24–25 are a sad note on human nature. Jesus knew better than to trust the applause of the crowd, because he "knew what was in man." He understood the fickleness and selfishness of which we are all capable, and he knew it could rise in an instant at the least provocation. The very people who would shout "Hosanna" as he rode into Jerusalem would be crying for his crucifixion only a few days later.

Against the ephemeral nature of popular approval, we can better evaluate the devotion of the few disciples who remained faithful to Jesus through his ministry, trial, and death. They clung to him not because of what they had seen but because of what they understood about the coming of a new order. This is why John so preferred the title of rabbi for Jesus—he taught the disciples understanding.

If I understand why Jesus was wary of popular acclaim, Lord, it is because I know the fickleness of my own heart. Like the people of Jerusalem, I am inclined to be more excited about outward signs than inner meanings. Teach me to be quiet and to study hidden connections, that I may be faithful in all things. Through Jesus the Christ. Amen.

Week 2: Monday

John 3:1–12 A Teacher of Spiritual Things

There was drama in this brief encounter. It occurred at night. It was between Jesus and a member of the Sanhedrin, the seventy ruling elders of Israel. And it pitted one teacher against another—a wonder-working newcomer against an established interpreter of the Law.

Nicodemus came to Jesus at night. Perhaps he did not wish to be seen in the company of the rabbi from Galilee; or maybe he chose that time because Jewish elders enjoyed discussing the Law at night. But we must not overlook the symbolism of light and darkness in John. When John describes the scene in which Jesus confronted Judas about betraying him, he concludes by saying that Judas went out into the night (13:30). Jesus is the light of the world (8:12), and those who are not with him are children of darkness.

Nicodemus began the conversation respectfully. It was obvious, he said, that Jesus had God's authority behind him—else he could not have done the wonders he had been doing. Jesus' answer, though, was not about wonders but about the kingdom of God. A truly spiritual teacher, he implied, one born from above, would have recognized that that was what he was about.

The Greek word *anōthen* means both "again" and "above." It has often been interpreted in the sense of "again" by those who use the phrase "born again." But that is the way Nicodemus misinterpreted it, so that he asked, "How can a man be born when he is old? Can he enter a second time into his mother's womb and be born?" (v. 4) Jesus' remark in verse 5, that one must be born "of water and the Spirit," reflects his real intention in the word: to participate in the kingdom of God, one must be born (or receive *begottenness)* from above, from the world of the Spirit.

"It is like the wind," said Jesus, making another word-play (the Greek word *pneuma* means both "wind" and "Spirit"). "It blows where it wishes, and you hear its voice, but you don't know where it comes from or where it is going" (v. 8, P).

In other words, the Spirit world is a mystery too deep for mere human teachers to understand. Nicodemus may have been an expert in the Law, but even a natural force like the wind was beyond his powers of explanation. How could he hope to understand the kingdom of God? And, if he did not know what to make of Jesus' teachings up to this point, how could he possibly comprehend the deeper spiritual truths Jesus was capable of imparting?

We should consider the effect of this story on John's audience of Christian Jews. Nicodemus was one of the most learned men of Israel—one of the great teachers—and he appeared as a mere school child in the presence of the Master. Why would any Christian choose to return to Judaism, forsaking such a teacher as Jesus? Nathanael was clearly a wiser Jew than Nicodemus; he not only called Jesus Teacher, he also called him Son of God and King of Israel (1:49). No wonder Jesus called Nathanael, not Nicodemus, "a true Israelite." It was through him, and others like him, that the kingdom of God would be realized.

Nicodemus will make two later appearances in the Gospel. In 7:50–51, he will try to restrain the Pharisees in their immoderate attempt to silence Jesus. And in 19:38–42, he will come with Joseph of Arimathea, carrying a great mixture of burial ointment, to prepare the body of Jesus for entombment. The effect of these two references is to assure us that Nicodemus became a crypto-disciple, a secret follower of Jesus. But there is something sad about the stealthiness of his discipleship. It suggests that those who have most to lose are least likely to identify themselves wholeheartedly with Jesus. Being born from above is not as easy for them as for the simple folk like Simon and Nathanael. Their risk is greater, and they are inclined to approach Jesus more cautiously.

O God, it frightens me that I may know many things, as Nicodemus did, and still miss the truths of the Spirit. Teach me to be open to your presence, that I may discern what you are doing in my world and worship you. Through Jesus your Son. Amen.

Week 2: Tuesday

John 3:13–21 A Word from the Author

These verses have traditionally been treated as part of Jesus' words to Nicodemus. It is entirely possible, however, that they are a gloss by the author himself—a short sermon prompted by Jesus' encounter with the Jewish ruler. Ancient manuscripts employed no quotation marks or paragraph indentations to guide us in making such determinations; we must simply judge by the words themselves.

Verse 13, "No one has ascended into heaven but he who descended from heaven, the Son of man," makes little sense if spoken by Jesus. The Latin manuscripts and some Greek manuscripts of the Gospel add to the end of the sentence the words "who is in heaven." This, as well as the verses to follow, seems fitting if the speaker is not Jesus but rather the author of the Gospel.

When the Israelites were in the wilderness, they complained of the lack of food and water. God sent a plague of serpents among them, and many persons died. When the people repented, Moses prayed for them. God instructed Moses to make a brazen serpent and set it on a pole for bearing standards; anyone who looked at it would live (Num. 21:4–9).

Now John picks up this ancient image and applies it to Jesus' being lifted up. As it was a serpent that saved the people from the bites of serpents, it is a human being, the incarnate Word, who will save people from themselves and the human situation. The word for "pole" in Numbers 21:9 is also the word for "sign," and this was surely in John's mind. The real sign that Jesus gives, finally, is his being lifted up, both in his crucifixion and in his ascension. And anyone who regards this sign faithfully will have not only life but *eternal* life.

John is the Gospel of eternal life. Again and again this theme predominates. The phrase means more than everlasting life, though that is part of it. Understood cumulatively throughout the

Gospel, it signifies a special quality of life—an unusual nature conferred on those who are born from above, not by the will of the flesh but by the will of God.

God loved the world, says John; he sent his only begotten Son into the world so that the world could be saved. The emphasis is not on the *whole* world, as one sometimes hears in sermons, but on the world as the opposite of the Spirit. We are back at the Wisdom theme of 1:1–18—Jesus has come as the light of the world in order to save us from darkness.

The people who have seen the great sign—Jesus' being lifted up and received back into the bosom of the Father—have escaped the condemnation of the darkness. Those who have not accepted the sign—presumably the Jewish leaders—are condemned for loving the darkness more than the light.

O God of brightness and glory, I tremble to think how I am inclined to darkness and shadow in my life. My spirit is lazy and my deeds are often selfish. Forgive me, I pray, and teach me to love the light who has come into the world. For he has been lifted up and set above all darkness forever and ever. Amen.

Week 2: Wednesday

John 3:22–30 The Friend of the Bridegroom

When we think of joy, it is usually in terms of growing or expanding—of having more friends, receiving more acclaim, making more money. In this passage we encounter a contrary phenomenon. John the Baptist says that his joy is most complete at the moment when Christ's popularity must increase and his own decrease.

John and his disciples were baptizing at Aenon, probably a settlement along the Jordan River (the location is uncertain today), when a certain Jew engaged the disciples in conversation about purification rites. The Gospel does not tell us which rites were in question. Probably the discussion was related to some difference between what John taught about baptism and what Jesus taught about it. (We know from Mark 2:18–22 that people questioned the differences between John's and Jesus' teachings about fasting; and the same metaphor, of the bridegroom, figures strongly in that passage.)

The disciples, possibly with new information obtained from the Jew, came to John in a state of disturbance. The crowds were leaving John and going to Jesus, they reported.

John's reply was calm and confident. It had two parts.

First, Jesus was receiving the people because God had given them to him. This is a consistent theme in John's Gospel (6:39, 10:29, 17:2, 9, 11, 24). God is sovereign, and all those he gives to Jesus must come to him; conversely, any who are not given may not come.

Second, Jesus was the bridegroom of the kingdom and John was only the friend of the bridegroom. It was the friend's job, in Jewish culture, to prepare the wedding feast and have everything in readiness for the nuptials. It would have been the grossest impropriety for the friend of the groom to have tried in any way to take the groom's place with the bride. Instead, the friend waited with the bride until other friends of the groom came and brought her to the groom. Then the friend rejoiced to hear the sound of the groom's voice, and turned his charge over to the groom. At that moment, the groom became everything to the bride, and it was time for the friend to fade away. Therefore John said, "He must increase, but I must decrease" (v. 30).

The author may have included this remarkable passage to remind disciples of John the Baptist that John deferred to Jesus and surrendered his ministry to him. But it is also an effective reminder to us about our own places in the kingdom. We worry more than we should about being recognized for our contributions to Christ's ministry in the world. But Christ is the bridegroom and we are only his friends; it is appropriate for us to do our duty and then retire from the limelight. The real focus of spiritual joy is on Christ and his church.

Thank you, God, for this beautiful picture of the relationship between Jesus and John. Help me too to be a friend of the groom and do everything I can for his bride. In his glorious name. Amen.

Week 2: Thursday

John 3:31–36 The Witness from Above

This is another of John's editorial comments. Just as he followed the account of Nicodemus' visit with the short sermon about Jesus (3:13–21), now he follows the story of John's waning popularity with a brief homily.

"He who comes from above is above all," says John. The emphasis is similar to that in Jesus' words to Nicodemus, that one must be born *from above* to see the kingdom (3:3). Jesus is above all earthly teachers—John the Baptist as well as Nicodemus—and whoever accepts his teachings has eternal life.

Verses 32–33 appear to contain contradictory statements. First we read, "no one receives his testimony," and then we see, "he who receives his testimony sets his seal to this, that God is true." Apparently the first statement is hyperbolic—an exaggeration. "Practically *nobody* is paying attention to Jesus' teachings. But"—and this gives force to the second statement—"any who *do* pay attention are receiving life from above."

The Jerusalem Bible translates the passage in a way to resolve the difficulty:

> He who comes from heaven
> bears witness to the things he has seen and heard,
> even if his testimony is not accepted;
> though all who do accept his testimony
> are attesting the truthfulness of God (31–33).

It is interesting that John gives this insight into the popularity of the faith. Several times in the Gospel we receive the impression that great crowds flocked about Jesus. Perhaps this remark indicates a feeling of depression experienced by many Christians through the ages because so few persons, considering the size of the population, have responded to the light.

Verse 36 is a statement parallel to verse 18—whoever believes in the Son has eternal life, but whoever does not is already experiencing the wrath of God. In the Synoptic Gospels, the wrath of God was spoken of as occurring in the future. In John, it is already operative, just as eternal life is a quality of being in believers' lives now, not only in the life beyond death.

Lord, I am concerned about all the people who are even now experiencing your wrath. How terrible it must be to live from day to day with darkness and hopelessness. I pray for your grace in their lives, that somehow they may turn to the light and find a new quality of being. Through Jesus Christ. Amen.

Week 2: Friday

John 4:1–15 A Greater than Jacob

This is the beginning of a longer story with several interesting highlights. You may wish to read the entire narrative, verses 1–42, on each of three successive days while we are examining sections of it. There are so many things to notice that each reading will prove richer and more interesting than the last.

We are told that Jesus "had to pass through Samaria" (v. 4). Geographically this was not true, especially if Jesus and the disciples had been baptizing in the Jordan River; they could have followed the valley north into Galilee. But perhaps John was speaking of another kind of constraint—the spiritual necessity that appears to have governed Jesus throughout the Gospel. In other words, the meeting with the woman at the well could have been more than a coincidence; it may have been divine destiny.

It was noontime, and Jesus was tired. He had probably been traveling since daybreak or before. In good rabbinical fashion, he sat by a wayside well to rest while his disciples went into town to purchase food. The town was called Sychar, apparently the settlement known in modern times as Shechem, directly on the north-south route between Jerusalem and Galilee.

Noon was an odd time for the woman to be coming for water. Water for household uses was normally drawn early in the morning or late in the day. We know, however, that the woman had a loose reputation. Perhaps she came at an hour when she expected to encounter no one in the vicinity of the well. It is true that we often meet God's messengers when we least expect them.

Jesus violated tradition by asking the woman for a drink. She was a Samaritan, and there had been ill will between Jews and Samaritans for centuries. Jews considered the Samaritans half-breeds, as the Jews who had once lived in Samaria were systematically intermarried with Babylonians and Medes after the fall of the Northern Kingdom in 722 B.C. The average Jew would have deemed a Samaritan's cooking utensils or drinking vessels unclean—ritually impure for eating or drinking—and Jesus asked to drink from the woman's water jar. But the biggest scandal of all, as evidenced by the disciples' amazement in verse 27, was that Jesus should speak publicly to a woman, whatever her race. Most men of that day would not address even their own wives in a public place, much less a strange woman like this.

Like the authors of the other Gospels, John apparently viewed Jesus' behavior as an evidence of his messiahship. The Lord of creation transcended the parochial rules by which other men lived.

"If you knew the gift of God," said Jesus when the woman did not immediately give him the drink he requested, "and who it is that is saying to you, 'Give me a drink,' you would have asked him and he would have given you living water" (v. 10). "The gift of God" probably means "the Spirit of God" or "the Spirit of truth," which in the Johannine literature is always treated as a divine gift. Had the woman only been aware that the final age had come and that she was standing in the presence of the Lord of that age, she would have been seeking the water of life from him.

As is typical in John, what Jesus is saying is misunderstood (cf. the interview with Nicodemus in 3:1–12). The woman's reply in verse 11, about his having nothing to draw with, indicates that she has taken his words "living water" to mean mere "running water" or "flowing water," not the water of eternal life. Is he greater than their common ancestor Jacob, she asks, who discovered the well where she draws water? Even for Jacob it was not a place of running water, but a *phrear*, a mere cistern, from which water had always been drawn by hand.

Jesus' reply underscores the difference between the Old Order and the New: "Every one who drinks of this water will thirst again, but whoever drinks of the water that I shall give him will never thirst; the water that I shall give him will become in him a spring of water welling up to eternal life" (vv. 13–14). The Greek word for "welling up" *(hallesthai)* means "leaping or springing up" and implies great liveliness and activity. What a declaration this must have been to Christian Jews who were tempted to forsake their Christianity in order to return to the synagogues. The faith that had come to them through Jacob and the patriarchs would leave them always thirsting for more; what had come to them in Jesus was fully satisfying, and would be so forever.

Again typically, the woman didn't understand. She thought they were still talking about mere physical water. But she was so impressed by the words of the stranger that she asked him for the water that would end her trips to the well.

Is there a reference to Christian baptism in this passage about "living water"? Interpreters disagree. But it is hard to believe that John, who was extraordinarily sensitive to the meaning of words and symbols, would not have reflected on the relationship between the "spring of water welling up to eternal life" and the words Jesus had spoken only shortly before to Nicodemus: "Truly, truly, I say to you, unless one is born of water and the Spirit, he cannot enter the kingdom of God" (3:5).

God, I am as guilty as "the Jews" of forgetting how far above tradition Jesus is—how much nearer the center of your being, how much wiser, and how much more compassionate. Let me now, in the quietness of my meditation, experience his transcendent glory, that my life may be transformed by his presence. For his name's sake. Amen.

Week 2: Saturday

John 4:16–26 The Meaning of True Worship

We recall that the woman at the well, beginning to believe the words of Jesus but still not fully understanding them, asked him to give her the water that would quench her thirst for all time (v. 15). Jesus' response was to tell her to go and bring her husband.

The woman said she had no husband. Jesus said she had spoken truly, for she had had five husbands and was presently living with a man who was not her husband. John may have been using words with double meanings again, as he did in the exchange between Jesus and Nicodemus. The Hebrew word for husband was *ba'al*, which was also the popular word for deity. When Jesus said that the woman had had five husbands, he might also have been saying she had had five gods, and that the god she now worshiped was not her god at all.

Supposing that the conversation was only about husbands, however, we see something of the woman's moral character and how truly unsatisfying her religious faith had been in her personal life. The law forbade Jewish women to marry more than three times. Although the woman was a Samaritan, she had obviously married more often than women generally did.

Jesus exhibited the kind of insight into the woman's affairs that he had shown with Nathanael (1:45–51) and Nicodemus (3:1–12). As John said in 2:25, he "knew what was in man." His extraordinary power of perception led the woman to guess that he was a prophet, and she initiated a conversation about worship.

The Samaritans had always worshiped on Mount Gerizim, at whose base stood the town of Sychar and Jacob's well. There had even been a temple on the mountain until a Maccabean king, John Hyrcanus, destroyed it about a century before Jesus. Orthodox Jewish worship, on the other hand, had long been centralized in Jerusalem. Jews worshiped in synagogues, but the temple was considered the absolute focus of their worship.

The woman alluded to the fact of religious pluralism: people had different ideas about where they should worship. But Jesus used her words as a springboard for the most important truth of these few verses—that the hour was now at hand when worship at all holy places was superseded by a new kind of worship. "God is spirit," he said, "and those who worship him must worship in spirit and truth" (v. 24).

This was precisely the message needed by Christians being forced out of synagogue worship—that the time had come when God's rule was everywhere and there was no more requirement for sacred locations. The coming of the kingdom had rendered the old dependence on holy places null and void.

The woman's understanding was growing, as Nathanael's had. Did she dare hope that Jesus was the messiah—the one called Taheb in her religion? "I know that Messiah is coming," she said; "when he comes, he will show us all things" (v. 25). "I who speak to you," said Jesus, "am he" (v. 26).

Egō eimi are the Greek words—"I am." It is a phrase we shall meet again and again in John. "I am the bread of life" (6:35). "I am the light of the world" (8:12). "I am the door of the sheep" (10:7, 9). "I am the beautiful shepherd" (10:11, 14, P). "I am the resurrection and the life" (11:25). "I am the way, and the truth, and the life" (14:6). "I am the vine" (15:1, 5). Used alone as in this passage, without any modifier, the words I AM carry a definitive, regal impact—as when God said to Moses, when Moses asked his name, "I AM WHO I AM" (Exod. 3:14).

The one speaking to the woman at the well was the eternal Word, present at the creation of the world!

Lord, it often seems easy to worship you in church, where everything reminds me to look for your presence. Teach me, I pray, to expect you everywhere; for every place is holy if you are there, and there is no place where you may not be found. Amen.

WEEK 3

Week 3: Sunday

John 4:27–42 The Beginning of the Harvest

When the woman saw the disciples returning, she left her water jar and ran into the city to tell the people about the extraordinary stranger she had met. Why did she go so abruptly? Perhaps because the appearance of the disciples convinced her that Jesus was a special person; or because she knew they would not approve of her talking with their Master. Some interpreters have seen in the forsaken water jar a symbol of her inadequate religion, similar to the symbolic meaning of the six stone jars at the wedding feast in Cana (2:6). For the moment, at least, she had lost all interest in water from the well of Jacob; she had discovered the one who could give her "living water."

"Come," the woman exclaimed to the townspeople, "see a man who told me all that I ever did. Can this be the Christ?" (v. 29)

Had Jesus indeed told her everything? If so, we have received only fragments of the conversation. Considering the time required for the disciples to purchase food, we can imagine a much more extensive interchange. Jesus apparently touched the deepest feelings of the woman, causing her to become excited and voluble about the experience.

Meanwhile, the disciples set food in front of Jesus and were worried that he didn't eat. "Rabbi, eat," they said. But Jesus said, in effect, that he was feeding on something else. He was beholding the coming of the kingdom, and the vision nourished him.

Others had sown the seeds of the kingdom. Now he and the disciples were reaping the harvest. They had entered fields prepared by others, and the disciples' labors would bring them eternal life.

The Samaritan village was among the first fruits of the harvest time. The people entreated Jesus to stay with them, and he remained in their midst for two days. When he left, they said to the woman, "At first we believed because of what you said; now we believe because we have experienced the man himself, and are convinced that he is the Savior of the world" (v. 42, P).

Lord, it was this way in my life, too. At first I believed because others spoke of you. Then I experienced your presence for myself. It was like nothing else that has ever happened to me. Grant, dear Master, that the memory of the event may remain strong and fresh in my mind, and that your presence may continue with me always. For your name's sake. Amen.

Week 3: Monday

John 4:43–54 More Fruits of the Kingdom

Leaving the Samaritan village, Jesus continued his journey into Galilee, where, according to verse 45, he received an enthusiastic welcome. Some Galileans had been in Jerusalem for the Passover and had obviously brought back to their region tales of the signs Jesus had given there. Verse 44, the saying about a prophet's being without honor in his own country, seems out of place here, and logically antithetical to verse 45; many scholars believe it to be the insertion of a redactor who unwisely put it in here because of the mention of Galilee.

Apparently Jesus stayed again in Cana, the home of Nathanael. Perhaps he lodged with the couple at whose wedding feast he had turned water into wine. The references to that sign in verse 46 and to the two signs performed in Galilee, in verse 54, indicate that John saw a special connection between the two stories.

The official whose son was ill in Capernaum, about twenty miles from Cana, was called a *basilikos*, a term meaning "ruler" or "servant of a ruler." If there are parallels of this story in Matthew 8:5–13 and Luke 7:2–10, as some commentators believe, the man was probably a centurion, a Roman officer, for that is what he is in both Synoptic accounts. In those accounts, however, it was a servant or a slave who lay ill, not a son; John's account is more intensely personal than theirs.

The man may have heard reports of Jesus' powers all the way from Jerusalem. We can imagine his hesitance, if he was a Roman, to come to a Jewish rabbi for help. But his son lay dying, and his compassion for the boy overcame any reluctance. He came to Jesus and begged for help. Jesus' reply appears tinged with rebuke, recalling his reaction in Mark 7:27 and Matthew 15:26 to the Syrophoenician woman who asked a miracle for her sick daughter. Putting the kindest interpretation on it, it is a momentary demurring lest people fasten upon "signs and wonders" and not receive the truth of the kingdom lying behind them. But the man importuned Jesus. "Sir," he said, "come down before my child dies" (v. 49). The Greek word *kurios* means both "sir" and "lord." It is possible that the man had moved to a deeper level of respect and expectation, and that this indication of faith in the kingdom, as well as compassion for the dying boy, led Jesus to do as he asked.

"Go," said Jesus; "your son will live."

Content that it was so, the man began his descent from the hills to the seacoast around Capernaum. While he was still on his way, his servants met him with news that his son had survived the crisis. At what hour did he begin to improve, asked the father. At the seventh hour, the servants said—probably an hour past noon. The father remembered, that was the hour when Jesus had said his son would live. "And he himself believed," says John, "and all his household" (v. 53).

There are two significant things about this passage.

First, assuming that the *basilikos* was a centurion, or a Gentile, the passage completes an idea begun in chapter one when Jesus called the disciples and in chapter three when he was visited by Nicodemus. Jesus presented himself first to the Jews, then to the Samaritans (the woman at the well and the people of her village, in 4:1–42), and finally to the Gentiles. This is the model of the gospel's progress as noted in Acts 1:8: "You shall be my witnesses in Jerusalem and in all Judea and Samaria and to the end of the earth." And the conversion of the man's household foreshadows a pattern found in Acts 10:2, 11:14, 16:15, 31, 34, and 18:8. So the passage is an example of the way Christianity moved out from Jerusalem and Jesus became identified as "the Savior of the world" (John 4:42).

Second, the emphasis of the passage is on *life*, a central theme in John. "In him was life," said the prologue, "and the life was the light of men" (1:4). "Truly, truly, I say to you," Jesus will say in chapter five, "the hour is coming, and now is, when the dead will hear the voice of the Son of God, and those who hear will live" (5:25). This story of the ruler's son forms a transition to a section of the Gospel even more strongly concerned with the subject of life than the one we have been reading.

O God, it is so easy for me to confuse mere living with life itself. Like the child's father in this story, I become concerned about survival. Help me to see my own existence more from your perspective than from mine, and to be able to say, "Whether I live or whether I die, I am the Lord's." Then I shall praise you as the Lord of life—eternal life—and never worry about death. For you are the God of the living, not the dead. Amen.

Week 3: Tuesday

John 5:1–9a A Healing on the Sabbath

An early Greek tradition identifies the "feast of the Jews" in verse 1 as Pentecost, the Feast of Weeks. There would be a certain appropriateness in this, because Pentecost was the festival celebrating Moses' reception of the Law on Mount Sinai, and the passage to follow (5:2–18) represents Jesus' superiority to the Law in performing a sign on the sabbath.

The sign occurred at the site of an ancient pool near an area where sheep were brought for sacrifice in the temple—hence the reference to the Sheep Gate. The pool and the five marble porticos surrounding it have been excavated in this century, and visitors may descend to the waters by two rather precipitous stairways. It is theorized that the pool is fed by a deep spring that once flowed intermittently, causing the water to roil up as if stirred by an angel. Some old manuscripts contain an extra clause between verses 3 and

4 saying that an angel did indeed stir the waters, and that the first crippled or paralyzed person into the waters after such a visitation was healed of his affliction. While textual evidence for this information is weak, it may nevertheless represent a legend about the pool that actually existed.

We can imagine the scene around the pool on a typical day. There would have been dozens of poor, unfortunate people sitting or lying about on their mats. Most would have shown signs of poverty or squalor. Some would have had twisted limbs. Others would have suffered various degrees of paralysis. For hours at a time, they would have lain there, some waiting quietly, others moaning or talking.

Whenever the waters of the pool began to move, those who lay closest would scream and claw to get in. Relatives or friends waiting nearby would hasten to help their loved ones into the water, hoping to be part of a miracle.

Jesus singled out a man who had lain often by the pool but had never been able to get into the water ahead of the others. The man had been lame for thirty-eight years, and Jesus surely knew his circumstances in the same way he knew all about Nathanael (2:47) and the woman at the well (4:39). Stopping before the man, Jesus looked at him intently. "Rise," he said; "take up your mat, and walk" (v. 8, P).

Immediately the man was healed and did as he was told.

How surprised he must have been to feel life surging in his long-unused limbs! What trembling steps he must have taken, as if he were a baby first learning to walk. And what a wave of shock and excitement must have swept over all those who lay about the old pool.

"Why, we have seen that man here for years," some probably said. "We never thought he would walk again!"

The early church evidently saw a symbolic relationship between this story and Christian baptism, because the scripture, along with the story of Nicodemus in 3:1–21 and that of the blind man in 9:1–40, was one of three Johannine passages used to prepare new Christians for their baptismal rites. Perhaps the story was viewed in the same manner as was the water-into-wine story of 2:1–11, as showing the superiority of Jesus over the old order of Judaism. The man had lain by the pool with five doorways (symbolizing the Pentateuch, or five books of the Law) for thirty-eight years, and Jesus, the Son of the new order, had healed him in a moment!

Lord, my heart swells for what happened to this man by the pool. What power you have to transform the lives of those who were dependent on insufficient forms of religion! Touch the areas of my life that have not responded to you, I pray, and cause them to respond to your glory. For you are the hope of all who have waited a long time. Amen.

Week 3: Wednesday

John 5:9b–18 The Fury of the Jews

How do you feel when something good happens to someone else? Are you delighted in the person's good fortune? Do you feel almost as happy and excited as if it had happened to you?

That is the way it ought to be. Our love and regard for others should enable us to participate in their joy and happiness as if it were our own.

But that is not the way it was with "the Jews" when the lame man was healed by the pool of Bethzatha. Instead of rejoicing in the man's new wholeness as a human being, they became upset and angry because they saw him carrying his little mattress through the streets of Jerusalem. An article in the Mishnah, part of the embellishment on the Law, expressly forbade carrying an empty bed on the sabbath. Caring more for the Law than for the crippled man who was healed, "the Jews" immediately attacked the man for transgressing the sabbath rules.

The man responded to this attack by saying he was only doing what his benefactor had commanded him to do. The man who healed him had told him to take up his pallet and walk away. This simple-minded man was not attempting to fix the blame on Jesus; he was merely describing how he had come to be walking through the streets of Jerusalem with his mat under his arm.

"The Jews" demanded to know the name of the man's benefactor. The man did not know. In his excitement, he had not even bothered to learn the name of the one who had helped him.

Later, Jesus saw the man in the temple, possibly making a sacrifice of thanksgiving for his healing. "Ah, you are all right now," said Jesus. "Take care not to sin, lest something worse befall you" (v. 14, P).

(This last sentence is difficult to interpret, for it is directly opposed to Luke 13:1–5 and John 9:3, in which Jesus refuses to draw a connection between sin and human affliction. Perhaps it was added by a well-meaning scribe who thought this was a good place to inject a little moral lesson for people who are in a healthy condition. On the other hand, the idea of retributive welfare is consistent with sayings in John about children of the light seeking the light because their deeds are good, while others seek the darkness because their deeds are evil [3:19–21, 11:9–10, 12:35–36].)

Having seen Jesus again, the man went to "the Jews" and told them it was Jesus who had healed him. He had no apparent motive for doing this, and seems to have been ignorant of any consequences of the act. Characteristically, in John's Gospel, people do what they have to do in order to fulfill the drama of salvation.

"The Jews" then went to Jesus and raised objections to the sabbath healing. His reply was pointed: God did not stop working on the sabbath; why should he, as the Father's Son? This naturally irritated "the Jews" even more. Not only did Jesus heal on the sabbath, he claimed to be equal with God. John had said in the prologue of the Gospel that Jesus was in the beginning with God and participated in the creation of everything. But this was something "the Jews" could never believe. Therefore a conflict between them and Jesus was inevitable and would lead eventually to Jesus' death.

O Lord, grant that I may never care more about religious rules and practices than I do about any human being. As Jesus transcended all earthly forms and places of worship, so let my spirit rise above all petty and parochial concerns, that you may be glorified in a loving care for all the world. Amen.

Week 3: Thursday

John 5:19–30 The Authority of the Son

These verses continue a discourse obviously begun in verse 17, when Jesus answered "the Jews" after healing a crippled man on the sabbath. They explain in more detail the authority of the Son to heal and give life, as well as to condemn those who refuse to believe in him.

The argument, as C. H. Dodd has pointed out, is essentially from analogy. In primitive Israel, sons learned their fathers' trades; they could literally do only what their fathers did before them. "Truly, truly, I say to you," said Jesus, "the Son can do nothing of his own accord, but only what he sees the Father doing" (v. 19). In other words, if Jesus were not the Son of God, and had not seen God healing on the sabbath, he would have been unable to do it himself.

But Jesus goes further. Not only has he learned to do what the Father did, but now the Father has turned his work over to Jesus, much as an earthly father retires and puts his son in charge of the business. "The Father judges no one, but has given all judgment to the Son, that all may honor the Son, even as they honor the Father" (vv. 22–23).

Judgment here means positive as well as negative judgment—judgment to life as well as to death. God's work is seen principally as the work of judgment—of making decisions about the life or death of men.

Now that Jesus is in charge of the judging, those who hear him and believe his word receive eternal life; those who do not are condemned accordingly. Moreover, this power of Jesus extends not only to the living but to the dead. Even people in their tombs will hear the voice of the Son and come forth to be judged by him. Those who have led good lives will receive "resurrection of life" *(anástasin zōēs)* and those who have done evil will receive "resurrection of judgment" *anástasin kriseōs)*. That is, the good will go on living and the bad will have their evil deeds raised against them, and, presumably, return to their torpid states.

The guarantee of the Son's justice lies in the fact that he does none of the judging for himself, according to his own will, but does it all for the Father who sent him. Again, it is the good name of the Father that insures the validity of the Son's work.

Teach me, O God, to do your work as Jesus did. Not that I may be set as a judge over others, but that I may be used to bring life to those who do not have it. Let me show love to those who have not experienced it freely, and joy to those whose hearts are sullen. Through Jesus the Son. Amen.

Week 3: Friday

John 5:31–40 Witnesses to Jesus' Authority

In the continued discourse on his authority, Jesus refers to a principle in the Law that calls for more than one witness in a civil case (Num. 35:30; Deut. 17:6, 19:15). If he were the only one testifying to his authority, he says, his word would be untrue. But he is not the only one. "There is another who bears witness" (v. 32). Some interpreters have taken this to mean John the Baptist, of whom Jesus speaks in the next verse. But the sense of the passage requires it to be God, for the reference to John is parenthetical to a longer reference to God. Jesus appears to think of John after mentioning God.

"You sent to John," he says, "and he has borne witness to the truth" (v. 33). Compare John 3:25–30, in which the Baptist said, "I am not the Christ, but I have been sent before him." Not that the word of a mere human being is adequate, says Jesus; he cites John's witness only because "the Jews" seemed to delight in him and because, if they could believe through him, they would be saved.

It is really the Father's testimony that counts most, and the Father has witnessed to Jesus' authority in three ways:

(1) By letting Jesus do the works he has done in their midst. The purpose of the signs has been to lead people to belief.

(2) By bearing personal witness to Jesus' sonship. The reference is possibly to John 1:32–33, in which the Spirit of God descended like a dove on the Son.

(3) By the witness of the scriptures, which foretold the coming of the Son and the things he would do.

"The Jews," however, are insensitive. They have seen the signs and wonders in their midst but have not believed. They cannot hear the voice of God and so do not accept God's confirmation of the Son. And, though they search the scriptures constantly, hoping to find eternal life, they miss the clues and do not come to the Son, who can give them life.

Lord, teach me to listen faithfully for your voice, that I may learn to trust it above my own opinions or the opinions of those around me. Let your witness be the measure by which I evaluate all other voices. For you have the words of eternal life. Amen.

Week 3: Saturday

John 5:41–47 The Glory of God

The Jews in Jesus' day accorded exceptional honor to famous rabbis, and many rabbis lived like princes among their countrymen. They were given large banquets and were attended by the wealthiest citizens of whatever town they visited. Their words were repeated in the best society, and they were respected as the wisest men in the world.

The rabbis themselves contributed to this aura by the way they continually quoted one another's words and praised one another's sagacity. They had, as it has been called, a "mutual admiration society."

Jesus, as John indicates, did not take part in this self-serving exchange of praise. His glory was not the cheap demi-glow of human commendation, but the glory and honor of God himself. Yet, because he did not play the little game the rabbis played, they did not speak well of him, and "the Jews" did not accept him.

"I know," said Jesus, "that you do not have God's love in you, for I have come in his name and you have refused to receive me. But if some rabbi comes among you in his own name, puffed up with human conceit, you fall over yourselves to receive him. You are full of pride, and love to exchange praise for one another instead of seeking the glory of God" (vv. 42–44, P).

What shame verse 44 strikes into our hearts if we but ponder it! For which of us is not guilty of having had more regard to what other persons think of us than what God thinks? Even in Christian congregations, we are often influenced more by what the minister or other well-placed persons think than by what God desires. We should commit this verse to memory and meditate on it often during the coming week.

The final verses of the passage contain added irony if the "feast of the Jews" in verse 1 was indeed the Feast of Pentecost, honoring Moses and the Law. "Don't think I am the one accusing you to God for your error," says Jesus. "It is your beloved Moses who accuses you, for he wrote of me and you do not believe him" (vv. 45–46, P).

Lord, I am certainly guilty of caring what others persons think of me. I know I have done things to receive their honor and good opinion when I should have done them for you and the kingdom alone. Forgive me, and restore a right spirit within me. Through Jesus, who knows what is in the hearts of people. Amen.

WEEK 4

Week 4: Sunday

John 6:1–14 Communion by the Sea

This is the only miracle of Jesus recorded by all four Gospels (Matt. 14:13–21; Mark 6:32–44; Luke 9:10–17), and John's account is probably the best loved, for it alone provides the detail about the small boy who surrendered his lunch to feed the multitude. The boy's example has been hailed again and again in sermon and story.

Actually, there are numerous significant details in the story, including the information that Passover was at hand. Passover was the most important Jewish feast, as it celebrated the escape of the Jews from bondage in Egypt and the subsequent founding of their nation. Even Christian Jews would have continued to attend special synagogue services and eat the Passover meal. Perhaps John's note about Passover in verse 4 was intended for these particular Jews, as a way of saying to them that, though they were no longer permitted to attend Passover services in the synagogues, Jesus had given Christians another meal, the Eucharist or communion, as a celebration of enormous significance.

Reminders of the Eucharist abound in the story. First, Jesus gave thanks over the bread. The Greek word for giving thanks, *eucharisteō*, is the very word from which the Eucharist derives its name. Second, Jesus himself distributes the bread, just as he will at the Last Supper. (In the Synoptic accounts, it is the disciples who do the distributing.) Third, the Greek word for fragments, *klasma*, is the same word used in the *Didache*, our earliest manual of church practice, for the eucharistic bread remaining after the meal. And, fourth, Jesus told the disciples to gather up the fragments "that nothing may be lost," foreshadowing a practice of conserving the leftover bread.

The multiplication of fish as well as bread is interesting. In Numbers 11, the Israelites are represented as complaining in the wilderness that they had only manna to eat. "O that we had meat to eat!" they cried (v. 4). Moses was despondent. "Where am I to get meat to give to all this people?" he asked. "For they weep before me and say, 'Give us meat, that we may eat.' . . . Shall all the fish of the sea be gathered together for them, to suffice them?" (11:13, 22) Is it possible that Jesus' giving the people both bread *and* fish was John's way of saying to Jewish Christians, "Here is one greater than Moses"?

The fact that the boy's lunch consisted of barley loaves and fish indicates a background of poverty. This may have symbolized the economic standing of the early Christians, many of whom were slaves and mendicants. Nevertheless, they were rich in Christ. He fed them until they had "eaten their fill"—and still there was an abundance left over. Twelve basketsful of fragments were collected, recalling the twelve tribes of Israel and the twelve disciples.

The reaction of the crowd is important. Following the miraculous sign, the people all acknowledged that Jesus must be "the prophet who [was] to come into the world." In popular belief, a prophet like Moses or Elijah would appear before the end, heralding a new age. And the appearance would occur at Passover. Unfortunately, as we shall see in the next reading, the people misunderstood the sign of the loaves and fishes. Jesus came as a spiritual leader, and they tried to make him a temporal king.

O Lord, I am thankful for John's inclusion of the small boy in this wonderful story. It reminds me of the way you can use my poor gifts if I will only yield them to you. Let me be as generous as the boy, I pray, that I may see miracles around me every day. In Jesus' name. Amen.

Week 4: Monday

John 6:15 The Temptation in the Wilderness

The Gospel of John does not contain a full-blown narrative of the temptation of Christ such as the one we find in Luke 4:1–13. Luke says that Jesus was led by the Spirit to the wilderness and tempted three times. First, he was challenged to turn stones into bread and satisfy his hunger. Second, he was taken to a high mountain and shown the kingdoms of the world. "If you will worship me," said the devil, "it will all be yours" (Luke 4:7). Third, the devil whisked Jesus to the pinnacle of the temple and bade him to test God's protection by throwing himself down.

The portrait of Jesus in the Gospel of John is of a confident, self-assured Christ almost above temptation. He is human enough to weep (11:35) and thirst (19:28). But he is also the eternal Word, and shows no signs of an inner struggle with the Tempter.

Yet this single verse (6:15) is a hint that John knew the tradition of the wilderness temptations, for it barely masks a temptation similar to the second temptation in Luke's account, to become a king without going through the horror of the cross. Curiously, too, it follows the story of the multiplication of loaves and fishes as the second temptation in Luke followed one associated with turning stones into bread.

The eloquence of John's statement lies in its terseness and simplicity. Jesus saw the mounting enthusiasm of the people for the miracle he had performed, and, not wishing to be a political king, withdrew to the mountain by himself. Some ancient manuscripts used the word *pheugei*—he actually *fled* to the mountains.

To understand the full irony of the verse, we must turn ahead to Jesus' trial before Pilate, in which he was accused of making himself King of the Jews (18:33–37). To Pilate's question "Are you the King of the Jews?" Jesus eventually responded, "My kingdom is not of this world." And later, when Jesus was crucified, Pilate defied "the Jews" by placing a sign on the cross that read "Jesus of Nazareth, the King of the Jews" (19:19).

The true qualities of royalty in any person are unrelated to the approval of the crowds. They are inner qualities, qualities in the bone and marrow. Jesus showed his character by refusing to be swept into a position of earthly power by people who did not understand his real mission among them. His retreat to the mountains, where he could be alone with the Father, ought to be an example for us whenever we are about to submit to a popular temptation. The real values of life are not found in the acclaim of the crowd but in the quiet of the lonely heart.

O God, in whose deep silences all truths become clear, teach me to depend less on my own wisdom and more upon yours. For you have ordained that poverty may be riches, weakness strength, and loneliness the ground of true companionship. Through Jesus Christ our Lord. Amen.

Week 4: Tuesday

John 6:16–21 Crossing the Sea

If you are familiar with parallel passages in Matthew 14:22–27 and Mark 6:45–51, you are probably disappointed in John's account of the storm at sea and Jesus' walking on the water. In the Synoptic versions, the disciples thought they were seeing a ghost on the water and cried out in terror. In Matthew, there is the added story of Peter's disastrous attempt to walk on the water to Jesus. And, in both Matthew and Mark, the winds suddenly died down when Jesus stepped into the boat.

Much of the drama seems to be missing in John's story. Jesus came walking on the sea. The disciples were frightened. Jesus said, "It is I; don't be afraid." They gladly received him into the boat, and—a curious detail—immediately "the boat was at the land to which they were going." It almost seems that John had no interest in the story and has condensed it in order to be quickly done with it.

Reflection, however, may convince us otherwise.

First, let's recall the total setting of the passage, within the feeding miracle (6:1–15), and the important discourse on the bread of life (6:25–59). All of this occurred, we are told in verse 4, at Passover time. The feeding story therefore had an obvious relationship to Jewish memories, always rehearsed at Passover, of God's having sustained his people with manna in the wilderness. Another significant Passover memory was of the crossing of the Red Sea, when God saved the Israelites from the pursuing Egyptian army. One of the synagogue readings for Passover was Isaiah 51:6–16. It included these verses:

> Was it not thou that didst dry up the sea,
> the waters of the great deep;
> that didst make the depths of the sea a way
> for the redeemed to pass over? (10)
>
> . . . .
>
> For I am the Lord your God,
> who stirs up the sea so that its waves roar—
> the Lord of hosts is his name (15).

John's brief account of the stormy crossing, in other words, evoked powerful associations with the crossing of the Red Sea. For the New Israel, the church, it symbolized a moment of passage as important as the original crossing. Orthodox Jews might continue to celebrate the old crossing in their synagogues; Christians could celebrate the more recent crossing, and rejoice to know that the messiah was in the ship with them.

This brings us to another important detail in John's account—the *egō eimi* saying in verse 20. These Greek words, which occur also in the Synoptic versions, are usually translated "It is I." Literally, however, they mean simply "I am." We have commented earlier that they are reminiscent of God's self-identification to Moses in Exodus 3:14 as "I AM WHO I AM." "Say this to the people of Israel," God told Moses, "I AM has sent me to you." Of all the Gospels, John certainly lays most emphasis on the phrase *egō eimi*. His Jesus repeatedly employs the formula in introducing some facet of his messiahship—"I am the bread of life," "I am the resurrection and the life," "I am the door of the sheep," etc. It is impossible to read this passage about the storm at sea and not recognize in Jesus' "I AM" a declaration of power and transcendence, and an identification with the Father who has given him authority to perform signs and wonders.

Of course the disciples were "glad to take him into the boat"! They must have felt like the Jews described by Isaiah 51:11, in the Passover reading:

> And the ransomed of the Lord shall return,
> and come to Zion with singing;

everlasting joy shall be upon their heads;
they shall obtain joy and gladness,
and sorrow and sighing shall flee away.

And what about the curious ending of the passage—"immediately the boat was at the land to which they were going"? Is that a mere fairytale touch—zip! and they were at their destination? Or does it have a more esoteric meaning? Say, that they needed wait no longer for the fulfillment of God's promises to Israel, for the Savior had already come and was with them!

O Lord, there are such spiritual depths in this small passage that I feel like the disciples floundering in the waves. Let Christ come to me amid the threatening waters and join me in my frail vessel, that I may not be afraid, but may rejoice as the early Christians did, with singing and everlasting joy. Amen.

Week 4: Wednesday

John 6:22–40 A Sermon about Bread

It is impossible to believe that all five thousand people who were fed from the barley loaves and fishes followed Jesus in boats across the sea. They would have constituted a veritable armada! Probably John meant to indicate that a group of them—possibly a few dozen—took passage in some fishing boats and came looking for Jesus on the other side of the lake.

When they found him, their first question was about how he managed the crossing. They had seen the disciples leave in the only boat the disciples had, and they knew Jesus did not sail with them.

Jesus' answer betrays the impatience he felt for their failure to perceive the spiritual nature of his having fed them. "You seek me," he said, "not because you saw signs, but because you ate your fill of the loaves" (v. 26). That is, the miraculous healings (v. 2) and the multiplication of loaves and fishes were not signs to them because the events did not point beyond themselves to the mysteries of the kingdom. The people merely saw in Jesus a perpetual meal ticket—a king who could feed them even when food was scarce.

We should understand this, for we often behave the same way.

We too are more interested in having a government able to feed us—one that provides a favorable economic climate and a guaranteed income—than we are in the designs of God for our lives. Our stomachs carry a stronger vote than our souls.

"Don't spend your life's energies on the kind of food that perishes," said Jesus, "but seek the food that means eternal life for you" (v. 27, P). The Son of man will *give* us this imperishable food, he said.

Trying to understand, the people asked what they had to do to get the eternal bread. They were still trying to behave like their fathers, who had had to obey the laws of God for the manna in the wilderness. But Jesus told them what God's real work for them was—to believe in the Son who had come to them.

Like the simple folk they were, the people cited the only similar instance they knew—Moses' feeding of their fathers on manna in the wilderness. It was their recollection of this that had spurred them, the day before, to hail Jesus as a prophet and try to make him a king.

No, said Jesus, Moses did not give them the bread; God did. And it was God who was now trying to give them the true bread from heaven, not some mere sign such as the manna or the multiplication of loaves and fishes. "For the bread of God is that which comes down from heaven, and gives life to the world" (v. 33).

Apparently the people understood at last. "Lord, give us this bread always," they asked (v. 34).

In response to their humble supplication, Jesus spoke the words in verses 35–40.

"I am the bread of life," he said. "Whoever comes to me will neither hunger nor thirst. And I will keep that person and raise him up at the last day. For it is my Father's will that whoever sees the Son and believes in him have eternal life, and be raised up at the last day" (v. 35–40, P).

Lord, give me this bread, that I may neither hunger nor thirst. Help me to see beyond mere physical tokens to the food that is eternal. Let my praise be always for the gifts of the Spirit, more than gifts of the flesh. For they shall not perish or fail me. Amen.

Week 4: Thursday

John 6:41–59 The Mystery of the Bread

As the last verse indicates, this exchange between Jesus and "the Jews" occurred in the synagogue at Capernaum, not among the simple folk by the sea. Word had reached some of the elders of the synagogue that Jesus had said to the people, "I am the bread which came down from heaven."

"Why," they whispered among themselves as Jesus began to teach, "we know this man's background. He is the son of Joseph of Nazareth. How can he say that he came down from heaven?" (v. 42, P).

Jesus scolded them for murmuring. They couldn't understand, he knew, because God had not given them understanding; only those whom the Father drew could come to him. Like their fathers, who had eaten manna in the wilderness, they would die. But all of those who came to the Son believing would have eternal life.

The comparison of bread and manna was similar to the one in John 4, in Jesus' discussion with the woman at the well. There Jesus had said, "Every one who drinks of this water will thirst again, but whoever drinks of the water that I shall give him will never thirst" (4:13–14). Here, in this passage, Jesus said, "Your fathers ate the manna in the wilderness, and they died. This is the bread which comes down from heaven, that a man may eat of it and not die" (vv. 49–50).

Unlike the common people by the sea, who said, "Lord, give us this bread always" (v. 34), "the Jews" in the synagogue stumbled at the idea of Jesus' being bread and giving his flesh to eat. "How can this be?" they wanted to know. But they were unable to understand the mystery.

Let us remember again that John composed his Gospel especially for Jewish Christians being exiled from the synagogues. We can imagine the effect this passage had on them. It portrays the leaders of the synagogues as being dull and unperceptive, unable to grasp in faith the teachings accepted by the simple people at the seashore.

"You see," the passage said in effect to these Jewish Christians, "those in the synagogues do not understand the mysteries of our beliefs because God has not given them the gift of understanding. Our Eucharist is folly to them, for they do not see how a man born of human flesh can have come down from heaven. But we understand, and know that we have eternal life by eating the flesh and drinking the blood of Christ."

What a wonderful gift it is, Lord, to see you in the communion—to know, in some mysterious way, that when I eat the bread and drink the cup I am feeding upon you. Nourish me today that I may dwell with you forever. And let my life become food for others, for your name's sake. Amen.

Week 4: Friday

John 6:60–71 Some Disciples Go Away

The "hard saying" of verse 60 is the word of Jesus in verses 51–58 about eating his flesh and drinking his blood. The mystery of the sacramental body was anathema to Jews. Paul said the Cross was "a stumbling-block" for them (1 Cor. 1:23),. They simply could not tolerate the idea of another human being's becoming a sacrificial lamb for them.

Even some of Jesus' disciples "murmured" about the saying (v. 61), as "the Jews" had in the earlier passage (v. 43). Jesus' question to them, "Do you take offense at this?" or, "Are you scandalized at this?," employs the verb from the same root as the noun Paul used in 1 Corinthians 1:23. They reacted as "the Jews" in the Gospel generally did.

The reference in verse 62 to the ascension is equivalent to saying, "What if you were to see the one who will die and give his flesh as an eternal meal rising to be with the Father? Then would you realize the connection between this bread and spiritual reality?"

"It is the spirit that gives life," said Jesus; "mere flesh doesn't understand such paradoxes. My words *are* spirit and life. But some of you still don't believe" (vv. 63–64, P).

The disciples Jesus was addressing were obviously a larger group than the twelve. Luke 10:1 refers to "the seventy." Probably these were the ones referred to in this section of John. But, after this confrontation about spiritual matters, many "drew back" and no longer followed—all of them, apparently, except the twelve.

John, in keeping with his heavenly image of Jesus, carefully points out that Jesus knew all along which disciples did not believe and which one would eventually betray him (literally, "hand him over"). We were told in 2:25 that Jesus "knew what was in man." Perhaps this is why the question in verse 67—"Will you also go away?"—is worded in the Greek to imply a negative answer. Jesus knew the twelve would remain, and that Judas would be the one to turn him over to the enemies.

What a sad picture, Lord, of the humanity you came to save. There is weakness and treachery in the best of us—even those who have been with you as disciples. The bright note is your own presence in our midst, manifested in the bread and wine of communion. Forgive our shortcomings and feed us on your eternal self, that we may not fall away or betray you. Amen.

Week 4: Saturday

John 7:1–13 Going to Jerusalem

The Gospel of John is much more centered in Jerusalem than the other Gospels. In the Synoptics, most of Jesus' ministry occurred in Galilee. John, with more than two-thirds of his Gospel to go, shifts our attention at this point to the ministry in Jerusalem. Jesus will go briefly to Transjordan (10:40) and spend some time at Ephraim near the desert (11:54), but there will be no further mention of his going to Galilee. The stage is already being set for his great conflict with the authorities and for the crucifixion.

It seems odd that Jesus' brothers should bait him to go up to Jerusalem for the Feast of Tabernacles—they did not believe in him despite the signs he had done—and that he should at first refuse to go. Raymond Brown has seen an interesting parallel between their urging the trip and the devil's third temptation of Jesus in Matthew 4:1–11 and Luke 4:1–13. The three temptations in the Synoptics were: (1) to rule the kingdoms of the world; (2) to turn the stones to bread; and (3) to display his power by leaping from the pinnacle of the temple in Jerusalem. In John 6:15, Jesus fled lest the people try to make him a king (temptation #1). In John 6:31, the people asked him for miraculous bread (temptation #2).

And, in the passage we are considering, his brothers tried to persuade him to go to Jerusalem and demonstrate his power (temptation #3).

Jesus' answer to his brothers was that his time had not come. The Greek word for time, *kairos*, is charged with theological significance. It means "fullness of time"—ripeness—as contrasted with another Greek word, *chronos*, which means mere clock or calendar time. In the Gospel of John, *kairos* is used almost interchangeably with the word "hour"; compare, for example, Jesus' words to his mother at the wedding in Cana, "My hour has not yet come" (2:4). The "hour" and the "time" would come at the same moment—when everything was ready.

Later, after the brothers had gone to Jerusalem, Jesus apparently decided that the time had come and went secretly to the city. This agrees with Mark 9:30–31, which reports that Jesus didn't want anyone to know he was going to Jerusalem and that he used the time on the journey to explain to the disciples that he would be killed there.

"The Jews" were expecting him at the feast. Probably they were already at work attempting to turn the populace against him. John says there was "much muttering about him among the people" (the word for "muttering" is the same one used in 6:41 and 6:61 for "murmuring," with a negative denotation). Some people insisted that Jesus was a good man, but others said he was deceiving people. Apparently this was a standard charge made against him. Luke 23:2 refers to it as the formal accusation against him in the trial before Pilate ("We found this man perverting our nation"), and Matthew 27:63 has the Pharisees telling Pilate that Jesus is an "impostor" or "deceiver."

The phrase "for fear of the Jews" in verse 13 sets the tone for the confrontations to follow. These particular Jews—obviously the authorities in Jerusalem—are seen as being both treacherous and powerful. They are emissaries of the darkness, and are naturally opposed to the light of the world. Conflict is inevitable.

O Lord, even your own brothers in the flesh did not understand you. What a dark and ignorant place the world is! How blind we can be to one another and to the truth! I pray for a light in the darkness, for even a glimmer to follow in my own personal dealings. Let me not fail to understand those close to me, for in serving them I am able to serve you, and in loving them I show my love to you. Amen.

WEEK 5

Week 5: Sunday

John 7:14–36 The Greatest Rabbi of All

The Feast of Tabernacles lasted seven days, except when it began on a sabbath; when it began on a sabbath, it ran through the following sabbath, for a total of eight days. Jesus probably began to teach in the temple on the third or fourth day of the feast.

The people were amazed at the depth and perception of his teaching, particularly in light of the fact that he had studied under no other rabbi. In those days, men became rabbis by following other rabbis and learning to speak as they did. There was a standard rabbinical lore, consisting primarily of the sayings of famous rabbis. But Jesus exhibited none of the traditional lore; there was a freshness and incisiveness about his teachings. Luke 2:46–47 indicates that already at the age of twelve he was astounding the learned men of the temple. John did not bother to cite this detail, if indeed he knew it; for him, Jesus was the divine Wisdom incarnate in human form, and no other explanation was needed for his exceptional teachings. "My teaching is not mine," said Jesus, "but his who sent me" (v. 16).

In the course of his discussion, Jesus raised the issue of the plot to kill him. No plot had been made public, but Jesus knew of its existence as, in the Fourth Gospel, he knew other things. His enemies were caught off guard and said he was crazy—literally, that he had a demon, which at that time was the way of expressing dementedness.

Jesus pinpointed the reason for their hostility—it was the healing of the crippled man on the sabbath (5:2–18). "I did one deed," he said, "and it shocked you all" (v. 21, P).

Then Jesus used a rabbinical argument to justify the healing. The rite of circumcising a male child was supposed to occur on the eighth day after birth. If birth occurred on a sabbath, circumcision was permitted on the following sabbath (the eighth day, counting the first sabbath as day one). Circumcision affected only part of the body, though it was supposed to be efficacious for the total personality. Jesus' argument proceeded from a lesser to a greater benefit: if circumcision was permitted, why wasn't the healing of the whole body, which obviously did even more for the person affected? "Don't be superficial in your judgments about these matters," said Jesus; "really use your senses" (v. 24, P).

The people were confused. Jesus seemed so wise, so right, that it was hard not to believe he was the messiah. Yet they knew his family and where he came from. His brothers were right there in the crowds. Wasn't the messiah supposed to come in secrecy, from unknown origins? Nathanael had perhaps echoed a similar belief when he asked, "Can anything good come out of Nazareth?" (1:46)

"All right," said Jesus, in effect, "so you know me and know where I come from. But I don't come on my own. I was sent. And you *don't* know the One who sent me" (vv. 28–29, P).

It was an effective point, and carried the argument back to the center of the matter all along—that Jesus knew God and his enemies did not. Many people believed in him. "Could another messiah do more signs than this one?" they asked (v. 31, P). But the authorities intensified their efforts to arrest Jesus. Only the fact that his hour had not come deterred them; God would not give them the power they needed until the time was right.

Always in command, Jesus spoke words "the Jews" could not understand. "I shall be with you a little longer, and then I go to him who sent me; you will seek me and you will not find me; where I am you cannot come" (vv. 33–34). Later, he would speak the same words to the disciples in the upper room (13:33, 16:16). "The Jews" were confused. Was Jesus planning to escape from their territory and take up teaching in a Jewish colony elsewhere? Their minds were not spiritual enough to perceive that the one who had come from God was about to return to God.

O God, I know how the authorities felt. I too have trouble with the fact that Jesus came from Nazareth and had a family like my own. But that is because my spirit, like theirs, is too earthbound and prosaic. When I am in prayer, and am no longer hindered by human rationality, I know he is the Christ, and that I am part of his kingdom. Grant that the mood of my praying may more and more dominate the rest of my life, that I may live for the kingdom every hour, and with every ounce of my being. For his name's sake. Amen.

Week 5: Monday

John 7:37–52 The Baptism of the Spirit

To understand the impact of Jesus' words on the final day of the feast, it is important to know a little about the feast itself. The Feast of Tabernacles, together with Passover and Pentecost, was one of three major Jewish festivals. Occurring in the autumn, it was associated with the harvest, but it also commemorated the years of wilderness wanderings, when the Israelites lived in tents or tabernacles. The people celebrated it with special religious services and by erecting small huts or booths reminiscent of the wilderness dwellings.

One of the central images of the feast was *water*. Finding water to drink had been a primary concern of the Israelites in the wilderness, and water for crops was always a concern after they reached the promised land. Therefore many of the scripture readings for synagogue services during the feast contained references to fountains, springs, and rivers. One reading, for example, Zechariah 9–14, describes the coming of the messianic king and God's giving men "showers of rain,/ to every one the vegetation in the field" (10:1). "On that day," said the prophet, "living waters shall flow out from Jerusalem, half of them to the eastern sea and half of them to the western sea; it shall continue in summer as in winter. And the Lord will become king over all the earth" (14:8–9).

In keeping with the emphasis on water, a special ceremony was observed during each morning of the feast. A procession descended from the temple to the fountain of Gihon, where a priest filled a golden pitcher with water as the choir sang Isaiah 12:3—"With joy you will draw water from the wells of salvation." Then the procession climbed the hill to the temple, singing the Hallel psalms (113-118), and marched around the altar in front as they sang:

> Save us, we beseech thee, O Lord!
> O Lord, we beseech thee, give us
> success! (Ps. 118:25)

Finally the priest mounted the ramp to the altar and poured the water into a silver funnel that allowed it to return to the ground. On the last day of the feast, the circling of the altar occurred not once but seven times.

It was probably at this moment on the final day of the feast ("the great day," as John calls it in verse 37) that Jesus stood up and cried out (the same verb is used for John the Baptist's crying out in the wilderness): "If anyone thirst, let him come to me and drink. He who believes in me, as the scripture has said, 'Out of his heart shall flow rivers of living water'" (vv. 37–38).

We can imagine the dramatic impact of such an announcement, especially at a time when the people were so divided in their opinions about Jesus and were talking about him constantly.

Curiously, there is no particular verse of scripture that says, "Out of his heart shall flow rivers of living water." Numerous theories have been proposed to explain the quotation. One of the Hallel psalms, 114, sung during the procession to the temple, says:

> Tremble, O earth, at the presence of the Lord,
> at the presence of the God of Jacob,
> who turns the rock into a pool of water,
> the flint into a spring of water (vv. 7–8).

The psalm's reference is to Moses' striking the rock and bringing forth water (Exod. 17:6, Num. 20:11). It is possible, too, that Jesus was referring to Zechariah 14:8, which we have already cited, "On that day, living waters shall flow out of Jerusalem."

Regardless of whatever scripture Jesus was citing, he probably adapted it in such a way as to refer to a phenomenon noted only in the Fourth Gospel, the issue of blood *and water* from the right side of the crucified (19:34). This would give meaning to "out of his heart" in the saying under question.

John, however, was untroubled by the source problem. He concentrated instead on the symbolism of Jesus' words. Jesus was really speaking, he said, about the pouring out of his Spirit on believers, which would occur after Jesus' death. Considering the fact that the outpouring of the Spirit occurred at Pentecost, when Jews from all over the Diaspora were gathered in Jerusalem, and thence reached many nations, John may indeed have been thinking of Zechariah 14:8 when he wrote Jesus' saying—on that day, living waters would flow out of Jerusalem to the east and the west!

When the temple police returned to the chief priests and Pharisees without Jesus, their leaders demanded to know why they had not arrested him. The police were unanimous in their reply: "No man ever spoke like this man!" (v. 46). The Pharisees were irate. Had the police found any inclination among them, the rulers of the people, to believe in Jesus? No, it was only the crowds who believed—the common people—and they were bewitched.

But one member of the Sanhedrin spoke courageously. It was Nicodemus, the ruler who had come to Jesus by night. Jesus had spoken to him about baptism "of water and the Spirit" (3:5). Did Nicodemus recognize a connection between that nocturnal conversation and Jesus' announcement at the feast about "rivers of living water" (v. 38)? Nicodemus' point was a telling one: their very Law provided for hearing a man before judging him (cf. Exod. 23:1 and Deut. 1:16–17). But the others were beyond reason. As tools of the darkness, they were trying to put out the light.

Lord, what a glorious scene this must have been, when you stood up at the feast and announced the "rivers of living water"! How prone I am to choke with thirst, when you are ready to provide your Spirit in measureless abundance. Help me this day to live with the image of the rivers, and to come to you repeatedly for my baptism of joy. Amen.

Week 5: Tuesday

John 7:53—8:11 The Woman Taken in Adultery

Most modern translations of the Fourth Gospel confine this passage to italics or small print to indicate its dubious place in the canonized text. No early manuscripts of reliability included it as a part of the Gospel. We are not certain precisely when it was inserted into the text, and some ancient manuscripts even place it in Luke, following 21:38, rather than in John. But through the centuries it has become a beloved part of the Gospel, told again and again to illustrate the tender forgiveness of Christ, and we shall do well to ponder it today regardless of its origin.

Verses 7:53 and 8:1 picture the disciples as going to various places of lodging about the city of Jerusalem, while Jesus went to his own place, somewhere on the Mount of Olives. Luke 21:37 says that "at night [Jesus] went out and lodged on the mount called Olivet," and this probably accounts for the passage's having been allocated in some manuscripts to this spot in Luke.

Early in the morning Jesus crossed the valley and climbed to the temple again, where he sat to teach. The day has always begun quite early for the people of Jerusalem, especially in the warmer months. They then become inactive at midday, when the temperature has risen, and resume a busier pace in the late afternoon.

The scribes and Pharisees brought a woman caught in the act of intercourse with a man who was not her husband. She was either an engaged woman or a woman already married, for the Law said nothing about adultery between a man and an unmarried woman who was not engaged. Leviticus 20:10 specified that both the man and the woman should be put to death, but in this case either the man was being held separately or he had escaped.

It is not clear whether the men who brought the woman to Jesus really intended to abide by whatever he decided about her. What *is* clear is that they expected to trap Jesus by whatever he said. If he said to release her, he would be countering a commandment of Moses; if he said she should be stoned, he would be in trouble with the Romans, who appear to have rescinded the Sanhedrin's power of capital punishment before this time. It was a dilemma similar to that of Mark 12:13–17, where Jesus was asked if it was lawful to pay taxes to Caesar.

Jesus stooped down and wrote on the ground with his finger. What did he write? The question has puzzled interpreters through the ages. Perhaps he wrote the word "witnesses," and was thinking of Deuteronomy 17:7, which says, "The hand of the witnesses shall be first against him to put him to death, and afterward the hand of all the people. So you shall purge the evil from the midst of you." It was a text about a situation like this.

At any rate, Jesus stood and gave his judgment: "Let him who is without sin among you be the first to throw a stone at her" (v. 7). And once more he knelt to write on the ground.

One by one, beginning with the eldest, the accusers left. It is an interesting detail that the eldest went first. They, more than the younger persons, would understand the complexity of sin and evil in the world. As Georges Bernanos once wrote, "We inhale it in the very air we breathe."

Jesus looked up. "Where are they?" he asked. "Has no one condemned you?" "No one, Lord," she said. "Nor do I," said Jesus. "Go, and do not sin again" (vv. 10–11, P).

Some scholars believe this passage may have existed in the Fourth Gospel at an early stage and then been expunged for fear it would produce an air of easiness toward sin. Certainly it seems less astringent about morality than the letters of Paul and other early Christian writings. But Jesus did command the woman not to commit sin again, and the judgment he executed cut the accusers as well as the woman, suggesting that true morality is a matter the Law cannot finally regulate or guarantee.

There is one very good reason that we have not mentioned for the story's inclusion in the Fourth Gospel. That is its relationship to the Wisdom theme in John. The dilemma posed to Jesus was not unlike the one set before Solomon in 1 Kings 3:16–28, when two women claimed the same child. When Solomon solved the problem, the people stood in awe of him, "because they perceived that the wisdom of God was in him, to render justice." Many people have felt the same way about Jesus because of the sensitive way he handled the problem thrust upon him.

Teach me, O Christ, to number my own sins before counting the sins of others. Then let me wait upon your presence until I have received the judgment given to this woman. And I shall praise you for your great victory, which is from everlasting to everlasting. Amen.

John 8:12–30 The Light on High

We are still dealing, in this section, with the Feast of Tabernacles, and again the ceremonies of the feast help us to understand the text. Traditionally, *light* was important in the ceremonies in much the same way that *water* was. The Israelites in the wilderness had been guided by a pillar of fire by night. And Zechariah, who provided a scriptural background for the water symbolism, likewise said this about light in the coming Day of the Lord: "There shall be continuous day (it is known to the Lord), not day and not night, for at evening time there shall be light" (14:7).

As there was a ritual involving water during the time of Tabernacles, there was one about light. It centered on the lighting of enormous candles in the Court of the Women, an outer part of the temple. There were four great golden candlesticks, each with four golden bowls on top that were reached by ladder. Floating in oil in these bowls were wicks made from the girdles of the priests. When the wicks were lit, the light reflected by the burnished bowls was said to illumine the entire city of Jerusalem.

It may well have been in the context of such a ceremony that Jesus said, "I am the light of the world."

We can imagine the scene. The people were gathered in the vicinity of the temple. Psalms were sung, and other scriptures were recited. The priests chanted prayers. Then, at a climactic moment, young men climbed the ladders and lit the special wicks. Out of the hush of the crowd rose an exclamation of wonder as the highly polished bowls caught the reflection of light and magnified it over the night sky. Even people who had witnessed the lighting for years were filled with awe.

And Jesus, standing among his disciples, spoke firmly and assuringly, loud enough for others to hear: "I am the light of the world; he who follows me will not walk in darkness, but will have the light of life" (v. 12).

Once more we have an *egō eimi* saying—one of the great messianic declarations of the Fourth Gospel. Like all the others, it is only a partial statement of the nature and work of Jesus. But, taken together, they imply the ultimate significance of his being.

The Pharisees challenged the assertion. As before, they accused him of being his only witness. Even so, he said, it was enough, because he knew whence he had come and where he was going (that is, from and to the Father), and that gave special character to his witness. "You Pharisees judge things according to the flesh," said Jesus, "I don't. And I don't judge by myself. The One who sent me judges with me" (vv. 15–16, P).

(These verses about judging may account for the story of the adulterous woman's being placed next to them. Jesus' saying he judged no one according to the flesh would seem most appropriate to the story.)

Again Jesus spoke of going away (v. 21). This time, instead of supposing he was planning to slip away to the Diaspora, as in 7:35–36, "the Jews" wondered if he spoke of killing himself. They could not understand, because, as Jesus said, they were from below and he was from above; his actions and speech were indecipherable to them. Only if they believed on him would they not die in their sins.

"Who are you?" they asked him. I am who I have told you from the beginning, he said—the one sent by the Father. "When you have lifted me up"—the same verb is used as in 3:14–15, about lifting the serpent in the wilderness—"you will realize that I AM, and that everything I do, I do in the authority of the Father" (v. 28, P).

Yet again we have an *egō eimi*, only this time used without a predicate modifier. The New English Bible translation is "you will know that I am what I am," which I find preferable to the RSV and Jerusalem Bible's "you will know that I am he." But the real significance of the statement must be seen against God's word to Moses, "I AM WHO I AM," and, "Say this to the people of Israel, 'I AM has sent me to you'" (Exod. 3:14).

Here we see why the author of the Fourth Gospel equates Jesus' being lifted up with his being exalted or glorified. For, after his death, people would realize that he was who he had said he was from the beginning of his ministry, namely, the Son of the Father, the I AM himself. Then there would be no question about his authority or the testimony he gave. People would know he was "the light of the world."

Meanwhile, the Son's chief comfort was this: "He who sent me is with me; he has not left me alone" (v. 29).

I know, Father, what Jesus meant; I cannot bow before the cross without realizing his identification with you. There is a power and a mystery there that energizes my life with faith. Mediate your presence to me through that image, and help me always to follow him who was crucified and raised from the dead. In his great name. Amen.

Week 5: Thursday

John 8:31–59 A Greater than Abraham

There is some question about who is being addressed in this passage. Verse 31 says "the Jews who had believed on him." But it soon becomes obvious that these Jews are not faithful followers and, in fact, hold positions of hostility to Jesus. There are two possible explanations: (1) their belief evaporated ("they *had* believed on him") or (2) the addresses mysteriously shift, between verses 31 and 34, from Jews who believed to "the Jews" who had been Jesus' enemies all along. Whichever explanation we accept, the meaning of the passage is the same: only in Jesus, not in Abraham, is there freedom and life.

The statement in verse 33, "We are descendants of Abraham, and have never been in bondage to any one," is odd, for the Jews had been enslaved by the Egyptians and the Babylonians, and were at the very time of speaking under the rule of the Romans. Possibly the speakers were thinking of spiritual bondage, for it was true that Jewish worship had been maintained even under most exilic conditions.

Jesus' argument ran this way: (1) Anyone who sins is a slave to sin; (2) the Jews were trying to kill him, and were therefore sinners; (3) they were therefore also slaves.

Jesus accused "the Jews" of being children of the devil and not of Abraham. "We were not born of fornication," they exclaimed; "we have one Father, even God" (v. 41). No, said Jesus; if they had been children of God, they would have known him as the Son of God. As children of the devil, they were at home with lies, not the truth; that is why they did not recognize the truth of Jesus' words (vv. 43–45).

"The Jews" retorted by calling Jesus a Samaritan and saying he was possessed of a demon (v. 48). The reference to Samaritans may have been a slur implying that Jesus was not even a good Jew. To have a demon was to be deranged.

On the contrary, said Jesus, God would be the judge of who he was. And anyone who kept his word would never see death (vv. 49–51). Was he still speaking to "the Jews who had believed in him," trying to elicit their support?

"Now we know you are crazy!" said "the Jews." "Abraham died, as did all the prophets after him, and you speak of never tasting death. Who do you think you are? Are you greater than Abraham and the prophets?" (vv. 52–53, P)

"Ah," said Jesus, "Abraham. Abraham rejoiced to see my day. He saw it and was glad" (v. 56, P). The meaning of this is not clear. Jesus may have meant that Abraham foresaw the fulfillment of God's promises to him—that he would be the father of a great kingdom (Gen. 12:1–3)—in the kingdom of Jesus. Or, some interpreters believe, he may have spoken of Abraham after death, being able then to see all things clearly.

"The Jews" scoffed. "You are not yet fifty years old," they said. "How could you have seen Abraham?" (v. 57, P) Luke 3:23 says that Jesus was about thirty years old when he began his ministry. These are the only two scriptural references to Jesus' age. Only if the ministry was much longer than the chronologists have figured could Jesus have been near fifty when he died. The saying may have been mere exaggeration, without any attempt to fix upon his correct age.

Jesus' next remark was the climax of the discourse. "Truly, truly," he said, "before Abraham was, I AM" (v. 58). It is the *egō eimi* again, and again without a predicate modifier. There is extreme majesty in the announcement, as if to say, "Fifty years? A trifle. Before Abraham was born, I already existed."

At this, "the Jews" took up stones to throw at him. This probably does not imply a decision to execute him on the spot—the Jews did not have the power of imposing the death penalty. Instead, it suggests the irateness of their spirits. Jesus had provoked them beyond their limits, and, in exasperation, they picked up stones to throw at him.

But, as Jesus had slipped into Jerusalem secretly at the beginning of the feast, now he hid himself, possibly behind piles of stone or building materials being used to finish the temple, and slipped away. If any of the people he was addressing had been followers, there was no longer any question of where their sympathies lay. He left the temple alone.

Lord, all of this talk about Abraham is quite mystifying to me, for I was never a Jew. But I understand about slavery and freedom. Help me to believe in order that I may be free from the bondage of sin, and, being free, to praise your name at all times. Amen.

Week 5: Friday

John 9:1–12 The Light of the World and the Man Born Blind

This is one of the most delightful stories in the Gospel. Jesus, the light of the world, came into contact with a man who had never seen light and opened the man's eyes to the world around him. Later, when others asked the man what he thought about Jesus, he said, "He is a prophet" (v. 17); then, when Jesus questioned him, he said he believed that Jesus was the Son of man (vv. 35–38).

When the man was first encountered, the disciples asked a typical rabbinical question: Whose sin made the man blind, his or his parents'? Disregarding such a question as inconsequential—people are always more significant than philosophical disputes—Jesus replied that the important thing was to do God's work for the man while there was still time. "Night comes," he said, "when no man can work" (v. 4). Woven throughout Jesus' speech at this time were references to his crucifixion, when evil and darkness would seem to overcome the light.

So Jesus spat on the ground, made a bit of mud, and anointed the blind man's eyes with it. (In Mark 8:22–26 there is a similar account in which Jesus used spittle to heal a blind man.) Then he told the man to go and wash in the pool of Siloam. Why did the messiah who was able to heal the sick even at long distance (4:46–54) bother with this primitive method of healing?

Since Jesus' interview with Nicodemus in chapter three, there have been references in the Gospel to "water and the Spirit." Washing in the pool of Siloam almost certainly had baptismal significance in the eyes of first-century readers. In fact, the early church adopted this passage as part of the educational preparation of persons approaching baptism. Depictions of the story appear several times in catacomb art, always in connection with Christian baptism. The French scholar F.-M. Braun has discovered that during the years when the early church followed the practice of scrutinizing candidates three different times before admitting them to baptism, this chapter was read on the day of the final scrutiny.

The early church also made a connection between baptism and light. Candles were lit and handed to persons who had just been baptized, as a symbol of their enlightenment in Christ. And baptismal liturgies always contained numerous references to light and illumination.

The man who had been blind from birth, then, was made to see, and became an example to all of those seeking sight through faith in Jesus. Obediently, the man went to the pool and washed as he was told. And others were astounded at the change in the man. They argued among themselves (v. 9) about whether he was even the same man they had always known!

Lord, I wonder if my faith and baptism have made this much difference in how I live and how others perceive me. Do I behave as one who has seen a great light shining in the darkness? Open my eyes daily, I pray, to the magnificence of Christ, that I may not dwell with a shadowed spirit. In his bright name. Amen.

Week 5: Saturday

John 9:13–41 The Blindness of the Sighted

One of the great ironies of the Gospels is that those who are blind often see more than the sighted persons around them, while the sighted, who should see most, are spiritually blind. It is the same paradox as that encountered in the poor who are rich toward God and the rich who are impoverished in spirit.

In this passage we see the great contrast between the man who was blind from birth, yet came to see Jesus as the messiah, and the Pharisees, supposedly the most enlightened of Jews, who were unable to perceive the messiah who had done so many signs in their midst. They were angry with Jesus for other reasons, but here their anger focused on two points: (1) he had again violated the sabbath, both by mixing clay and by healing; and (2) he appeared to be doing the works of God, though they disputed his claim to be from God.

First, the Pharisees tried to disprove the miraculous nature of the healing by arraigning the man's parents and questioning them. There had been other cases of blind persons seeing again, but none where the persons had been blind from birth. The bent of the Pharisees' questioning was to discover whether the man had really been blind since birth. But the parents were adamant. This was their son, and he had been born without sight.

Then the Pharisees called in the man himself and tried to persuade him not to give credit for the healing to Jesus. "Give God the praise," they said; "we know that this man is a sinner" (v. 24). The implication was that no sinner could have done such a miraculous work. The man refused to be drawn into their dispute with Jesus. "I know what I know," he said, "—that I was blind and now I can see" (v. 25, P).

Like prosecutors grilling a witness, the Pharisees turned back to questions they had already raised. The man's wit was quick: "What's the matter with you," he asked in effect; "do you wish to become his disciples?" Incensed, the Pharisees accused the man of being one of Jesus' disciples. They themselves, they proudly declared, were disciples of Moses. They knew God had spoken to Moses, but they didn't even know where Jesus had come from. The man twitted them. They didn't know where Jesus was from, yet he had done the most wonderful work ever spoken of! If they had any sense at all, they would know Jesus had to be from God. Otherwise he could do nothing.

The Pharisees were irritated beyond their control. "You presume to instruct us," they said, "—you who were born in miserable sin!" (v. 34, P) This may have been a reference to the man's blindness from birth; they concluded that his sin produced the affliction. "And they cast him out."

Casting the man out, in light of verse 22, probably meant his ejection from the synagogue. Even in the time of Jesus, ruling Jews had the power to exclude people from synagogue worship, either for brief disciplinary periods or on a permanent basis. This would have been a permanent exclusion, and would have spoken eloquently to the Christian Jews of John's time who were facing expulsion from the synagogues unless they recanted and became non-Christians again. Indeed, John's intention in relating the entire narrative may well have been to encourage the followers of Jesus, who had been baptized (gone to the pool of Siloam) and received their sight (their Christian enlightenment) not to deny their faith under threat of excommunication from Jewish places of worship.

The final scene between the man and Jesus summarizes the situation. The man who had been blind from birth could now see. What he saw clearly was that Jesus was the Son of man, the long-awaited messiah. And the Pharisees, who made such a point of being able to see life clearly and discriminately, were really blind to the most important thing in the world, the lordship of Jesus.

It frightens me, O God, to be a leader of others—a parent, a teacher, a professional—and have a reputation for seeing. For it is in my contentment with this reputation that I am in most danger of not *seeing—of being short-sighted, prejudiced, and wrong in my judgments. Teach me to rise each day and, recalling my darkness, humbly seek the light of Christ in my life. For he alone has seen you and knows the meaning of everything.* Amen.

WEEK 6

Week 6: Sunday

John 10:1–21 The Beautiful Shepherd

This passage is related to the foregoing narrative in chapter nine by references to thieves, robbers, and hirelings who do not care for the sheep but steal and slaughter them (vv. 1, 8, 10, 12–13). Jesus was surely thinking of the Pharisees who did not care for the man born blind, but were willing to sacrifice the poor and afflicted for the sake of mere rules and regulations.

He probably had in mind also Ezekiel 34, which begins: "The word of the Lord came to me: 'Son of man, prophesy against the shepherds of Israel, prophesy, and say to them, even to the shepherds, Thus says the Lord God: Ho, shepherds of Israel who have been feeding yourselves! Should not shepherds feed the sheep?'" (vv. 1–2). Aileen Guilding, in her book *The Fourth Gospel and Jewish Worship*, says that this text regularly served as one of the prophetic readings for the Feast of Dedication mentioned in John 10:22. Therefore, just as ceremonials at the Feast of Tabernacles provided the background for Jesus' announcements in chapter seven ("If any one thirst, let him come to me and drink") and chapter eight ("I am the light of the world"), the reading for the Feast of Dedication prompted his discourse on shepherding.

The accusation in Ezekiel denounces the shepherds of Israel for not healing the sick, binding up the crippled, or seeking the lost. Because the shepherds have sought only their own welfare, it says, God will take away their shepherding function and assume it himself. "I myself will be the shepherd of my sheep, and I will make them lie down, says the Lord God. I will seek the lost, and I will bring back the strayed, and I will bind up the crippled, and I will strengthen the weak, and the fat and the strong I will watch over; I will feed them in justice" (34:15–16).

It was in the setting of these words that Jesus announced his role as shepherd of Israel. "I am the beautiful shepherd," he said, "the one who lays down his life for the sheep" (John 10:11, P). Most translations offer the wording "the *good* shepherd," but the word *kalos*, which they translate "good," also means "beautiful." We have a derivation of the word in the English "calligraphy," which means "beautiful writing." The sense of "beautiful" in the text is "perfect," "right," "exemplary." In other words, Jesus was the shepherd Ezekiel had promised, who would truly care for the sheep of Israel.

The reference to "the door of the sheep" or "sheep-gate" in verses 7 and 9 seems an intrusion into the shepherd metaphor. Possibly it was a separate utterance of Jesus edited into the sayings about shepherding because of its apparent affinity. Some interpreters have attempted to reconcile the images by suggesting that the shepherd lay down in the doorway at night to guard the sheep, thus becoming in effect the "door" to the sheep. This would certainly harmonize with the saying that the beautiful shepherd lays down his life for the flock.

There was a real intimacy, Jesus suggested, between him and the members of his flock. "I know my own and my own know me, as the Father knows me and I know the Father" (vv. 14–15). The sheep recognize the shepherd's voice and follow him when he calls them (v. 3). If the people were not following the Pharisees, it was because the Pharisees were thieves, robbers, and hirelings—not true shepherds.

Verse 16 has long taxed the imagination of commentators: "I have other sheep, that are not of this fold; I must bring them also, and they will heed my voice. So there shall be one flock, one shepherd." Given the audience of Jewish Christians to whom John was writing the Gospel, these words may well have meant that Jesus had followers in many places, not only among Jews in the synagogues, and that he would eventually bring them all together into a single flock. Then there would be "one flock, one shepherd." (The Greek is a clever play on words, for "flock" is *poimnē* and "shepherd" is *poimēn*; hence one *poimnē*, one *poimēn.)*

The emphasis on the smitten shepherd is strong in the passage because Jesus was approaching the time of his death. The Feast of Dedication was in December; Jesus was crucified at Passover in the spring. But references to resurrection and ascension were also strong. "I lay down my life, that I may take it again. No one takes it from me, but I lay it down of my own accord. I have power to lay it down, and I have power to take it again; this charge I have received from my Father" (vv. 17–18). John is the Gospel of *life*, not death. The shepherd would be slain for the sheep; but even in death he would prove triumphant.

O beautiful Shepherd, who laid down your life for me, I want to follow you wherever you lead. With you, even barren places become lush pastures, and the valley of the shadow of death becomes a field of resurrection! Amen.

Week 6: Monday

John 10:22–42 The Consecrated One

The Feast of Dedication *(Hanukkah)* celebrated the victory of Judas Maccabeus over the Syrians. In 167–164 B.C., the Syrians erected an idol on the altar of the temple, constituting what the Jews called "an abomination of desolation" (Dan. 9:27). When the Maccabeans defeated the Syrians, a new altar was built and the temple was rededicated. The memory of this important occasion was relived annually in the Feast of Dedication.

Against this background, it is interesting that Jesus, confronting "the Jews," referred to himself as the one "whom the Father consecrated and sent into the world" (v. 36). The word for "consecrated" is the same one used for consecrating an altar or a temple. Jesus, at a time when Jewish minds turned to the consecration of holy places, offered himself as the holy person dedicated by God himself.

"How long will you keep us in suspense?" asked "the Jews." "If you are the Christ, tell us plainly" (v. 24). They did not want to know if he was the Christ; he had already told them as much, and, besides, they could see the works he did. They wanted him to make an official claim, so they could hail him before the authorities.

"You don't believe me," said Jesus, "because you are not part of my flock. My sheep know me, and follow me. I give them what you cannot have, eternal life, and will keep them forever. My Father joins me in protecting them, because he and I are one and the same" (vv. 27–30, P).

At this declaration of unity with the Father, "the Jews" picked up stones to hurl at him, just as they had when he said he existed before Abraham (8:59). For which of his "beautiful works" (again it is the word *kalos)* were they going to kill him? It was not for the works, they said, but for the blasphemy—making himself God.

Jesus stayed the barrage of stones by engaging "the Jews" in a rabbinical argument. He cited Psalm 82:6,

> I say, "You are gods,
> sons of the Most High, all of you;
> nevertheless, you shall die like men,
> and fall like any prince."

The setting of the speech, made by God, was in a paganlike council of gods, where the gods were guilty of aiding the strong and not the weak. God turned to the other deities present and denounced them for their injustice. They might be gods, he said, but they would die like human beings.

If God called even minor deities "gods," Jesus was arguing, why should "the Jews" think he was blaspheming—he whom the Father had set apart and sent into the world—when he said he was the Son of God? If his works were not the Father's works, then they should not believe him; but if the works were what the Father would do, then they should understand that he was who he said he was.

"The Jews" tried to arrest Jesus, we are told, but he escaped again as on previous occasions (7:30, 44), because his hour had not come. He went into Transjordan, to the area where John had baptized, and for a while enjoyed the acceptance of the simple people of the land.

Lord, I want to be a simple person. Remove all my pretension and unnecessary complexity. Let me meditate on you until all of my life is focused and plain. And then let others see you through me, shining through the aperture of my faith. For your kingdom's sake. Amen.

Week 6: Tuesday

John 11:1–44 The Resurrection and the Life

In the previous message (10:22–42) Jesus spoke about doing the works of the Father. In an earlier discourse, he had told "the Jews": "As the Father raises the dead and gives them life, so also the Son gives life to whom he will" (5:19–24). Here, in the present passage, we see the most dramatic picture of this life-giving mission in the entire Gospel and we reach the climax of all the *egō eimi* sayings, when Jesus declares, "I am the resurrection and the life" (v. 25).

This chapter is pivotal to the Gospel. The raising of Lazarus was the most important sign Jesus could give, for death is the final enemy of man. It was therefore natural, once the sign had been given, that it should intensify the opposition to his ministry and his antagonists should seek ways not only of arresting him but of putting him to death.

John wished, in this unusual story, to emphasize three things: Jesus' love for his friends, the absolute deadness of Lazarus, and the immediacy of life in Christ.

(1) *Jesus' love for his friends.* Mary, Martha, and Lazarus lived in the small hillside village of Bethany, scarcely two miles from Jerusalem. Luke mentioned that Jesus visited in Martha's house while Mary also was present (10:38–42). And John, anticipating his own narrative in the next chapter (12:1–3), identified Mary as the one who anointed Jesus' feet with precious ointment. All the references indicate that there was a close personal relationship between Jesus and these three persons in Bethany, and that it was probably natural for him to visit them when he was in the area of Jerusalem. Mark 11 suggests that during the final week of his life he taught in Jerusalem by day and returned to Bethany each evening. It was not extraordinary, therefore, that the two sisters sent to Jesus when their brother lay gravely ill. They knew Jesus had strange powers, and they believed he could heal their brother. Jesus was

touched by the message. John noted that he loved the three friends. The proof of his love was his willingness to go back to Bethany so soon after "the Jews" had tried to stone and arrest him. "Rabbi," said the disciples, "the Jews were but now seeking to stone you, and are you going there again?" (v. 8). Apparently the family was well known in Jerusalem, and the disciples knew there would be many people from the city coming to see them. But Jesus had recently said that "the beautiful shepherd lays down his life for the sheep" (10:11). There was no question about his going back!

An additional evidence of Jesus' love and humanity was his weeping at Lazarus' tomb (vv. 33–35). Commentators have long sought to explain why he wept though he knew he would raise Lazarus from the dead. Some have suggested that he wept at the human situation, so filled with grief; others, that he wept for the dead man's sake, that Lazarus should have to come back to this life after tasting the one beyond. But regardless of the reason, the fact that Jesus wept at the tomb of a friend is an eloquent touch in the portrait of the eternal Word who became fully human.

(2) *The absolute deadness of Lazarus.* In none of Jesus' other resuscitation miracles was such care taken to emphasize the full reality of death's presence. John wished there to be no doubt of Lazarus' deadness or of Jesus' power to raise the dead. Instead of responding immediately to the sisters' message about their brother's illness, Jesus purposely tarried until the brother was not only dead but "in the tomb for four days." He had been no more than thirty or thirty-five miles away, yet procrastinated until there was no doubt of Lazarus' demise. Other touches confirm the presence of death: the stone rolled across the mouth of the tomb, the wailing of the mourners, the bandages on the corpse, and Martha's warning that, if they rolled away the stone, there would be an odor, because Lazarus had been dead four days. This was no case of mere revival a few minutes after death; Lazarus was firmly in the grip of death.

(3) *The immediacy of life in Christ.* This was the major point of the entire story, as of the Gospel itself. Jesus did not respond immediately to the sisters' plea for help because he wished to provide the greatest sign of his power and purpose as the messiah. Not even the sisters understood his power. When he arrived, he saw them in turn, and each lamented that if he had only been there their brother would not have died (vv. 21, 32). To Martha, who was the first to greet him, he said, "Your brother will rise again" (v.

23). Martha replied with the common faith of those who believed in the resurrection at the time, "I know that he will rise again in the resurrection at the last day" (v. 24). But Jesus was going to show her something better than that. "I am the resurrection and the life," he declared; "he who believes in me, though he die, yet shall he live, and whoever lives and believes in me shall never die" (vv. 25–26). Going to the tomb, and pausing to give thanks for always being heard by God, he cried out into the hollowness of the burial vault, "Lazarus, come out!"

"The dead man came out," says the scripture, still emphasizing his deadness, "his hands and feet bound with bandages, and his face wrapped with a cloth."

"Unbind him," said Jesus, "and let him go" (vv. 43–44).

Nowhere in the Gospels is there a more stunning story—or one more central to the purposes of the Incarnation. Christ is clearly the resurrection and the life!

O Christ, my rational mind is shocked by this story; it is like nothing I experience in daily life. Yet its very outrageousness convinces me of its truth, and of the fact that I **should** *experience it in daily life. Help me to know you so intimately through prayer and meditation that even my rationality shall come to understand and glorify you. For you are the Lord of both life and death.* Amen.

Week 6: Wednesday

John 11:45–57 A Misuse of Authority

In John's Gospel, people judged themselves according to their reaction to Jesus. Here is a primary example of this theological truth. The raising of Lazarus was Jesus' greatest sign of his union with the Father. Yet the members of the Sanhedrin, the council of Jewish elders, instead of accepting Jesus' messiahship, intensified their efforts to accomplish his death.

Like any group of "responsible citizens," the chief priests and Pharisees of the Sanhedrin cloaked their designs in civic respectability. They were worried about what the Romans would do if Jesus continued to perform miracles and recruit followers. The

Romans might become nervous, it was argued, and destroy the temple; or they might even lay waste the entire nation. We can almost hear the clacking of voices as the old men discussed their "duties" under the present state of emergency!

In the end, it was the words of the high priest that summed up the council's will: Jesus must die in order to avert a national disaster. Those words, "it is expedient for you that one man should die for the people, and that the whole nation should not perish" (v. 50), became an important preaching text to the early Christians. Caiaphas did not know how truly he spoke, or that what he had said would be given a spiritual interpretation by future generations.

The decision of the Sanhedrin to go all out in seeking Jesus' life was supposed to be a judgment on Jesus. As it turned out, it was a judgment on the council members themselves. How many times, in how many places, have people in authority committed a similar transgression of justice because some individual or group of individuals constituted a threat or an affront to their positions or self-interest? Even parents are prone to misuse authority in this way, as a means of bolstering the self and its ways.

As his opposition intensified, Jesus continued to be careful, waiting for the hour when he would give his life for his sheep. John says he went to a town called Ephraim, near the wilderness—a place so remote that scholars today argue over which small village it may have been. There he stayed with the disciples until the Feast of Passover. And, in Jerusalem, suspense was building among the people. The word was out that the Sanhedrin was set to arrest Jesus. Would he dare to come for the feast?

Lord, I know I have been guilty of abusing my authority as a parent, as a teacher, as a minister. I do it without thinking. There is a question, someone steps out of line, I haven't the time or energy to deal with the crisis, and I swing my weight. I have injured not only those with whom I was peremptory, but myself as well. Even worse, Lord, I have injured you. Forgive my self-centeredness and help me to be more constantly loving and considerate. For no position is worth the smallest act of inhumanity or the least betrayal of your trust. Amen.

Week 6: Thursday

John 12:1–8 A Prophetic Anointment

Accounts similar to this one are contained in Mark 14:3–9 and Luke 7:36–38. In Mark, the anointing occurs two days before Passover, in the house of Simon the leper, a resident of Bethany, and is performed not on Jesus' feet but on his head. In Luke, it occurs in Galilee, during the ministry there, at the home of Simon the Pharisee, and is done by a nameless sinful woman who first weeps on Jesus' feet, dries the tears with her hair, and then anoints his feet with perfume. Scholars have strained themselves to harmonize these accounts with the narrative in the Fourth Gospel, but with only modest success. John tells the story with his own set of details (the names of Mary, Martha, and Lazarus, and Judas' anger about the waste are found only in his version) and for his own theological purposes.

The suggestion has been offered, attempting to reconcile John with Mark's information about a dinner at Simon's house, that Simon was the father of Mary, Martha, and Lazarus. That is a plausible suggestion, and would account for Martha's serving at table. Martha's serving and Mary's act of worship also accord well with Luke's portrait of the two sisters (10:38–42), in which Martha "was distracted with much serving" while Mary "sat at the Lord's feet and listened to his teaching."

Here the action centers on Mary's sacrifice of a pound of nard on Jesus' feet. Nard, also known as "spikenard," was a kind of perfume extracted from the roots and spikes of the nard, a plant that still grows in northern India. It was, as the text indicates, extremely expensive, and was used sparingly in various perfumes, medicines, incenses, and burial lotions.

If a denarius was worth a day's wages, as we are informed by Matthew 20:2, then the flask of nard Mary used was worth nearly a year's wages. Judas, as keeper of the disciples' treasury, was understandably dismayed at the extravagance. He was not identified, in Mark's Gospel, as the one who objected; there the text says, "There were some who said to themselves indignantly, 'Why was the ointment thus wasted?'" (14:4). Either John represents a further development of the story in which Judas was purposely vilified or John had personal knowledge of Judas' objection which the other

Gospel traditions did not have. The former may have been true, for John has all along portrayed Judas as a devil (6:70) and will say in 13:2, 27, that he was cohabited by Satan. John alone among the Gospel writers gives the information that Judas was a thief and was accustomed to stealing from the group's money box (v. 6).

Jesus' comment in verse 7 that the anointment was for his burial indicates the prophetic nature of Mary's act. He would soon die for his beloved sheep. That it was a prophetic gesture would explain why Mary anointed his feet instead of his head, as in Mark. Perfume was normally put on the head or face to give a pleasant aroma to the person wearing it. A corpse, on the other hand, might be anointed on the feet as well as the head, for in the case of the dead the aroma was for other persons to smell, not the one who had died.

Some persons have been troubled by Jesus' apparent nonchalance about the poor in verse 8, "The poor you always have with you, but you do not always have me," and point out that this statement is much unlike Jesus' usual sentiments about the poor. Joachim Jeremias, however, has helpfully called attention to a distinction in rabbinic thought between two kinds of good works—those pertaining to mercy (including the burial of the dead) and those pertaining to justice (including alms for the poor). Actions related to mercy were always considered more important than those related to justice. Jesus was confirming an acceptable standard of piety, not a single action that happened to benefit him.

One important factor in Mary's behavior must not be overlooked, and that is the raising of Lazarus as narrated in chapter eleven. Mary could well part with the valuable perfume she was saving for her own burial because *she no longer felt the need of it*. Jesus had raised her brother from the dead. He had said, "I am the resurrection and the life." In a wonderful display of faith, she was "wasting" the precious ointment reserved for her funeral preparations, confident that Jesus had made it unnecessary. In what better way could she demonstrate her newfound understanding that he was the Lord of eternal life? The fact that Judas did not see the "logic" of her gesture meant that he was one of the sons of darkness. Like the Pharisees and high priests, he belonged to the evil one.

O God, I have always admired the spontaneity and generosity of Mary's act and wished that I could behave as she did. Now that I see her motivation—the transforming of life under the Prince of resurrection—perhaps I can be like her. Let me see what she saw, I pray, that I may be as she was. Through Jesus, who lives eternally. Amen.

Week 6: Friday

John 12:9–19 The Falseness of the Crowds

These verses are like little winds gusting before a storm. They contain the mounting tension and frenzy of the final days before Jesus' crucifixion.

First, we are shown the crowds that came to Bethany to see Jesus and Lazarus. Lazarus had become a tourist attraction; no one had ever before heard of a dead man raised to life, much less beheld one. This provoked the authorities in Jerusalem to connive to put Lazarus to death again. Merely being associated with Jesus was becoming dangerous.

Then we see the crowds in Jerusalem—the thousands of pilgrims who had arrived for Passover—going out to meet Jesus as he came down the road from Bethany. They brought palm branches, probably imported from the Jordan Valley for the Passover ceremonies, and greeted him with words from Psalm 118:26–27—

> Blessed be he who enters in the
> name of the Lord!
> We bless you from the house of the Lord.
> The Lord is God,
> and he has given us light.
> Bind the festal procession
> with branches,
> up to the horns of the altar!

The last sentence may have been a liturgical direction not originally part of the psalm. It would explain the appropriateness of the palms. They were used to welcome pilgrims to the temple. In the Palm Sunday context, however, Jesus was no mere pilgrim. He was the Son of God, the spiritual King of Israel, and, in a sense anticipated by the psalm, the light of the world.

The phrase "even the King of Israel" is not part of Psalm 118. It is probably a reference to Zephaniah 3:14–20, which includes the promise, "The King of Israel, the Lord, is in your midst," and speaks of a time when the lame will be cured and the outcasts gathered together.

In parallel passages in Matthew 21:8, Mark 11:8, and Luke 19:36, the crowds spread their cloaks and (in Matthew and Mark) the palm branches on the road before Jesus, giving an air of triumphalism to the entry. John does not mention the cloaks or the laying down of palm branches. In his Gospel, Jesus has been in Jerusalem many times, and John is less concerned with a triumphal entry than with the drama to come.

Verse 15 is a prophecy from Zechariah 9:9 that Israel's king would come riding on the foal of an ass. The comment in verse 16 that the disciples understood the significance of this only later, after Jesus had been glorified, is indicative of the early Christians' process of assimilating all that had happened: they recalled what had occurred and was said during Jesus' ministry and reflected on it in the light of scripture.

Reflecting on Jesus' entry into Jerusalem, John realized that many of those who cried "Hosanna!" were also in the crowd that shouted "Crucify him!" They went out to greet Jesus, not because they understood him to be the Son of God, but because they heard he was a miracle-worker. Crowds often follow a good show. The Pharisees despaired, however, when they saw the crowds. "Look," they said, "the whole world has gone after him" (v. 19). John saw the irony of this. Jesus' real hour of glory would be when he was lifted up on a cross and the crowds had fallen away—not now, when they were running to greet him.

O Christ, I am so easily blinded by the world's values that I fail to understand what is eternal and true. Teach me to see the world as you saw it, through the eyes of God, that I may not waste my time and energy pursuing the things that will neither last nor matter. For your name's sake. Amen.

Week 6: Saturday

John 12:20–36 The Arrival of Jesus' Hour

Throughout the Gospel, there have been references to Jesus' "hour" (2:4, 7:30, 8:20) and his "time" (7:6, 8). Now the hour has finally come. Jesus is ready to enter the fatal confrontation with the authorities in Jerusalem and to lay down his life for his sheep.

Perhaps the coming of the Greeks signaled the moment he had been waiting for. They came first to Philip, possibly because he would have spoken Greek, and asked to see Jesus. It must have been regarded by Philip as a momentous occasion, for he did not go directly to Jesus. Instead, he consulted his brother Andrew, and together they went to tell Jesus. The suggestion is that Jesus was in hiding, as he had been on other recent occasions (8:59; 10:40, 11:54), and the disciples felt some uncertainty about whether to take the strangers to him. We don't know if the Greeks ever did see Jesus. John was not interested in pursuing the story. What he cared about was the fact that Jesus saw their coming as an indication that his time had come to be lifted up.

Jesus' metaphor to the disciples about a grain of wheat falling into the ground and dying was an important lesson. He would be their great example, and they would later learn to give their lives as he gave his. "What good is saving your life," he asked in effect. "If you do that, you destroy it. It is only by living generously—by sowing your life profligately, as wheat is sown—that you enable the future to spring from your deeds!"

Jesus had come to this hour to die and be lifted up. It would have been pointless to flee, now that the hour was upon him. Instead, he prayed, "Father, glorify thy name." There was a sound like thunder. Those who were merely part of the crowd attracted by the raising of Lazarus assumed it was indeed thunder. But those who had faith said otherwise; they heard a voice say, "I have glorified it, and I glorify it again" (v. 28).

As Jesus had told Nicodemus that the Son of man must be lifted up like the serpent in the wilderness (3:14), now he repeated the necessity of his being lifted up in crucifixion (v. 32). The crowd, as usual, was uncomprehending. How could the Son of man be lifted up? Surely the real messiah would be above such a natural death.

Jesus' answer was simple: Walk in the light while you can, and become children of the light.

John had said in the prologue to the Gospel, "In him was life, and the life was the light of men. The light shines in the darkness, and the darkness has not overcome it" (1:4–5). In a little while, the light would seem to waver and go out.

Father, it takes a lot of living to understand what Jesus meant about dying. In selfishness, I try to preserve my life; but the minute I do that, I lose something. Teach me to live generously, loving the world as you have loved it. Then I shall not fear dying, or that I am leaving anything behind, for it will all be invested in you, who have never suffered any good thing to be lost. Amen.

WEEK 7

Week 7: Sunday

John 12:37–50 A Time for Summing Up

In the year of King Uzziah's death, Isaiah had an unforgettable experience of the mystery of God. He was in the temple and had a vision of God sitting on his throne. God's train—his retinue of angels—filled the entire temple. The angels were singing "Holy, holy, holy is the Lord of hosts," and when God spoke the very foundations of the doors trembled.

Afterwards, God sent Isaiah to speak to the Israelites. He was to say to them:

> Hear and hear, but do not understand;
> see and see, but do not perceive (Isa. 6:9).

God wanted Isaiah to make the people's ears heavy and cause them to shut their eyes,

> lest they see with their eyes,
> and hear with their ears,
> and understand with their hearts,
> and turn and be healed (6:10).

* * *

The people were already condemned by their sinfulness; God merely wished to increase their condemnation for not seeing and hearing.

John understood the Jews' failure to receive the Son of God in the framework of Isaiah's experience. He too, like Isaiah, had seen something almost beyond description—the incarnation of the eternal Word and a ministry filled with signs and wonders. Yet people had callously behaved as if Jesus were no more than a wandering magician. Their eyes beheld the glory of the Son of God, but they did not see him for who he was.

Some members of the Sanhedrin, John knew, believed Jesus was the Son of God. Nicodemus (3:1–14) was probably one of these. Joseph of Arimathea (Mark 15:43) was another. But they were afraid of being ejected from the synagogue if they confessed what they believed. They cared more for their reputations among men than for their reputation with God (v. 43). Worrying about what others think, John knew, could be spiritually fatal. "How can you believe," he wrote in 5:44, "who receive glory from one another and do not seek the glory that comes from the only God?"

Words like these must have scored a direct hit on people who were afraid of being expelled from their synagogues if they confessed to belief in Christ. Their fears would have put them in the class with the high-ranking Jews who never crossed over the line to become true disciples of Jesus.

Jesus' words in verses 44–50 are a kind of summary of what he has taught to this point of the Gospel. Many interpreters think they are out of place here, for Jesus has gone into hiding again (v. 36) and there is no one to hear them. But John saw them as an appropriate recapitulation before commencing the Passover narrative.

Those who believed in Jesus were really believing in the One who sent him. He was the light of the world, and those who followed him would not walk in darkness. He did not judge people, but people judged themselves by how they responded to him. And nothing he said was his own word, but was given to him by the Father.

The hardest part, for John, was to understand how people could see and hear what they had seen and heard, and still not believe.

Lord, I too am guilty of seeing and hearing and not believing. Your signs and testimonies in my life have been amazing, and have caused me to say again and again that I believe. Yet I live my life as if this were not so—as if I had seen and heard nothing. Forgive me, Lord, and let me stand once more in your presence. Renew an excited spirit within me. And this time help me not to forget so quickly. For your kingdom's sake. Amen.

Week 7: Monday

John 13:1–20 Sent by the Master

The tradition has been to read this passage principally as a narrative about humility: Jesus washed the disciples' feet, and we all should treat others in the same self-effacing manner. But interpreters in recent years have noted several difficulties in the passage. Three of these difficulties have to do with (1) the date of the Lord's Supper, (2) the significance of the foot-washing, and (3) the relationship of the washing to Judas the betrayer.

(1) *The date of the Lord's Supper.* The Synoptic Gospels clearly indicate that the meal eaten by Jesus and the disciples was a Passover meal. John says it was eaten "before the feast of the Passover" (v. 1). Later, John will allude to the day of crucifixion as the day of preparation for the Passover (19:14). Pilate handed Jesus over to the Jews for crucifixion at noon that day—the very hour when the priests were slaying the Passover lambs. Either there was a misunderstanding about the date—meaning that John or the Synoptic tradition was incorrect—or John purposely rearranged the date to give it a special theological significance. John the Baptist, upon seeing Jesus, had exclaimed to his disciples, "Behold, the Lamb of God, who takes away the sin of the world!" (1:29) By having the Last Supper *before* Passover and shifting the crucifixion to the day of preparation, the author of the Fourth Gospel could exalt Jesus as the true paschal Lamb, slain at the official time for slaughtering lambs for the Passover meal.

(2) *The significance of the foot-washing.* On the surface, at least, Jesus washed the disciples' feet as a lesson in humility. Laying aside his clothes and wearing a towel, as if he were a servant, he performed a menial task which Jewish masters were not even allowed to require of their slaves. But Jesus' words, "What I am

doing you do not know now, but afterward you will understand" (v. 7), assure us that John saw a deeper, symbolic meaning in the washing. Some interpreters believe it referred to baptism. Verse 10 seems to endorse such a view; the word for "bathe" *(louein)* has cognates used for "baptize" in several New Testament references (e.g., Acts 22:16, 1 Cor. 6:11, Titus 3:5).

There is, however, a simpler interpretation. Only five days earlier, at another supper, Mary had anointed Jesus' feet in preparation for his death and burial (12:1–8). I suggested in the discussion of that passage that the customary place for anointing the body was the head, and that Mary anointed the feet as one might perfume the feet of a corpse. Suppose Jesus washed the feet of the disciples as a sign of their eventual martyrdom for the gospel. This would fit well with Origen's interpretation that the footwashing was related to preaching the gospel, and with the scripture

> How beautiful upon the mountains
> are the feet of him who brings
> good tidings,
> who publishes peace, who brings
> good tidings of good,
> who publishes salvation,
> who says to Zion, "Your God
> reigns" (Isa. 52:7).

If it is indeed a correct interpretation, we might well include footwashing as a part of the ordination ceremony for those being commissioned to preach the Word.

(3) *The relationship of the washing to the betrayer.* The footwashing was obviously related to Judas' forthcoming act of betrayal. Jesus told the disciples, "You are clean, but not every one of you" (v. 10). John said this was because Jesus "knew who was to betray him" (v. 11). If our earlier interpretation is correct, that the footwashing was a preparation for dying for the gospel, then Judas would not have been "clean," even if his feet had been washed, for he would never preach the gospel.

The proof that the footwashing pertained to the disciples' coming deaths by martyrdom and not merely to humility is contained in verses 12–20. Jesus reclothed himself and took his place at the table with the disciples. He *first* spoke to them of what he had done as an example, that they too should be servants as he was a servant (vv.

15–16). Once more he exempted Judas from what he was saying, lest the disciples afterward think he did not know he harbored a betrayer in his midst. "I tell you this now," he said, "before it takes place, that when it does occur you may believe that I AM" (v. 19, P). Here again was the divine signature, the *egō eimi* without a modifier. *Then*, after talking about the exemplary nature of his act, Jesus added this important word about it: "Truly, truly, I say to you, he who receives any one whom I send receives me; and he who receives me receives him who sent me" (v. 20). In other words, the footwashing had to do with sending the disciples out. Jesus anointed their feet as a preparation for them to go out and preach—and subsequently to die for the gospel, as he was about to die.

Lord, prepare me to pay the price for the gospel of the kingdom you yourself were willing to pay. Let me say with Simon Peter, "Not my feet only, but also my hands and my head!" Let me give heart and soul and life for your kingdom's sake, and I shall be happy beyond words. For yours is the power and glory forever. Amen.

Week 7: Tuesday

John 13:21–30 The Drama of Betrayal

Jesus had emphasized to the disciples his foreknowledge of Judas' treachery. But the disciples themselves did not know, and were doubtless puzzled by his repeated references to a traitor in their midst. Thus, when Jesus openly said at the table, "I emphatically assure you, one of you will betray me" (v. 21, P), they looked around at once, wondering who the betrayer could be.

Jesus and the disciples were probably dining in the Roman fashion, lying on couches drawn up around three sides of the table. The disciple "whom Jesus loved"—probably John who wrote the Gospel—was "lying close to the breast of Jesus" (v. 23). As it was traditional to recline on the left elbow, John was undoubtedly on Jesus' right side, in a position where he could simply lay his head back to recline on Jesus' breast. Because John was so close and was a favorite disciple, Peter motioned to him to press the question with Jesus and learn the identity of the betrayer.

"Lord, who is it?" asked John (v. 25).

"The one to whom I give this morsel," said Jesus (v. 26, P). And he gave it to Judas.

The morsel may have been bread dipped in herbs or wine. Some interpreters have read into this a reference to communion, especially the form of communion known as intinction, in which the bread is dipped into the wine and the two are served together. This scene, in which Judas brazenly accepted the morsel from Jesus as a token of honor, would thus connect easily with Paul's warning in 1 Corinthians 11:27–29 that any one who eats the bread or drinks the cup of the Lord unworthily "eats and drinks judgment upon himself."

The drama at the table must have been intense as Jesus offered the morsel to Judas. Judas may still have been uncertain about whether to betray his master. (Verse 27 says that Satan entered into him only *after* he took the morsel.) If he had repented and confessed the treachery in his heart, his outcome might have been far different. But he received the morsel, ate it, and then determined to go ahead with his plans.

Judas may have been almost as close to Jesus at the table as John, for Jesus had handed him the morsel. As treasurer of the group, he probably held a place of importance, perhaps even on Jesus' left hand. It is likely, when Jesus spoke to him, that the others did not hear. "What you are going to do, do quickly," said Jesus (v. 27). And Judas went out.

Some of the disciples assumed that Jesus had sent him to acquire provisions for the Passover meal or had directed him to take some money to the poor, for he kept the money box.

There is an ominous note in John's words "and it was night" (v. 30). Jesus had come as the light of the world, and he was opposed by the darkness (1:4–5). Near the end of his public ministry, Jesus had warned: "Night comes" (9:4). "If any one walks in the night," he said, "he stumbles, because the light is not in him" (11:10). Now Judas had gone out into the darkness. Soon the darkness would appear to overcome the light.

Lord, my heart has always cried for Judas. Why should one be given to darkness and another to light? What is there in me, that I deserve your favor when another doesn't? Help me to be more worthy, that I may not betray the trust you have given me. Through Jesus, who suffers from all betrayal. Amen.

Week 7: Wednesday

John 13:31–38 Jesus' Farewell Speech

The farewell speech was a well-defined genre of Old Testament literature. It can be seen in the stories of such famous persons as Jacob (Gen. 47:29–49:33), Moses (the entire book of Deuteronomy), Joshua (Josh. 22–24), and David (1 Chron. 28–29). Certain features were always present in the farewell speech. They include: an announcement of the speaker's departure; comfort for those remaining behind; a review of the speaker's life and achievements; a reminder to keep the commandments of God; a call for unity and love among those left behind; a promise that the speaker's spirit will be close to those remaining; and a prayer for the ones remaining.

There can be little doubt that Jesus' long discourse at the Last Supper was intended as this kind of classical farewell speech. Jesus called the disciples "little children" (v. 33), as a man would speak to those he was leaving behind at death; it is the only time the term is used in the entire Fourth Gospel. He announced his departure (v. 33) and instructed the disciples to "love one another" (v. 34). And, in subsequent parts of the discourse, he would include all the other features of farewell speeches listed above.

"A new commandment," Jesus called his directive that the disciples love one another. Was it really a *new* commandment? Jewish scholars have often observed that the Old Testament likewise stressed the importance of love. When Jesus was asked to name the greatest commandment (Matt. 22:34–40; Mark 12:28–31), his response included Leviticus 19:18, that one is to love his neighbor as himself. Leviticus 19:34 even extended such love to foreigners: "The stranger who sojourns with you shall be to you as the native among you, and you shall love him as yourself; for you were strangers in the land of Egypt: I am the Lord your God."

Perhaps the "newness" in Jesus' commandment lay not in the commandment itself but in the motivational clause attached to it: "Love one another *as I have loved you*." In the Old Testament, the statement of the commandments began with the words "I am the Lord your God" (Exod. 20:2). The motivation to keep the commandments stemmed from the covenant relationship with God. Suppose, in Jesus' farewell discourse, he was citing a new, more intimate kind of motivation. He had described himself as the "beautiful shepherd" who lays down his life for the sheep (10:11). Now, in his final words to the disciples, he was saying, in effect, "Make this the basis of a new commandment: even as I have loved you, and given my life for you, love one another."

God had been more or less remote from the people of the Old Covenant. But he had come and stood in the midst of the people of the New Covenant. Now he was going to show them his love through the death of the Son. What stronger appeal could be made for their observing a commandment to love one another? People would know the disciples were followers of Jesus if they loved one another, for love was the distinguishing mark of his relationship to all of them.

Peter, characteristically, wanted to know where Jesus was going. He could not believe that the one who raised Lazarus from the grave should be speaking of his own death. Apparently he began to understand, however, for he swore he would lay down his life for Jesus. It was a case of the sheep's being willing to die for the shepherd.

But only the Shepherd's will was as good as his word. Peter would deny his relationship to Jesus three times before morning, and Jesus would give his life for the sheep on the following day.

Lord, I am gripped by Jesus' linking the love commandment to what he has done for me. How can I not love others, given such a reminder? Yet I do not. I forget what he has done, and, like Peter, deny him without thinking. Remind me, Lord. Keep me this day before the Cross. For his love's sake. Amen.

Week 7: Thursday

John 14:1–14 Words of Encouragement

The disciples were predictably distressed at Jesus' announcement of his departure. But his "comfortable teachings," many of them reminders of things he had said in his ministry, were drawn together as words of encouragement.

"Don't let your hearts be anxious," he said. "Believe in God and believe in me. There are rooms for all of you in my Father's house; otherwise, would I go to prepare a place for you?" (v. 1–2, P)

The word for rooms *(monē)* was customarily used for rest stops or temporary dwelling places, not for permanent homes. Early church fathers took this to signify a continuance of growth after death. The picture is of one's moving from level to level in understanding and of appropriating God's presence in the afterlife. Jesus goes ahead to prepare a place, and will come again to lead his disciples into these new realms of discipleship. If we remember the "beautiful shepherd" passage (10:1–18), we may imagine this as the shepherd's conducting the sheep into new, rich pasturelands.

(It is interesting, in the light of this passage, to recall the testimonies of many persons who have had "life after life" experiences—who were clinically dead and then returned to life with memories of the time while they were dead. Most of them have spoken of encountering a "guide" in the life beyond who would lead them into fresh understandings in their new environment. And, for many of them, this "guide" was Jesus.)

This time it was Thomas who led the way to further clarification of a saying of Jesus. "Lord," he said, "we do not know where you are going; how can we know the way?" (v. 5) Jesus' response to the question was another *egō eimi* saying, this time combining three great predicate modifiers: "I am the way, and the truth, and the life; no one comes to the Father, but by me" (v. 6).

"*I AM the way.*" Jesus had already identified himself as "the door of the sheep" (10:7). The disciples did not need to worry about finding their way to God when Jesus was gone. He was the way, and, as long as they remained in him and his teachings, they would have no trouble arriving at their spiritual home.

"*I AM the truth.*" Rabbis were constantly trying to discover truth and impart it to their followers. Jesus did not have to search for truth. He was the eternal Word, the Wisdom of God in the flesh, the Light that enlightens everyone who comes into the world. Hence he could say, without equivocation, "I AM the truth."

"*I AM the life.*" The entire Gospel has been about life. Jesus has identified himself as "the water of life" and "the bread of life." Those who drink the water he gives them will never thirst (4:14); those who eat his bread will never hunger (6:35). Any who believe in him will not perish, but will have eternal life (3:16). The disciples would not only have life in the world to come; in Jesus, they had it already, for he *was* the life.

What did Jesus mean, "No one comes to the Father, but by me"? Is this a declaration of exclusivism, a way of saying there is absolutely no salvation outside the Christian faith? Jesus had all along identified himself as the Son of the Father, who did the works of the Father (see especially 5:17, 19–24). He and the Father, he said, were one. Therefore, to come to the Father was to come to the Son. And, conversely, to come to the Son was to come to the Father. "If you had known me, you would have known my Father also; henceforth you know him and have seen him" (v. 7).

Philip still did not understand. "Show us the Father," he asked. "Have I been with you so long," replied Jesus, "and you don't understand? If you have seen me, you have seen the Father. You have beheld the works I do. They are not my works, but the Father's. Don't you see? I am the very extension of the Father. He is in me and I am in him" (vv. 9–10, P).

There was more. Not only was Jesus in the Father, so that he did the Father's works, but the disciples, who were in Jesus, would also do the Father's works. The extraordinary power of the Creator would flow from them as it had flowed from the Son. Anything they asked *in his name* would be done.

"In my name." Many of our prayers have come to be signed "in Jesus' name." It is not that there is magic in the formula, but that there is power in the reality to which it attests. It speaks of our being in communion with the One whose name we employ, so that we signify, by speaking his name, that we are extensions of his work in the world. And there is nothing in the world, as the raising of Lazarus demonstrated, that can resist the power of the Son and the Father!

Heavenly Father, I am prone to wish power for my own sake, and to pray in Jesus' name without really dwelling in his spirit. What a dangerous thing it is to pray in his name if I really mean it; then I am like a toy sailboat swept out to sea on a bottomless tide! Help me to pray the phrase and to mean it—whatever the cost. Amen.

Week 7: Friday

John 14:15–24 Children of the Covenant

"A new commandment I give to you, that you love one another," Jesus said; "even as I have loved you, that you also love one another" (13:34). Now he says, "If you love me, you will keep my commandments" (14:15). Both verses suggest that we are dealing in this passage with a new covenant situation. In the Old Testament, the Jews identified themselves with God by keeping his commandments; Jesus expects his followers to identify with him the same way.

Covenant-keeping followers will be given a special "Spirit of truth" as a counselor and guide, and the Spirit will dwell in them. Jesus calls the Spirit "*another* Paraclete" (or "counselor"), suggesting that he himself has been the first. This Paraclete will help them to understand all that has happened. As we shall see, the notion of the second Paraclete is not fully developed, as the doctrine of the Trinity would be at a later date, but appears to be a way of saying that the Spirit of the Father and the Son will be with them. "I will not leave you desolate," says Jesus; "I will come to you" (v. 18). The Jerusalem Bible and The Living Bible translate more literally: "I will not leave you orphans" (Greek *orphanous*). Earlier, Jesus called the disciples "little children" (13:33); now he promises not to forsake them as children with no leadership or provision.

What does it mean that Jesus will come to them? Is this the *parousia*, or Second Coming? Possibly so, but not as the Synoptic Gospels interpret the Second Coming. John is more inclined to think of Jesus' return as his spiritual reappearance to the disciples after his resurrection. Soon the world will not see him; but the disciples will see him (v. 19). Then they will know that he is in the Father (v. 20), and he will show himself to them (v. 21). Not only that, but both Jesus and the Father will come and make their home with the disciples (v. 23).

The word for "home" in verse 23 is the same word used in verse 2, "In my Father's house are many homes" (or "dwelling-places"). The idea is circular, to express the central truth of the new covenant. God will dwell with his children and they will dwell with him. And the disciples will understand all these things later, after the resurrection has occurred.

O Lord, these matters are hard to understand unless one has felt *them. Help me to feel them more deeply and certainly from day to day, and to lead others to experience them too, that we may dwell together with you in perfect unity. Through him who gave his life that we might know you as you are.* Amen.

Week 7: Saturday

John 14:25–31 The Great Bequest

This passage concludes the first section of Jesus' farewell speech, and Jesus emphasizes his departure in verse 25 ("These things I have spoken to you, while I am still with you") and verse 30 ("I will no longer talk much with you").

Again he speaks of the Paraclete, this time using the full phrase "the Holy Spirit." The Father will send the Holy Spirit "in my name," says Jesus, reminding us of the phrase in verse 13 ("Whatever you ask in my name, I will do it") and once more emphasizing the unity theme of the entire discourse. The Spirit's work will be to continue teaching the disciples and to cause them to remember all of Jesus' words and understand them in the light of what transpires. (Cf. 13:7, "What I am doing you do not know now, but afterward you will understand.")

Jesus then makes his final bequest to the disciples—his peace (v. 27). Most persons about to die make parting gifts to those closest to them. Jesus is an itinerant rabbi, with nothing of great worldly value to leave behind. But he gives the disciples a priceless inheritance—his blessing of fullness. In Jewish thought, the word "peace" (Hebrew *shalom*) meant more than the absence of conflict; it meant fullness of being. Jesus knew it was a special gift: "not as the world gives do I give to you" (v. 27). And peace, along with grace, was to become a part of the standard Christian greeting after Jesus' death and resurrection. It is a Christian's most precious possession, something, as Paul said, that passes all ordinary understanding (Phil. 4:7).

In further consolation for what is to happen, Jesus tells the disciples that if they only understood his love and their union with him, they would be glad he is going to the Father, for the Father is greater than he (v. 28). This is not a statement about unequal powers within the Trinity, any more than the talk of a Paraclete was a full-grown trinitarian statement. Jesus simply means that he is returning to the One who sent him, who, in the sense of being the originating parent, always takes precedence. Later, Paul will reflect the same attitude of rejoicing about going to the Father and the Son: "For to me to live is Christ, and to die is gain. If it is to be life in the flesh, that means fruitful labor for me. Yet which I shall choose I cannot tell. I am hard pressed between the two. My desire is to depart and be with Christ, for that is far better" (Phil. 1:21–23).

The ruler of this world, says Jesus, does not really have the power he will appear to have. Evil will seem to control everything—even the destiny of the one who is the Light of the World and the Beautiful Shepherd. But the control is an illusion. Jesus submits to death not at Satan's command but at the Father's, in order that the world may understand the nature of true obedience—or, as Jesus puts it, "so that the world may know that I love the Father" (v. 31).

Finally, Jesus bids the disciples to rise and go out with him, terminating this part of the discourse. Some interpreters suggest that the second part—chapters fifteen and sixteen—occurs on the way to Gethsemane, and that the image of the vine and the branches in 15:1–11 was occasioned by their passing either some vines or a pile of dead branches pruned away from the vines. Others believe that the entire discourse took place in the upper room and the command to rise and go out was merely a displaced instruction. Either way, the sentence marks a clear division in the final discourse.

In the storms of life, O Christ, give me your peace and I shall be content. Nothing matters as much as your presence. Teach me to be still and know you, that I may no longer fear the wind and the waves. For you are the Lord of all. Amen.

WEEK 8

Week 8: Sunday

John 15:1–11 The Vine and the Branches

Here is another *egō eimi* passage, with Jesus this time using the grapevine as an image of his life and work. We recall that his images often reflected the failure of Israel and his own supplanting of old traditions. Thus, the well of Jacob was insufficient, but Jesus was the giver of "living water" (4:7–15); the manna of Moses was unfilling, but Jesus was "the bread of life" (6:25–35); the special candles lit at the Feast of Tabernacles illuminated the city of Jerusalem, but Jesus was "the light of the world" (8:12); the shepherds of Israel cared only for their own comfort and prosperity, but Jesus was "the beautiful shepherd" who laid down his life for the sheep (10:11–15).

By calling himself "the true vine" or "the real vine," Jesus was reflecting again on the failure of national religion in Israel. There are many references in the Old Testament to Israel as a vineyard (cf. Isa. 5:1–7, 27:2–6; Jer. 5:10, 12:10–11) or as a vine (cf. Ps. 80:8–11; Ezek. 17:1–10). Most of these references are negative; they deal with Israel's breaking of her covenant with God and God's consequent destruction of the vineyard or the vine. Jesus, by contrast with the unfaithful nation, was the genuine stock of the vineyard, the one for whom God cared and who would bear fruit for the great vinedresser.

Therefore it was important that the disciples remain in him, and not seek their life in another vine or another vineyard. This was a clear word to Christian Jews facing expulsion from the synagogues. Only by keeping their attachment to Jesus would they have life. Away from him, they would become like the branches pruned from the trunk and thrown away to wither.

There is even an ominous note for those who do remain in Jesus but bear no fruit. They too will be cut away and destroyed, so that they do not inhibit the better branches from bearing fruit. Judas, we assume, was thus removed. The other disciples had been made clean (that is, in the way fruit-bearing branches were trimmed to give more nourishment to the fruit) by "the word" Jesus had spoken to them. The word was the *logos* of chapter one—the Wisdom of God addressed to the disciples through Jesus' teachings.

The image of the vine and the branches fits beautifully with the entire theme of unity in the farewell discourse. Over and over, Jesus stressed the importance of remaining in him as he remained in the Father, and drawing on his love as he drew on the Father's love. If the disciples only continued in him, they would have Jesus' joy in them—the creative excitement of knowing they were at the center of God's will for human life—and their joy would be full (v. 11).

Lord, help me to remain in you and follow your commandment to love others as you have loved me, that I may shout with joy at what I see and know. For yours is the life for ever and ever. Amen.

Week 8: Monday

John 15:12–17 The Greatest Motivation of All

"No longer do I call you servants," said Jesus, "for the servant does not know what his master is doing; but I have called you friends"—the Greek is *beloved* or *loved ones*—"for all that I have heard from my Father I have made known to you" (v. 15).

What a touching scene this is—a man about to die, giving his farewell discourse, and saying to his servants, the menials who have tended to the basic needs of his life, "You are no longer my servants, you are my dearly prized friends, my loved ones"! What a sense of unity it implies! And what consequences it would have in the disciples' lives!

We hear a lot today about motivation. Firms search for ways of motivating employees. Teachers try to motivate students. Advertising agencies wish to motivate consumers. But here is the greatest example of motivation in the world.

Jesus was the incarnate Wisdom of God, the eternal Son, the King of Glory. Yet he loved his disciples with such intense passion that he laid down his life for them and called them his dearly beloved friends. "You didn't choose to follow me," he said, "but I chose you, because I knew you would be fruitful for the Father. Now, continue in my love by walking in the way I have shown you, and love one another in the way you see me loving you, and the Father will care for all your needs, in my name" (vv. 16–17, P).

Is it any wonder the disciples went to the ends of the earth, suffered in prisons, or died on crosses for him? Who wouldn't have done the same?

In the stillness, O Christ, I know that you have loved me as you did your first disciples. The words you said to them are spoken to me as well. How can I love you, Lord? Let me withhold nothing of myself, but give you everything. For you have given all for me. Amen.

Week 8: Tuesday

John 15:18–16:4a The World's Hatred for the Disciples

If Jesus had testified to the disciples of his love for them, he had also to warn them of the world's hatred for them. The hatred would stem from the fact that they bore his name and were identified with the works he did. After all, he had many times revealed himself as the I AM of God—the one whose presence makes all earthly institutions appear shabby by comparison. And those who had anything to uphold or protect in those institutions would be innately opposed to him, as the darkness is opposed to the light.

"The Jews" would hate the Christians because Christ threatened their authority in religious matters. The Romans would hate them because they worshiped Jesus instead of Caesar. Jesus said he was hated to fulfill the word of Psalm 35:19 and Psalm 69:4 about "those who hate me without cause." From a spiritual perspective, neither "the Jews" nor the Romans had just cause to hate him. But the perfidious thing about hate is always its baselessness and ridiculousness. "To understand everything," said Voltaire, "is to forgive everything." Had "the Jews" and Romans only understood, they would have loved instead of hated.

The Paraclete, said Jesus, would help to teach the disciples about these things and would bear witness to him. There would be times when they would need that witness, lest they think they had followed a madman and bargained poorly with their souls.

As we have noted all along, the Fourth Gospel was written primarily to encourage Christian Jews being put out of synagogues. In 16:1–14, Jesus said that the main purpose of his farewell speech was to prevent their falling away from the faith. He knew they would be expelled from the synagogues. Worse, the time would come when some Jews would even seek their deaths as worship or service to God (the Greek *latreia* meant both "worship" and "service"). But they were to remain in him, as branches in the true vine, and he and the Father would care for them and give them eternal life.

Lord, I have seldom felt persecuted for my faith. Does this mean that my faith has not been radical enough to provoke the fear and envy of others? Help me to ponder this question today and face its implications in my daily life. For your name's sake. Amen.

Week 8: Wednesday

John 16:4b–15 The Role of the Spirit

It was not necessary, as long as Jesus was with the disciples, that he tell them all the things he put into his farewell speech. Before leaving them, however, he wished them to be conscious of these matters.

Did hearing them make the disciples sad? It shouldn't, because

Jesus' going to the Father would be to their advantage. He would send the other counselor of whom he had spoken (14:16) and the counselor would convict the world of its sin, injustice, and wrongdoing (v. 8).

The Greek words I have translated as "to convict" have a variety of meanings. They can mean "expose," "bring to light," "correct," or even "punish." The King James or Authorized Version reads "reprove"; the Revised Standard Version and Living Bible, "convince"; and the New English Bible, "confute." The Jerusalem Bible translation of the entire passage is interesting:

> And when he comes,
> he will show the world how wrong it was,
> about sin,
> and about who was in the right,
> and about judgment (v. 8).

The idea is that the Spirit would set everything in a new perspective, so that many would understand that Jesus was not a self-willed impostor but the true Son of God. They would know that they sinned in not believing in Jesus; that they were unrighteous, because the Son of righteousness was killed and left in their midst; and that they were under judgment, because the prince of this world, their ruler, had been judged.

The Spirit would also reveal many things to the disciples they could not presently bear—either because there was too much for them to remember or because the sayings would tax their understanding. The Spirit's revelations would come as they needed them. "Whatever he hears he will speak" (v. 13) probably refers to the divine council—the Spirit repeats to the disciples what he has heard in the presence of the Father and the Son. "He will declare to you the things that are to come" (v. 13) does not mean that the Spirit predicts the future but that he interprets whatever happens. The verb translated "declare" means "to reannounce" or "republish," as if the Spirit's function is to remind the disciples of what has already been declared and help them see its relationship to everything occurring in the present. He will glorify Jesus by bringing to mind everything belonging to the Son.

Teach me, O Spirit, to listen to you about Jesus and the world. Help me to understand—to feel deeply—the things that matter about his incarnation and what it means to the world, that I may be your servant in all things. Through him who walked the land and sailed the sea. Amen.

Week 8: Thursday

John 16:16–24 The Joy Beyond the Pain

"A little while, and you will see me no more; again a little while, and you will see me" (v. 16). What did Jesus mean by these words? The disciples were rightly puzzled. Looking back, we can easily see what was meant by the first statement; it referred to Jesus' impending death. But did the second statement refer to his reappearance after the resurrection, to a second coming at some future time, or to the disciples' reunion with Jesus in the afterlife?

Jesus' analogy in verses 21–22, of the woman who goes through anguish in giving birth and then forgets the anguish in her joy for the child, almost certainly interprets the words as applying to his post-resurrection appearances to the disciples. They would suffer great pain at the time of the crucifixion, but it would be forgotten in their ecstasy at seeing him afterward.

"So you have sorrow now, but I will see you again and your hearts will rejoice, and no one will take your joy from you" (v. 22).

Again, Jesus spoke to the disciples of asking "in my name." They had not done this before, he said; in the future, they should do it, and see how full their joy was. He was not giving them the key to self-indulgence, so they could ask indiscriminately for whatever they wished. His words must be interpreted in light of the entire discourse and its emphasis on unity—on being in him and in the Father. A person in that intimate spiritual relationship does not desire things for the self. He or she wishes what the Father and Son wish—the healing of cripples, the sight of the blind, the raising of the dead, the love of all people for one another. "Ask these things in my name," Jesus was saying to the disciples, "and you will have what you ask, and your joy will overflow."

Lord, I know your words were not meant for the disciples alone, but for all followers. I want to be part of the unity you described, so that my desires are transformed by your love and your truth. Help me to will the things you will, and to will them so devotedly that I may see them come to pass. For your name's sake. Amen.

Week 8: Friday

John 16:25–33 A New Stage of Relationship

"I have said this to you in figures," said Jesus. To what does "this" refer? To the foregoing verse, which speaks of asking in Jesus' name and having joy? To the whole final discourse? Or to Jesus' entire ministry, in which he has characterized himself by such figures of speech as "the bread of life," "the light of the world," and "the beautiful shepherd"?

Perhaps it does not matter, as Jesus spoke in figures throughout his relationship with the disciples. The important thing is that their relationship was about to transcend all figures and become so intimate that it would not need language at all. Jesus would be in their hearts, speaking the language of the heart, and assuring them directly of the Father's love.

Jesus would no longer pray to the Father for them. Being in the Son and Father, they would ask what they wished in the Son's name—"for the Father himself loves you, because you have loved me and have believed that I came from the Father" (v. 27).

Jesus had come from the Father to do the Father's work, and he was going back to the Father now that the work was done. Suddenly the disciples seemed to understand. "Now we know that you know all things, and need none to question you; by this we believe that you came from God" (v. 30). The phrase "need none to question you" is a puzzling one. It may refer to the way the disciples and others constantly questioned Jesus in order that he could give them the truth; now, as Spirit, he would impart truth in another way, directly and without need of a rabbinical structure.

Again Jesus warned the disciples of difficult times to come. They would be scattered as sheep without their shepherd. Yet they were not to be concerned about the shepherd. God would not leave him alone. However desolate he might appear to be, the Father was with him. Luke would picture him, in the final moments of life, saying, "Father, into thy hands I commit my spirit" (23:46). There was no reason for John to report these words; Jesus had told the disciples many times of his relationship to the Father; they knew he would not be abandoned.

Jesus predicted the disciples' scattering (this may also have been a reference to the Dispersion throughout the Empire) and told of his being with the Father to assure them of their continued blessing in him and the Father. The world might hate them and give them enormous difficulty, but Jesus would continue to give them peace and joy, for he had overcome the world.

The tense of the last verb suggests that his overcoming did not even await the resurrection. His "hour" had come, and God was glorifying him through everything that transpired—even his trial and death!

Lord, I am grateful for the figures that have taught me how to see you. It is wonderful to picture you as light and bread, shepherd and true vine. Yet the most thrilling moments of all are those when I annihilate all thought and feel you warm and strong as a presence without images or figures at all. Then I know you as the disciples did, and understand your triumph over the world. Give me such a moment now, Lord, for your name's sake. Amen.

Week 8: Saturday

John 17:1–5 Jesus' Great Pastoral Prayer

This is the longest prayer by Jesus recorded in the Gospels. It extends through the entire chapter. Structurally, it is part of the farewell speech begun near the end of chapter thirteen. Farewell speeches in the Old Testament frequently included a prayer for those being left behind, and it was natural for Jesus to follow the pattern.

John, unlike the Synoptic Gospels, includes no prayer of Jesus in Gethsemane—that, if it be the Father's will, the cup might pass from him. The Jesus of the Fourth Gospel is far more triumphant than the Jesus of the Synoptics. He does not agonize over the cross. Instead, he sees the cross as his hour of glory, when he will return to the Father. God has given him "power over all flesh" (v. 2); he is already the cosmic Christ. Therefore the prayer he offers is a great pastoral prayer—the prayer of the "beautiful shepherd" for his sheep.

The prayer is divided into three sections. First, Jesus addresses the Father and speaks of the hour of his glory (vv. 1–5). Then he prays for the disciples (vv. 6–19). Finally, he prays for all who are to become followers in the years ahead (vv. 20–26). Someone has observed that the prayer thus resembles one offered by Aaron, the high priest, in Leviticus 16:11–17. Aaron first prayed for himself, then for his priestly family, and finally for the whole people. John may well have been conscious of these parallels when he set down the prayer of Jesus, for, as Aaron was the great high priest of the old covenant, Jesus was the great high priest of the new!

Jesus begins the prayer by addressing the Father and asking for his glorification. Glory is a quality of Godhood. It emanates from God in the same way the energy of our solar system emanates from the sun. As the Son of God, Jesus had shared in that glory before coming into the world. Now, returning to the Father, he asks to share in it once more.

Seeing the Son's glory enables people to have eternal life. "This is eternal life," says Jesus, "that they know thee the only true God, and Jesus Christ whom thou has sent" (v. 3). *Knowing*, in the Hebrew world view, meant more than cerebral awareness; it meant *participation* in what was known. To know something was to be intimately involved with it. Thus, to know Jesus was to have one's destiny entwined with his—to be one with him and the Father.

We are prone, after centuries of emphasis on salvation through Jesus' death on the cross, to exalt that aspect of his work. But John saw the importance of the post-resurrection state of Jesus—of his triumph over the world and return to the bosom of the Father. John did not neglect a detailed account of the Passion; he simply emphasized the eternal nature of Christ and the completion of his work by rejoining the Father in glory.

The Orthodox Church, which has followed John's Gospel more closely than the Synoptics, to this day retains a strong sense of resurrection and triumphalism in its worship. The center of its services is the exalted Christ, not the humble Jesus of Galilee. The figure most often found in its church buildings is the Pantocrator Christ—the glorified Messiah with arms outstretched over the world. One can almost hear him say, when viewing it, “Be of good cheer, I have overcome the world” (16:33).

Lord, as the moon possesses no glory of its own, but reflects the brilliance of the burning sun, help me in my darkness to receive the glory of your presence and reflect it to those who dwell in a land of shadows; for yours is the kingdom and the power and the glory forever. Amen.

WEEK 9

Week 9: Sunday

John 17:6–19 The Prayer for the Disciples

In some ways, this section of Jesus' great pastoral prayer seems to have been uttered not before Jesus' death but after his resurrection—indeed, many years later. Jesus speaks of the disciples' having kept God's word (v. 6) and having been hated by the world (v. 14). At the time of the prayer's setting, between the Last Supper and the visit to Gethsemane, these things can hardly have come to pass. In fact, Jesus has only moments earlier (15:18–27) warned the disciples that they will be hated, and has promised them the Holy Spirit for encouragement. We can but suppose that John, with the liberty of a creative editor, has written the prayer not only as it applied to the disciples when Jesus prayed it but as it came to apply to them and other disciples years after Jesus' return to the Father.

"I manifested thy name," says Jesus, "to the men whom thou gavest me out of the world" (v. 6). Was this Jesus' mission, to reveal God's name? A name, among the Hebrews, was supposed to contain the very essence of a person. Yahweh, the holiest name of God, was for that reason not lightly spoken. The people never uttered it in common speech. Only the high priest was allowed to speak it—and then only on the Day of Atonement. Jesus had made his disciples familiar with God's name and personality—something unheard of among ordinary people.

God's name, in the Fourth Gospel, may be related to Jesus' frequent use of the phrase *egō eimi*—I AM. It did correspond to God's giving the name Yahweh to himself in speaking to Moses at the burning bush, for Yahweh meant I AM. Jesus not only gave the disciples the holy name, he coupled it with images that revealed the holy personality. I AM was the bread of life (6:35), the light of the world (8:12), the door of the sheep (10:7), the beautiful shepherd (10:14), the resurrection and the life (11:25), the true vine (15:1), the way, the truth, and the life (14:6). He came walking on the stormy sea in the dark of night (6:20). He made the crippled spring up (5:2–9), the blind see (9:1–12), and the dead live (11:1–44). Surely the disciples were overwhelmed by Jesus' revelation of the "name" of God. It is no wonder they believed he was sent from the Father.

Like the great shepherd he is, Jesus has kept the disciples given to him—all except Judas, "the son of perdition." Now, going away from them, he prays for their continued unity in him and the Father. He does not ask that they too be taken out of the world—only that they be kept from the evil one while they are in the world.

"As thou didst send me into the world," says Jesus, "so I have sent them into the world" (v. 18). Against the background of the entire Gospel that has preceded it, this is a remarkable statement. The Father sent the Son into the world to do his works. He and the Son were one in everything. At the end of his mission, the Son went back to the glory of the Father. It will be the same for the disciples. They will take up the works of the Son. They will be one with him in everything. And, finally, they will join him in glory, leaving yet more disciples to do the works of the Son and the Father.

What a name you have revealed to us, O Lord. It is a name of music and poetry, a name of life and love and joy, a name surpassing every name. Help me to live daily in its great mystery, until my life is fully converted to your way, and I am yours for ever and ever. Amen.

Week 9: Monday

John 17:20–26 A Prayer for Future Believers

Jesus' great pastoral prayer finally includes all of those who would come to believe in him through the ministry of the disciples. It is essentially the prayer offered for the disciples themselves—that they may all be one with him and the Father.

We can imagine how encouraging this prayer was to the Jewish Christians who were being put out of their synagogues and separated from the Jewish communities. They must have read the words again and again, drawing hope and joy from the thoughts of being in Christ.

In verse 24, Jesus expresses a desire for both his present and future followers to be with him in the life after the resurrection, so they can behold the glory he had with the Father before the creation of the world. As believers, they already know something of this glory. But in the life beyond death they will be in the presence of eternal Wisdom in all its glory, with no barriers to their understanding.

Phillips Brooks once spoke of the division between this life and the next as a curtain. Sometimes, he said, we see the curtain tremble—especially if a loved one has recently gone beyond. It is enough to remind us of the life on the other side. But when we die we ourselves pass beyond the curtain, and nothing will then inhibit us from seeing and knowing all things.

Jesus was anxious for his followers to join him beyond the curtain. Then they would see all they had believed and hoped, given form in the heavenly world. The "name" Jesus had revealed to them—that of the great I AM himself—would be fulfilled in the unspeakable presence to which it alluded. The love with which they had been loved would see them safely home to the bosom of the Father, who would then be "all in all."

I can live my life more fully, Lord, knowing that its ultimate destiny is to dwell with you forever. Let my words and deeds remind others of this knowledge, that they too may come to know you and live in your love. For your kingdom's sake. Amen.

Week 9: Tuesday

John 18:1–12 Jesus Taken Captive

Having given his farewell speech and prayer, Jesus went with the disciples to the garden where he often met with them. Luke also said it was Jesus' "custom" to go there (22:39), but John alone calls the place a garden. The Synoptics all speak only of "the Mount of Olives" and "a place called Gethsemane." Perhaps John wished to emphasize the symbolism of the place, and relate it to the garden where Adam and Eve first sinned against God.

To reach the garden, Jesus and the disciples crossed the little brook Kidron. It was called "winter-flowing Kidron" because it was a mere wadi, or stream bed, and was dry except at the time of the late winter rains, in February and March. John may have mentioned the Kidron for two reasons. One is prophetic: in 1 Kings 2:37, Solomon warned Shimei, "On the day you go forth, and cross the brook Kidron, know for certain that you shall die." The other reason is prophetic too, but in a different way: during Passover, the brook flowed with the blood of lambs slain at the temple.

Because Jesus was accustomed to going with his disciples to the garden, Judas knew where to find him, and came leading "a band of soldiers and some officers from the chief priests and the Pharisees" (v. 3). The word for "band," literally, is "cohort." A cohort was six hundred Roman soldiers. It seems unlikely that Pilate would have dispatched so many men to arrest Jesus; therefore the translators have preferred a less precise term. John's is the only Gospel involving the Romans in Jesus' arrest; in the other Gospels, it is the temple guard that comes. Some interpreters think John may have been universalizing Jesus' enemies in this way—and underlining what Jesus said to the disciples about being hated by "the world" (15:18). The other Gospels, however, may have wished to downplay the Roman part in the arrest to avoid difficulties with the government, and John's account may be the more accurate one.

The soldiers and police came with "lanterns and torches and weapons." John probably liked this touch in his narrative, for it emphasized again the darkness out of which they came to Jesus, who was the light of the world. Their weapons would have been clubs and swords, and possibly spears. One can imagine the scene, as they swarmed over the hillside of the Mount of Olives, their lanterns and torches forming winding paths of light among the rocks and olive trees and grape vines, and their armor clinking audibly in the night.

In the Synoptic accounts, Judas came forward to Jesus and identified him for the police. Here, Jesus is in complete command, as we would expect him to be in John's Gospel; "knowing all that would befall him," he stepped forward to the searchers and said, "Whom do you seek?" "Jesus of Nazareth," they replied. "I am he," said Jesus. Literally, in the Greek, the words were *egō eimi*—I AM. The searchers recoiled and fell to the ground. Some suppose this was because Jesus had uttered the name of God—the name no one but the high priest was allowed to speak. It is unlikely that a cohort of Roman soldiers would have been so affected by the name of a Hebrew deity unknown to them. Instead, it was probably Jesus' personal bearing that at first frightened and intimidated them—though we cannot be sure it was not the other.

Again Jesus asked whom they sought. It was as if he did so to revive them, to start up the drama again. This time, when they told him whom they sought, he said once more that it was he, but that they should let his disciples go. "This," says John, "was to fulfill the word which he had spoken, 'Of those whom thou gavest me I lost not one'" (v. 9).

John repeatedly emphasizes Jesus' not losing any disciples (6:39; 10:38; 17:12); in 17:12, he has Jesus excepting Judas, for Judas was foreordained to be lost. This accent on the security of those in Jesus was surely for the benefit of Jewish Christians having to choose between Christ and the synagogue. The synagogue was willing to turn them out, but Jesus would never lose those whom God had given him.

Simon Peter, who in all the Gospels has a reputation for impetuousness, drew a sword and struck the slave of the high priest, Malchus, cutting off part of his ear. The word for ear, *ōtarion*, suggests an earlobe, not the entire ear. As Judas was in league with the high priest, he was probably close to the high priest's slave, together with those who commanded the soldiers and police. Peter was most likely striking into the midst of the enemy leadership.

But again Jesus was in command. His hour had come and he was ready to drink the cup his Father gave him. In the Synoptic accounts, he prayed in the garden for the cup to pass. Here, however, he seems eager for the cross to come, that he may join the Father in glory. So he tells Peter to put up the sword, and permits the soldiers and police to bind him and take him away.

Lord, this was a dramatic encounter, when you faced your enemies and did not use your great power to overcome them. Teach me your calmness of soul before those who would be my enemies, that I may not be disturbed by the evil of the world. For you are my strength and my redeemer. Amen.

Week 9: Wednesday

John 18:13–18 The Infidelity of Peter

Bound by the soldiers and police, Jesus was taken to the home of Caiaphas, the high priest. Caiaphas's aged father-in-law Annas, who had been high priest a few years earlier and still wielded much political force among the Jews, was also there. Some historiographers believe that Caiaphas' and Annas' homes adjoined one another, possibly with this infamous courtyard between them.

The focus is temporarily turned not on Jesus but on Peter, who in the garden had offered resistance to the soldiers and police and then followed the crowd to Caiaphas' house when Jesus was brought there. There is a mystery disciple in the passage, whose presence gained entrance for Peter into the high priest's courtyard. He was "known to the high priest," says John, and "entered the court of the high priest along with Jesus" (v. 15). Speculation about the mystery disciple's identity has centered principally on three persons.

Some think it was the beloved disciple John, who consistently hesitated to mention his own name in the Gospel. If it was not John, then why does the account fail to identify the disciple? The author surely knew the man's name, for he even had the name of the unfortunate slave whose ear was severed in the garden.

Other commentators suggest that the unnamed disciple was Nicodemus, who is pictured in 19:39 coming with spices and ointments to anoint Jesus' body for burial. Nicodemus was apparently a crypto-disciple, and would have been well known in

Caiaphas' house, so that he could have gained entrance for Peter. But why would John have failed to name him? He would not have been more endangered by identification here than in chapter twenty.

The third possibility is that the unknown disciple was Judas. Judas certainly was known to the high priest, having negotiated with him for the betrayal of Jesus, and would almost surely have followed with the soldiers and police he had led to the garden. The maid at the gate knew that the mystery figure was a disciple, for she asked Peter if he was also a disciple. Peter's denial indicates that it was not safe to admit to discipleship, which means that John could not have gone there freely. Judas could, for he had sold out his master. But would he have helped Peter gain entrance?

The Gospel is not concerned with answering our questions about this unidentified person. Its entire focus is on Peter and his act of infidelity. No story in the annals of discipleship was more important to the distraught Jewish Christians than this one. If Peter could fluctuate so greatly in a matter of hours, from single-handedly attacking the soldiers to denying that he was a follower of Jesus, then the falling away of other Christians was an understandable act of human frailty. And if Peter could be restored to fellowship—even to leadership—then there was always hope for those who had denied Christ in the synagogues, that they could be forgiven and rejoined to the fledgling Christian community.

Lord, this is my hope too. How often I deny you in my self-centeredness, my forgetfulness of others, and my doubts and fears. I am not worthy to be called your follower. Yet you forgive me and anoint me again with your Spirit and send me forth to do your bidding. Let me not fail you today, I pray, but live honestly and openly for you, for my friends' and family's sake. Amen.

Week 9: Thursday

John 18:19–24 Jesus before Annas

There is apparent confusion in this passage about who interrogated Jesus. We were told in verse 13 that Jesus was led to Annas, the father-in-law of Caiaphas, and are informed in verse 24, when the interrogation was ended, that Annas "sent him bound to Caiaphas the high priest." But verse 19 says "the *high priest* then questioned Jesus about his disciples and his teaching"—before he was sent to Caiaphas. It seems impossible to separate the tangle, further complicated in verse 28, where we are told that Jesus was led from the house of Caiaphas to the praetorium, without any word of his being questioned there.

But some light is shed on the matter by Acts 4:6, which refers to "Annas the high priest and Caiaphas and John and Alexander, and all who were of the high-priestly family." Annas was clearly the head of a priestly dynasty. In all, he had five sons who became high priests. Caiaphas held the office in the year of Jesus' trial and crucifixion. But always it was Annas—the crafty, powerful patriarch of the family—who took precedence in important matters. For this reason, he continued to be known as the high priest even while his sons were in office.

It is probable, therefore, that the high priest referred to in verse 19 was Annas. The old patriarch himself was up in the middle of the night, questioning Jesus about "his disciples and his teaching."

Persons brought before the powerful old priest would normally have cowered and answered his questions submissively. Jesus radiated confidence and self-possession. "I have not conducted my ministry in secret," he said in effect. "Why am I being dealt with secretly here?" His demand that others be asked about him was tantamount to requesting an open trial.

One of the temple police, unaccustomed to such boldness before the old man, struck Jesus in the face and asked, "Is that how you answer the high priest?" (v. 22) In the Synoptic Gospels, Jesus received even worse treatment: he was spit upon, blindfolded, and made to prophesy who hit him (Matt. 26:67–68; Mark 14:65; Luke 22:63–64). John would surely have been troubled to report such indignities to the eternal Word; a slap in the face was all he would allow himself to describe.

Not even a blow in the face, however, curbed Jesus' spirit. "If I was wrong," he said, "then take me to trial. If I was not, then why am I struck?" (v. 23, P).

Annas was surely not satisfied by Jesus' answers, but could do nothing else. So he sent him to his son Caiaphas—either in another part of the house or in a house adjoining. His son was now officially the high priest—*he* would have to deal with Jesus.

Lord, it is sad that religious leaders can be part of the web of evil and darkness in the world. I suppose any of us can, even without intending to. Teach me to live in such daily humility before you that I may never offend you while thinking I am performing my duty. For yours is a name above every name, both in heaven and on earth. Amen.

Week 9: Friday

John 18:25–27 Afraid in the Courtyard

For the second time, John mentions that Peter was warming himself at the charcoal fire in the courtyard of the high priest (vv. 18 and 25). Jerusalem is half a mile above sea level, and the spring nights are often quite chilly. The confrontation between Annas and Jesus may have required an hour or more, for Annas probably spent time conferring with his associates about what should be done with the Nazarene. Peter, having nothing to do but wait in the courtyard, undoubtedly grew cold and moved to the fireside.

We can imagine what was going through his head. Jesus had been marched off as a captive. The longer he was gone, the more frightened Peter became. Was Jesus less powerful than he had believed? Why didn't he strike his enemies a mortal blow and walk out of the high priest's house? The constant movement of soldiers and police in the courtyard must have been unnerving to an outsider.

The girl who watched the gate had asked Peter if he was a disciple of Jesus and he denied it (v. 17). Now, when others standing about the fire thought they recognized him, he denied it again. Then one of the servants of the high priest, studying Peter's face in the firelight, decided Peter must be the man who had attacked his cousin in the garden. "Didn't I see you in the garden with Jesus?" he asked (v. 26, P). Once more Peter denied his association with Jesus, and instantly he heard a cock crowing.

Peter's mind must have flashed back at once to the conversation at supper. "I will lay down my life for you," he had said to Jesus. "Will you lay down your life for me?" Jesus had asked. "Truly, truly, I say to you, the cock will not crow, till you have denied me three times" (13:37–38).

Sometime between his burst of bravado in the garden and the crowing of the cock—as early as 3 a.m. in Jerusalem—Peter had lost his courage. With Jesus by his side, nothing could daunt him, not even a cohort of legionnaires. But alone in a courtyard, with a fire casting shadows on strange faces, it was a different matter. Something went out of him, and he was afraid.

I know the feeling, Lord; it happens to me. When I have been faithful at prayer, and feel your presence, I am ready for anything. My pulse races to do your will. But when I have been unfaithful and feel as if I'm on my own, it is another story. Help me today to be faithful, that no shadows may frighten me. For your name's sake. Amen.

Week 9: Saturday

John 18:28–32 A Fateful Meeting

"I believe in God the Father Almighty, maker of heaven and earth, and in Jesus Christ his only Son, our Lord, who was conceived by the Holy Ghost, born of the Virgin Mary, suffered under Pontius Pilate. . . ." Thus begins the Apostle's Creed, the most widely used affirmation of faith in Christendom. The entire creed names only two human beings beside Christ. One is his mother Mary. The other is Pontius Pilate, the Roman governor of Judea whom we meet in this section of John's Gospel.

Pilate was procurator or governor of Judea from A.D. 26–36. His reputation among Jewish authors of the period is a sordid one. Philo associated his name with robbery and murder, and Josephus accused him of horrible atrocities against the Jews. While it was his order that eventually resulted in Jesus' crucifixion, the Christian writers of the period were, curiously, less condemning. They pilloried the Jewish authorities as the real villains in the drama, and left the impression that Pilate was a more or less helpless pawn in the judicial process of the day.

The procurator's primary base was in Antioch, not Jerusalem. But Pilate had doubtless come up to the garrison headquarters in Jerusalem for the Passover feast, to be on hand to quell any disturbance that might arise during the festival. What a fateful move that was for Pilate! Who would remember his name today if he had not gotten involved with Jesus?

We do not know precisely how much power the Romans allowed the Jewish Sanhedrin in settling its own affairs. Some scholars think they were not permitted to impose the death penalty (as verse 31 attests), and so brought Jesus before Pilate on a charge of sedition against the government. Others refer to the accounts of stoning in the Gospel (8:3–5; 8:59; 10:31) and the Book of Acts (particularly the stoning of Stephen in 7:58–60) to argue that the Jews could execute by stoning, but in Jesus' case desired death by crucifixion, which carried a curse from God (Deut. 21:23) and would discredit Jesus in the eyes of his followers. Verse 32, "This was to fulfill the word which Jesus had spoken to show by what death he was to die," seems to support the latter contention. (John's reference, of course, is to 3:14, which said the Son of man must be "lifted up.")

"The Jews"—members of the Sanhedrin and their police—took Jesus to Pilate very early in the morning. The Greek indicates it was in the last division of the night, from 3:00 A.M. to 6:00 A.M. It was not uncustomary for Roman officials to be at work this early, finishing their agendas well before noon.

Ever punctilious in their religious observances, "the Jews" took Jesus only as far as the outside of the praetorium, or Roman hall, where Pilate was. Numbers 9:6 indicates that "unclean" Jews could not take the Passover meal when it was regularly celebrated, but must delay a month to allow for cleansing. Either these officials and police thought they would be contaminated by entering a house where there was leaven present (they were forbidden to come into contact with leaven at the time of the feast of unleavened bread) or they believed that entering a Gentile house would make them impure.

This was always the picture of observant Jews in the Gospels—they ridiculously tithed their little herb gardens of mint and cumin while failing to observe the weightier matters of the Law, namely, loving God and their neighbors. Raymond Brown has put it even more pointedly about these particular Jews: "They fear that ritual impurity will prevent their eating the Passover lamb, but unwittingly they are delivering up to death him who is the Lamb of God."

Pilate, perhaps impatient with the scruples shown by the Jewish mob, went outside to meet them, and asked what official judgment they had brought against Jesus. The implication is that he was not surprised by their coming. This would be explained by the presence of the soldiers in the garden a few hours earlier—he had already collaborated with the local officials by lending them a cohort of men to overpower Jesus and the disciples.

The answer given by "the Jews" hardly disguises their disdain for the Roman ruler: "If this man were not an evildoer, we would not have handed him over" (v. 30). The word for "handed over" is the same one used frequently in John to describe Judas' betrayal of Jesus. "The Jews" too were betraying him as their countryman by giving him over to the Romans.

Pilate, dissatisfied with the answer, ordered "the Jews" to take Jesus back and judge him by their own laws. It was Roman policy to leave jurisdiction as much as possible within the hands of local authorities. But they could not impose the death penalty they really desired, probably by crucifixion—implying that Jesus was a dangerous subversive and that Pilate himself should examine the case.

O God, I am often unaware of the most fateful meetings in my own life, as Pilate was. I never know when some casual conversation or minor relationship will become the turning point of my entire existence. Guide me into real awareness, that I may not miss the important connections you prepare for me, but may be ever ready to meet them with wisdom and joy. Through Jesus Christ my Lord. Amen.

WEEK 10

Week 10: Sunday

John 18:33–38a What Is Truth?

The main theological question of Jesus' trial was the nature of his kingship. "The Jews" had apparently told Pilate that Jesus designated himself "King of the Jews." This was probably an insurrectionist title, calculated to brand Jesus as a popular revolutionary who wished to overthrow the Romans and reestablish Jewish rule over Israel.

"Are you the King of the Jews?" asked Pilate.

"Are they your words," replied Jesus, "or did someone else supply them?" (v. 34, P)

Pilate's response (v. 35) indicates a certain helplessness. After all, he was not a Jew. How could he understand the thinking and customs of the Jews? "Your own people have handed you over," he said. "What have you done?" (v. 35, P)

"My kingship is not of this world," said Jesus; "if it were, my subjects would have fought to prevent my falling into the hands of the authorities" (v. 36, P). The word for "subjects" (RSV "servants") is *hypērētes*, the same word John used for the temple police, who were the subjects of the Sanhedrin. In other words, Jesus had his own forces, as the Sanhedrin did. But he did not use them for conflict in a worldly manner, as his kingdom was not an earthly kingdom. There was possibly an indictment of "the Jews" in these words—their subjects *had* been employed in a worldly manner.

Jesus had spoken of his kingship, so Pilate legitimately concluded he was a king, or thought he was, albeit not King of the Jews.

"*You* say I am a king," said Jesus. "But I didn't come into the world for that. I came in order to witness to the truth, and my subjects are those who are of the truth" (v. 37, P). In 9:39, Jesus said he came into the world for judgment. Judgment and truth are not uncomplementary terms. Truth, in the biblical sense, is always the basis for judgment; and carries judgment with it.

Pilate's musing question "What is truth?" was a pathetic one. Facing this compelling man whom the authorities wished to execute, he probably wondered where the truth really lay. As procurator, he had a special responsibility to render truthful judgments. In the legal sense, at least, he did come to a right judgment. But he was about to go down in the annals of infamy for lacking the moral courage to *do* the truth he recognized.

How often, Lord, have I stood in Pilate's shoes, wondering what to do! And how many times I have erred as he did—guessing the truth but failing to do it! Let me wait before you until wisdom becomes courage and I learn to act out the truth, not merely discern what it is. For you are the way, the truth, and the life. Amen.

Week 10: Monday

John 18:38b–40 Jesus or Barabbas

Innocent: this was Pilate's verdict. A world traveler, a hardened soldier, a seasoned administrator, he was a wary man. How many times had he faced men before—corrupt officials, offending soldiers, habitual criminals? He had seen enough to know men, and he knew Jesus was not the kind of criminal he was accused of being.

So Pilate announced to the waiting authorities and police outside the praetorium that he found no guilt in Jesus.

But—Pilate was not through. The Jews had a custom that the procurator should release one prisoner to them at Passover. Did they wish him to release Jesus?

There is no evidence outside the Gospels of the existence of such a custom, but all the Gospels refer to it. Matthew 27:15 calls it a custom of the *governor*. Mark 15:6 and Luke 23:17 say it was *Pilate's* custom. Only John speaks of it as a custom of the Jews. Perhaps Pilate had made it an annual custom as a gesture of good will to the captive nation, and thus referred to it as *their* custom.

"The Jews" shouted down the idea of releasing Jesus. "Not this man," they cried, "but Barabbas!" (v. 40).

Barabbas is not really a name but a patronym, a kind of surname referring to the father of the man. The prefix *bar* means "son," as in the name Simon *Bar*jonah, or Simon the son of Jonah. So Barabbas meant "son of Abbas." The Aramaic word *abba* meant "father," so the name may have betokened "son of the father." This would have been ironic, for "the Jews" would have been asking for "son of the father's" release while seeking the death of the real Son of the Father! Some ancient manuscripts even gave Barabbas the first name of Jesus, which would have underlined the parallelism even more.

John calls Barabbas a *lēstēs*—a robber or bandit. Jewish literature of the time frequently used this word to describe insurrectionist guerrillas who roamed the countryside making daring raids and sometimes killing people as they plundered. Mark and Luke both identify Barabbas as a murderer, and Matthew says he was "a notorious prisoner" (27:16). John shows surprisingly little interest in Barabbas; for him the drama is clearly centered on Jesus and Pilate.

Could Pilate conceivably have believed that "the Jews" would ask for the release of Jesus, when they had brought Jesus to him with the express purpose of having him condemned and executed? One biblical scholar, A. Bajsić, has advanced the thesis that Pilate tried to release Jesus in order to avoid giving up Barabbas, who was apparently a popular figure in Jerusalem. As we shall see in the next few days' readings, however, Pilate was apparently convinced of Jesus' innocence. And, more than that, he seems to have taken an unusual interest in the most extraordinary prisoner he ever faced. "The Jews" may have charged Jesus with posing as a king; but Pilate, who knew about kings, recognized something royal in the man's demeanor.

Lord, Pilate said he found no crime in Jesus, yet did not use his authority to set Jesus free. Why do so many of us lack the courage to do what we know is right? Help me to live today so that what I believe is enacted in my deeds, that you may be glorified and I may rejoice in my own integrity. Amen.

Week 10: Tuesday

John 19:1–5 Behold the Man!

Scourging was the worst form of Roman beating. There were three classes of beatings—ordinary beatings, floggings, and scourgings. The third was the most barbarous. Inflicted with a leather whip into which were imbedded bits of stone and metal, it was reserved for capital offenses. It was torture, in other words, attached to execution.

The cruelty of the soldiers was not uncommon. Stationed in a foreign country where they were disliked by the populace, and subjected to strong discipline by superior officers, they often released their pent-up hostilities on unfortunate prisoners. In Jesus' case, they had a subject of abuse whose charge was that he had tried to become a king. They could therefore vent their anger on him as if he were a fallen superior.

Draping a purple robe around him and fashioning a crown of thorns for his head, they pretended he was royalty and mocked him with cries of "Hail, King of the Jews!"—as if he were a caesar and they were greeting him, "Hail, Caesar!" Circling about him in revelry, they struck him in the face—something they probably longed to do with real superiors but never dared to try.

After the beating and mockery, which he had surely observed, Pilate emerged again before the praetorium and told "the Jews," "I am bringing him out to you, that you may know that I find no crime in him" (v. 4). This is a doubly curious statement. Pilate had already announced Jesus' innocence of the charge (18:38). The scourging, moreover, was normally the prelude to execution. Had Pilate decided to have Jesus crucified, then changed his mind during the scourging? Perhaps Jesus' behavior during the beating and mocking convinced him that he could not go through with the execution.

"Here is the man!" said Pilate as the beaten figure in purple robe and crown of thorns was pushed out in their midst. *Ecce homo*, as the Latin phrase translated it—"Behold the man!"

What did Pilate mean by these words? Did he say them proudly, defiantly, as in "See what a man you are dealing with!" Or did he say it with pathos in his voice, as if to imply, "Look, he is only a broken man; why do you wish to crucify him?"

Whatever Pilate's intention in the utterance, there can be little doubt as to John's thought in including it in the passion narrative. Throughout the Gospel he has been at pains to demonstrate the humanity of the eternal Word. Jesus has thirsted, wept, loved, and now suffered. "Behold the *man*." Not an angel or a spirit, but a man. John is not losing the chance to remind us that God has been in our midst in human flesh, loving us person to person!

O Christ, I am ashamed of the pain and indignities you suffered—you, of all people. But I realize you still suffer whenever any of your little ones are subjected to pain or indignities. Make me more aware of where this is happening today, Lord, and give me a chance to help you there. For you are the King of my life. Amen.

Week 10: Wednesday

John 19:6–11 The Limited Power of Pilate

Again the Jewish authorities refused to accept the release of Jesus. Pilate, it is clear, really desired to set Jesus free. He must have recognized in him a depth of being far beyond that of men he was accustomed to sentence. But the Jews were persistent. They had wanted Jesus' death for a long time, and were not about to let it slip through their hands now.

"Crucify! Crucify!" they shouted.

Pilate was angry. "Crucify him yourselves," he said. "I have found him innocent" (v. 6, P).

They could not do it, of course. They had brought Jesus to Pilate in the first place because only the Romans had the power of crucifixion. So they raised another issue for Pilate to consider. They had been accusing Jesus of being a political revolutionary, thinking that was a charge Pilate could not ignore. Now they shifted ground and accused him of the real basis of their animosity all along, that he had made himself the Son of God. The Jews had a law about that, they said, that carried death with it. They were probably referring to Leviticus 24:16, "He who blasphemes the name of the Lord shall be put to death." (They did not remind

Pilate, cagily, that the kind of death prescribed was death by stoning.)

This change of direction on the part of "the Jews" was tantamount to saying, "Look, we made a mistake in trying to get what we wanted by pretending that Jesus is a political insurgent. He may be innocent of that. But he is not innocent of blasphemy, and our law requires that he die. We are counting on you to help us see that he does."

Pilate, upon hearing this, was "the more afraid" (v. 8). There have been no previous references to fear on Pilate's side. What does this suggest? Perhaps Pilate was worried now for Jesus' sake. The matter of Jesus' release was becoming more complicated.

Once again Pilate took Jesus into the praetorium to question him. "Where are you from?" he asked (v. 9). Luke reports that Pilate asked Jesus if he was a Galilean and used the fact that he was as a reason to send him to Herod for judgment, as Herod was tetrarch of Galilee (23:6). John may have used the same words to indicate a totally different question. We have been reminded again and again that Jesus was from the Father, to whom he would return following the resurrection. Pilate's question is a rhetorical reminder of Jesus' true origin, not a mere question of geographical location.

Why did Jesus remain silent and not reply to the question? In the Synoptics, he remained silent through most of his interrogation, fulfilling an image of the Suffering Servant in Isaiah 53:7 who was mute like a sheep before its shearers. Here, the silence may be for one of two reasons: (1) to emphasize Jesus' regal control of the exchange with Pilate, or (2) because Jesus thought it futile to reply. He had not convinced the Jews of his heavenly origin. How could he expect the Roman prefect to understand?

Pilate chided him for his silence. "Don't you realize," he asked, "that I have the power to set you free or to crucify you?" (v. 10, P).

"No," said Jesus, in effect, "you don't. Yours is a limited power, a proscribed power. Only God, the one sending me, has power over me. The only power you have is the power he lets you have. Whatever happens, therefore, is not really your fault; it is 'the Jews'' fault. I let them take me in the garden because it was my time to do so. They are really the ones who are challenging the power of God."

Lord, I sympathize with Pilate. He was dealing with matters he could not comprehend. Much of my life seems to be lived the same way, dealing with things beyond my understanding or control. Be merciful to me, a sinner, and let me live with love and courage. For your name's sake. Amen.

Week 10: Thursday

John 19:12–16 The End of the Trial

Pilate had considered the charge that Jesus was a political enemy and had dismissed it. He had investigated the possibility that Jesus was a religious criminal and decided he was not. Once more, he went outside to "the Jews" and attempted to persuade them to let him release Jesus.

But "the Jews" were crafty. If they could not achieve Jesus' crucifixion by defaming him, they would do it by personal threats to Pilate. Jesus had admitted he was a king, and any one who set himself up as a king—even a spiritual one—was challenging Caesar, who claimed to be both a temporal and spiritual ruler. "If you release this man," said "the Jews," "you are not Caesar's friend" (v. 12).

Pilate must have blanched at this. "The Jews" were threatening to accuse him officially before Caesar. He would be subject to investigation. There was no telling what errors or corruption in his prefecture would come to light. At the very least, a cloud of suspicion would be thrown over his name. Future appointments would be jeopardized. Even his present authority might be terminated or impaired.

Some scholars believe there was a special order in the Roman Empire known as the Friends of Caesar—that it was held by those who had done special favors for Caesar or were politically well related to him. If this was so, Pilate was being taunted as well as threatened. He was not, "the Jews" were pointing out, behaving as a true Friend of Caesar. He was permitting his special regard for this Nazarene prisoner to make him forget his ordinarily unswerving allegiance to the Emperor. And any sign of softness in his administration would be ill taken by Rome!

This was the argument that crumbled Pilate. He would withstand his clever adversaries no more. Peter had denied his Lord three times. Pilate had tried three times to save him. Now Pilate could—or would—do no more.

Jesus was brought outside onto the *lithostrotos*, the place of wide paving stones. Such stones were always an evidence of an official building or a palace, for individuals could not afford them in common residences. The Hebrew word *gabbatha* is not an obvious translation of the word for pavement. Instead, it seems to mean "high" or "elevated." Possibly the porch of wide stones was elevated from the street level.

(There is an old fortress in Jerusalem, called Antonia, where excavations have revealed such a place of wide paving stones; many archaeologists favor it as the site of Pilate's confrontations with "the Jews.")

Pilate seated himself on the judgment bench, from which official sentences were decreed. John is careful to note the hour—it was twelve noon. The trial lasted six hours, including the time of the scourging and mocking of Jesus. Mark 15:25 sets the time of crucifixion at 9 a.m. But John is interested in the symbolism of a noontime crucifixion on the day before Passover—it was the very hour when the priests in the temple began to slay the thousands of lambs required for the Passover meal.

In ancient times, the lambs had been killed on the evening of the day before Passover. The law in Exodus 12:6 required that they be kept alive till then. But in more recent years, the swelling of the population in Jerusalem by tens of thousands of visitors made it impossible for the priests to get all the lambs slain between sundown and darkness. So liberal interpretation had decreed that evening might begin with the beginning of the sun's decline at noon, and that was when the priests commenced the enormous task of slaughtering thousands of animals.

"Here is your King!" said Pilate at the hour of the slaughtering. Is there an echo of John the Baptist's voice in 1:29, "Behold, the Lamb of God"? Both statements begin with the Greek *ide*, "behold" or "here is."

But "the Jews" were not having the Lamb for their King. "Away with him, crucify him!" they shouted. "Shall I crucify your King?" asked Pilate—clearly indicating that the crucifixion had to be done by Roman order. "We have no king but Caesar," replied "the Jews."

It was a damning admission—one the Jews had always been loath to make. God was the King of Israel, according to 1 Samuel 8:7, and God had only allowed Israel an earthly king as an accommodation to her blindness and wickedness. Now the authorities of Israel were owning a completely foreign king—and one who claimed to be a divinity!

The drama of the trial was over. Jesus, garbed in purple and a crown of thorns, was delivered to his crucifiers. "The Jews" had judged themselves by rejecting the eternal Word.

O Lamb of God, who takest away the sins of the world, be my King, now and forever. Amen.

Week 10: Friday

John 19:17–22 Pilate Has the Last Word

All the Gospels are remarkably taciturn about the execution of Jesus. They expand in varying degrees upon the events leading up to the crucifixion, and upon the sayings and events which follow it. But they provide little detail about the actual placing of Jesus on the cross. Either they could not bear to describe it or they revered it too much to expatiate on it.

Jesus bore his own cross, says John. This would probably have been only the crossbar; the upright beam was normally left standing at the place of execution. The Synoptics all report that Simon of Cyrene was compelled to help Jesus carry his cross. Possibly Jesus began carrying the cross alone and Simon was encountered on the way to Golgotha, which was outside the city walls. To John, it may have been theologically important to picture Jesus bearing the cross alone—he was the regal Son of God.

The place of crucifixion was known as "the place of a skull." *Golgotha* was the Hebrew word for "skull," and *calvaria* the Latin word. Tradition assumes that the crucifixion occurred on a skull-shaped hill, though the place may have been so designated because of a skull left there to mark it as a forbidden site. Ancient Christian legends attest that Adam was buried on the site, and Jesus, the bringer of eternal life, shed his blood on the skull of the first man.

"Two others" were crucified with Jesus. Mark and Matthew identify them as *lēstai* (the word used for Barabbas) or robbers, and Luke says they were criminals. Pilate may have ordered that Jesus be given the middle cross as a place of honor. The Gospels' care in observing that one man was killed on either side of Jesus may also have related to the request of James and John that they be permitted to sit on either side of him in the kingdom (Matt. 20:20–28; Mark 10:35–45; Luke 22:24–27). Jesus replied to their request by asking if they could drink the cup that he must drink, referring to the suffering of the cross.

The dominant motif of this particular Johannine passage is the information that it was Pilate who caused an inscription to be put on the cross (Matthew 27:37 says it was over Jesus' head) naming Jesus as King of the Jews. The inscription was in three primary languages, so that anyone who could read at all would comprehend the words. Apparently it was the plaque bearing a criminal's accusation, commonly carried ahead of the man or hung by a cord about his neck.

All the Gospels refer to the inscription, but only John attributes it to Pilate. His information forms a fitting climax to the drama of Pilate's struggle for the release of Jesus. Failing to persuade "the Jews" to accept the release, he printed the words of accusation on a public placard. "The Jews" objected that what he printed was inaccurate—Jesus only *said* he was King of the Jews. "What I have written I have written," said Pilate (v. 22).

It was almost a confession of faith on Pilate's part. Perhaps he did not fully understand the significance of the title—he was a foreigner and probably not a religious man. But there was something about Jesus that compelled his respect and wonder. For him, Jesus *was* the King of the Jews, even though his throne was a cross.

O Lord, how did Pilate live with what he saw that day? I am grieved merely to read about it. Grant that I may never stray very far from this tragic scene, except to experience the joy of your resurrection. For you are the Risen One with nailprints in your hands. Amen.

Week 10: Saturday

John 19:23–25a The Tunic of Jesus

John alone has told us that the soldiers who crucified Jesus were a quaternion—a band of four. It is possible that a quaternion was assigned to each man being crucified.

When the soldiers had put Jesus on the cross, they exercised their privilege of dividing his belongings among themselves. Scholars have written entire books speculating on what the four garments were. There is agreement that three would have been a *tallith*, or robe; a cincture or girdle; and a head covering of some kind, probably like a modern *kafia*. The fourth article was probably Jesus' sandals, unless he was wearing an undershirt beneath his tunic.

The tunic was a garment usually worn next to the skin. The seamlessness of Jesus' tunic did not indicate that it was particularly expensive or valuable. It was merely in keeping with a law in Leviticus 19:19 that forbade wearing a garment woven of two kinds of material. Tunics and robes that had not been pieced together were common in the marketplace, for this showed at a glance that the law was honored.

The soldiers cast lots for the tunic to avoid cutting it up for division. John saw this as fulfilling a prophecy in Psalm 22:18 about a man's enemies dividing his possessions among them. Psalm 22, incidentally, is the one beginning "My God, my God, why hast thou forsaken me?," cited by Mark 15:34 as one of Jesus' words from the cross. John would not have quoted this verse of the psalm because of his emphasis on the constant unity of the Son with the Father. (Several early church fathers, it should be noted, saw in the seamless tunic a symbol of the unity theme so prominent throughout the Gospel.)

One can hardly resist speculating about the soldier who won the toss and received Jesus' tunic. Did he wear it as his own undergarment, against the skin? Did he feel the aura of its last owner, and did it lead to any dramatic effects in his life?

Jesus was apparently left naked on the cross, as most men wore either a tunic or a breechcloth beneath their clothing, but not both. He died therefore as he had come into the world—without property or clothing.

O Lord, you were the victim of such humiliation, yet turned it into glory and triumph. Help me to love you so much that I will not worry about my own defeats in the world, but will rejoice in the light of your victory. For yours is the kingdom forever. Amen.

WEEK 11

Week 11: Sunday

John 19:25b–27 The True Holy Family

The previous scene (verses 23–25*a*) revealed four soldiers. This one has four women—Jesus' mother, his aunt, and the two other Marys. According to one scholar who has studied the matter thoroughly, the families of those crucified were usually permitted to remain by the side of their dying relatives. We know from the Synoptics that Jesus traveled in the company of a number of women, as well as his disciples, and that his mother was often in the group.

Looking down from the cross, Jesus saw his mother among the women standing there. At a slight distance stood also the beloved disciple John. "Woman," Jesus said—the word he had used to address her at the wedding in Cana (2:4)—"behold, your son!" To John, he said: "Behold, your mother!"

It was a transaction similar to ancient contract scenes in which a dying man made provision for a wife or children or parents being left behind. Perhaps Jesus, who had known what kind of death he must die, had made the arrangements earlier, and now, in the final hour of his consciousness, was sealing what had been decided.

The Gospel of John has no birth narrative for Jesus, and so contributes nothing to the story of the holy family as found in

Matthew and Luke. But it has this touching scenario in which Mary, the mother of Jesus, is given into the care of the disciple John. In other words, it gives us the picture of another kind of holy family—one built on the mutual love and commitment of the members.

In this sense, the picture prefigures the nature of all Christian fellowship. Those of us who are one with Jesus and God are also one with each other. Jesus has commanded us to love one another (15:17). We are to care not only for Jesus but for all those who are of his family.

What a tender picture, O God, of the life in your Son. How different it is from the world, where we dwell in isolation and loneliness. Grant that I may truly care for others in the fellowship, and share whatever I have with them, for your Son's sake. Amen.

Week 11: Monday

John 19:28–30 It Is Finished

We have dwelled at length upon these brief passages of the Gospel because they are so filled with meaning and importance. Here, in a mere forty-five words (in the Greek), John describes the final minutes of Jesus' dying, including two of the seven sayings on the cross.

Knowing the work he had been sent to do was completed, Jesus said, "I thirst."

Three observations may be offered:

(1) This fulfilled a prophecy, as John points out. The probable allusion is to Psalm 69:21, "For my thirst they gave me vinegar to drink."

(2) To this point, Jesus had held himself in rigorous self-control. He retained regal composure throughout the trial and crucifixion. With his work finished, he now indulged a personal need and asked for a drink.

(3) With this detail, absent from the other Gospels, John was once more enforcing his theme of the humanity of Jesus. The messiah who had described himself to the Samaritan woman as the

giver of "living water" (4:10) was also a man of flesh and blood, with appetites like those of ordinary persons. This was no docetic Christ. He was a human being in the fullest sense of the words.

A jar or bowl of vinegar stood near the cross. The word for vinegar, *oxos*, means a diluted, vinegary wine drunk by common people and soldiers. The jar may have been placed there by custom for the dying men, or it may simply have belonged to the soldiers or someone else. The fact that the wine was not merely held to Jesus' mouth, but was poured on a sponge and extended to him on a stick, is the clearest indication we have that the cross was a high one.

The word *hyssop* has caused commentators some concern. The hyssop bush was not uncommon, but its stalk was not notably strong, and seems an unlikely kind of stick to have used for the task of extending a sponge soaked in wine. Some scholars therefore think there may have been a scribal error in copying the word and that it was originally *hyssos*, a javelin or spear. But it is probable that John intended the word *hyssop*, because the hyssop plant was used at the time of the exodus to sprinkle the blood of the paschal lamb on the doorposts of Israelite families (Exod. 12:22). Jesus was the Lamb of God, taking away the sins of the world (1:29). It would have been extraordinarily fitting for a hyssop plant to have come in contact with his suffering body in the final moments of the crucifixion.

Having received the vinegary wine, fulfilling the scripture, Jesus said, "It is finished," bowed his head, and gave up his spirit. His work was done. If John had been present at the cross during Jesus' most agonizing moments, when he said "My God, my God, why hast thou forsaken me?" (Matt. 27:46; Mark 15:34), or if he knew the tradition of the saying, he omitted it from his narrative. Similarly, he did not mention Jesus' crying with a loud voice, "Father, into thy hands I commit my spirit!" (Luke 23:46) His Jesus simply bowed his head in a quiet manner and gave up the spirit.

John had emphasized all along the unity of the Son and the Father. This was the hour of the Son's glory. He did not vent his agony, or in any way voice misgivings about what was transpiring. For this cause he had come into the world.

Lamb of mercy, I wait reverently before this image of your crucifixion and listen as you say, "I thirst." Would, Lord, I could give you everything for which you thirst: an end to human suffering, a universal community of love, the joy of your whole creation. At least let me give you no cheap wine, but the very best I have. For your love's sake. Amen.

Week 11: Tuesday

John 19:31–37 The Wounded Side

The Jews did not like to have bodies left on crosses overnight because of a law in Deuteronomy 21:22–23 saying that the land would be defiled by a corpse remaining on a tree all night. They especially did not want the bodies of Jesus and the other men crucified with him left on their crosses, because Passover that year coincided with the sabbath, making it a particularly holy occasion. So they went to Pilate and asked that the legs of the crucified men be broken to hasten their dying.

The Romans were usually in no hurry to remove the bodies. Sometimes people died slowly, over a period of days. Besides, corpses left on crosses were a deterrent to crime. But apparently Pilate wanted no trouble from these bothersome people who had threatened to report him to Rome (19:12), so he sent the delegation they requested.

Breaking an executed man's legs was not an unusual practice. Called the *crurifragium*, it was accomplished with a large mallet. The skeleton of a first-century man discovered in recent excavations in Jerusalem had both legs broken, leading archaeologists to suspect that he had died as a criminal.

Jesus' legs were not broken, because the soldiers saw that he was already dead. True to John's portrait of him, he remained in control of his own death, dying before the soldiers came.

One of the soldiers, however, apparently to be sure Jesus was dead, plunged a spear into his side. At once, says John, "there came out blood and water" (v. 34).

Much has been written of the blood and water, by both medical doctors and biblical scholars. The doctors have been at pains to show how blood and water could possibly have flowed from the side of a dead man, as blood does not generally flow after the heart stops beating, and the water is even more difficult to explain. The biblical scholars have taxed their minds to cite theological reasons for the unusual event. One of the simplest of these is found in the Gospel itself, when Jesus stood at the Feast of Tabernacles and spoke of "rivers of living waters" flowing from the faithful person (7:38).

The early church fathers may have had the best attitude. They regarded the event as a miracle, and saw verse 35, about the witness (surely John himself), as proof of this. An ordinary event, they reasoned, would not have required the special testimony of a witness.

Whether it was a natural occurrence or a miraculous happening, John doubtless had a symbological reason for including it in his narrative. The water is rich in associations—the water from the rock struck by Moses in the wilderness (Num. 20:10–11)—the water of life—the water of baptism. The coming of the Spirit was also associated with water, as John 3:5 attests: "Truly, truly, I say to you, unless one is born of water and the Spirit, he cannot enter the kingdom of God." And the imagery of blood is just as strong as that of water in Hebrew lore—the blood of the Passover lambs—the blood of covenants—the blood containing the spirit of life.

Considering the great sacramental passages of John—references to baptism and new birth in 3:3–7 and to the Eucharist in 6:1–14, 25–59—there is a likelihood that the author intended this reference to blood and water to be sacramental also. Jesus had finished the work the Father gave him by dying on the cross. Thus both baptism and the Lord's Supper would ever after derive their real meaning from the drama of Calvary—a drama that in its climax contained references to both of them.

The soldiers had not broken Jesus' legs, and they had pierced his side. The scriptures, said John, foretold both. Exodus 12:46 says, of the Passover lamb, "you shall not break a bone of it." And Zechariah 12:10 says, "I will pour out on the house of David and the inhabitants of Jerusalem a spirit of compassion and supplication, so that, when they look on him whom they have pierced, they shall mourn for him, as one mourns for an only child, and weep bitterly over him, as one weeps over a first-born."

The passion story would indeed invoke the tears of those who belonged to the true Jerusalem, the new Israel. Not because Jesus had died—the resurrection would cancel all grief for that—but because he had suffered so for the sins of others.

"They shall look on him whom they have pierced." What had John said in 3:14—that as the serpent was lifted up in the wilderness and the people were saved by looking at it, so Jesus must be lifted on the cross? Now it would happen. People would look and be saved.

O Jesus, born to die but alive forevermore, help me to turn my eyes upon you. "Let the water and the blood, from thy wounded side that flowed, be of sin the double cure, save from wrath and make me pure." Amen.

Week 11: Wednesday

John 19:38–42 The Secret Disciples

How encouraging this passage must have been to Jewish Christians afraid to confess Jesus in the synagogues! At last, two members of the Sanhedrin, the council that had sought Jesus' death, came forward to claim his body and display their allegiance to him. Mark 15:43 and Luke 23:50 both identify Joseph as a member of the council, and we know from John's report of the meeting between Nicodemus and Jesus (3:1–14) that Nicodemus was too.

Jesus had said in 12:32, speaking of his death on the cross, "When I am lifted up from the earth, I will draw all men to myself." Was this part of what he meant—that even the secret followers among the rulers of Israel would come out of hiding to own their discipleship?

Matthew 27:60 says the place of burial was in Joseph's "own new tomb." As Mary had used her burial ointment to anoint Jesus (John 12:1–8), Joseph was surrendering his own resting place. The body was washed, covered in the mixture of myrrh and aloes, and wrapped in linen cloths. The amount of myrrh and aloes was very great—enough, in fact, to indicate that Nicodemus regarded Jesus as a person of royal status. The fact that the tomb was in a garden also betokens the royal nature of the burial—kings and rulers were usually buried in such surroundings, while common people were buried in ordinary burial grounds. It was only fitting, after the emphasis on Jesus' kingship throughout the trial and crucifixion, that he be interred in a royal manner.

To comprehend the daring of Joseph and Nicodemus in

preparing the body and burying it, we need to remember the Jewish associations of death and defilement. "He who touches the dead body of any person," says Numbers 19:11, "shall be unclean seven days." This meant that the two men could not eat the Passover meal the evening of Christ's death. Their families and friends would know they had been defiled. There was no way of keeping their devotion secret any longer.

We can only suppose they had discovered something that made their risk worthwhile—that the one who died on the cross was the real Passover Lamb, who takes away the sins of the world!

Lord, I have seen the pilgrims in Jerusalem kneeling to kiss the stone where your body was prepared for burial. I wanted to join them, but decided it was probably not the very stone on which you were laid. Give me a simple faith, I pray, that I may feel at all times the mystery of your presence and serve you as the King of my life. For your kingdom's sake. Amen.

Week 11: Thursday

John 20:1–10 The Empty Tomb

This passage is so vibrant with meaning and mystery that it is difficult for a Christian to read it without trembling. For two chapters, we have been reading about the capture, trial, and execution of Jesus. The material was heavy, sorrowful, dirgelike. Now the pace quickens and the material lightens. Suddenly people are running and speaking breathlessly to one another. There is excitement, hope, the dawning of belief. The entire atmosphere is different.

It was early Sunday morning, the day after Passover sabbath. Mary of Magdala, a small town in Galilee only a few miles from Capernaum, came to the tomb where Jesus was laid on Friday evening. She had stood with Jesus' mother near the cross less than forty-eight hours earlier (19:25). Now she was coming to mourn his death—to weep and wail in the Israelite fashion. (In 11:31, the Jews who saw another Mary rise and go out to meet Jesus assumed she was going to weep at Lazarus' tomb.) Some interpreters assume she was not alone, because of the plural pronoun when she said "we do not know where they have laid him" (v. 2). Perhaps the mother of Jesus and the other women were with her or followed at a short distance.

At any rate, Mary found the stone rolled away from the mouth of the tomb and ran to inform the disciples. "They have taken the Lord out of the tomb," she said (v. 2). We cannot be sure who she meant by "they," if indeed she had a specific group of persons in mind. Perhaps she believed the soldiers or the Jewish authorities had done it. Or she may have thought grave-robbers were responsible, for there is evidence to show that corpse-stealing was a serious problem in those days.

Peter and John ("the other disciple, the one whom Jesus loved") ran toward the tomb. John, perhaps because he was younger and more excitable, arrived first. By this time, the first rays of the sun had broken over the garden. John knelt to peer through the small opening, and saw the linen cloths used to wrap Jesus' body lying there on the stone shelf that ran around three sides of the cavernous tomb.

Before John could recover from the sight, Peter had arrived and plunged through the opening into the interior of the tomb. True to his impetuous nature, he was not worried about ceremonial defilement from contact with the dead. In the shadowy half-light, he saw not only the linen cloths but the *soudarion*, or head covering, which instead of lying with the linen cloths was rolled up and lying by itself. Unable to believe his senses, Peter doubtless shouted this information to John. If robbers had stolen the body, they would not have troubled to unwrap the spiced grave clothes and lay the head covering neatly to the side. The disciples were clearly dealing with something greater than a body-theft!

John soon followed Peter inside and saw the evidence too. "Then the other disciple, who reached the tomb first, also went in, and he saw and believed" (v. 8). Many scholars have argued on the basis of these words that John came to faith in the resurrected Jesus before Peter did. It seems probable, however, that Peter's belief is implied in the narrative. The word *also* is the same in Greek as the word *and*, and the construction of verse 8 permits us to read "he also saw and believed." This interpretation is strengthened by verse 9, "for as yet they did not know the scripture, that he must rise from the dead." The plural pronoun has the force of implying that *both* Peter and John had seen and believed inside the tomb.

That the disciples did not know "the scripture" pertaining to the resurrection may strike us as very unusual, for in the Synoptic Gospels Jesus often alluded to his resurrection and New Testament writers often combed the Old Testament for possible allusions to the resurrection. But we should remember that John has consistently emphasized Jesus' reunion with the Father, not his resurrection as such. Repeatedly, in the farewell speech and prayer of chapters fourteen to seventeen, Jesus spoke of going away and being with the Father—not of shortly returning to the disciples.

It was natural, therefore, that the two disciples, on making the astounding discovery of Jesus' resurrection, returned to their homes (v. 10). (They were not, apparently, living at the same address in Jerusalem.) Their heads were filled with the wonder of what they had seen, but they did not anticipate seeing Jesus again before they too went to be with the Father. They were probably quite content with the evidence that Jesus was triumphant over death.

Lord, my heart beats faster and faster as I contemplate this marvelous scripture. How simply and beautifully it describes the wonder of that irrepeatable scene! I can enter the amazement of it as if I were there. Thank you for this vivid memory from the two disciples and what it has meant to believers through the ages. Let it remain strong and active in my mind throughout this day and the days to come, transforming the way I view the world and my role in it. For you have overcome everything—even my lethargy. Amen.

Week 11: Friday

John 20:11–18 The Appearance to Mary Magdalene

This is surely one of the tenderest scenes in the entire Bible. There is little wonder it supplied the inspiration for C. Austin Miles's famous hymn "In the Garden," with its description of intimate companionship with Jesus.

Mary apparently followed Peter and John back to the tomb, arriving after they had departed for their homes (v. 10). Her "weeping" would not have been the usual mourning for the dead, as she was still concerned about the missing body. It was probably a combination of sadness, despair, and confusion.

In a distraught state of mind, she stooped, as John had, to peer into the tomb, and had a parapsychological experience. Sitting on the stone shelf where the body of Jesus had been were two angels. "Woman, why are you weeping?" they asked her. "Because they have taken away my Lord," she said, "and I do not know where they have laid him" (v. 13).

Still in the grip of the experience, Mary turned, aware of a figure behind her. In her stooping position, she did not see the figure directly, and assumed it was the keeper of the garden. (She may have seen the keeper elsewhere in the garden when she entered.) The voice behind her repeated the question of the angels: "Woman, why are you weeping? Whom do you seek?" (v. 15)

Supposing it was the gardener, Mary asked if he knew where the body was. Perhaps, as the keeper of the place, he had for some reason removed it and laid it in another tomb.

Jesus spoke her name: "Mary."

Instantly she turned and knew him.

"Rabboni!" she exclaimed.

It was the Hebrew word for teacher or master, but in a special form of the word indicating an affectionate relationship. Perhaps we can translate it "Dear Master." During Jesus' ministry, his followers probably called him rabbi more than anything else. It was instinctive of Mary to greet him as her rabbi—only she gave it this intimate form.

It has always interested readers that Mary recognized Jesus the moment he spoke her name. The passage suggests the intimate relationship that always exists between Jesus and the individual believer. And it echoes something Jesus had said in the Beautiful Shepherd passage: "The sheep hear [the shepherd's] voice, and he calls his own sheep by name" (10:3).

Apparently, as there is no evidence of Mary's having risen from her stooping position, Mary clutched at Jesus' feet when she recognized him. It would have been an appropriate gesture—prostrating oneself before an exalted master.

But Jesus said, "Don't try to hold onto me—I haven't yet ascended to the Father. Instead, go to my brothers and tell them I am ascending to my Father and your Father, my God and your God" (v. 17, P).

"Do not hold me." Jesus was probably alluding to the very nature of psychic experiences like this one. Mary was still flesh and blood. She could not remain in this ecstatic state indefinitely, any more than any of us can. What was important was that she had seen the resurrected Lord and was to witness about this to the disciples.

The nature of the resurrection appearances in John's Gospel is already becoming clear. Jesus' rejoining the Father—his Father and ours, as verse 17 emphasizes—was the thing of supreme importance to John. The appearances were only brief manifestations to Jesus' followers in evidence of his ascension, so they would not be tempted merely to think the body had been stolen or appropriated by the authorities.

Therefore there is no real contradiction in Jesus' telling Mary not to hold him (v. 17) and then instructing Thomas to handle his wounds (v. 27). Everything is told to verify the one overriding claim of the Gospel, that the Word that became flesh has overcome the world and been reunited with the Father.

Mary, like a faithful witness, went back and reported to the disciples what she had seen and heard. This time she did not use the word *Rabboni*. She said: "I have seen the Lord."

Like Mary, Lord, I want the reality of sacred moments to linger forever, so that it transcends all other realities. But, like Mary, I cannot hold you. The world is too much with me. Only in prayer and meditation can I experience the union with you and the Father that overcomes the world. Therefore help me to pray as constantly as possible, and to retain the sense of having prayed even when I must be doing other things. For there is nothing like being in your presence, which even the tomb could not contain. Amen.

Week 11: Saturday

John 20:19–23 The Recommissioning of the Disciples

In the early morning, when Peter and John had discovered the mystery of the empty tomb with the grave clothes lying neatly inside, they had returned to their separate places of residence. Then, in the evening, they were with the other disciples—all except Thomas—in the same place. Probably it was in the upper room where they had eaten the Last Supper. The doors were shut, and probably locked, "for fear of the Jews" (v. 19). Possibly they were afraid, now that the sabbath was over, that the authorities would round up Jesus' associates—or that they would be blamed for the disappearance of the body!

We can imagine their excitement as they pondered what Peter and John had seen that morning and talked of Mary Magdalene's experience with the Master in the garden. Surely they were trying to recall all of Jesus' words the night before the crucifixion, when he spoke so much about being one with the Father and going to prepare a place for them.

Suddenly, as they talked, Jesus appeared in their midst. There is no mention of the doors being opened. Instead, he simply appeared to them. "*Shālōm hālēkem*," he said—"Peace be with you." It was the formula spoken by God to Gideon in Judges 6:23 when Gideon was frightened at seeing the Lord's angel. Only now it bore the added meaning given by Jesus in his farewell speech when he said, "In me you may have peace. . . . I have overcome the world" (16:33).

After showing the disciples his hands and side—emphasizing the brokenness of the body now raised up before them—Jesus repeated the words "Peace be with you." They were to understand that God's peace keeps even one whose body is mutilated in the kingdom's service. And this time Jesus added the Johannine form of the Great Commission: "As the Father has sent me, so I send you." The Father had sent the Son into a world of resistance and cruelty, where he had had nails driven into his hands and a spear thrust into his side. Now Jesus was sending his disciples into the same world. He had already warned them that the world would hate them as it had hated him (15:18–20).

When he had said this, Jesus breathed on the disciples and said: "Receive the Holy Spirit" (v. 22). Literally, the words may be read, "Receive holy breath," for the Greek word *pneuma* may mean either "breath" or "spirit" and there is no definite article in the sentence. Whichever way the phrase is translated, the meaning is essentially the same: Jesus was imparting his essential being to the disciples, that they might continue his work in the world. They would have his power to forgive or not forgive sins in the people they encountered.

To understand this final part of the commission (v. 23), we can turn to a similar saying of Jesus in Matthew 16:19, following Peter's confession that Jesus was the Christ: "I will give you the keys of the kingdom of heaven, and whatever you bind on earth shall be bound in heaven, and whatever you loose on earth shall be loosed in heaven." The image is of a master giving a steward the keys to all his possessions, so that the steward can act in the master's behalf for members of the household or others who require anything. The gift of his Spirit was Jesus' way of conferring total stewardship on the disciples.

One of the fascinating things about this brief passage is the number of references it bears to the form of early Christian worship, so that we could almost take it as a prototype of a worship service. *First*, the meeting took place on the first day of the week, as Christian worship did. *Second*, it occurred behind closed doors (early Christians often met in hiding). *Third*, the followers of Jesus were probably talking about their earlier experiences of Jesus. *Fourth*, Jesus manifested himself to them, as Christians believed he would in the Eucharist (*Maranatha*, "Our Lord, come," was the standard eucharistic prayer). *Fifth*, Jesus said, "Peace be with you," the formula greeting used in the Eucharist from earliest times. *Sixth*, the followers received the gift of the Spirit. And, *seventh*, they were empowered to represent Jesus in their dealings with others.

Lord, the scripture says the disciples were glad when they saw you. I too am glad when I feel your presence. Come, I pray, behind the closed doors of my life, and breathe your Spirit upon me, that I may feel empowered to represent you in the world. For your peace is all the armor I need. Amen.

WEEK 12

Week 12: Sunday

John 20:24–29 The Great Confession

How did Thomas feel about being absent when Jesus appeared to the disciples? He must have been terribly disappointed—perhaps even resentful. We can imagine his saying, "What had you been drinking? I can't believe you really saw him." When the disciples protested that Jesus had even shown them his wounded hands and side, Thomas replied: "I would not believe it unless I could actually touch the nailprints and put my hand in his side" (v. 25, P).

But Thomas was not left out. One week later (the Jews counted the present day when figuring time, so that the eighth day corresponded to our seventh), Jesus appeared again to the disciples. This time Thomas was present. The similarities of the passage in verses 19–23 to a service of worship and the emphasis on the fact that both appearances were on Sunday or the Lord's Day suggests that these two occurrences were regarded by John as the original experiences of Christian worship.

Again, as before, Jesus came when the doors were shut, and said, "Peace be with you" (v. 26). Then, as he had earlier shown the disciples his wounded self, he offered himself to Thomas. "Put your finger here," he said, "and see my hands; and put out your hand, and place it in my side; do not be faithless, but believing" (v. 27).

Even more certainly than in verses 19–23, because of the repetition, we are dealing with references to the Eucharist. Jesus' hands represent his body or the bread, while the wounded side, from which flowed blood and water (19:34), represents the blood or the wine. The injunction to have faith, and not be disbelieving, would be especially relevant to persons approaching the sacred table. With faith, they would recall the Lord's presence in the elements. He would come and stand in their midst.

Thomas's response to the invitation of Jesus was precisely the one desired of every follower of Christ: "My Lord and my God!" It was the highest word of personal confession spoken in the entire Gospel. Jesus had been called Lamb of God, Teacher, Lord, and King of Israel. He had called himself the Bread of Life; the Light of the World; the Resurrection and the Life; the Gate of the Sheep; the Beautiful Shepherd; the Way, the Truth, and the Life; and the True Vine. But Thomas's confession topped them all. It was the climax of understanding toward which the whole Gospel had been moving. And it is the insight to which every follower should rise each time he or she participates in Christian worship: "My Lord and my God!"

"Have you believed becaue you have seen me?" asked Jesus. "Blessed are those who have not seen and yet believe" (v. 29). In the Eucharist, we all see by faith. We have not really seen, as Thomas did—not literally, with our eyes. But we have seen with our hearts, and that was finally how Thomas had to see too.

My Lord and my God: it is a staggering confession, and I feel the weight of it as I make it. It changes the center of my life. I am no longer there, but you are. Come, Lord Jesus, and take full possession of me. For you are the one who died and is alive, and I want no life outside of yours. Amen.

Week 12: Monday

John 20:30–31 Life in His Name

These verses are actually a formal conclusion to the first twenty chapters of the Gospel, suggesting the possibility that the Gospel originally ended here and an editor subsequently added chapter twenty-one. This does not mean that chapter twenty-one is not authentically Johannine—only that it was appended later to the first version of the Gospel. The stories in chapter twenty-one may well have been told by John and preserved by one of his disciples until they were safely included in the written narrative.

"Jesus did many other signs in the presence of the disciples," the ending says. Some of these marvelous events are doubtless recorded in other Gospels. But it is thrilling to think that what was written in the Gospels was only a portion of what Jesus did and said during his ministry with the disciples. Imagine! There were probably dozens of major healings and dramatic encounters—perhaps hundreds—that did not get into the pages of the Gospels. The authors selected only the stories and sayings needed to present a true picture of Jesus' power and personality.

The "signs" included in his Gospel, says John, were put there so that the reader "may believe that Jesus is the Christ, the Son of God, and . . . have life in his name" (v. 31).

Scholars disagree about whether the verb "to believe" *(pisteuēte)* is an aorist or a present subjunctive. John's customary use of causal relationships in other places argues for the present subjunctive. In this case, the verb should be translated "keep believing" or "continue to believe." That is, "these are written in order that you may continue to believe that Jesus is the Christ, the Son of God," etc.

This would agree with our contention that the entire Gospel was written primarily to encourage Jewish Christians to continue in the faith, even if expelled from their synagogues, not to make new Christians. It would also help to explain why John presents a more exalted image of Jesus than the other Gospels—it was purposely intensified to appeal to persons who already had a basic introduction to the faith but needed a more "spiritual" narrative to deepen their perceptions of Christ and his faithfulness as the shepherd of the Christian flock.

The object of all this? That readers might have life in Jesus' name. As we said in the beginning, John's is the Gospel of eternal life—of a quality of existence that is truly extraordinary. And people discover that dimension of life through faith in the One who came among us as the Wisdom of God.

Lord, when I think how many wonderful signs have been done in your name, both during your ministry and since you breathed your Spirit into the disciples, my mind is boggled! They continued to be done throughout the world every hour! Give me eyes to see and ears to hear, that I may always have life in your name. For you are the Christ, the Son of God. Amen.

Week 12: Tuesday

John 21:1–11 An Amazing Catch

This chapter has long perplexed scholars. It is obviously an appendage to the first twenty chapters, which ended with 20:31. The language and usages are largely Johannine, however, suggesting that the material was added by a disciple of John if not John himself. But why was it added? And why, after the Gospel was so largely centered in Jerusalem, was this episode set in Galilee by the seashore?

The answer may lie in the symbolism of the sea and the fish, and their relation to the universal mission of the church. The first twenty chapters of John were concerned with the ministry of Jesus and its immediate effect on the faith of the disciples. But Jesus, after his "hour" had come, was returning to the Father. He had breathed his Spirit into the disciples (20:22). Now they were to carry on his work in the world. Chapter twenty-one was necessary to dramatize the opportunities and responsibilities of their ministry. And, as the Sea of Galilee bordered on Gentile territory, it was a natural setting for a long, enacted parable about the work of the disciples and the early church.

Interestingly, there were only seven disciples who went fishing on the Sea of Tiberias or Galilee. This in itself is a clue to the meaning of the narrative. Seven, in Jewish numerology, was a universal number. It was believed there were seventy Gentile nations—seven (for universal) times ten (for wholeness or completeness).

Peter and his friends went fishing at night—a natural time to go, as fishermen usually brought in their catches to sell early in the morning. But we remember that night and darkness in John are symbolic of the world and its opposition to God. So, when the disciples caught nothing, we know why: they were fishing in their own power.

Jesus appeared with the daybreak. The Light of the World was standing on the beach. But, because it was the spiritual Jesus, who had been raised from the dead, the disciples did not recognize him. They were like the woman at the well (4:7–42), who did not know at first to whom she was talking.

"Children, have you any fish?" said Jesus. The Greek word used for children is *paidia*, which means "small boys" or "lads." It is the plural of the word used in 6:9 for the small boy brought to Jesus with the loaves and fishes, suggesting perhaps a link between the two "multiplication" stories.

Being told that the disciples had caught nothing, Jesus told them to drop their nets on the right side of the boat. Presumably they had been fishing from the left side. When they did as instructed, they caught such an amazing draft of fishes that they were unable to get the net into the boat.

The miraculous nature of the event is underlined by the fact that they were fishing essentially the same water they had fished moments earlier without success. They merely let down the nets on the opposite side of the boat.

It was John, the one who at the Last Supper had lain with his head at Jesus' bosom, who recognized the Master. Turning to Peter, who had been his companion at the empty tomb, he said, "It is the Lord!"

The picture of Peter—bold, impetuous, and impatient—is the one with which we have become familiar. Learning the identity of the One on the shore, he could not wait for the boat to get there, but dove into the sea and struck out for his Lord! We are reminded of Matthew 14:28–33 and the story of Peter's walking on the water to come to Jesus. The oddity of Peter's pausing to put on his clothes is probably best explained in terms of the difficulty of the Greek text, which can also mean "to tuck in" one's clothes. Peter was fishing in his cincture and tunic, both undergarments. When he realized that the Stranger was Jesus, he tucked up his tunic in his cincture and plunged into the water.

When the disciples got the boat to land, they found bread and a fire with a fish cooking on it. Jesus instructed them to bring some of the fish they had caught. Again Peter was the active one. Returning to the boat, he loosened the end of the net and dragged it ashore, teeming with fish.

There has been much speculation about whether the number 153 is symbolic, and, if so, what it was intended to mean. Jerome, one of the early interpreters, said that Greek zoologists recorded 153 varieties of fish in the seas and that therefore the number indicated the fullness of the church's evangelistic promise. Augustine said that 153 is the sum of all the numbers from 1 to 17, and that 17 is a combination of 7 (universality) and 10 (completeness). A more recent interpreter has observed that the number can be represented by three equilateral triangles with sides of 17 dots, combining the number 17 with the Trinity. John may have intended only to indicate a great number of fish; but, if we conclude that there was special significance in the number, it seems doubtless that the symbolism had to do with fullness or completeness.

An interesting detail is provided in verse 11, that "although there were so many, the net was not broken." This is in contrast to Luke's version of a miraculous catch, when there were so many fish that the nets broke (Luke 5:6). As we are obviously dealing with references to "catching men" (Luke 5:10 makes this plain), there is surely significance in John's information. Its most likely reference is to Jesus' faithfulness in keeping all those who believe, as expressed in 17:11–12, "And now I am no more in the world, but they are in the world, and I am coming to thee. Holy Father, keep them in thy name, which thou hast given me, that they may be one, even as we are one. While I was with them, I kept them in thy name, which thou hast given me; I have guarded them, and none of them is lost but the son of perdition, that the scripture might be fulfilled."

This passage, then, is clearly about the work of the early church as it set out to evangelize the world. Without Christ, the disciples would have been powerless. With him, they brought in great numbers of people. And, because of the unity of converts with the Son and the Father, true believers were never lost—"the net was not torn."

Thank you, Lord, for this graphic picture of the ministry of the early church. Help me to ponder it in considering the mission of the church today—and to take my place at the nets. For you are the Lord, and we listen to your voice. Amen.

Week 12: Wednesday

John 21:12–14 Breakfast by the Sea

Having made his point about the missionary enterprise of the early church (vv. 2–11), John now turns to the manner in which the early church would be sustained, and shows us this beautiful picture of Jesus feeding his disciples. It is the only story we have, in any of the Gospels, of a breakfast meal.

The wording of verse 13, "Jesus came and took the bread and gave it to them, and so with the fish," is particularly suggestive of the serving of the Eucharist. That the meal consisted of bread and fish, and not bread and wine, is not a strong impediment to this interpretation, for we know from early Christian art (in the catacombs, for instance) that fish were often pictured as part of the communion meal. Perhaps John or his editor, noting that there was a story about wine without bread early in the Gospel (2:1–11), decided to balance the accounts near the end of the Gospel with a story about bread without wine.

The fact that all the disciples "knew it was the Lord" (v. 12) is further support for the eucharistic reference. In Luke 24:30–31, it was in the breaking of bread that the two disciples from Emmaus recognized the risen Lord. There was probably a general connection, in the minds of early Christians, between eating the Eucharist and discovering the presence of Christ—a connection to which we alluded in discussion 20:20–22 and 26–28.

This was the third time, says John, that Jesus revealed himself to the disciples after the resurrection (v. 14). This overlooks the revelation to Mary Magdalene (who of course was not one of the twelve), and numbers the two Lord's Day appearances to the disciples in Jerusalem. The stress on its being the third occasion may well mean that it too occurred on a Lord's Day, underlining once more the eucharistic reference of the passage.

The Gospel may have provided us, in the two Upper Room visits of Jesus, each on the first day of the week, and in this breakfast visit by the sea, with a normative picture of worship life in the early Christian community. From the first Sunday after the crucifixion—that is, Easter Day itself—the Christians did not fail to meet, break bread together, and experience the presence of Christ in their midst!

O Lord known in the breaking of bread and drinking the cup, I am grateful for these powerful reminders of your suffering, and for the promise that whenever we share them in your name, you will be there, ministering to us as before. Grant that Christians everywhere may give more reverence to this sacred occasion, and that, sensing your presence, we may return doubly faithful to our mission in the world. Amen.

Week 12: Thursday

John 21:15–19 A Touching Interrogation

We have observed many times through the Gospel that it was especially directed at converts who were tempted to fall away from their faith rather than be excluded from Jewish worship in the synagogues. Apostasy (the church's word for falling away) was a widespread problem in the early church, and the Gospel writers were often concerned to encourage people not to desert Christ. By the same token, they wished to encourage those who had apostatized to return to the fold.

No example was more powerful in this encouragement than Simon Peter's, for Peter had flagrantly denied Jesus not once but three times, and then had returned to favor and become the leader of the church in Jerusalem. In the commentary on Matthew 14:22–33, I pointed out that Peter's sinking in the water when he tried to walk to Jesus, and being subsequently caught and helped into the boat by Jesus, was in fact an allegorical portrait of Peter's defection and restoration to faith.

Here, in verses 15–19, we have one of the tenderest and best-loved pictures of Peter's restoration and recommissioning by Jesus.

Three times Peter had denied his Lord (18:17, 25–27); three times his Lord questioned him, "Simon, son of John, do you love me?" The use of Peter's old name, Simon, is interesting. Perhaps, as it was his name when he first came to Jesus and, when coupled with his father's name, was his more formal designation, Jesus was using it in a legal, contractual sense. Scholars have shown that repeating questions and vows three times was often done in ancient times to indicate the contractual status of a verbal exchange. The entire scene may therefore have constituted a formal commissioning of Peter to special responsibilities in the fledgling church.

The first time Jesus questioned Peter, he said, "Lovest thou me more than these?" We cannot be certain what "these" refers to, for there is no clear antecedent. Some interpreters think it infers "things"—that is, "Lovest thou me more than these things?" If that was the case, Jesus probably gestured toward the boat, the nets, and the sea, and Peter was having to choose between his old occupation and a new one. Others believe Jesus meant the disciples—did Peter love him more than they did? He *had* sworn, before his denials, that he would lay down his life for Jesus (13:37). This interrogation accords well with verses 18–19, which speak of Peter's future death in the service of Christ.

Each time that Peter replied to a question, "Yes, Lord, you know that I love you," Jesus directed him to care for his (Jesus') sheep. The first time, Jesus said, "Feed my lambs." The second time he said, "Tend my sheep." The word "tend" (Greek *poimainain)* is a broader word than "feed" (Greek *boskein)*, and means "lead," "guard," and "provide for" as well as "feed." The distinction between feeding lambs and tending sheep may have been intended, for, as any shepherd knows, the lambs follow the flock and require less attention than the sheep themselves. But the third directive, "Feed my little sheep" (not merely "sheep," as in the RSV; the Greek word is different), returns to the verb used in the first directive, minimizing the probability of a strong distinction.

Peter's responses are touching, particularly the third time, when we are told that he was hurt by Jesus' repetition of the question "Do you love me?" and replied, in a final burst of desperation, "Lord, you know everything; you know that I love you" (v. 17). How could Peter prove it? He had already denied his Lord after promising to die for him. Now the only appeal was to Jesus' intimate knowledge of him. Surely Jesus knew what was in his heart, and understood how faithful he would be now that Jesus was alive forever more!

Jesus' replies, on the other hand, that Peter should feed and care for his little ones, were his way of accepting Peter's love and giving him responsibility at the same time. It was tantamount to saying, "Yes, I know you love me, and you shall show it through my flock which I entrust to you."

"Truly, truly," said Jesus, "I say to you, when you were young, you girded yourself and walked where you would; but when you are old, you will stretch out your hands, and another will gird you and carry you where you do not wish to go" (v. 18). This, says John, was to signify what kind of death Peter was to die.

It was natural for Jesus to connect death with the feeding of sheep, for they had been connected in his own ministry. When he identified himself as the Beautiful Shepherd, he added immediately, "The beautiful shepherd lays down his life for the sheep" (10:11). The servant, he had told the disciples, is not greater than the master (15:20).

There may have been an old proverb behind Jesus' saying. If there was, it has been lost. But the meaning is clear. When Peter was younger, he was self-determinant—he hitched up his belt, went where he wanted, and did what he wished. Now that he had the responsibility for Christ's little ones, it would not be so easy. The time would come when he would stretch forth his hands, be bound by others, and carried where he had no desire to go. This was the way it had been with Jesus; he had been bound in the garden of Gethsemane and taken to Annas and Pilate. And Peter would have a similar experience, leading to his own crucifixion.

Finally Jesus said simply, "Follow me."

Follow him where? Wherever he led. Back to Jerusalem. To Joppa. To Macedonia. To Rome. Eventually to death and complete union with the Father.

Lord, this is a model commissioning service. Peter is tested, he answers that he loves you, you tell him to care for your sheep, and you predict his death in the ministry. Help me to love you so much that I too will be ready to die in your service. For you are the Beautiful Shepherd and you have laid down your life for me. Amen.

Week 12: Friday

John 21:20–23 What about the Other Person?

There has been much speculation about the reason for the existence of this brief passage. Was it written to correct the impression that John would live until the *parousia* or return of Jesus? Was it intended to settle a dispute among followers of Peter and followers of John as to which was greater in the kingdom? The answers are not easy.

On the surface, it is merely a little story about Peter's interest in what the beloved disciple would do while Peter was following Jesus. "Lord, what about this man?" (v. 21) Perhaps Peter wished to have John at his side. They had experienced much together as disciples—especially the discovery of the empty tomb and folded grave clothes. Or, as seems more likely, in the light of Jesus' mild rebuke, Peter wanted to know what Jesus planned for John while he himself was feeding Jesus' sheep and being led away captive.

How easy it is to understand that! We are forever trying to condition our service to Christ on what others are or are not doing for the kingdom. We give or withhold gifts on the basis of what others are giving. We go or refuse to go on the basis of whether they are going. We would do well to mark the words of Jesus addressed to Peter: "What is that to you? Follow me!" (v. 22).

Once more we need to remember the effect of the Gospel on Jewish Christians facing expulsion from their synagogues for the faith. How would they have interpreted this passage? Surely they would have heard in it the warning we have heard—to follow Christ faithfully without making the behavior of others the model for our own actions. Some Christians who read the text were actually facing death for Christ. They were not to hesitate because others were not put in the same situation. Their devotion was to Christ, not to some kind of moral consensus.

"Suppose," said Jesus in effect, "I said to John, 'You stay right here until I return for you.' Would that make any difference in what I have asked you to do? No. I have told you to follow me. You have said you love me. Now follow me!" (v. 22, P).

The rumor apparently circulated that John was not to die, but was to remain behind until Jesus returned to earth.

Those who believe the passage was written to quell competitive feelings of two groups of disciples suppose that Peter's death by martyrdom impelled his followers to feel superior to John's followers, whose master lived to old age. The words of Jesus, in that case, would have given divine sanction to John's not being a martyr.

Those who think the passage had to do primarily with the delay of Jesus' return suggest that it was designed to dispel the anxieties of Christians who had actually believed that John, as the youngest disciple, would not die at all, but would greet Jesus' royal return. In Matthew 16:28, Jesus told the disciples: "Truly, I say to you, there are some standing here who will not taste death before they see the Son of man coming in his kingdom." And, significantly, this was part of the passage about Peter's confession of Jesus' messiahship and Jesus' giving him the keys of the kingdom (16:13–28). In other words, Peter's commissioning and the word about someone's living until the return of Jesus were connected in Matthew as they are in John.

But John defuses the question, whatever its motivation, by saying that Jesus did *not* say to the beloved disciple that he would not die, only that it was no business of Peter's if he did say that (v. 23).

John's own view of the Second Coming is usually different from the view often held by early Christians. His emphasis was on the constant union of believers with Jesus and the Father, not upon a visible return of Jesus to earth. That is the point of the appearance narratives in the Fourth Gospel: Jesus comes to his followers as they worship and eat the eucharistic meal. They are not to pine for the end of the world and a new age. A new age dawned with the coming of Jesus and the imparting of his Spirit. Eternal life is a possession of all who believe in his name.

Guilty, Lord. I am guilty of having waited to see what others would do for you. What if you had waited for someone else to love me and die for me? Forgive me, Lord, as you forgave Peter. And use me in whatever way you wish, for your kingdom's sake. Amen.

Week 12: Saturday

John 21:24–25 The Final Word

We come at last to the second or final conclusion of the Gospel. "This is the disciple who is bearing witness to these things," says the writer, "and who has written these things; and we know that his testimony is true" (v. 24). "The disciple" is the one described with Peter and Jesus in verses 20–23, namely John the beloved. The "we" of the second part of the verse suggests that at least this final passage, if not the entire twenty-first chapter, was written by an editor. His reference to John is in the third person: "his testimony is true."

Perhaps this writer was one of John's disciples, and, in ruminating on the stories of Jesus he had heard John tell, decided that the ones in chapter twenty-one should be added to the Gospel originally written or dictated by John himself. Therefore he appended the narratives of the fishing expedition, the meal at the seashore, the commissioning of Peter, and Peter's asking what John was to do.

And, when he got through, this nameless disciple imitated the conclusion in 20:30–31, attesting from all the stories he had heard John tell that there were countless narratives yet to be told. In fact, he said, the world itself could not contain all that might be written.

Suppose all these things had been written. Would it make the lordship of Jesus more credible? Probably not. "The Jews" had not believed, even though they saw many of the signs and wonders occur in their very midst. One of the points often made by the Gospel is that faith is a gift, and no one can believe who is not drawn by God to do so (6:44).

But what wonders those who are drawn do see!

Do you remember the calling of Nathanael in chapter one of the Gospel? Nathanael was astounded that Jesus knew him under the fig tree. "Did that make you believe?" asked Jesus. "Wait until you see the heavens opened, and the angels of God ascending and descending on the Son of man!" (1:50–51, P)

Before the Gospel narrative was over, Nathanael had seen this. He had seen Jesus' oneness with the Father, and the way Jesus' Spirit could bring that oneness among the disciples themselves. He had seen a man raised from the dead, blind men given sight, lame men made to walk again. He had seen the risen Christ in the midst of the disciples, showing his wounds from the crucifixion and causing a skeptic like Thomas to cry out, "My Lord and my God!"

In other words, Nathanael's way of seeing had been completely transformed. He no longer saw a mere man who had extraordinary powers of personality—he saw the very presence of God, as though heaven itself were opened and angels were ascending and descending on the Son of man!

This is what the Gospel is able to do in our own lives if we believe. It is no ordinary book, for it is about no ordinary life. Its theme is life eternal, and it has a power to change everything for us, if we only believe in the One at its center.

"Have you believed because you have seen me?" Jesus asked Thomas. "Blessed are those who have not seen and yet believe" (20:29).

That is our cue. We are the ones he was talking about. And this Gospel has helped to make it possible. Because John bore witness, and talked of some of the things he had seen, we can believe too. We, like Thomas, can exclaim, "My Lord and my God!"

How wonderful, Lord, was the witness of John! He has made me see and feel and understand things I did not know. Grant that I, in turn, may be the kind of witness he was, and share your life-giving presence with my world. For you are the Resurrection and the Life, and there is none like you; no, not one. Amen.

ABOUT THE AUTHOR:

John Killinger is pastor of the First Presbyterian Church in Lynchburg, Virginia. For fifteen years he was professor of preaching, worship, and literature at Vanderbilt University Divinity School in Nashville, Tennessee. He received the S.T.B. in theology from Harvard Divinity School, the Ph.D. in English from the University of Kentucky, and the Th.D. in homiletics from Princeton. Dr. Killinger has had a broad background as a pastor, academic dean, and professor of English, as well as theologian. He is author of more than twenty books, including *Bread for the Wilderness, Wine for the Journey; Prayer: The Act of Being with God;* and *Christ in the Seasons of Ministry.*